The Pauline History of Hebrews

CULTURES OF READING IN THE ANCIENT MEDITERRANEAN

Series Editors
William A. Johnson and Chris Keith

This book series presents a home for original scholarship on the reading cultures of the wider ancient Mediterranean world. Broadly chronological—from the Iron Age to Late Antiquity—and geographical—from Western Europe to Mesopotamia—the series welcomes new work at the intersection of Classics, papyrology, epigraphy, Jewish Studies, early Christian studies, early Islamic studies, and ancient media culture.

Jeremiah Coogan, *Eusebius the Evangelist: Rewriting the Fourfold Gospel in Late Antiquity*

Anna M. Sitz, *Pagan Inscriptions, Christian Viewers: The Afterlives of Temples and Their Texts in the Late Antique Eastern Mediterranean*

Warren Campbell, *The Pauline History of Hebrews*

The Pauline History of Hebrews

WARREN CAMPBELL

OXFORD
UNIVERSITY PRESS

Oxford University Press is a department of the University of Oxford.
It furthers the University's objective of excellence in research, scholarship,
and education by publishing worldwide. Oxford is a registered trade mark of
Oxford University Press in the UK and in certain other countries.

Published in the United States of America by Oxford University Press
198 Madison Avenue, New York, NY 10016, United States of America.

© Oxford University Press 2025

All rights reserved. No part of this publication may be reproduced, stored in a retrieval system,
transmitted, used for text and data mining, or used for training artificial intelligence, in any form or
by any means, without the prior permission in writing of Oxford University Press, or as expressly
permitted by law, by license or under terms agreed with the appropriate reprographics rights
organization. Inquiries concerning reproduction outside the scope of the above should be sent
to the Rights Department, Oxford University Press, at the address above.

You must not circulate this work in any other form
and you must impose this same condition on any acquirer.

CIP data is on file at the Library of Congress.

ISBN 9780197769256

DOI: 10.1093/9780197769287.001.0001

Printed by Integrated Books International, United States of America

The manufacturer's authorized representative in the EU for product safety is
Oxford University Press España S.A., Parque Empresarial San Fernando de Henares,
Avenida de Castilla, 2 – 28830 Madrid (www.oup.es/en).

For Troy Kenny

Acknowledgements

This book is a reminder to me of my many debts. I am indebted to a host of wonderful colleagues at various departments whose friendships and insights have been invaluable to me. I want to thank Paul Wheatley, Robert Edwards, Kacie Klamm, Greg Fewster, Kai-Hsuan Chang, Jeremiah Coogan, Samuel Johnson, Jason Yuh, Raleigh Heth, Eric DeVilliers, Andrew King, Cory Louie, Bruce Worthington, James Schetelich, and Angela Zautcke. You have all shaped my understanding deeply, and I am incredibly privileged to have worked alongside you and to have drawn from your expertise over the years. To Bruce and Greg in particular, our overlap in Toronto was formative for me and many of the ideas that structure this book grew out of midnight hockey under the CN Tower in 2016. To my many professors over the years, I could not be more appreciative of your teaching, scholarship, and guidance. From my early graduate school days, I want to thank Libbie Groves, Matt Dudreck, Judith Newman, Ann Jervis, John Marshall, and Terry Donaldson. From the University of Notre Dame, I thank David Lincicum, Jennie Grillo, Christopher Baron, Adam Carter Bremmer-McCollum, John Fitzgerald, Blake Leyerle, and Tzvi Novick. Special thanks go to Tzvi, Blake, and John for serving as members of the dissertation committee. I am especially privileged to have worked closely with Lincicum as the supervisor of this project, whose erudition, humility, and encouragement is unmatched. I continue to aspire to his model of scholarship and collegiality.

I want to thank the Manfred Lautenschlaeger Award committee for selecting this project for the 2024 prize and for hosting the awardees. I am deeply grateful to Prof. Michael Welker and Prof. Matthias Konradt for their warm reception and kind remarks in Heidelberg. This project was also funded by the University of Notre Dame's Presidential Fellowship and the Social Sciences and Research Council of Canada's Doctoral Fellowship.

My two older sisters, Sarah Mor and Lindsay Thornton, have always been inspiring to me and deeply supportive. I am still a little brother admiring their strength of character and hoping to be more like them. Most of all, it is an honor to name and thank Nicole Campbell publicly. I continue to be inspired by her bookishness and intellectual curiosity. Her insights on the art of writing and the framing of this project are countless, and it has been a joy to work through them while chasing Oliver and Jubilee (and later Florence). Coley, I have learned more from you than any book.

Warren Campbell

Pascha, 2025

Contents

1. Introduction: The Letter to the Hebrews and the Study of Paul   1
2. The Invention of Paul's Letter to the Hebrews   19
3. Clement of Alexandria's (Dis)engagement with Hebrews   60
4. Origen's Letter on the Nature of Jewish Reading   100
5. Prefacing Hebrews and the Institutionalization of Paulinity   143
    Epilogue   181

Appendix   187

Bibliography   189
Index   223

1

Introduction

The Letter to the Hebrews and the Study of Paul

The Letter to the Hebrews is not really a letter, it does not name an author, its title lacks specificity, and many of the rudimentary questions surrounding its destination, date, and provenance seem impermeable. Despite these perplexities, Hebrews was included in Pauline letter collections, perhaps around the turn of the first century, and was read by Christians in second-century Alexandria and third-century Palestine as a Pauline letter that was written to Jews. By the fourth century, the Pauline status of Hebrews is observed across the ancient Mediterranean in Latin, Syriac, and Greek contexts and was subsequently transmitted and read as Pauline until the fervent and humanistic textual scholarship of the early sixteenth century would lay the foundations for slowly untangling the association between Paul and Hebrews, at least theoretically. Though Hebrews has this rich history of Pauline ascription, transmission, and use, it is the anonymity of this text that has transfixed the scholarly gaze.

Throughout the second and third centuries CE, Christian readers across the Mediterranean sought to retrofit Hebrews with a people and a place. By the mid-third century, Hebrews was affiliated with no less than four authorial personae: Barnabas, Clement of Rome, Luke (as a translator), and Paul. Under the auspices of a burgeoning philological criticism, the anonymity of the Letter to the Hebrews, coupled with the variety of ancient testimonies on the authorship of Hebrews preserved in Eusebius of Caesarea—a fourth-century chronicler and historian—provided an endless fountain of reconstructive possibility for nineteenth-century scholars. With its precursors in Erasmus, Luther, Calvin, Andreas, Simon, and Michaelis, a "freer investigation" of Hebrews arose in the nineteenth century with a renewed criticism of the available evidence.[1] This was an era of scholarship in which a new set

---

[1] On this point see Otto Michel, *Der Brief an die Hebräer*, KEK 13 (Göttingen: Vandenhoeck & Ruprecht, 1947), 39–40. Nineteenth-century scholarship set the stage for almost all subsequent

of historical reconstructions were made possible, and indeed, today, as long as it is called "today," there are many historical configurations of the letter's purpose and argument, its destination and provenance, the social and ethnographic features of its recipients, its date, and, of course, author.[2]

In surveying what was already a distant landscape of apostolic origins by the fourth century, Eusebius was interested in asking, "Who thought Paul wrote Hebrews (and who did not)?" Eusebius is not exactly cryptic about his aim to amass testimony from those who used Hebrews as a Pauline letter in order to build a case for the letter's status as one of the ὁμολεγούμενα, the accepted texts.[3] Yet authorial reconstructions have done little to erase the anonymity that unavoidably persists, and so the question "Who?" is posed without the possibility of an answer. Despite B. F. Westcott's challenge in 1903 that scholarship on this question is content to "combine and repeat" the data preserved in Eusebius into a host of new assemblages, logging authorial claims onto an "accepted or rejected" Eusebian paradigm continued throughout the twentieth century.[4] The value of this catalog of votes on Pauline

---

consideration of the ancient pieces of evidence on the reception of Hebrews. See esp. F. Bleek, *Brief an die Hebräer* (Berlin: Dümmler, 1828), 82–436; W. M. L. de Wette, *Kurze Erklärung der Briefe an Titus, Timotheus und die Hebräer* (Leipzig: Weidmannische Buchhandlung, 1844), 161–70; G. Lünnemann, *Kritisch exegetisches Handbuch über den Hebräerbrief*, KEK 13 (Göttingen: Vandenhoeck & Ruprecht, 1855), 1–56; Karl Wieseler, *Eine Untersuchung über den Hebräerbrief namentlich seinen Verfasser und seine Leser. Erste Hälfte* (Kiel: C. F. Mohr, 1860), 1–48; Franz Overbeck, *Zur Geschichte des Kanons: Zwei Abhandlungen* (Chemnitz: Ernst Schmeitzner, 1880); B. Weise, *Kritisch exegetisches Handbuch über den Brief an die Hebräer* (Göttingen: Vandenhoeck and Ruprecht, 1888), 1–19; Theodor Zahn, *Geschichte des neutestamentlichen Kanons, Erster Band: Das Neue Testament vor Origenes. Erste Hälfte* (Erlangen: Deichert, 1888), 262–302; B. F. Westcott, *The Epistle to the Hebrews* (London: Macmillan 1892), lxii–lxxix.

[2] For a sample of this literature see F. F. Bruce, "'To the Hebrews': A Document of Roman Christianity?," *ANRW* 2.25.4 (1987): 3496–521; Hans-Friedrich Weiss, *Der Brief an die Hebräer*, KEK 13 (Göttingen: Vandenhoeck & Ruprecht, 1991), 35–132; Pamela Eisenbaum, "Locating Hebrews Within the Literary Landscape of Christian Origins," in *Hebrews: Contemporary Methods, New Insights*, ed. Gabriella Gelardini, BibInt 75 (Leiden: Brill, 2005), 213–38; Walter Schmithals, "Über Empfänger und Anlass des Hebräerbriefs," in *Eschatologie und Schöpfung: FS für Erich Grässer zum siebzigsten Geburtstag*, ed. M. Evang, H. Merklein, and M. Wolter, BZNW 89 (Berlin: de Gruyter, 1997), 321–42; Wolfgang Kraus, "Zu Absicht und Zielsetzung des Hebräerbriefes," *KD* 60.1 (2014): 250–71; Gert J. Steyn, "Hebrews in an Egyptian Setting?," in *The Epistle to the Hebrews: Writing at the Borders*, ed. Régis Burnet, Didier Luciani, and Geert Van, BETL 85 (Leuven: Peeters, 2016), 103–22.

[3] Eusebius, *Hist. eccl.* 3.3.5.

[4] Westcott, *Epistle to the Hebrews*, lxv. Commentarial highlights from the twentieth century include H. Windisch, *Der Hebräerbrief*, HNT 14 (Tübingen: Mohr Siebeck, 1913); James Moffatt, *The Epistle to the Hebrews*, ICC (Edinburgh: T. & T. Clark, 1924); Michel, *Der Brief an die Hebräer*; Ceslas Spicq, *L'Épître aux Hebreux*, I. Introduction, II. Commentaire, Études Bibliques (Paris: Libraire Lecoffre, 1952); Harald Hegermann, *Der Brief an die Hebräer*, ThHK 16 (Berlin: Evangelische Verlagsanstalt, 1988); Harold W. Attridge, *Hebrews: A Commentary on the Epistle to the Hebrews*, Hermeneia (Philadelphia: Fortress, 1989); Eric Gräßer, *An die Hebräer*, EKKNT 17/1 (Zürich: Neukirchener, 1990); Weiss, *Der Brief an die Hebräer*.

authorship from the second, third, and fourth centuries is limited to customary discussions of the nonlinear development of canonicity or as a rite of prolegomenous passage in the ever-burgeoning commentaries on Hebrews. Precisely because the Pauline authorship of Hebrews predominates the *ancient* discussions of the text, *modern* scholarly engagement with Hebrews, which reads the ancient attribution as historical fantasy, has become enraptured with its own fantasy of history, setting itself to producing a growing catalog of *other* possible authors for the text—Apollos, Philip, Timothy, Jude, Aristion, Epaphras, Silvanus, Priscilla, et cetera.[5]

Exploring anonymity as a constituent feature within imperial Roman literature with unique affordances, Tom Geue describes the "anathema" that is anonymity for traditions of classical historicist scholarship—something to be fixed.[6] Indeed, the Eusebian frame for the question of Hebrews considers anonymity to be a problem in need of solution, a lack in the text that cannot remain. Amid this quest of an author, we have forgotten that Hebrews was a Pauline letter *in use*. Rather than a marginal appendage, the placement of Hebrews within collections of Paul's letters has consequences for the history of reading and imagining Paul. Through participation within a unifying corpus, Hebrews ripples out and blends in with other Paulines, influencing and being influenced by other texts within the collection. While we rightly no longer think seriously about the Pauline authorship of Hebrews, and, though there are attempts to read Hebrews as an intentional imitation of Paul, we rarely, if ever, focus attention on the significance of Hebrews as a Pauline letter in later Christian appropriation. We have been content to consider *who* encountered and "accepted" Hebrews as Pauline, but we have not focused attention on the *Pauline* history of Hebrews conceived as an account of the image of Paul continually negotiated in the reception and transmission of his letter to Jews. After all, Hebrews is not like other Pauline letters.

The Deutero-Paulines are marked by explicit strategies of imitation and invite consideration of the shifting social circumstances that give meaning to imitating Paul. The Pauline authorship of Hebrews is something that later readers must (re)constitute, justify, and otherwise preserve as they

---

[5] Literature on these authorial ascriptions is collected and discussed in various places. See especially, Lünnemann, *Kritisch exegetisches Handbuch*, 1–56; Attridge, *Hebrews*, 1–6; Andrew W. Pitts and Joshua F. Walker, "The Authorship of Hebrews: A Further Development in the Luke-Paul Relationship," in *Paul and His Social Relations*, ed. Stanley E. Porter and Christopher D. Land (Leiden: Brill, 2013), 143–44.

[6] Tom Geue, *Author Unknown: The Power of Anonymity in Ancient Rome* (Cambridge, MA: Harvard University Press, 2019), 4.

appropriate a letter as Paul's without Paul's name or style. Not only is the contextual frame of this text invariably Jewish, given its title, but *because* it also has no name and lacks Pauline stylistic features, its "Paulinity" must be fashioned in ways that Pauline imitations simply do not require. The letter, in this sense, is a kind of pure Pauline fiction in that every Pauline marker is a secondary feature, a byproduct of its inclusion within the corpus. Later readers take up these markers and add others, giving the letter an origin story, a narrative account of its context of production designed to explain its strangeness. Rather than configure anonymity as a problem, this book considers the anonymity of Hebrews as a vantage, a site from which to observe the processes by which the Pauline authorship is forged and sustained.

This anonymous text became Paul's letter *Ad Hebraeos*. How? How was this text read and written as a Pauline text, and is there a discernible relationship between written and readerly modes of creating authorship? How do texts and readers sustain and mobilize Hebrews as a Pauline letter, and what "Paul" emerges from this history of engagement?

As an anonymous text with a Pauline title, a Jewish audience, and positioned within collections of Paul's letters, a robust Pauline history of Hebrews must account for these three dimensions: image, ethnicity, and corpus. Image refers to the predetermined ideas about Paul that inform how readers may defend, describe, and use Hebrews, as well as the traditions about Paul that influence material presentations of the text within the *corpus Paulinum*, such as prefaces and superscriptions. Ethnicity accents how, given its title, Hebrews uniquely invites discussion of Paul's Jewishness, often in connection with the role Paul is made to play in configuring the relationship and separation between "Christianity" and "Judaism." Finally, "corpus" brings to the fore how material contexts participate in the Pauline history of Hebrews much like readers, shaping and being shaped by interpretation about Paul. A comment on each of these categories provides the larger scholarly context in which this book is situated, as well as its core methodological commitments.

1. Image: Which Paul Wrote the Letter to the Hebrews?

It is increasingly difficult to talk about Paul as he "really was" and not Paul as always and ever a figure mediated through the compounding layers of reception: centuries of interpretive traditions, complex textual transmission and editorial shaping, the intractable difficulties in what constitutes the "data" of Paul.[7] Time and textuality are formidable foes to traditional modes of historicism, especially as scholars have widened the scope of what is considered to be study of the "reception of Paul." Even while Paul was still alive, there were clashing interpretations of this figure, and the biographical and other kinds of self-descriptive comments found in letters blessed with authenticity are selective and conditioned by an intense particularity.[8] Can the ways in which one represents oneself, asks Judith Lieu, be the only measure of who one "really" is?[9] How Paul was understood and interpreted by the individuals and communities receiving these contextually specific letters and how the eventual formation of a Pauline corpus directs readers to a singular, authorial Paul who emerges from the totality of a varied epistolary collection add further layers of memory and text that obstruct one's vision of the "real" Paul.[10]

In recognition of the vibrancy and instability of social memory and textual transmission, as well as the ways in which discourses surrounding the authentic Paul operate within questionable ideological lineages, Pauline scholars have been asking the question, "Which Paul?"[11] For nineteenth- and much of twentieth-century scholarship, "Which Paul?" was perhaps not a complicated question, and he certainly was not going to be found in the second century CE. For an earlier generation of scholars, the early Christian

---

[7] Samuel Vollenweider, "Paulus zwischen Exegese und Wirkungsgeschichte," in *Die prägende Kraft der Texte. Hermeneutik und Wirkungsgeschichte des Neuen Testaments: Ein Symposium zu Ehren von Ulrich Luz*, ed. Moises Mayordomo, SBS 199 (Stuttgart: Katholisches Bibelwerk, 2005), 142: "The history of effects is not a factually irrelevant appendix of historical-critical biblical interpretation, but an indispensable and epistemologically relevant discipline of its methodological ensemble" (die Wirkungsgeschichte kein sachlich irrelevanter Appendix historisch-kritischer Bibelauslegung ist, sondern eine unverzichtbare und erkenntnisrelevante Disziplin ihres Methodenensembles darstellt). See also Samuel Vollenweider, "Paul entreexégèse et histoire de la réception," in *Paul, une théologie en construction*, ed. Andreas Dettwiler, Jean-Daniel Kaestli, and Daniel Marguerat, MoBi 51 (Geneva: Labor et Fides, 2004), 441–59.
[8] Jens Schröter, Simon Butticaz, and Andreas Dettwiler, "Introduction," in *Receptions of Paul in Early Christianity: The Person of Paul and His Writings Through the Eyes of His Early Interpreters*, ed. Jens Schröter, Simon Butticaz, and Andreas Dettwiler (Berlin: de Gruyter, 2018), 5–6.
[9] Judith M. Lieu, "The Battle for Paul in the Second Century," *ITQ* 75 (2010): 7.
[10] See the collection of essays in *Recovering an Undomesticated Apostle: Essays on the Legacy of Paul*, ed. Christopher B. Zeichmann and John A. Egger (Montreal: McGill-Queen's University Press, 2023).
[11] Benjamin L. White, *Remembering Paul: Ancient and Modern Contests over the Image of the Apostle* (New York: Oxford University Press, 2014), 174; Karlfried Froehlich, "Which Paul? Observations on the Image of the Apostle in the History of Biblical Exegesis," in *New Perspectives on Historical Theology: Essays in Memory of John Meyendorff*, ed. Bradley Nassif (Grand Rapids: Eerdmans, 1996), 279–99; Martinus C. de Boer, "Comment: Which Paul?," in *Paul and the Legacies of Paul*, ed. William S. Babcock (Dallas: Southern Methodist Press, 1990), 45–54.

reception of a simultaneously genuine and false Pauline letter collection, coupled with the absorption of the portrait of the apostle in the Acts of the Apostles, irrecoverably damaged the possibility of discerning the "thought" of the historical Paul, represented by more or less seven authentic letters (*Hauptbriefe*).[12] That Adolf von Harnack, Walter Baur, and Hans von Campenhausen considered Paul to be the apostle "held captive" by the Gnostic heretics as their cherished apocalypticist, and so avoided by the "proto-orthodox" out of direct opposition or embarrassment by association, only minimized the vitality of reception further.[13] It is precisely the relationship between this "historical Paul" and this "second-century Paul" that has been significantly reconsidered, and the wall dividing them, while still apparent, is increasingly perforated. Calls for the study of "Paulology"—how Paul is constructed and how Paul functions—reflect this more robust sense of "reception history."[14] Paul is not available to us as though these layers of mediation did not exist.

The groundwork for advances in the study of the reception of Paul began in the late 1970s, when Andreas Lindemann, Ernst Dassmann, David Rensberger, and Donald Penny variously pursued and parsed out the literary reception of Paul in the second century and together argued that the so-called proto-orthodox were more familiar with Paul's letters than was previously appreciated.[15] Out of this reassessment of the second century arose work that focuses not on the degree to which these readings of Paul cohere with contemporary interpretations, that is, framing reception in terms of fidelity to or corruption of other readings, but how second-century interpretations of Paul construct and work with images of Paul gleaned from earlier layers of tradition in order to address contemporary

[12] White, *Remembering Paul*, 27.
[13] On the history of this "captivity narrative" see White, *Remembering Paul*, 20–41.
[14] See Cavan W. Concannon, "Paul Is Dead. Long Live Paulinism! Imagining a Future for Pauline Studies," *Ancient Jew Review*, November 1, 2016, https://www.ancientjewreview.com/read/2016/11/1/paul-is-dead-long-live-paulinism-imagining-a-future-for-pauline-studies, 2022/06/1.
[15] Andreas Lindemann, *Paulus im ältesten Christentum: Das Bild des Apostels und die Rezeption der paulinischen Theologie in der frühchristlichen Literatur bis Marcion*, BHT 58 (Tübingen: Mohr Siebeck, 1979); Andreas Lindemann, "Der Apostel Paulus im 2 Jahrhundert," in *The New Testament in Early Christianity, La reception des écrit néotestamentaires dans le christianisme primitif*, ed. Jean-Marie Sevrin, BETHhL 86 (Leuven: Leuven University Press, 1989), 39–67; Andreas Lindemann, *Apostel und Lehrer der Kirche: Studien zu Paulus und zum frühen Paulusverständnis* (Tübingen: Mohr Siebeck, 1999); Ernst Dassmann, *Der Stachel im Fleisch: Paulus in der frühchristlichen Literatur bis Irenäus* (Münster: Aschendorff, 1979); David Rensberger, "As the Apostle Teaches: The Development of the Use of Paul's Letters in Second-Century Christianity" (PhD diss., Yale University, 1981); Donald N. Penny, "The Pseudo-Pauline Letters of the First Two Centuries" (PhD diss., Emory University, 1979).

questions.[16] Early engagement with the concept of "images of Paul" focused on the canonical moments of imitation and the Paul of Acts of the Apostles.[17] Other epistolary imitations and narrated depictions of Paul in acts and apocalyptic texts were then increasingly situated within the history of Paulinism, each as sites of interpretive representation, whether these readings of Paul service anti-Pauline traditions or contexts of valorization and cult devotion.[18]

Benjamin White's work *Remembering Paul* narrates the rise of this developing area of Pauline scholarship most thoroughly while also showing how the nineteenth-century discourses on the "real" Paul in contrast to the corrupted Paul of the second century came to receive trenchant criticism.[19] When White asks, "Which Paul?" it is with the conviction that we should

---

[16] C. K. Barrett was an early voice drawing attention to the presence and impact of Pauline legends that develop outside of the extant epistolary corpus. "Pauline Controversies in the Post-Pauline Period," *NTS* 20 (1974): 229–45. See also Christian Grappe, "De quelques images de Paul et da la manière dont elles se déploient au cours de deux premiers siècles," *FoiVie* 94 (1995): 49–59; Judith M. Lieu, "'As Much My Apostle as Christ Is Mine': The Dispute over Paul between Tertullian and Marcion," *EC* 1 (2010): esp. 42; Lieu, "The Battle for Paul," 3–14.

[17] Martinus C. de Boer, "Images of Paul in the Post-Apostolic Period," *CBQ* 42 (1980): 359–80, was an early voice drawing attention to the image of Paul in Colossians, Ephesians, Acts, and the Pastoral Epistles. See also Klaus Wegenast, *Das Verständnis der Tradition bei Paulus und in den Deuteropaulinen* (Neukirchen-Vluyn: Neukirchener Verlag, 1962); G. Schille, *Das älteste Paulus-Bild: Beobachtungen zur lukanischen und zur deuteropaulinischen Paulus-Darstellung* (Berlin: Evangelische Verlagsanstalt, 1979); Joachim Gnilka, "Das Paulusbild im Kolosser- und Epheserbrief," in *Kontinuität und Einheit: Festschrift für Franz Mussner*, ed. Paul-Gerhard Müller, Werner Stenger, and J. C. van Kesteren (Freiburg: Herder, 1981), 179–93; Annette Merz, *Fiktive Selbstauslegung des Paulus: Intertextuelle Studien zur Intention und Rezeption der Pastoralbriefe*, NTOA 52 (Göttingen: Vandenhoeck & Ruprecht, 2004); Jens Schröter, "Kirche im Anschluss an Paulus: Aspekte der Paulusrezeption in der Apostelgeschichte und in den Pastoralbriefen," *ZNW* 98 (2007): 77–104; Eve-Marie Becker, "Von Paulus zu 'Paulus': Paulinische Pseudepigraphie-Forschung als literaturgeschichtliche Aufgabe," in *Pseudepigraphie und Verfasserfiktion in frühchristlichen Briefen*, ed. J. Frey, J. Herzer, M. Janßen, and C. Rothschild, WUNT 246 (Tübingen: Mohr Siebeck, 2009), 363–86; Daniel Marguerat, *Paul in Acts and Paul in His Letters*, WUNT 310 (Tübingen: Mohr Siebeck, 2013); J. Jervell, "Paulus in der Apostelgeschichte und die Geschichte des Urchristentums," *NTS* 32 (1986): 378–92; Niels Hyldahl, "The Reception of Paul in the Acts of the Apostles," in *The New Testament as Reception*, ed. Mogens Müller and Henrik Tronier, JSNTSup 230 (Sheffield: Sheffield Academic Press, 2002), 101–19; Gregory E. Sterling, "From Apostle to the Gentiles to Apostle of the Church: Images of Paul at the End of the First Century," *ZNW* 99 (2008): 74–98.

[18] Important texts here include the *Acts of Paul and Thecla*, the *Martyrdom of Paul*, the *Apocalypse of Paul*, the *Coptic Apocalypse of Paul*, the *Epistula Apostolorum*, *Third Corinthians*, the *Letter to the Laodiceans*, the Paul-Seneca Correspondence, the Pseudo-Clementine *Homilies* and *Recognitions*. See esp. Gerd Lüdemann, *Paulus, der Heidenapostel*, vol. 2: *Antipaulinismus im frühen Christentum*, FRLANT 130 (Göttingen: Vandenhoeck & Ruprecht, 1983); David Eastman, *Paul the Martyr: The Cult of the Apostle in the Latin West* (Atlanta: Society of Biblical Literature, 2011); David Eastman, *The Death of the Apostles: Ancient Accounts of the Martyrdoms of Peter and Paul (Latin, Greek, Syriac)* (Atlanta: Society of Biblical Literature, 2015). On Pauline veneration, see Hanns Christof Brennecke, "Die Anfänge einer Paulusverehrung," in *Biographie und Persönlichkeit des Paulus*, ed. E.M. Becker and P. Pilhofer, WUNT 1 /Reihe 187 (Tübingen: Mohr Siebeck, 2005), 295–305; Laura Nasrallah, "'Out of Love for Paul': History and Fiction and the Afterlife of the Apostle Paul," in *Early Christian and Jewish Narrative: The Role of Religion in Shaping Narrative Forms*, ed. Judith Perkins and Ilaria Ramelli (Tübingen: Mohr Siebeck, 2015), 73–96.

[19] See White, *Remembering Paul*, 20–69.

ask ancient writers not only about the lines of continuity with the past that they wield in order to advance a picture of Paul—the available textual and oral traditions about Paul—but how social and theological conditions provide the context within which literary depictions and commentarial interpretations of Paul are shaped and have value.[20] White wants to critically engage the Paul that is constructed out of a complex mixture of textual sources and non-textual traditions and how shifting social situations give rise to different Pauls, who miraculously emerge in order to address them.[21] White focuses on the ways in which Paul is constructed out of past traditions to address contemporary questions in two second-century literary contexts, *Third Corinthians* and Irenaeus of Lyons.

In *Third Corinthians*, White observes a second-century pseudepigraphon positioning Paul against the founding leaders of (what would become) rival Christian thinkers by evoking the language of the Pastoral Epistles and aligning Paul as a subordinate authority within the larger network of apostolic tradition.[22] With Paul depicted as the defender of the "deposit" of apostolic tradition (1 Tim 6:20, 2 Tim 1:12, 14), *Third Corinthians* attempts to stabilize interpretations of 1 Corinthians 15:50 from rival readings ("flesh and blood cannot inherit the kingdom of God, nor does the perishable inherit the imperishable"). What White emphasizes here is that the Paul of *Third Corinthians* becomes the defender of second-century proto-orthodox perspectives not through direct counter-interpretation

---

[20] White, *Remembering Paul*, 174. White points to the work of Michael Kaler, Louis Painchaud, and Marie-Pierre Bussières as exemplary of this dual view. Kaler, Painchaud, and Bussières argue that the expanded ascent vision of 2 Corinthians 12:2–4 in the *Apocalypse of Paul* and the discussion of Paul's ascent in Irenaeus (*Adv. Haer.* 2.30.7) are both conditioned by Valentinian speculation about the heavenly journey: "The Coptic *Apocalypse of Paul*, Irenaeus' *Adversus Haereses* 2.30.7, and the Second-Century Battle for Paul's Legacy," *JECS* 12.2 (2004): 173–93.

[21] Notable collections include Michael F. Bird and Joseph R. Dodson, eds., *Paul and the Second Century* (London: T&T Clark, 2011); Kenneth Liljeström, ed., *The Early Reception of Paul* (Helsinki: Finnish Exegetical Society, 2011); Manfred Lang, ed., *Paulus und Paulusbilder: Konstruktion—Reflexion—Transformation*, ABG 31 (Leipzig: Evangelische Verlagsanstalt, 2013); Tobias Nicklas, Andreas Merkt, and Joseph Verheyden, eds., *Ancient Perspectives on Paul* (Göttingen: Vandenhoeck & Ruprecht, 2013); Schröter et al., *Receptions of Paul*.

[22] White, *Remembering Paul*, 108–34. White notes here that a "dependent" Paul is but one interpretive option available with texts like 1 Corinthians and Galatians, which themselves lack systemization and proffer a complex picture of Paul's relation to contemporary authorities (132). Cf. also Benjamin L. White, "Reclaiming Paul? Reconfiguration as Reclamation in 3 Corinthians," *JECS* 17.4 (2009): 497–523; as well as Steve Johnston, "La correspondance apocryphe entre Paul et les Corinthiens: Un pseudépigraphe paulinien au service de la polémique anti-gnostique de la fin du IIe siècle," in *Colloque international "L'Évangile selon Thomas et les textes de Nag Hammadi"*, ed. Louis Painchaud and Paul-Hubert Poirier, BCNH 8 (Quebec: Presses Université Laval, 2007), 226–29; Vahan Hovhanessian, *Third Corinthians: Reclaiming Paul for Christian Orthodoxy*, StBibLit 18 (New York: Peter Lang, 2000).

of 1 Corinthians 15:50 but by depicting Paul as occupying a particular stream of Pauline tradition(s) that was understood to be effective for addressing the needs of these later interpretive battles.[23] White finds a similar strategy of depiction in Irenaeus. Working with Gérard Genette's notion of *peritext*, White points to the importance of the title of Irenaeus' lengthy project—*Adversus Haereses*—and the centrality given to 1 Timothy 6:20 with its encouragement to avoid the (the Marcionite sounding) "antitheseis," "falsely called knowledge" (ἀντιθέσεις τῆς ψευδωνύμου γνώσεως). These prefatory comments work within the same Pauline images informing the interests of *Third Corinthians*. For White, despite the generic differences between Irenaeus and *Third Corinthians*, the heresy-combating Paul of the Pastoral Epistles deeply informs both contexts. Asking if they "got Paul right" assumes a static Paul available for interpretation in what is in fact a tension-filled early layer of tradition.[24]

To ask, "Which Paul wrote the Letter to the Hebrews?" recognizes the productiveness of these lines of scholarship, the tricky dynamics of reception they highlight, and the need to think critically about the Paul who is remembered and constructed in order to meet the needs of subsequent interpretive, theological, and communal contexts. Recent arguments that the Pauline ascription of Hebrews develops as a natural byproduct of the internal claims to Pauline authorship within the text of Hebrews complicate how one conceptualizes the origins of Paulinity.[25] Is Hebrews an imitation of Paul like *Third Corinthians*, where the Pauline association is bound up with the earliest contexts of production, or does the "Paulinity" of the text have a different sphere of origins? The ancient readers who appropriate Hebrews as Pauline *assume* the lack of intentional imitation (anonymity and stylistic difference). Unlike Ephesians and 2 Timothy, for example, Hebrews generates a discourse about Pauline authorship precisely because it lacks distinctive Pauline features. Why is Paul's name absent from this text? Why is the style of this text markedly different from other Paulines? Why is Paul writing to "Hebrews," and who are they? In asking and answering these kinds of questions, ancient readers generate a Paul fit to be the author of "To the Hebrews." This project asks, who is *that* Paul?

---

[23] White, *Remembering Paul*, 133.   [24] White, *Remembering Paul*, 164.
[25] Clare K. Rothschild, *Hebrews as Pseudepigraphon: The History and Significance of the Pauline Attribution of Hebrews*, WUNT 235 (Tübingen: Mohr Siebeck, 2009).

In order to see "that" Paul, one must look beyond the overt ways of engaging with Hebrews as Pauline, the explicit quotations and discussions of the letter, and pay attention to the subtle transactions between a reader's image of Paul, image of Jews, and conceptions of Christian difference. How does Hebrews function as a *Pauline* letter within the context of a given corpus? Does Hebrews guide the interpretation of other Pauline texts and vice versa? Irenaeus and *Third Corinthians* value the Paul of the Pastoral Epistles insofar as *that* Paul aligns with their heresiological goals. What function does "a Paul who wrote to Hebrews" provide, or not provide, for later readers? These questions accent the importance of the ethnic valence of Hebrews. Subsequent readers taking up this text are confronted not only with an anonymous Pauline letter but one that is addressed to Jews. The reception of this text, then, is particularly illuminative for exploring how Paul's Jewishness was variously parsed and weighed.

2. Ethnicity: A Jewish Apostle Writing to Jews

Pauline scholars have worked hard to unshackle Paul from the moorings of a distinctly Protestant conceptualization of Judaism exemplified by Weber, Bousset, and Schürer at the turn of the nineteenth century.[26] In conversation with advances in the study of Second Temple Judaism more broadly, many have been reimagining the implications of a thoroughgoingly Jewish Paul who is not working contrastively against a religion known as "Judaism." Some of the early voices working to develop a new perspective on Paul argue that the apostle challenged the ways in which Jewish ethnic identity markers were praised and practiced, and (by implication) the set of assumptions regarding uniqueness and election that justify protecting them.[27] Others, finding a "deficient Judaism" as the primary impetus of Paul's convictions still lingering in this reading,[28] push further, giving way to readings of Paul

---

[26] Ferdinand Weber, *System der altsynagogalen palätinischen Theologie aus Targum, Midrash und Talmud* (Leipzig: Dörffling & Franke, 1880); Wilhelm Bousset, *Die Religion des Judentums im neutestamentlichen Zeitalter* (Berlin: Reuther & Reichard, 1903); Emil Schürer, *Geschichte des jüdischen Volkes im Zeitalter Jesu Christi* (Leipzig: Hinrichs, 1866–90).

[27] James D. G. Dunn, *The New Perspective on Paul: Collected Essays*, WUNT 185 (Tübingen: Mohr Siebeck, 2005).

[28] Matthew Thiessen notes elsewhere that there is a striking affinity between the "New Perspective" and the work of F. C. Baur regarding the contrast between Pauline universalism and Jewish particularism (*Paul and the Gentile Problem* [Oxford: Oxford University Press, 2016], 173 n. 16 citing Baur, *Paul the Apostle of Jesus Christ*, 1:308–9). See also Matthew Thiessen, "Conjuring Paul and Judaism Forty Years After Paul and Palestinian Judaism," *JJMJS* 5 (2018): 10.

that emphasize the thoroughgoing eschatological framework within which the relationship between Torah and (the inclusion of) pagans (as worshipers of Israel's God) is conceptualized.[29] These convictions have led to the emergence of alternative angles on well-worn questions concerning circumcision, eschatology, and the *ethnē*.[30] Yet these exciting and necessary renovations are faced with the dilemma that the judgments of authenticity that determine what constitutes the data of this historical Paul emerge from the very scholarship on Paul and the Jews that is being rewritten.

While the Baur-inspired *Hauptbriefe* have long been the agreed textual battleground for scholars whose work is framed as a concern for the historical Paul,[31] the history of Paul's Jewishness is increasingly valued as a way of thinking not only about shifting legacies of Paul but larger questions about the emerging distinction between "Christianity" and "Judaism" in these formative centuries.[32] Indeed, Paul's Jewishness is variously imagined in subsequent literary traditions.[33]

---

[29] See Lloyd Gaston, *Paul and the Torah* (Vancouver: University of British Columbia Press, 1987); Lloyd Gaston, "Paul and the Torah," in *Antisemitism and the Foundations of Christianity*, ed. Alan T. Davies (New York: Paulist Press, 1979), 48–71; Stanley Stowers, *A Rereading of Romans: Justice, Jews, Gentiles* (New Haven: Yale University Press, 1994); John Gager, *Reinventing Paul* (Oxford: Oxford University Press, 2000); John Gager, *Who Made Early Christianity? The Jewish Lives of the Apostle Paul* (New York: Columbia University Press, 2017); John Marshall, "From Small Words: Reading Deixis and Scope in Romans," *JJMJS* 4 (2017): 20.

[30] See Matthew Novenson, *Paul, Then and Now* (Grand Rapids: Eerdmans, 2022); Matthew Thiessen, *Contesting Conversion: Genealogy, Circumcision, and Identity in Ancient Judaism and Christianity* (Oxford: Oxford University Press, 2011); Thiessen, *Paul and the Gentile Problem*; cf. also Pamela Eisenbaum, *Paul Was Not a Christian: The Original Message of a Misunderstood Apostle* (New York: HarperCollins, 2009); Paula Fredriksen, *Paul, the Pagans' Apostle* (New Haven: Yale University Press, 2017); "Judaizing the Nations: The Ritual Demands of Paul's Gospel," *NTS* 56 (2010): 232–52; Paula Fredriksen, "Paul's Letter to the Romans, the Ten Commandments, and Pagan 'Justification by Faith,'" *JBL* 133 (2014): 801–8; Paula Fredriksen, "Why Should a 'Law-Free' Mission Mean a 'Law-Free' Apostle?" *JBL* 134 (2015): 637–50; Paula Fredriksen, "How Jewish Is God? Divine Ethnicity in Paul's Theology," *JBL* 137 (2018): 193–212.

[31] According to the index, there are no citations from Ephesians, Colossians, 2 Thessalonians, 1 Timothy, 2 Timothy, or Titus in Mark D. Nanos and Magnus Zetterholm, *Paul Within Judaism: Restoring the First-Century Context to the Apostles* (Minneapolis: Fortress, 2015). For Baur, this letter collection included Romans, 1–2 Corinthians, and Galatians. The tradition would ultimately include Philippians, 1 Thessalonians, and Philemon. Voices prior to Baur questioning the authorship of the now-disputed Paulines include Edward Evanson, Friedrich Schleiermacher, and W. M. L. De Wette. Relevant here is Christof Landmesser, "Ferdinand Christian Baur as Interpreter of Paul: History, the Absolute, and Freedom," in *Ferdinand Christian Baur and the History of Early Christianity*, ed. Martin Bauspiess, Christof Landmesser, and David Lincicum (Oxford: Oxford University Press, 2017), 147–76.

[32] Jens Schröter, Simon Butticaz, and Andreas Dettwiler together ask, "What can the history of ancient reception contribute to this re-examination of Paul's relationship with Judaism and its focus on both continuity and discontinuity between the apostle and his natal milieu?" (*Receptions of Paul*, 18). On the place of *Wirkungsgeschichte* in Pauline studies and in this *Schule* more particularly, see Matthew Novenson, "Whither the Paul Within Judaism Schule?" *JJMJS* 5 (2018): 87.

[33] On the "Judaism" of Paul, see esp. Jörg Frey, "Das Judentum des Paulus," in *Paulus: Leben—Umwelt—Werk—Briefe*, ed. Oda Wischmeyer, 2nd ed., UTB 2767 (Tübingen: FranckeVerlag, 2012), 25–65; Simon Butticaz, "Paul et le judaïsme: Des identités en construction," *RHPR* 94 (2014): 253–73.

The second-century Gospel-like text *Epistula Apostolorum* describes Paul as a circumcised Jew according to the Law and the object of prophecy (*Ep. Apos.* 31; cf. Phil 3:5). The Roman philosopher Seneca is made to describe Paul as one who left Judaism through conversion (Epistle of Paul to Seneca 5.3). In the Acts of the Apostles, one finds Paul declaring himself "ceremonially clean" (Acts 24:18), that he has "committed no offense against the law of the Jews or against the temple or against Caesar" (Acts 25:8), and introducing himself as "a Jew" (Acts 22:3). In the *Apocalypse of Paul*, Paul throws himself to the ground in thankfulness to the divine beneficence that "delivered me from the race of the Hebrews."[34] Clement of Alexandria's Paul can speak of a former time in his life when "I *was* a Jew."[35] Epiphanius describes a so-called Ebionite view of Paul that more flatly denies his Jewishness altogether, claiming he was a Greek born of Greek parents who was circumcised in order to marry the daughter of the high priest, but turned against the circumcision and the Sabbath after these plans were stymied (*Pan.* 30.16.9). Paul's Jewishness was continually remembered and imagined, and this process need not have a "beginning" at the Rubicon between texts deemed as authentic and those that are pseudonymous. Paul's description of Jewishness in Philippians 3 has just as much of a context as the image of Paul in Ephesians and Acts.

How these Pauline texts recreate, inflect, distort, emphasize, or otherwise mention Paul's Jewishness has been of recent interest, motivated, in part, by the renewed value granted to the portraits of Paul in the second and third centuries.[36] But why is reception history of value on this question? While Peter Schäfer has isolated Hellenistic Egypt as the seedbed of ancient expressions of anti-Semitism, John Gager and Paula Fredriksen point to the complexities of reception and appropriation of Paul, together with Gospel texts, as the impetus for the development of distinct form(s) of Christian

---

[34] C. Tischendorf, *Apocalypses Apocryphae, Mosis, Esdrae, Pauli, Iohannis, item Mariae Dormitio, additis evangeliorum et actuum apocryphorum suplementis* (Leipzig: Mendelssohn, 1866), 67: ἐμοῦ λυτρωσάμενος ἐκ τοῦ γένους τῶν Ἑβραίων.

[35] Henri-Irénée Marrou and Marguerite Harl, eds., *Le pédagogue*, vol. 1, SC 70 (Paris: Éditions du Cerf, 1949), 172: ὅτε ἤμην νήπιος, τουτέστιν ὅτε ἤμην Ἰουδαῖος.

[36] See here Tet-Lim N. Yee, *Jews, Gentiles and Ethnic Reconciliation: Paul's Jewish Identity and Ephesians* (Cambridge: Cambridge University Press, 2005); Isaac W. Oliver and Gabriele Boccaccini, eds., *The Early Reception of Paul the Second Temple Jew*, LSTS 92 (London: Bloomsbury, 2018); Gabriele Boccaccini and Carlos A. Segovia, *Paul the Jew: Rereading the Apostle as a Figure of Second Temple Judaism* (Minneapolis: Fortress, 2016); as well as the relevance of the remembered Paul for the history of Jewish-Christian relations: Daniel R. Langton, *The Apostle Paul in the Jewish Imagination: A Study in Modern Jewish-Christian Relations* (Cambridge: Cambridge University Press, 2014).

anti-Semitism.[37] The processes of reception are creative and generative and need historical description. The received or remembered or imagined Paul is also an access point into thinking about the morphology of Pauline traditions. John Marshall suggests that the "Jewish error" ascribed to Marcion by later critics like Tertullian and Justin—that Jesus of Nazareth was not the object of prophecy found in Israel's scriptural texts, which refer to a different "Christ"—is a subtle line of continuity with the *Sonderzeit* (formerly *-weg*) Paul of Lloyd Gaston.[38] Isolated moments of interpretation have antecedents and afterlives that are important to register for (re)tracing the history of interpreting Paul.

Here, again, Hebrews invites, or even demands, ancient readers articulate a link between Paul and Jews in unique ways. This link illuminates a larger set of assumptions about Jews and "Judaism" within these early Christian literary projects. How was the unavoidable ethnic valence of the title "To the Hebrews" conceptualized and historized by readers of this text? What hermeneutical postures do early readers find in and employ for Hebrews as a Pauline letter written to a Jewish audience? How was Paul's Jewishness remembered and (re)configured in light of this appropriation? Hebrews facilitates discourse on Paul's Jewishness in unique ways. But it is also vital to note that the title, "To the Hebrews," is what instantiates the Jewishness of the letter and is the product of editorial shaping and collection. Hebrews not only functions as a Pauline letter when read and used but is also written and transmitted as Pauline too, and a Pauline history of Hebrews must attend to ways in which *writing* is Paulinizing.

3. Corpus: Hebrews as a Pauline *Text*

Margaret Mitchell makes the important point that the production of a corpus of Pauline letters reverses their intense particularity and grants to them a new set of literary contexts; one piece within a corpus of letters and, later,

---

[37] John Gager, *The Origins of Anti-Semitism* (Oxford: Oxford University Press, 1983); Paula Fredriksen, "The Birth of Christianity and the Origins of Christian Anti-Judaism," in *Jesus, Judaism, and Christian Anti-Judaism: Reading the New Testament After the Holocaust*, ed. Paula Fredriksen and Adele Reinhartz (Louisville: Westminster John Knox Press, 2002), 8–30.

[38] John Marshall, "Misunderstanding the New Paul: Marcion's Transformation of the Sonderzeit Paul," *JECS* 20 (2012): 1–29. For Marshall, Marcion's insistence that an expected Christ who would reestablish the "Jewish kingdom" is a sign of the authority still afforded to Israel's scriptures (17). Tertullian's issue is that Marcion's law and gospel are not organized along a temporal axis of replacement but stand side-by-side as parallel spheres of salvation (Tertullian, *Marc.* 4.6).

a corpus of letters as a piece within a larger collection of authorized texts.[39] The collection of letters into a corpus produces an "epistolary Paul" for later readers to engage and imagine.[40] Since this "epistolary Paul" features a pseudonymously inclusive corpus of texts and is also joined by a diverse set of images and legends of Paul that may or may not have links to the epistles, François Bovon referred to Paul the "Monument" and Paul the "Document."[41] Daniel Marguerat rightly points out that epistolary imitations of Paul are also containers of the "Monument," and indeed others have developed fuller typologies of reception.[42] But Bovon's formulation is instructive for thinking about Paul as, quite literally, a "Document."

Seizing on Heather MacNeil's notion of *archivalterity*—the interconnectivity of archival and textual scholarship— Gregory Fewster points out that the editorial strategies employed in the production of a Pauline corpus facilitate notions of authenticity and coherence.[43] Fewster notes how editorial practices and modes of control over Pauline letters such as collection, corpus, and canon work toward the production of authenticity and exert an interpretive pressure on subsequent readers.[44] In thinking about this "spectral" presence of Paul within and behind the editions of Pauline texts, Fewster draws attention to titles and subscriptions in Codex Coislinianus—a sixth-century manuscript with paratextual devices—that unify disparate texts together as a "corpus."[45] The well-decorated and information-rich superscriptions together with titles of chapter summaries (*kephalaia*) are constant reminders of Paul's authorial presence. Reading, it turns out, is a complex

[39] Margaret M. Mitchell, "Paul and Judaism Now, Quo vadimus?" *JJMJS* 5 (2018): 66.
[40] As part of a formative conference, "Legacies of Paul," Martinus de Boer pointed out that for early readers of Paul like Ignatius, Polycarp, and *1 Clement*, differing configurations of Paul's letters each have their own "epistolary" apostle ("Comment: Which Paul?," 48–49).
[41] François Bovon, "Paul comme Document et Paul comme Monument," in *Chrétiens en conflit: L'Épître de Paul aux Galates*, ed. J. Alaaz, Essais bibliques 13 (Geneva: Labor et Fides, 1987), 54: "Paul survivra soit sous forme de document, soit sous forme de monument; c'est-a-dire soit comme texte, soit comme figure."
[42] Daniel Marguerat, "Paul après Paul: Une histoire de réception," *NTS* 54 (2008): 322. Judith Lieu refers to three poles of reception: the narrated Paul, the letter-writer Paul, and Paul the thinker or theologian ("The Battle for Paul," 78). Similarly, Samuel Vollenweider divvies up reception along the life of Paul, the collection of Paul's letters as a canon, and "the overall phenomenon of the Apostle and his theology" (das Gesamtphänomen des Apostels und seiner Theologie) ("Paulus zwischen Exegese und Wirkungsgeschichte," 153).
[43] Gregory Fewster, "Archiving Paul: Manuscripts, Religion, and the Editorial Shaping of Ancient Letter Collections," *Archivaria* 81 (2016): 101–28.
[44] Fewster, "Archiving Paul," 101–23.
[45] Greg Fewster, "Dying and Rising with the Author: Specters of Paul and the Material Text," in *Biblical Exegesis Without Authorial Intention? Interdisciplinary Approaches to Authorship and Meaning*, ed. Clarissa Breu, BibInt 172 (Leiden: Brill, 2019), 169–73.

event.⁴⁶ Pauline scholars like Benjamine Scherbenske and T. J. Lang are likewise attuned to these shaped and shaping dynamics of reading.⁴⁷

Framing the relationship between interpretive tradition and the material presentation of the *corpus Paulinum* as "paratextual hermeneutics," Eric Scherbenske underscores three material contexts that are marked by and invite further interpretive reflection.⁴⁸ Scherbenske's work reminds us that Paul's letters are shaped by editorial practices that are conditioned by assumptions of about the "authentic" Paul, but also that the same results of editorial shaping go on to have a determining force that encourages certain kinds of reading. Reading is shaped by the technologies of textual presentation. Similarly, T. J. Lang explores this dynamic with respect to the Priscillian canons that align Pauline texts to various creedal statements. For Lang, though these canons are designed to oppose certain theological currents, the residual network of cross references facilitates the creative production of Pauline theologies that move well beyond the particularity of earlier theological battles.⁴⁹

The Letter to the Hebrews, no less than other Paulines, is subject to these kinds of unifying configurations. Superscriptions and chapter divisions are later met with prefaces (*hupothéseis*) and marginal commentary. What is the role of the title in the reception of the text as Pauline? What other

---

⁴⁶ See Brian Tucker, "The Invisible Movement That Reading Is: Three Chapters in the History of a Liberal Art," Charles D. LaFollette Lecture Series, 2017, http://www.wabash.edu/lafollette/tucker2017/.

⁴⁷ Exemplifying this work in early Christian studies and focusing on the literary technologies used to map relations between canonical gospels, Jeremiah Coogan also registers this shaped and shaping dynamic of the physical text in *Eusebius the Evangelist: Rewriting the Fourfold Gospel in Late Antiquity. Cultures of Reading in the Ancient Mediterranean* (New York: Oxford University Press, 2022). For Coogan, the tables of cross references between Gospel texts developed by Eusebius of Caesarea and later transmitted in late antique and medieval manuscripts not only are readings of those very Gospel texts but also facilitate a certain set of readings in subsequent use. By creating pathways between *certain* texts, these Eusebian canon tables enable a *certain* kinds of reading practices.

⁴⁸ Eric Scherbenske, *Canonizing Paul: Ancient Editorial Practice and the Corpus Paulinum* (Oxford: Oxford University Press, 2013), 4. Scherbenske argues that the editorial shaping of Marcion's early second-century Pauline collection was grounded in certain theological principles derived from other Marcionite texts, the *Antitheses* and the Marcionite *argumenta*, texts that continue to exert interpretive pressure on subsequent readers (71–115). Likewise, the later "Euthalian" edition of Paul—an edition that features biographical texts, prologues, martyrdom accounts, *kephalaia*, and summaries of Paul's letters—have paraenetic and catechetical interests that together work toward the production of a distinct "Christian polity" (116–74). Editions of Paul might also contain a variety of hermeneutical interests, as Scherbenske points to the *Primum quaeritur* in Codex Fuldensis—a prologue affiliated with Rufinus for Paul's letters as part of a revision to the Latin Vulgate—which harbors lingering vestiges of Pelagian, anti-Pelagian, *and* Marcionite hermeneutics.

⁴⁹ T. J. Lang, "Arts of Memory, Ancient Manuscript Technologies, and the Aims of Theology," *Religions* 13.5 (2022): 1–13.

editorial strategies "Paulinize" Hebrews within collections of Paul's letters, especially as systems for organizing the Pauline corpus begin to emerge in the fourth century? The transmission of the Letter to the Hebrews as a Pauline epistle is a distinct mode of curation and not a static holder of a text awaiting authorial configuration by readers. If material transmission has a shaped-by and shaping feature, that is, if Pauline manuscripts are sites of interpretations of Paul, physical hermeneutics for facilitating readings of Paul, then consideration of the image of Paul in the Pauline history of Hebrews is only partially registered if it limits itself to "what is said about" Hebrews and not also what the material dimension "says" about Pauline authorship. In order to pursue a thicker description of the Pauline history of Hebrews, one must attend to the ways in which the processes of collection and editorial shaping of the text work toward the production of Paulinity. How do physical copies of Hebrews facilitate its reception as a Pauline object and with what kinds of editorial interventions? What traditions of interpretation do material contexts adopt and forward and what kinds of reading do they invite among subsequent readers?

4. Chapter Summary

This book analyzes how *Ad Hebraeos* became a Pauline letter through material configuration and readerly appropriation. The following four chapters isolate the earliest contexts of the Pauline authorship of Hebrews (Chapter 2), the first appropriations of Hebrews as a Pauline letter (Chapters 3 and 4), and the transmission history of Hebrews as Pauline (Chapter 5).

Chapter 2 provides an account of the invention of Hebrews as a Pauline letter by reexamining the origins of the title, the postscript, and the earliest papyrological evidence, its circulation as a letter of Barnabas, its varying life within collections of Paul, as well as the first discussions of this unusual Pauline text. While the earliest associations between Hebrews and Paul are lost to us, the title, "To the Hebrews," is the first marker of Paulinity and is a product of editing Hebrews for placement within collections of Paul. The earliest extant Christian voices to discuss this letter show that they are already confronted with a text titled and collected as Pauline. Discourse on the Pauline authorship of Hebrews assumes this material priority. The narratives developed to explain the origins of the letter build upon the title, which directs readers to Acts 21, where Paul addresses Jews in the Ἑβραΐδι διαλέκτῳ.

Though the Pauline authorship is continually discussed in the second and third centuries, the ultimate stabilization of Hebrews in Latin and Greek collections was not the result of successful argumentation that the letter is in fact Paul's, but an outworking of a scribal willingness to shift the position of Hebrews within collections of Paul to accommodate developing theories of Paul's letters. The openness to pushing Hebrews outside of Paul's letters to (seven) churches allowed the text to linger on in the outer range of the corpus.

Chapters 3 and 4 take up the two earliest readers to leave us sustained evidence of their reading activity of Hebrews as Pauline, Clement and Origen, both from Alexandria in Egypt. The third chapter focuses on Clement's engagement with Hebrews in concert with his image of Paul, image of Jews, and the function of Israelite history in his configuration of Christianity. Here I take note of Clement's avoidance of the Letter to the Hebrews, which is most often evoked as an anonymous and supplementary letter within Clement's *corpus Paulinum* and only occasionally used as *Pauline* against rival second-century teachers like Basilides and Valentinus. Rather than evoke and position this letter as Pauline, Clement finds in Hebrews an archive of scripture citations that he freely excerpts and repurposes in order to imitate his image of Paul as the recipient of "unwritten" gnosis from the *logos* that is symbolically laden within the "old" scriptures. As Clement excerpts Paul's scriptural citations from Romans and 1 Corinthians, for example, he mimics the epistolary sequence of these citations, maintaining something of the "original" Pauline logic. Hebrews, on the other hand, is excerpted and repurposed without reference to the original sequence of citations. This distance at which Clement holds Hebrews is also informed by his reading of the ethnic valance of the title "To the Hebrews." Clement characterizes Jews as "fleshly" and contextualizes the audience of Hebrews along these stereotypical lines despite otherwise using "Hebrew" as a term free from the connotations of "Jew." So, too, Clement uses the term "Hebrew" to ground Paul's ethnicity and free the apostle from the connotations of being a *Ioudaios*. Clement's reading of the Jewish audience and occasion for the Letter to the Hebrews contrasts with and refracts Clement's image of Paul as a former Jew.

Origen's appropriation of Hebrews a few decades after Clement, in Alexandria and subsequently in Caesarea, is the focus of the fourth chapter. With Clement, Origen imagines the Jewish reader as "earthly" and "literal," but, unlike Clement, Origen finds in Hebrews a definitive Pauline description of Jewish reading practices and, by extension, a way of describing the core of Christian uniqueness. Origen seizes upon the language of Hebrews 8:5, which describes the wilderness Tabernacle as a "shadowy copy" (ὑποδείγματι καὶ σκιᾷ) of a true, heavenly counterpart. This text defines Christian and Jewish reading practices simultaneously; Jews read the shadows while Christians understand that there is a higher, heavenly reference. The centrality of this conception of reading is registered as Origen presents Jesus and Paul as the inventor and practitioner of the reading method articulated in Hebrews; difference in reading becomes the crux between Judaism and Christianity. Though Origen is thought to have a robust lived experience with third-century Jews in Caesarea and deep familiarity with Jewish exegetical traditions, I claim that Origen builds his conception of Jewish-Christian difference around the art of reading informed by the language of Hebrews 8:5. Since Hebrews provides Origen with the hermeneutical leverage to assert the uniqueness of Christian reading practices, it is an integral text within his *corpus Paulinum*.

The fifth chapter shifts from these reading engagements with Hebrews to note the institutionalization of the Pauline authorship of Hebrews within the newly burgeoning prefatory practices of the fourth century. As Hebrews is the object of commentary and homily, the preface or *hypothesis* is the new location for comments about this strange Pauline text. As fourth-century prefaces emerge from Ephrem the Syrian, Rufinus, and John Chrysostom, we see these authors recycle the information preserved in Eusebius into slightly new combinations. Still, since *hypotheses* are not only a product of commentaries but are also positioned within editions of Paul's letters, I draw attention to the Euthalian *hypothesis* to Hebrews that forwards Origen's reading of Hebrews 8:5 and configures the purpose of Hebrews around the language of the shadow. As the form of commentary known as *catena* develops in the sixth century—commentaries built upon excerpts from previous interpreters organized together to form a "chain" of comments—one finds Chrysostom's preface repeatedly revisited as a way of framing Hebrews, but it is ultimately overwhelmed by the presence of the Euthalian hypothesis in later catena manuscripts as the most common prefatory comment on the letter. In the end, while Hebrews is initially configured as Pauline through titling practices, to which readers react, the history of transmission reveals the return of reading traditions that sustain and institutionalize the Pauline status of Hebrews. Origen's reading of Hebrews as a description of Jewish reading practices follows Hebrews throughout its medieval and early modern afterlife.

The Pauline History of Hebrews. Warren Campbell, Oxford University Press. © Oxford University Press 2025.
DOI: 10.1093/9780197769287.003.0001

2

The Invention of Paul's Letter to the Hebrews

The Letter to the Hebrews was the most contentious Pauline text to circulate in the second and third centuries CE.[1] Eusebius of Caesarea looks back upon the landscape of possible evidence from the vantage of the early fourth century and is open about his interest in shoring up the letter's authorial status with testimonies of its Pauline appropriation:[2]

> Paul's fourteen epistles are well known and undisputed. It is not indeed right to overlook the fact that some have rejected (ἠθετήκασι) the Epistle to the Hebrews, saying that it is disputed by the church of Rome, on the ground that it was not written by Paul. But what has been said concerning this epistle by those who lived before our time I shall quote in the proper place.

True to his word, Eusebius weaves remarks about Hebrews throughout the *Historia*—curating the received opinions of Gaius of Rome, Irenaeus of Lyon, Origen, and Clement of Alexandria—even from those who "reject" (ἀθετέω) Hebrews as a Pauline letter.[3] Leaving no stone unturned, Eusebius

---

[1] There is a cross-confession between those who want to appropriate Hebrews as Pauline and those who do not. Philastrius of Brescia, for example, who writes against Hebrews as a Pauline letter (referring to the "heresy of Paul's letter to the Hebrews"), acknowledges that "it is read by some" (*Haer.* 89, *esti legitur a quibusdam*). From the other direction, Amphilochius (*Iambi ad Seleucum*, ll. 308–9) in defending Hebrews as a Pauline letter acknowledges that "some say that the Letter to the Hebrews is spurious." Cf. Eusebius, *Hist. eccl.* 3.25.4–5, 6.13.6, referring to Clement of Alexandria's comments on τὰς ἀντιλεγομένας (disputed writings), which include Hebrews, *Wisdom of Solomon, Sirach, Barnabas, 2 Clement*, and Jude.

[2] *Hist. eccl.* 3.3.5. Greek text found in Eduard Schwartz and Theodore Mommsen, eds., *Eusebius Werke* II/1, *Die Kirchengeschichte*, ed. Friedhelm Winkelmann, 2nd ed., GCS N.F. 6.1 (Berlin: Akademie Verlag, 1999), 190: τοῦ δὲ Παύλου πρόδηλοι καὶ σαφεῖς αἱ δεκατέσσαρες· ὅτι γεμήν τινες ἠθετήκασι τὴν πρὸς Ἑβραίους, πρὸς τῆς Ῥωμαίων ἐκκλησίας ὡς μὴ Παύλου οὖσαν αὐτὴν ἀντιλέγεσθαι φήσαντες, οὐ δίκαιον ἀγνοεῖν· καὶ τὰ περὶ ταύτης δὲ τοῖς πρὸ ἡμῶν εἰρημένα κατὰ καιρὸν παραθήσομαι.

[3] See 3.38.1–4, 5.26.1, 6.13.6, 6.14.2–4, 6.20.3, 6.25.11–14.

claims that even the Therapeutae described by Philo (*On the Contemplative Life*) were in possession of the Gospels and the writings of the apostles, including the Epistle to the Hebrews among other letters of Paul.[4]

Subsequent recognition that Hebrews is simply absent in the surviving works of Cyprian, Novatian, and Ambrose, as well as in the Muratorian fragment, the Marcionite Prologues, and the Latin commentaries of one called "Ambrosiaster," among others, led to the development of a much larger narrative that Hebrews was "rejected" in the "West," that is, among those who wrote primarily in Latin in places like Rome and Carthage. By the late fourth century, it is argued, the capitulation of Jerome and Augustine to the growing "acceptance" of Hebrews in the "East," that is, by those writing in Greek in cities like Alexandria and Caesarea, led to the letter's acceptance as Pauline across the Mediterranean until the time of its de-Paulinization a millennium later in the hands of Erasmus and others. The basic duality of this narrative, the accept-reject and West-East pairing, imposes a deeply reductionistic framework upon the ancient discussion.

The language of acceptance and rejection first emphasized by Eusebius assumes and empowers the image of autonomous ancient readers as the final arbiters of authorial ascription and obscures a more dynamic process of authorization in which readers encounter and engage the signs of Paulinity found in the editorial shaping and transmission of Hebrews as a Pauline *text*.[5] Accordingly, this chapter focuses on the origins and ongoing curation of Hebrews as a Pauline letter with particular attention to the interplay between text and reader.

1. Origins of the Pauline Ascription: The Triumph of a Pseudepigraphon?

The ἀμήν in Hebrews 13:21 has long seemed like a suitable ending for a text with such distinctive and widely recognized rhetorical and homiletic

---

[4] *Hist. eccl.* 2.17.12. See here Sabrina Inowlocki, "Eusebius of Caesarea's *Interpretatio Christiana* of Philo's De vita contemplative," *HTR* 97.3 (2004): 305–28.

[5] For a recent challenge to disentangle the conflation of authorial attribution and textual production see Gregory Fewster, "Authoring Manuscripts," in *The Oxford Handbook of the New Testament in the Roman Empire*, ed. Harry O. Maier, Heid Wendt, and Emiliano Rubens Urcuioli (Oxford: Oxford University Press, forthcoming).

features.[6] Yet, to the frustration of later interpreters, an "I" voice (re-) emerges in Hebrews 13:22–25 and addresses the audience in markedly personal terms:[7]

Παρακαλῶ δὲ ὑμᾶς, ἀδελφοί, ἀνέχεσθε τοῦ λόγου τῆς παρακλήσεως, καὶ γὰρ διὰ βραχέων ἐπέστειλα ὑμῖν. Γινώσκετε τὸν ἀδελφὸν ἡμῶν Τιμόθεον ἀπολελυμένον, μεθ' οὗ ἐὰν τάχιον ἔρχηται ὄψομαι ὑμᾶς. Ἀσπάσασθε πάντας τοὺς ἡγουμένους ὑμῶν καὶ πάντας τοὺς ἁγίους. Ἀσπάζονται ὑμᾶς οἱ ἀπὸ τῆς Ἰταλίας. Ἡ χάρις μετὰ πάντων ὑμῶν.

I appeal to you, brothers, bear with the word of exhortation, for I have written to you briefly. I want you to know that our brother Timothy has been set free, and if he comes in time, he will be with me when I see you. Greet all your leaders and all the saints. Those from Italy send you greetings. Grace be with all of you.

Stylistic, linguistic, as well as situational and contextual dissimilarity between this postscript and Hebrews 1–12 has fueled an ongoing and seemingly irresolvable discussion regarding the textual development of

---

[6] Some early examples of this view include Franz Overbeck, *Zur Geschichte des Kanons: Zwei Abhandlungen* (Chemnitz: Ernst Schmeitzner, 1880), 16; Richard Perdelwitz, "Das literarische Problem des Hebräerbriefs," *ZNW* 11 (1910): 59–78; C. C. Torrey, "The Authorship and Character of the So-Called 'Epistle to the Hebrews,'" *JBL* 30 (1911): 152. On rhetorical features of Hebrews see Jerome H. Neyrey, "Syncrisis and Encomium: Reading Hebrews Through Greek Rhetorics," *CBQ* 82 (2020): 276–99; Walter Übelacker, "Paraenesis or Paraclesis—Hebrews as a Test Case," in *Early Christian Paraenesis in Context*, ed. James Starr and Troels Engberg-Pedersen, BZNW 125 (Berlin: de Gruyter, 2012), 319–52. In fact, Hebrews 13 as a whole is a site of a number form-critical excavations, which divide the chapter into various layers of editorial development. See E. D. Jones, "The Authorship of Hebrews xiii," *ExpTim* (1934–35): 562–67 (a detached leaf added to Heb 1–12); Jean Héring, *L'Épître aux Hébreux*, Commentaire du Nouveau Testament, 12 (Neuchatel-Paris: Delachaux & Niestlé, 1954) (added to Heb 1–12); Harald Hegermann, *Der Brief an die Hebräer*, ThHKNT 16 (Berlin: Evangelische, 1988) (an *inclusio* between Heb 1:1–4 and 12:25–29); George W. Buchanan, *To the Hebrews*, AB 36 (New York: Doubleday, 1972) (Heb 13 itself split between 1–19 and a later hand in 20–21 and 22–25); Torrey, "The Authorship and Character," 137–56 (13:1–7 added to flow with chapters 1–12, which resume in 13:8). Defenses of the authenticity of Hebrews 13 include Ceslas Spicq, "L'authenticité du chapitre XIII de l'Épître aux Hébreux," *ConNT* 11 (1947): 226–36; and Jukka Thurén, *Das Lobopfer der Hebräer: Studien zum Aufbau und Anliegen von Hebräerbrief 13*, Acta Academiae Aboensis 47 (Åbo: Akademi, 1974).

[7] Greek text from *Novum Testamentum Graece*, ed., Eberhard Nestle, Erwin Nestle, Barbara Aland, Kurt Aland, Johannes D. Karavidopoulos, Carlo M. Martini, and Bruce M. Metzger, 28th ed., Institut für neutestamentliche Textforschung (Stuttgart: Deutsche Bibelgesellschaft, 2012), 684. On Hebrews 13:21–25 as a "postscript" see Walter Übelacker, *Der Hebräerbrief als Appel: Untersuchungen zur Exordium, Narratio und Postscriptum (Hebr 1–2 und 13,22–25)*, ConB 21 (Stockholm: Almqvist & Wiksell, 1989).

Hebrews.[8] The degree of stylistic difference warranted by the generic difference of a postscript is a common point of discussion here, as are the other uses of "amen" followed by παρακαλῶ (Rom 11:36, Eph 3:12) or a greeting (ἀσπάσασθε in Phil 4:20–21, 2 Tim 4:18–19) in various Pauline texts.[9] The epistolary postscript in 1 Peter 5:10–14 also follows an "amen" and complexifies the discussion of the origins of the postscript in Hebrews further.[10] Even if Hebrews 13:22–25 was corrected in 𝔓[46], in which a later hand squeezed the omitted και παντας τους αγιους in the space between the final two lines—a kind of correction found frequently in the text of Hebrews in 𝔓[46]—there is no manuscript evidence of a "shorter" ending of Hebrews.[11]

---

[8] Harold W. Attridge, *Hebrews: A Commentary on the Epistle to the Hebrews*, Hermeneia (Philadelphia: Fortress, 1989), joined a long line of scholarship going back to Westcott and Wrede at the turn of the twentieth century that sees Hebrews 13, specifically vv. 22–25, as integral to the text. Subsequent commentarial scholarship has seized upon Attridge's estimation and some refer to a "consensus" on the authenticity of Hebrews 13:21–25. However, the copiousness of commentaries skews perception of the field, which remains divided. Those who view the "postscript" as an addition include A. J. M. Wedderburn, "'Letter' to the Hebrews and Its Thirteenth Chapter," *NTS* 50 (2004): 390–405; Gert J. Steyn, "The Ending of Hebrews Reconsidered," *ZNW* 103 (2012): 235–53; Walter Schmithals, "Der Hebräerbrief als Paulusbrief: Beobachtungen zur Kanonbildung," in *Die Weltlichkeit des Glaubens in der Alten Kirche: Festschrift für Ulrich Wickert zum siebzigsten Geburtstag*, ed. Dietmar Wyrwa (Berlin: de Gruyter, 1997), 319–37; Eric Gräßer, *An die Hebräer, 1 Teilband (Hebr 1–6)*, EKKNT 17/1 (Zürich: Benziger, 1990), 16–18.

[9] See, for example, Wedderburn, "'Letter' to the Hebrews," 392, who highlights a wide variety of differences between the final chapter and the body of Hebrews: abrupt shifts, "miscellaneous exhortations," "tersely formulated, almost staccato in its string of direct or implied exhortations and commands" (394), different terms in Hebrews 13 for near synonyms in 1–12 (397–98), as well as situational and contextual differences. Others point out that epistolary parenesis requires or at least permits stylistic difference. See, for example, Clare K. Rothschild, *Hebrews as Pseudepigraphon: The History and Significance of the Pauline Attribution of Hebrews*, WUNT 235 (Tübingen: Mohr Siebeck, 2009), 52; Brian R. Dyer, "The Epistolary Closing of Hebrews and Pauline Imitation," in *Paul and Pseudepigraphy*, ed. Stanley E. Porter and Gregory P. Fewster, Pauline Studies 8 (Leiden: Brill, 2013), 276–78.

[10] On 1 Peter 5 and Hebrews 13 see Frumentius Renner, *"An die Hebräer"—ein pseudepigraphischer Brief*, Münsterschwarzacher Studien 14 (Münsterschwarzach: Vier-Türme, 1970), 115–19. Notice also the similar language of "written briefly" in 1 Peter 5:12 (δι' ὀλίγων ἔγραψα παρακαλῶν) and in Hebrews 13:21 (διὰ βραχέων ἐπέστειλα ὑμῖν). L. Paul Trudinger "'ΚΑΙ ΓΑΡ ΔΙΑ ΒΡΑΧΕΩΝ ΕΠΕΣΤΕΙΛΑ ΥΜΙΝ': A Note on Hebrews XIII.22," *JTS* 23 (1972): 128–30, reads Hebrews 13:21 as a reference to Hebrews 13, not the whole of Hebrews. For comparison between 1 Peter and Hebrews see Hermann von Soden, *Hebräerbrief, Briefe des Petrus, Jakobus, Judas*, 3rd ed. HCNT 3/2 (Tübingen: Mohr Siebeck, 1899), 3–4.

[11] This correction is also noted in H. C. Hoskier, *A Commentary on the Various Readings in the Text of the Epistle to the Hebrews in the Chester-Beatty Papyrus* 𝔓[46] *(circa 200 A.D.)* (London: Bernard Quaritch, 1938), 65. Steyn considers whether the start of the postscript on a new line in 𝔓[46] is suggestive of an addition. Of course, there are a number of other active questions concerning the redaction in other Pauline letters. See Walter Schmithals, "Zur Abfassung und ältesten Sammlung der paulinischen Hauptbriefe," *ZNW* 51 (1960): 225–45, translated as "On the Composition and Earliest Collection of the Major Epistles of Paul," in *Paul and the Gnostics*, trans. J. E. Steely (Nashville: Abingdon, 1971), who finds an anti-Gnostic context for the redaction of Pauline letters. For a response see Harry Y. Gamble, "The Redaction of the Pauline Letters," *JBL* 94 (1975): 409–14, and, more generally, Thomas Schmeller, "Ungetrennt und unvermischt? Die Frage nach Kompilationen und Interpolationen in den echten Paulusbriefen," in *Receptions of Paul in*

Those who are otherwise split on the question of authenticity are more or less aligned on the *function* of the postscript as a marker of Paulinity. Clare Rothschild, for instance, has recently reignited and extended William Wrede's thesis, arguing that Hebrews as a whole was written as a Pauline pseudepigraphon and the postscript (an original feature of the text) is but the final sign.[12] Aside from stylistic and generic differences between Hebrews and other Pauline letters, the challenge in reading the entirety of the Letter to the Hebrews as an instance of Pauline pseudonymity is that the self-description in Hebrews 2:3—which claims to know "the voice of the Lord" from "those who heard"—is a quintessentially non-Pauline genealogy of tradition (cf. Gal 1:13).[13] This text alone was enough to dissuade Ephrem the Syrian of Pauline authorship in the fourth century. Indeed there are similarities—language of the seed of Abraham (Gal 3:29 / Heb 2:16), milk-meat metaphors (1 Cor 3:2 / Heb 5:13–14), a new covenant (2 Cor 3:6 / Heb 8)—but scholarship taking up the question of conceptual parallels between Hebrews and other Pauline letters typically finds insufficient conceptual or theological overlap to suggest imitation that amounts to an active attempt at pseudonymity.[14] So too, the second- and third-century readers who positioned, defended, or otherwise justified the Paulinity of Hebrews assumed the non-Pauline stylistic features and overarching lack of a Pauline authorial claim.[15]

The more common route to Paulinity, however, is to see the final postscript in Hebrews 13:22–25 as a later, secondary attempt to Paulinize an

---

Early Christianity: The Person of Paul and His Writings Through the Eyes of His Early Interpreters, ed. J. Schröter, S. Butticaz, and A. Dettwiler (Berlin: de Gruyter, 2018), 751–77.

[12] See Rothschild, *Hebrews as Pseudepigraphon*, 15–44, as well as William Wrede, *Das literarische Rätsel des Hebräerbriefs*, FRLANT 8 (Göttingen: Vandenhoeck & Ruprecht, 1906), esp. 39–45. Wrede famously claimed that there was a shift toward Pauline pseudepigraphy midway through the composition of Hebrews.

[13] Later prologues to Pauline letters also mention this counter to Pauline authorship. See the prologue to Hebrews in Hermann Freiherr von Soden, *Die Schriften des Neuen Testaments in ihrer ältesten erreichbaren Textgestalt hergestellt auf Grund ihrer Textgeschichte*, I. Teil: *Untersuchungen*, I. Abteilung: *Die Textseugen* (Göttingen: Vandenhoeck and Ruprecht, 1911), 347.

[14] Friedrich Schröger, "Der Hebräerbrief-paulinisch?," in *Kontinuität und Einheit: Festschrift für Franz Mussner*, ed. P. G. Müller and W. Stenger (Freiburg: Herder, 1981), 217–19; Kurt Erlemann, "Alt und neu bei Paulus und im Hebräerbrief: Frühchristliche Standortbestimmung im Vergleich," TZ 54 (1998): 345–67; Walter Schmithals, "Der Hebräerbrief als Paulusbrief: Beobachtungen zur Kanonbildung," in *Die Weltlichkeit des Glaubens: Festschrift für Ulrich Wickert zum siebzigsten Geburtstag*, ed. Dietmar Wyrwa, BZNW 89 (Berlin: de Gruyter, 1997), 334; Christian Grappe, "Hébreux et la tradition paulinienne," in Schröter et al., *Receptions of Paul*, 466–70. Cf. also Ceslas Spicq, *l'Épître aux Hebreux*, I. *Introduction*, Études Bibliques (Paris: Libraire Lecoffre, 1952), 145–66, for a classic treatment of Hebrews and Paul.

[15] See section 3 below.

otherwise anonymous text with an added epistolary frame, transforming the preceding content into a Pauline epistle, an instance of pseudepigraphy in the second degree. Yet, even as a secondary attempt at Paulinization, the postscript lacks a sense of urgency and clarity. Although the Timothy in Hebrews 13:23 might technically be an unknown figure to us, the figure is likely the same as the close affiliate of Paul and thereby invites some kind of Pauline proximity.[16] However, without a Pauline self-identification this personal reference might just as easily be read as the voice of an affiliate of Paul from subsequent Pauline circles. There was nothing holding back the circulation of Hebrews as a letter of Barnabas, for instance, who might also have known Timothy.[17] The postscript, as Gabriella Gelardini points out, "activates" several names.[18] Every other epistolary text that scholars have variously judged as attempts at Pauline pseudepigraphy names Paul in that attempt.[19]

Granted, the addition of a postscript to Paulinize a homiletical text is a much different literary situation than the kinds of unified epistolary imitations scholars find in texts like Colossians and 1 Timothy, and so the comparison between the two is limited. Still, the urgency for Paulinity at the end of 2 Thessalonians, for example, is not nearly as pronounced in Hebrews: "I, Paul, write this greeting in my own hand, which is the distinguishing sign ($\sigma\eta\mu\epsilon\hat{\iota}ον$) in all my letters. This is how I write" (2 Thess 3.17).[20] The suggestion that Paul was named as the author of Hebrews in a greeting that was later removed prompts us to account for the *removal* of a

---

[16] References to Timothy include Romans 16:21, 1 Corinthians 4:17, 16:10, 2 Corinthians 1:1, 1:19, Philippians 1:1, 2:19, Colossians 1.1, 2 Thessalonians 1:1, Philemon 1, as well as 1 Timothy and 2 Timothy.

[17] See section 4 below.

[18] Gabriella Gelardini, "'As If by Paul?' Some Remarks on the Textual Strategy of Anonymity in Hebrews," in *The Early Reception of Paul the Second Temple Jew: Text, Narrative and Reception History*, ed. Isaac W. Oliver and Gabriele Boccaccini (London: T&T Clark, 2018), 273.

[19] Ephesians 1:1 ("Paul, an apostle"), Colossians 1:1 ("Paul, an apostle"), 1 Timothy 1:1 ("Paul, an apostle"), Titus 1:1 ("Paul, a bondservant"), 2 Timothy 1:1 ("Paul, an apostle"), 2 Thessalonians 1:1 ("Paul, Silvanus, and Timothy"), *Third Corinthians* ("Paul, a prisoner"), *To the Laodiceans* ("Paul, an apostle"), various letters from Paul to Seneca ("Paul to Seneca, Greeting"). See also Dyer, "Epistolary Closing of Hebrews," 284; Buchanan, *To the Hebrews*, esp. 267–68.

[20] Steve Reece, *Paul's Large Letters: Paul's Autographic Subscriptions in the Light of Ancient Epistolary Conventions*, LNTS 561 (London: T&T Clark, 2017), 52, draws a comparison with Plato, *Letter* 3 (315a–c), which refers to the beginning of the letter as a "sign" or "symbol" ($\sigma\acute{\upsilon}\mu\beta\omicron\lambda\omicron\nu$) that it is indeed from Plato. 2 Thessalonians is, to be sure, a disputed text in contemporary scholarship. On pseudepigraphy see Trevor Thompson, "As If Genuine: Interpreting the Pseudepigraphic 2 Thessalonians," in *Pseudepigraphie und Verfasserfiktion in frühchristlichen Briefen*, ed. Jörg Frey, Jens Herzer, Martina Janssen, and Clare K. Rothschild (Tübingen: Mohr Siebeck, 2009), 471–88. See Cicero, *Att.* 10.11.1 on the use or nonuse of his personal seal and handwriting.

Pauline attribution on such an unusual text, one that suffers from a lack of authorial markers despite being read as Pauline in Egyptian communities.

The postscript, then, does not generate its own Paulinity, and the anonymity of the text is, in the end, inescapable. In light of these features and in resistance to erasing or escaping anonymity as a chosen feature, Michael Wolter inquires into the possible function of anonymity in distinction from pseudepigraphy. If, following Norbert Brox, pseudonymous claims are designed, at least in part, to authorize postapostolic teachings by means of apostolic continuity, Wolter explores the implicit locus of authority that anonymous texts assume.[21] Wolter positions Hebrews, as well as a number early Christian "nameless" texts, as active renunciations of the authority of a name, a "consciously intended anonymity" with literary and ideological underpinnings.[22] With Hebrews, the "author" is but a "hearer" of the *logos*, whose authority is channeled by anonymous human mediation.[23] The description used by the postscript for the content of Hebrews as a λόγος παρακλήσεως provides a slightly more tangible social and cultural context in which to think about anonymity as a chosen posture, since, in Acts 13:15, there is an open invitation by synagogue officials (οἱ ἀρχισυνάγωγοι) for someone to give a λόγος παρακλήσεως after the reading of the Law and the prophets.[24] Perhaps rendering this παρακλήσεως anonymous was an active

---

[21] Michael Wolter, "Die anonymen Schriften des Neuen Testaments Annäherungsversuch an ein literarisches Phänomen," *ZNW* 79 (1988): 2, referring to Norbert Brox, *Falsche Verfasserangaben: Zur Erklärung der frühchristlichen Pseudepigraphie*, Stuttgarter Bibelstudien 79 (Stuttgart: Katholisches Bibelwerk, 1975). There are a number advances in scholarship on pseudepigraphy since Brox. See David E. Aune, "Reconceptualizing the Phenomenon of Ancient Pseudepigraphy: An Epilogue," in Frey et al., *Pseudepigraphie und Verfasserfiktion*, 789–824; Armin D. Baum, "Authorship and Pseudepigraphy in Early Christian Literature: A Translation of the Most Important Source Texts and an Annotated Bibliography," in Porter and Fewster, *Paul and Pseudepigraphy*, 11–63; Hindy Najman and Irene Peirano Garrison, "Pseudepigraphy as an Interpretive Construct," in *The Old Testament Pseudepigrapha: Fifty Years of the Pseudepigrapha Section at the SBL*, ed. Matthias Henze and Liv Ingeborg Lied, SBLEJL 50 (Atlanta: Society of Biblical Literature, 2019), 331–55; *Ethopoiia: La représentation de caractères entre fiction scolaire et réalité vivante à l'époque impériale et tardive*, ed. Eugenio Amato and Jacques Schamp, Université de Fribourg, Groupe de recherches sur les rhétoriques de l'antiquité tardive, Cardo 3 (Salerno: Helios editrice, 2005); Patricia A. Rosenmeyer, *Ancient Epistolary Fictions: The Letter in Greek Literature* (Cambridge: Cambridge University Press, 2001).

[22] Wolter, "Die anonymen Schriften," 5: "einer literarische wie theologisch bewußt intendierten Anonymität interpretieren läßt."

[23] Wolter, "Die anonymen Schriften," 11. For an active realization of this theological view see Kurt Aland, "The Problem of Anonymity and Pseudonymity in Christian Literature of the First Two Centuries," *JTS* 12 (1961): 39–49. Interestingly Dio Chrysostom praises Homer for his anonymity, a quality that actually elevates the voice of the text investing it with divine capabilities (*Or.* 53).

[24] See Gabriella Gelardini, *Verhärtet eure Herzen nicht: Der Hebräer, eine Synagogenhomilie zu Tischa be-Aw*, Biblical Interpretation 83 (Leiden: Brill, 2007); Gabriella Gelardini, "Hebrews, an Ancient Synagogue Homily for Tisha be-Av: Its Function, Its Basis, Its Theological Interpretation,"

attempt to see if it might fall into the orbit of an even "higher" authority than the one that initially authorized it. Perhaps even an apostle.

Others read the postscript not as a signal of a Pauline epistle or the casting out of textual bait into the pool of apostolic fish, but as an added textual greeting for a new Christian assembly receiving the text of Hebrews as it was forwarded to them.[25] The addition of an epistolary postscript is then a way to greet those who must be a familiar group receiving this "word of exhortation" for the first time. Régis Burnet notes that the final postscript steps back and views the "word of exhortation" as a whole—not as "my" but as "the" λόγος—as though the preceding was not originally intended for what is *now* its next audience.[26] Burnet advances on the work of Albert Vanhoye in positing that the postscript functions as an accompanying letter in its own right, facilitating the process by which this exhortation is "resent" to another Christian group.[27] Elias Bickerman argued similarly a few decades earlier, pointing out, in part, that practices of epistolary forwarding can be found in Cicero (*Att.* 1.9; Thyillus asking Cicero to ask Atticus for books on the ritual of Eumolpidae), in Pauline networks (Col 4:16, 1 Thess 5:27), and between later Christian reading communities (*Phil.* 13; the Philippians ask Polycarp for copies of Ignatius).[28]

---

in *Hebrews: Contemporary Methods—New Insights*, ed. Gelardini (Leiden: Boston, 2005), 107–27; Lee Levine, "Synagogue Leadership: The Case of the Archisynagogue," in *Jews in a Graeco-Roman World*, ed. Martin Goodman (Oxford: Oxford University Press, 1998), 181–94.

[25] See, for example, Régis Burnet, "La finale de l'épître aux Hébreux: Une addition alexandrine de la fin du IIe siècle?," *RB* 120 (2013): 423–40, following Albert Vanhoye, *Exegesis Epistulæ ad Hebræos [ad usum privatum auditorum]* (Rome: Pontificium Institutum Biblicum, 1968), 15 (cited on 426–27); Christian Grappe, "Hébreux et la tradition paulinienne," in Schröter et al., *Receptions of Paul*, 466–70; Elias J. Bickerman, "En marge de l'écriture," *RB* 88 (1981): 39–40; Knut Backhaus, "Der Hebräerbrief und die Paulus-Schule," *BZ* 37 (1993): 183–208. Johann Gottfried Immanuel Berger is cited as the first to critically engage the postscript in Hebrews 13:21–25 and suggest that it arose in the process of sending "Hebrews" to a secondary audience; see "Der Brief an die Hebräer: Eine Homilie," in *Göttingische Bibliothek der neuesten theologischen Literatur*, ed. J. F. Schleusner and Carl F. Stäudlin, Dritter Band (Göttingen: Vandenhoeck & Ruprecht, 1797), 445: "Allein dieser Schluß [Heb 13:22–25] ist von der vorhergehenden Abhandlung so wohl durch seinen Inhalt als durch das vorgehende ἀμήν so sorgfältig abgesondert, daß man offenbar sieht, er gehöre nicht unmittelbar dazu. Es läßt sich daher die Schwierigkeit sehr gut dadurch heben, wenn man annimmt, die Rede sei entweder von ihrem Verfasser selbst, der sie, nachdem er sie gehalten hatte, aufgesezt habe, oder auch von einem andern, der sie entweder nachgeschrieben, oder ihre Gedanken so gut gefaßt hatte, daß er sie nachher aufsezen konnte, or irgend eine auswärtige Gemeine [sic], oder auch an mehrere geschikt [sic] worden." Citation noted in Grappe with original [sic] marks, "Hébreux et la tradition paulinienne," 479.

[26] Burnet, "La finale de l'épître," 425. Cf. Gräßer, *An die Hebräer*, 412 n. 96.

[27] Burnet, "La finale de l'épître," 426–27.

[28] See Bickerman, "En marge de l'Écriture," 39–40. In thinking about the lack of a title or greeting, Bickerman points to the transmission of the Ps-Clementines, which feature letters of transmission of a text without a title. Relevant here is the work of David A. Smith, *The Epistles for All*

In thinking about the ascension of Hebrews into a *corpus Paulinum*, there might be several "possibilities consistent with known evidence," to borrow a phrase from C. P. Anderson.[29] The postscript is certainly open to a Pauline reading, but triangulating the precise mechanism by which Hebrews was first connected to other Pauline letters is perhaps inaccessible to us. In his oft-cited work on Hebrews and the Pauline school, Knut Backhaus argued that although the postscript was not designed to imitate Paul, it was the textual evidence through which the letter was initially affiliated with the apostle.[30] Indeed, later scribes and copyists used material from the postscript to heighten the Pauline biography of the basic title, "to the Hebrews."[31] In the fifth-century Codex Alexandrinus the superscription reads πρὸς Ἑβραίους ἐγράφη ἀπὸ Ῥώμης, and in the sixth-century Codex Coislinianus it is πρὸς Ἑβραίους ἐγράφη ἀπὸ τῆς Ἰταλίας διὰ Τιμοθέου.[32] At the same time, the first to make the association between Paul and the details of the postscript was Ephrem the Syrian in the mid-fourth century, followed closely by John Chrysostom. Theodor Zahn pointed to the familiar idea of a shared liturgical setting as the basic catalyst for the beginnings of the Paul-Hebrews association.[33] The reading of Hebrews as Pauline in liturgical settings put pressure on figures like Clement, Origen, and Eusebius to shore up the Paulinity of the letter from known dispute. Incidentally, the texts of Romans and Hebrews have a higher concentration of liturgical markings in the earliest Pauline manuscript, 𝔓⁴⁶.[34]

A consideration of Hebrews apart from its context with the corpus Pauline reveals that it was not designed to be Pauline, that is, to bear explicit markers of Paulinity on "its own." Rather, Hebrews accrues markers of Paulinity from "elsewhere," namely, from the processes of inclusion within collections of Paul's letters.

Christians: Epistolary Literature, Circulation, and The Gospels for All Christians, BIS 186 (Leiden: Brill, 2020).

[29] C. P. Anderson, "Hebrews Among the Letters of Paul," *SR* 5.3 (1975): 259. Anderson argues that Hebrews is the Epistle to the Laodiceans recommended in Colossians 4:16, and that through this connection with Colossians, Hebrews began to be circulated as Pauline.

[30] Backhaus, "Der Hebräerbrief und die Paulus-Schule," 183–208. Grappe also argues that the epistolary postscript was read as Pauline, "Hébreux et la tradition paulinienne," 461–83, as does Gräßer, *An die Hebräer*, 17–19.

[31] For superscriptions to Hebrews see B. M. Metzger, *A Textual Commentary on the Greek New Testament*, 2nd ed. (Stuttgart: Deutsche Biblegesellschaft, 1994), 678.

[32] Metzger, *Textual Commentary*, 678.

[33] Theodor Zahn, *Geschichte des Neutestamentlichen Kanons, Erster Band: Das Neue Testament vor Origenes, Erste Hälfte* (Leipzig: Andreas Deichert, 1888), 302.

[34] Only Romans and Hebrews have secondary markings making sense divisions for what are likely liturgical readings.

2. Our First Copy of *Pros Hebraious*

The historical circumstances that gave rise to the earliest collection(s) of Pauline letters remain hidden, and our best reconstructions remain theoretical. Proposals range from elongated historical processes in which a core, or perhaps cores, of Pauline letters circulated throughout Asia Minor around which other letters were eventually magnetized, down to more punctiliar moments of collection in which specific locations like Ephesus, Corinth, and Alexandria, and even specific actors such as Timothy, Luke, Onesimus, or Paul himself, provide the context for collecting multiple letters together for circulation (cf. Cicero, *Att.* 16.5.5).[35] The material forms of these early collections are also inaccessible. The size of roll needed for even a ten-letter Pauline collection doubles the typical length of papyrus rolls in the first century.[36] Paul's letters might have been sent on a roll that was later copied and stored on various codex-related technologies as circulation of

---

[35] See here Kurt Aland, "Die Entstehung des Corpus Paulinum," in *Neutestamentliche Entwürfe*, ed. Kurt Aland (Munich: Chr. Kaiser Verlag, 1979), 302–50; Harry Y. Gamble, *The New Testament Canon: Its Making and Meaning* (Philadelphia: Fortress, 1985), 35–46; Patrick Hart, *Prolegomena to the Study of Paul*, SuppMTSR 15 (Leiden: Brill, 2020); Stanley E. Porter, "When and How Was the Pauline Canon Compiled? An Assessment of Theories," in *The Pauline Canon*, ed. Porter (Leiden: Brill, 2004), 95–127; D. C. Parker, *An Introduction to the New Testament Manuscripts and Their Texts* (Cambridge: Cambridge University Press, 2008), 249–56. Important pieces of scholarship in this discussion continue to be Zahn, *Geschichte des Neutestamentlichen Kanons*, 262–302; Adolf Harnack, *Die Briefsammlung des Apostels Paulus und die anderen vorkonstantinischenchristlichen Brief Sammlungen* (Leipzig: Hinrichs, 1926), 6–27; B. H. Streeter, *The Four Gospels: A Study of Origins* (London: Macmillan, 1930), 526–27; Kirsopp Lake, *The Earlier Epistles of St. Paul: Their Motive and Origin* (London: Rivingtons, 1911), 356–59. The champion of a personal involvement theory continues to be David Trobisch, *Die Entstehung der Paulusbriefsammlung: Studien zu den Anfängen christlicher Publizistik*, NTOA10 (Göttingen: Vandenhoeck & Ruprecht, 1989), with precursors in John Knox, *Philemon Among the Letters of Paul* (London: Collins, 1935); C. L. Mitton, *The Formation of the Pauline Corpus* (London: Epworth, 1955). Walter Schmithals' theory takes an early struggle with Gnosticism as the context for the production of what is currently an anti-Gnostic Pauline collection, *Paul and the Gnostics* (Nashville: Abingdon, 1972), 239–74.

[36] The upper length for Greek papyrus rolls, according to Frederic G. Kenyon, is about thirty-five feet, and an eighty-foot roll would be required for a Pauline collection. *Books and Readers in Ancient Greece and Rome* (Oxford: Clarendon, 1932), 51–52; see also Harry Y. Gamble, *Books and Readers in the Early Church: A History of Early Christian Texts* (New Haven: Yale University Press, 1995), 62–63. As noted by Kenyon, Egyptian rolls are much longer, exceeding one hundred feet in some cases, but they are all copies of the *Book of the Dead* (51). Accordingly, the roll-theory posits the idea of a two-volume archetype; see John Knox, *Philemon Among the Letters of Paul: A New View of Its Place and Importance* (Chicago: University of Chicago Press, 1939), 42; Luke Stevens, "The Two-Volume Archetype of the Pauline Corpus," *JSPL* 8.1 (2018): 102–26. Christians still made use of the roll, as Malcolm Choat and Rachel Yuen-Collingridge observe: "Among the 34 books (i.e., rolls or codices) of unidentified authorship on papyrus owned, written, or copied by Christians, from Egypt before 325 CE, 15 (ca. 44%) are on rolls." "Texts without Authors: Unidentified Texts in the Christian Tradition from Roman Oxyrhynchus," *EC* 10 (2019): 66. Still, as noted by Charles Roberts and others, there is no extant New Testament text on the recto of a roll. Roberts, "The Christian Book and Greek Papyri," *JTS* 50.199–200 (1949): 158.

the letters increased (Col 4:16, 1 Thess. 5.27, cf. Polycarp, *Phil.* 13). This process of collection then led to the production of papyrus codices to accommodate the corpus.[37]

It is in Egypt where Hebrews first emerges as a physical Pauline object. In fact, all of the manuscripts of Hebrews (and all of the codices of Paul before the fourth century) are Egyptian. Table 1 lists the seven known papyrus manuscripts of the Letter to the Hebrews dated prior to the fifth century CE.

The final four papyri in Table 1—$\mathfrak{P}^{114}$, $\mathfrak{P}^{17}$, $\mathfrak{P}^{126}$, and $\mathfrak{P}^{89}$—are single, fragmented codex folios.[38] Given the current state of preservation, one can

Table 1 The Earliest Papyri of Hebrews

Papyrus	Siglum	Date	Text	Location
P. Beatty 2, Mich., inv. 6238	$\mathfrak{P}^{46}$	200–225 CE	Hebrews 1:1–13:25	Aphroditopolis (Atfih)
P. Amh. I 3b	$\mathfrak{P}^{12}$	3rd c. CE	Hebrews 1:1	Arsinoite (Fayum)
P. Oxy. 4.657 / PSI 12.1292	$\mathfrak{P}^{13}$	3rd c. CE	Hebrews 2:14–15:5, 10:8–22, 10:29–11:13, 11:28–12:17	Oxyrhynchus (Bahnasa)
P. Oxy. 66.4498	$\mathfrak{P}^{114}$	3rd c. CE	Hebrews 1:7–12	Oxyrhynchus (Bahnasa)
P. Oxy. 8.1078	$\mathfrak{P}^{17}$	4th c. CE	Hebrews 9:12–19	Oxyrhynchus (Bahnasa)
PSI inv. 1479	$\mathfrak{P}^{126}$	4th c. CE	Hebrews 12:12–13, 19–20	Unknown
P. Flor. 292/ PLaru. IV 142	$\mathfrak{P}^{89}$	Late 4th c.	Hebrews 6:7–9, 15–17	Antaiopolites (el-Kebir)

[37] Quintilian, *Inst. Or.* 10.3.31, is held as the first reference to a notebook made of parchment called a *membranae*. Martial's "Christmas list" in *Epigrams* 14.183–95 uses *membrana* to describe small codices of Homer, Cicero, and Virgil (*Epigrams* 14.180) and a codex of Cicero in a *membranis* (14.188). See Kenyon, *Books and Readers*, 120–33. Gamble reads τὰς μεμβράνας in 2 Timothy 4:13 not as a reference to "parchments," which are called διφθέραις (cf. *Letter of Aristeas* 3, 176), or even περγαμηνή, after King Pergamon, but to parchment codices (*Books and Readers*, 50–51). On the supposed origins of the use of vellum see Pliny, *Nat. Hist.* 13.11–12. On the development, use, and spread of the codex see Kenyon, *Books and Readers*, 95–119; Gamble, *Books and Readers*, 54–66; C. H. Roberts and T. C. Skeat, *The Birth of the Codex* (London: Oxford University Press, 1983); E. R. Richards, "The Codex and the Early Collection of Paul's Letters," *BBR* 8 (1998): 151–66; Larry Hurtado, *The Earliest Christian Artifacts Manuscripts and Christian Origins* (Grand Rapids: Eerdmans, 2006), 43–93; David Stern, "The First Jewish Books and the Early History of Jewish Reading," *JQR* 98.2 (2008): 163–202; Roger S. Bagnall, *Early Christian Books in Egypt* (Princeton: Princeton University Press, 2009), 70–90; Matthew D. C. Larsen and Mark Letteney, "Christians and the Codex: Generic Materiality and Early Gospel Traditions," *JECS* 27.3 (2019): 383–415.

[38] For the publication of each papyrus manuscript in order of reference see W. E. H. Cockle, "4498. Epistle to the Hebrews I 7–12," in *The Oxyrhynchus Papyri*, vol. 66, ed. N. Gonis, J. Chapa, W. E. H. Cockle, D. Obbink, P. J. Parsons, and J. David Thomas (London: Egypt Exploration Fund, 1999), 9–11; Arthur S. Hunt, "1078. Epistle to the Hebrews IX," in *The Oxyrhynchus Papyri: Part*

only imagine how the larger context of these codices might have facilitated the Paulinization of Hebrews, whether through a title or superscription or by virtue of its order in the collection.[39] 𝔓[12] (P. Amh. I 3) is similar in regards to Paulinity. The manuscript is a bureaucratic letter onto which someone copied Hebrews 1:1, perhaps as a general exercise (perhaps for the making of an amulet).[40] The only manuscripts from this earlier period that reflect a *Pauline* text of Hebrews are 𝔓[13] and 𝔓[46].

𝔓[13] (itself comprising P. Oxy. 4.657, PSI 12.1292) is an opisthograph roll with an epitome of Livy's *Ab Urbe Condita* (P. Oxy. 4.668 / PSI 12.1291) on the recto and (portions of) Hebrews on the verso.[41] Rodney Ast notes how unusual it is to have a literary text on the verso of an unrelated literary text on the recto, since rolls with literary texts were not typically reused and, if they were, the verso often features documentary and "casual" texts in less practiced and more cursive bookhands.[42] Martial, for example, associates writing on the verso with lower quality in *Epigrams* 8.62. So too, the text of Hebrews shows many signs of nonprofessional use, and the numbered columns suggest it was used as practice from an exemplar, perhaps a codex

---

VIII, ed. Hunt (London: Egypt Exploration Fund, 1911), 11–13; Guido Bastianini, ed., "1497. NT HEBR. 13:12–13; 19–20," in *Papiri Greci e Latini*, vol. 15, *PSI* (Florence: Istituto papirologico G. Vitelli, 2008), 171–72; Rosario Pintaudi, "N.T. Ad Hebraeos VI, 7–9; 15–17," *ZPE* 42 (1981): 42–44.

[39] As Clivaz notes, 𝔓[126] is a fragmented codex folio numbered 161–62 in the codex. "A New NT Papyrus: P126 (PSI 1497)," *EC* 1 (2010): 158–62. 𝔓[89] is also fragmented on all sides, and so it is difficult to determine the size of a page, lines, columns, etc.; see Pintaudi, "N.T. Ad Hebraeos VI," 42.

[40] B. P. Grenfell and A. S. Hunt, *The Amherst Papyri I* (London: Oxford University Press, 1900), 28–31; see Gregory Peter Fewster, "Forgers and Critics of the *Corpus Paulinum*" (PhD diss., University of Toronto, 2020), 73–77; Claire Clivaz, "The New Testament at the Time of the Egyptian Papyri: Reflections Based on P12, P75 and P126 (P. Amh. 3b, P. Bod. XIV–XV and PSI 1497)," in *Reading New Testament Papyri in Context—Lire les papyrus du Nouveau Testament dans leur contexte. Actes du colloque des 22–24 octobre 2009 à l'université de Lausanne*, ed. C. Clivaz and J. Zumstein (Leuven: Peeters, 2011), 41–51. On Egyptian amulets see esp. Theodore de Bruyn and Jitse H. F. Dijkstra, "Greek Amulets and Formularies from Egypt Containing Christian Elements: A Checklist of Papyri, Parchments, Ostraka, and Tablets," *BASP* 48 (2011): 96–197; Theodore de Bruyn, *Making Amulets Christian: Artefacts, Scribes, and Contexts* (Oxford: Oxford University Press, 2017).

[41] Hebrews 2:14–5:5, 10:8–22, 10:29–11:13. Bernard P. Grenfell and Arthur S. Hunt, "657. Epistle to the Hebrews," in *The Oxyrhynchus Papyri. Part IV* (London: Egypt Exploration Fund, 1904), 36–48.

[42] Rodney Ast, "A New Fragment from Herodas' 'Mimes' and a Snippet of Homer (P.CtYBR inv.457)," *Museum Heveticum* 70.2 (2013): 146–47. In addition to P. Oxy. 4.657+668, Ast notes two other rolls with different literary texts on the recto and verso, name P. Oxy. 3448 (Homer on an unidentified prose text) and P. Tebt. 3.696 (Hesiod on a fragment of the *Odyssey*). Annemarie Luijendijk points to the parallel example of P. Oxy. 8.1075 and 8.1075, which contain Exodus 40:26–32 (recto) and Revelation 1:4–7 (verso): "Sacred Scriptures as Trash: Biblical Papyri from Oxyrhynchus," *VC* 64 (2010): 251 n. 121. However, this fragment might not be a roll but a codex; see Brent Nongbri, "Losing a Curious Christian Scroll but Gaining a Curious Christian Codex," *NovT* 55.1 (2013): 77–88.

THE INVENTION OF PAUL'S LETTER TO THE HEBREWS   31

with page numbers.[43] Since Hebrews 2:14 is found in column 47, there was certainly text before Hebrews on the verso of the roll, and there might be space for Romans, which would match the order of 𝔓[46]. In its current form, however, the wider Pauline order and context of the text of Hebrews is not visible to us. While it can be strongly inferred that the text of Hebrews is Pauline, there are no explicit signs. As of the present day, the only extant manuscript of Hebrews with concrete markers of Paulinity is 𝔓[46].

𝔓[46] is a single-quire papyrus codex with 86 extant numbered folios of what were originally 104 folios (or 208 pages) that emerged in Egypt in the 1930s from the southern city of Aphroditopolis.[44] The codex is typically dated to the early third century (200–225 CE, +/− 50).[45] The text of Hebrews is found on folios 21r–38v and features almost half of the total corrections in the manuscript.[46] The seven missing folios at the beginning and end of the codex have sparked a discussion whether there is room for three

---

[43] The eleven columns of Hebrews are numbered 47–50, 61–65, and 67–69. On the nonprofessional features of the hand, including re-inking the pen, see P. M. Head and M. Warren, "Re-Inking the Pen: Evidence from P. Oxy. 657 (P13) Concerning Unintentional Scribal Errors," *NTS* 43 (1997): 469–73; R. Yuen-Collingridge, "Between Autograph and Copy: Writing as Thinking on Papyrus," *Book History* 21 (2018): 1–28; Roberts, "The Christian Book," 158; AnneMarie Luijendijk, "Sacred Scriptures as Trash," 252, notes that the entirety of the manuscript was discarded.

[44] The details of the codex are well known and often cited. Some leaves of the manuscript are found in the Chester Beatty Biblical Papyri (Codex II) while others are in the University of Michigan Papyrus Collection (P. Mich. inv. 6238). On the acquisition of the Beatty Biblical Papyri see Brent Nongbri, *God's Library: The Archaeology of the Earliest Christian Manuscripts* (New Haven: Yale University Press, 2018), 119–30. For plates see Frederic G. Kenyon, ed., *The Chester Beatty Biblical Papyri: Descriptions and texts of Twelve Manuscripts on Papyrus of the Greek Bible: Fasciculus III Supplement Pauline Epistles, Plates* (London: Emery Walker, 1937), 21r–38v. The editio princeps is found in F. G. Kenyon, *The Chester Beatty Biblical Papyri: Descriptions and Texts of Twelve Manuscripts on Papyrus of the Greek Bible, Fasciculus III Supplement Pauline Epistles, Text* (London: Emery Walker, 1934), 21–51. Transcribed by Henry A. Sanders, *A Third Century Codex of the Epistles of Paul*, University of Michigan Studies, Humanistic Series 38 (Ann Arbor: University of Michigan Press, 1935), 39–118.

[45] On the date of 𝔓[46] see Nongbri, *God's Library*, 141–44, and his discussion of Young Kyu Kim, "Palaeographical Dating of P[46] To the Later First Century," *Biblica* 69 (1988): 248–57; as well as Brent Nongbri, "Grenfell and Hunt on the Dates of Early Christian Codices: Setting the Record Straight," *BASP* 48 (2011): 149–62.

[46] A total of four hands have been identified as correctors of 𝔓[46]. For description of 𝔓[46] as well as its corrections, omissions, transpositions, and harmonizations see James R. Royse, *Scribal Habits in Early Greek New Testament Papyri* (Leiden: Brill, 2008), 199–358 (on the hands of correction see vii–xxi, 221–22); Günther Zuntz, *The Text of the Epistles: A Disquisition upon the Corpus Paulinum*, Schweich Lectures 1946 (London: Oxford University Press, 1953), 17–57; Philip W. Comfort and David P. Barrett, *The Text of the Earliest New Testament Greek Manuscripts* (Wheaton: Tyndale House, 2001), 203–35; H. C. Hoskier, "A Commentary on the Various Readings in the Text of the Epistle to the Hebrews in Chester-Beatty," *RB* 46 (1937): 58–82; Frank W. Beare, "The Text of the Epistle to the Hebrews in P[46]," *JBL* 63.4 (1944): 379–96; Jacob W. Peterson, "Patterns of Correction as Paratext: A New Approach with Papyrus 46 as a Test Case," in *The Future of New Testament Textual Scholarship: From H. C. Hoskier to the Editio Critica Maior and Beyond*, ed. Garrick Allen (Tübingen: Mohr Siebeck, 2019), 201–29.

Pastoral Epistles after, presumably, 2 Thessalonians and Philemon. Most agree that the Pastoral Epistles would not fit in the now missing seven folios, but this has not prevented others from posing scenarios where these three texts might be included, such as adding sheets to a single-quire codex, and the discussion is still active.[47] Still, 𝔓[46] is one of three papyrus manuscripts containing more than one Pauline letter dated prior to the earliest extant fourteen-letter collection in Codex Sinaiticus (mid-fourth century) and much of the codex remains.[48] 𝔓[46] contains, in order, Romans, Hebrews, 1–2 Corinthians, Ephesians, Galatians, Philippians, Colossians, and 1 Thessalonians.

The position of Hebrews, second after Romans, is understood by Clare Rothschild as an indication of the hermeneutical function of Hebrews within this collection of letters, namely, as a reading guide to Romans.[49] Rothschild builds this argument on overlapping citations from the Septuagint and commonalities identified between the two postscripts (Rom 16 and Heb 13).[50] Gabriella Gelardini has logged significant challenges to

---

[47] This is also one of the main arguments made by Jeremy Duff, "P46 and the Pastorals: A Misleading Consensus," *NTS* 44 (1998): 578–90, who points to Nag Hammadi Codex I and the Tura Papyrus of Origen, in addition to the increase of letters per page toward the end of the quire. The discussion and framing of this question in Kenyon, *Chester Beatty Biblical Papyri, III Text*, x–xi, still holds. Disregarding the question of space, Jerome Quin, "P46—the Pauline Canon?" *CBQ* 36/3 (1974): 379–85, suggests that 𝔓[46] is strictly a collection of "church" letters not unlike Marcion's *Apostolikon* and thus the pastorals would have been excluded in principle. For consideration of a wider set of comparanda see Brent Nonbgri, "The Construction and Contents of the Beatty-Michigan Pauline Epistles Codex (𝔓[46])," *NovT* 64.3. (2022): 388–407.

[48] The two others are 𝔓[30] (1 and 2 Thess) and 𝔓[92] (Eph and 2 Thess). 𝔓[46] is also the only early witness to Galatians, Colossians, and 2 Corinthians. See James R. Royse, "The Early Text of Paul (and Hebrews)," in *The Early Text of the New Testament*, ed. Charles E. Hill and Michael J. Kruger (Oxford: Oxford University Press, 2013), 175–77, 200. Other fragmentary codex manuscripts of Paul include 𝔓[32] (P. Ryl. Gr. I 5) and the combination of 𝔓[49] (P. Yale 415) and 𝔓[65] (PSI 1373). On these manuscripts as codices see Emily Gathergood, "Papyrus 32 (Titus) as a Multi-Text Codex: A New Reconstruction," *NTS* 59.4 (2013): 588–606; William Henry Paine Hatch and C. Bradford Wells, "A Hitherto Unpublished Fragment of the Epistle to the Ephesians," *HTR* 51.1 (1958): 33–37. 𝔓[65] is published in Vittorio Bartoletti, *Papiri greci e latini della Società Italiana*, vol. 14 (Florence: Le Monnier, 1957), 5–7.

[49] See Clare Rothschild, "Hebrews as a Guide to Reading Romans," in Frey et al., *Pseudepigraphie und Verfasserfiktion*, 537–73; Clare Rothschild, "Hebrews as an Instructional Appendix to Romans," in Porter and Fewster, *Paul and Pseudepigraphy*, 245–68, with precursors in William Manson, *The Epistle to the Hebrews: An Historical and Theological Reconsideration*, 2nd ed. (London: Hodder & Stoughton, 1953) and in Dieter Georgi, "Hebrews and the Heritage of Paul," in Gelardini, *Hebrews*, 239–44. Cf. also Hanna Roose, "2 Thessalonians as Pseudepigraphic 'Reading Instruction' for 1 Thessalonians: Methodological Implications and Exemplary Illustration of an Intertextual Concept," in *The Intertextuality of the Epistles: Explorations of Theory and Practice*, ed. D. R. McDonald, S. E. Porter, and T. L. Brodie (Sheffield: Sheffield Phoenix, 2006), 133–51; Hanna Roose, "Der 2. Thessalonicherbrief im Verhältnis zum 1. Thessalonicherbrief: Ein Gedankenexperiment," in Schröter et al., *Receptions of Paul*, 443–59.

[50] Rothschild argues that the lack of pre-Pauline uses of Ἐφάπαξ (once for all) and its repeated use in Hebrews is indicative of "literary reliance," "intentional commentary," and the overarching

these proposed affiliations, at least insofar as they are suggestive of an intentional juxtaposition with Romans.[51] The position of Hebrews after Romans and before the Corinthian correspondence was likely determined principally by stichometry—the measurement of the length of a text based on lines and also the predominant logic of arranging the order of Paul's letters.[52] Since Hebrews is shorter than Romans but fits awkwardly between the lengths of the two Corinthians letters, it was decided that Hebrews be placed prior to 1 Corinthians to keep the correspondence intact. Whether that decision had larger hermeneutical influences remains to be seen. But what there should be no doubt on is that the positioning has hermeneutical consequences; the position of the text is a marker of Paulinity.

To facilitate the inclusion of this text within the collection, and as part of a larger editorial practice to provide coherence, this text was titled πρὸς Ἑβραίους.[53] Titles for ancient texts were generally in flux and might also be added in different ways to either rolls or codices: a tag with title used for rolls (*sillybos*), a colophon, a header, an authorial designation within a list of contents in codices, etc.[54] The seven missing folios at the beginning of the codex (as well as the end) preclude us from knowing how the letters in this collection were framed as Pauline, whether, for example, with a heading such as ΕΠΙΣΤΟΛΑΙ ΤΟΥ ΑΠΟΣΤΟΛΟΥ ΠΑΥΛΟΥ.[55] The various titles, πρὸς with an accusative plural noun for the audience, would then be an extension of this heading.

---

status of Hebrews as an "appendix" to Romans ("Hebrews as an Instructional Appendix," 248–59). Other unique instances of overlap include the use of ἱλαστήριον in Romans 3:25 and Hebrews 9:5, and Habakkuk 2:4 in Romans 1:16 and Hebrews 10:37–38.

[51] Gelardini, "As If by Paul?" 274–84, points to contextual differences in each of Rothchild's points of overlap.

[52] Jack Finegan, "The Original Form of the Pauline Collection," *HTR* 49.2 (1956): 97–103; Charles H. Buck, "The Early Order of the Pauline Corpus," *JBL* 68.4 (1949): 351–57. As an aside, H. F. D. Sparks, "The Order of the Epistles in P46," *JTS* 42 (1941): 180–81, speculatively suggests that when Hieracas moves from Romans to Hebrews and to 1 Corinthians, in the preserved quotation in Epiphanius, *Pan.* 67.2, he reveals a replicated order of Pauline epistles from 𝔓46. On stichometry see the classic work of James Rendel Harris, *Stichometry* (London: C. J. Clay & Sons, 1893); James Rendel Harris, "Stichometry," *American Journal of Philology* 4 (1883): 133–57, 309–31.

[53] On titles for New Testament texts in Greek papyri, see Garrick V. Allen, "Titles in the New Testament Papyri," *NTS* 68 (2022): 156–71, who finds ten papyri with twenty-six titles.

[54] See Simon Gathercole, "The Alleged Anonymity of the Canonical Gospels," *JTS* 69.2 (2018): 459; Appendix III, "Title of the Books of the New Testament," in Bruce Metzger, *Canon of the New Testament: Its Origin, Development and Significance* (Oxford: Clarendon Press, 1987), 301–4. On book titles see Eleanor Dickey, *Ancient Greek Scholarship* (Oxford: Oxford University Press, 2007), 129–30; F. Schironi, *TO MEΓA BIBΛION: Book-Ends, End-Titles, and Coronides in Papyri with Hexametric Poetry* (Durham, NC: American Society of Papyrologists, 2010).

[55] See von Soden, *Die Schriften des Neuen Testaments*, 296.

In its current form, then, there is a lingering tension between the broad, disassociated audience with its wide linguistic, geographic, and ethnic resonances and the marked particularity of the concerns of the text, which relate directly to the life experiences of the audience.[56] This tension invites hypotheses that see πρὸς Ἑβραίους as an abbreviated title of something that was much less mysterious.

While Adolf von Harnack is rightly remembered for suggesting the *probability* that Priscilla authored the Letter to the Hebrews, in the same essay, Harnack also joined forces with Theodor Zahn in popularizing the idea that Hebrews was sent to a group of Christians within the city of Rome, to "Hebrews" in the household church affiliated with Priscilla and Aquila mentioned in Romans and 1 Corinthians.[57] For Harnack, Priscilla's name was removed but the personalized postscript remained as it was put into circulation as a letter not from a woman to a house church back in Italy, but from an "older generation."[58] Harnack received quick approval for the idea of a Roman destination to a group of Hebrews. F. M. Schiele, for instance, saw in Harnack a way of accounting for the existence of the postscript and the lack of an initial greeting. Schiele too proposed that "Pros Hebraious" might reflect an abbreviated greeting, such as Πρίσκα καὶ Ἀκύλας, οἱ ἀδελφοί, τοῖς ἐκλεκτοῖς παρεπιδήμοις ἐπισυναγωγῆς Ἑβραίων, τοῖς οὖσιν ἐν Ῥώμῃ, κλητοῖς ἁγίοις. χάρις ὑμῖν καὶ εἰρήνη κτλ."[59] However, if in fact Hebrews was edited for redistribution and a longer greeting was abbreviated down into a Pauline title, then the editorial project seems conspicuously unfinished. Why leave the personal postscript without adding a new and informative greeting? Other anonymous texts of the period that are

---

[56] An audience is addressed in the second-person voice in Hebrews 5:12, 6:10–12, 12:4, 13:7, 13:17.

[57] Adolf von Harnack, "Probabilia über die Adresse und den Verfasser des Hebräerbriefs," *ZNW* 1 (1900): 16–41. On Priscilla and Aquila's household see Romans 16:5 (τὴν κατ᾽ οἶκον αὐτῶν ἐκκλησίαν) and 1 Corinthians 16.19 (ἀσπάζεται ὑμᾶς ἐν κυρίῳ πολλὰ Ἀκύλας καὶ Πρίσκα σὺν τῇ κατ᾽ οἶκον αὐτῶν ἐκκλησίᾳ). Another important feature of the view that Hebrews was sent to a subgroup of a larger network are the references to "your" and "all" the "leaders" (ἡγουμένους) in Hebrews 13:7, 17, and 24, which is read as a distinction between various leaders in the vicinity of Rome. The term ἡγούμενος is certainly well attested in Roman sources; see *1 Clem.* 1.3, 21:6; Hermas, *Vis.* 2.2.6; 3.9.7. See also Franz Laub, "Verkündigung und Gemeindeamt: Die Autorität der ἡγούμενοι Hebr 13, 7.17.24," *SNTSU* 6–7 (1981–82): 169–90.

[58] Harnack, "Probabilia," 37: "It was put into circulation with good reason not as a letter from Priscilla and Aquila to their house church, but as an anonymous edifying letter from the older generation" (Er wurde mit gutem Grunde nicht als Brief der Priska und des Aquila an ihre Hausgemeinde, sondern als anonymes erbauliches Schreiben aus der älteren Generation in Circulation gesetzt).

[59] F. M. Schiele, "Harnack's 'Probabilia' Concerning the Address and the Author of the Epistle to the Hebrews," *AJT* 9 (1905): 308.

broadly epistolary attract ascriptions to known figures, whether they originally held such titles (2 Clem*ent*, the *Epistle of Barnabas*, and the *Letter to Diognetus*).[60]

We are left then with a more minimalist reading, that πρὸς Ἑβραίους is designed to mimic other Pauline letter titles as exemplified in 𝔓[46] in order to add coherence to the collection.[61] Metzger, for example, pointed out that in 𝔓[46] (and others) "Colossians" is spelled differently in the title (Κολασσαεῖς) and in Colossians 2.1 (Κολοσσαῖς).[62] The title, πρὸς Ἑβραίους, is first witnessed in 𝔓[46] (P. Mich. inv. 6238 fol. 41r) and first mentioned (or at least implied) in book 6 of Clement's *Stromata* in the late second century.[63] It is an early and stable title apart from the normal kinds of variations in Pauline collections that build on this πρὸς + accusative formula, and was likely fixed around the turn of the second century.[64] As an added title, it is nevertheless unique in the way it names its audience. Who is meant by this designation? Who are the Hebrews?

The noun Ἑβραῖος has a modest usage in the Greek scriptures of the Hellenistic period and surrounding texts from the late Second Temple period, including Josephus and Philo, as well as some inscriptional evidence.[65] Graham Harvey's work on the use of the noun up through the first century CE suggests that it came to accent both a speaker of Hebrew or Aramaic as well as an archaizing reference, given its association with Abraham and the era prior to the Kingdoms of Israel and Judah.[66] Later Christians like Clement of Alexandria and Eusebius of Caesarea refer to Hebrew persons in ways that resemble the extreme of Harvey's second

---

[60] On this point see Theodor Zahn, *Introduction to the New Testament*, ed. Melancthon Williams Jacobus, trans. John Trout, William Mather, Louis Hodous, Edwards Worcester, William Hoyt Worrell, and Rowland Dodge, 2nd ed., from the third German edition (New York: Scribner, 1917), 2.311–12 n. 13.

[61] Gräßer, *An die Hebräer*, 17–18; E. J. Bickerman, "En marge de l'Écriture," *RB* 88 (1981): 31; Zahn, *Introduction to the New Testament*, 2.295; F. F. Bruce, "'To the Hebrews' or 'To the Essenes,'" *NTS* 9 (1963): 231.

[62] Metzger, *Canon of the New Testament*, 303.

[63] See *Strom.* 6.8.62 (τοῖς Ἑβραίοις γράφων).   [64] Metzger, *Textual Commentary*, 678.

[65] On origins of Ἑβραῖος from the cognate ʿapirû (עבר) (in fourteenth-century BCE Amarna letters, its subsequent interpretation as a term of legal-social status in the work of Gerhard von Rad, and later reading as a term for herders with limited ties with fixed towns by Daniel Fleming, see Jason Staples, *The Idea of Israel in Second Temple Judaism: A New Theory of People, Exile, and Israelite Identity* (Cambridge: Cambridge University Press, 2021), 71–72, esp. n. 55. See also Graham Harvey, *The True Israel: Uses of the Names Jew, Hebrew, and Israel in Ancient Jewish and Early Christian Literature* (Leiden: Brill, 2001), 104–47. Cf. Genesis 10:21, where Shem is the father of all the *eber* (וּלְשֵׁם יֻלַּד גַּם־הוּא אֲבִי כָּל־בְּנֵי־עֵבֶר אֲחִי יֶפֶת הַגָּדוֹל).

[66] Harvey, *The True Israel*, 146. Similarly, Simon Mimouni, "Le 'grand prêtre' Jésus 'à la manière de Melchisédech' dans l'Épître aux Hébreux," *Annali di Storia dell'Esegesi* 33 (2016): 81.

sense, reserving "Jew" as a negative descriptor distinct from the laudatory and patriarchal "Hebrew."[67] Jason Staples, however, finds that prior to the second century, that is, prior to the burgeoning Christian uses of the term, a "Hebrew" primarily connotes a speaker of Aramaic in the region of Palestine.[68]

Staples notes that as a designation for Aramaic speakers, the use of "Hebrew" is relatively mute in Hebrew and Aramaic contexts, such as Qumran, where the term is never used.[69] Uses of Hebrew (Ἑβραΐδι) in Acts 21:40, 22:2, and 26:14 are certainly linguistic, but so also might be Ἑβραῖος in Philippians 3:5 and 2 Corinthians 11:22. Staples follows Beatie and Davies in reading Paul's self-description in Philippians 3:5 less as a claim to be a "Jew's Jew" than an Aramaic speaker from a family of Aramaic speakers.[70] The difference between one who is a Ἑλληνιστής and a Ἑβραῖος in Acts 6:1–8:4 is also often conceived as primarily a division of spoken language and not, at least as far as we know, a division over lineage.[71] Still, even if the reference is first and foremost about language, the cultural and ethnic attachment to Abraham may contribute quite a bit to the cultural purchase of claiming language use, and the two senses work somewhat evenly in tandem (Artapanus, *fr.* 1). There may be finer and more complex layers of meaning when terms are traded among "insiders," as outside references to "Hebrew" in Lucian (*Alexander the Oracle-Monger* 32.13) and Pausanias (*Descriptions of Greece* 5.7.4, 6.24.8) emphasize a language and a land (Palestine)[72] Staples concludes that as a designation for a language and a region, "Hebrew" is closely affiliated with terms like *Ioudaios* and "Samaritan" and "Israelite," but that these are far from synonymous, much less branches of a larger and common "Judaism."[73] Most diaspora Jews were *Hellenes*, the Samaritans were not Jews but Israelites, and the Hebrews were, at the very least, Aramaic speakers.

---

[67] On Clement's use of this distinction see Chapter 3.
[68] Staples, *The Idea of Israel*, 73–83. [69] Staples, *The Idea of Israel*, 81.
[70] Staples, quoting D. R. G. Beattie and P. R. Davies, "What Does Hebrew Mean?," *JSS* 56 (2011): 73: "an Aramaic speaker from an Aramaic-speaking family." *Pace* Andrew Jacobs, "A Jew's Jew: Paul and the Early Christian Problem of Jewish Origins," *JR* 86 (2006): 258–86.
[71] See, for example, Martin Hengel, *Between Jesus and Paul* (Philadelphia: Fortress, 1983), 14–18; C. C. Hill, *Hellenists and Hebrews* (Minneapolis: Fortress, 1992).
[72] The same passage from Pausanias also refers to the grave of one Helen, a "Hebrew woman from Jerusalem," which was destroyed by the Roman emperor (8.16.5).
[73] Staples, *The Idea of Israel*, 80–83. This point is also anticipated by Otto Michel, who sees "Hebrew" as a differentiation from other communities that use conventional names like Israel and Judah. *Der Brief an die Hebräer*, KEK 13 (Göttingen: Vandenhoeck & Ruprecht, 1947), 41.

Returning to the critical fervor of the nineteenth century, Theodor Zahn was adamant that those who entitled the "Letter to the Hebrews" did not have "Hebrew speakers" in view, preferring to find a parallel with the Latin titles for 1 Peter and James as *ad Ponticos* and *ad Dispersos*, respectively.[74] On this reading, the lack of regional specificity invites seeing Hebrews as an address to Jews throughout the Mediterranean, paralleling Eusebius' description of 1 Peter as a letter "to the Hebrews who were in the dispersion of Pontus, Galatia, Cappadocia, Asia, and Bithynia."[75] However, if those responsible for the title conceptualized such a broad and wide ranging audience, why not entitle the letter πρὸς Ἰουδαίους, or πρὸς τοὺς ἀπὸ τῆς Ἀσίας Ἰουδαίους, or πρὸς Ἑλληνιστας, especially given the specificity of a "Hebrew" in the first century?

In thinking about later Christian contexts of use, Claire Clivaz juxtaposes the Letter to the Hebrews with the *Gospel According to the Hebrews* and suggests that whoever was responsible for the title understood "Hebrews" as relatively unknown, mysterious, and archaic.[76] From the distance of this Christian vantage, "Hebrews" suggests speakers of Aramaic in and around Jerusalem who are followers of Christ.[77] Indeed, later sources refer to Jews who are Christ-followers in the area of Palestine as Hebrews, especially those in Jerusalem. The reference to Hebrews in Jerusalem in Acts 6 was likely important for this development. Eusebius notes that the bishops of Jerusalem prior to Hadrian were Hebrews (Ἑβραίους φασὶν ὄντας ἀνέκαθεν).[78] In fact, "Their entire church consisted of Hebrews who had held out as faithful from the Apostles down to the siege" (τὴν πᾶσαν ἐκκλησίαν ἐξ Ἑβραίων πιστῶν ἀπὸ τῶν ἀποστόλων καὶ εἰς τὴν τότε διαρκεσάντων πολιορκίαν).[79] The *Epistula Clementis*, a third-century pseudonymous text attached to the Pseudo-Clementine *Homilies* and *Recognitions*, refers to James as "the lord and the bishop of bishops, who

---

[74] Zahn, *Introduction to the New Testament*, 297.
[75] Eusebius, *Hist. eccl.* 4.3.2 (τοῖς ἐξ Ἑβραίων οὖσιν ἐν διασπορᾷ Πόντου καὶ Γαλατίας Καππαδοκίας τε καὶ Ἀσίας καὶ Βιθυνίας γράφει).
[76] Claire Clivaz, "(According) To the Hebrews: An Apocryphal Gospel and a Canonical Letter Read in Egypt," in *Between Canonical and Apocryphal Texts*, ed. Frey Jörg, Clivaz Claire, Nicklas Tobias, and Röder Jörg, WUNT 1.419 (Tübingen: Mohr Siebeck, 2019), 281. On the *Gospel according to the Hebrews* see Andrew Gregory, ed., *The Gospel according to the Hebrews and the Gospel of the Ebionites* (Oxford: Oxford University Press, 2017), 3–167.
[77] The *Gospel according to the Hebrews* was also later understood to be a Greek translation of a Hebrew or Aramaic text. See Jerome, *Against the Pelagians*, 3.2.
[78] *Hist. eccl.* 4.5.2 (GCS N.F. 6.1, 304).   [79] *Hist. eccl.* 4.5.2 (GCS N.F. 6.1, 304).

rules Jerusalem, the holy church of the Hebrews."[80] Other Christian texts use "Hebrews" less for a connection to Jerusalem than for its archaizing connotation (Jesus was born among the Hebrews, Aristides, *Apol*. 2; Justin's Trypho is a Hebrew from the circumcision, *Dial*. 1.3).

There is little to suggest that the title Πρὸς Ἑβραίους is indicative of historical knowledge of the earliest intended audience of this text. Rather, it seems that the unique focus on the Levitical cult in Hebrews was read in such a way that the most likely audience imaginable was a group of Christ-devoted Jews in Palestine, and the language with which to express this idea was "Hebrews." The idea of an audience of Aramaic speakers is secondary to this more fundamental Christian layer. The title is, for Erich Gräßer, an expression of "perplexity," "a quick pen stroke" of a later collector that, in effect, is the shortest "commentary" on Hebrews, an interpretation of its content and audience.[81]

The title reflects a reading of the text as Jewish, that is, addressed to, concerned with, and otherwise regarding Jews. Perhaps the opening reference to "the ancestors" was sufficient to read what follows as matters concerned with and addressed to Jews and the calls for maintaining fidelity to Jesus throughout the text pushed the title-er to name the document "to the Hebrews in Jerusalem", or something similar. Increasingly, others like Wolfgang Kraus and Thomas Schenck suggest that the text we call "to the Hebrews" might have been addressed to Gentiles. Even if a Gentile audience is not historical and the title is not something that inverts the ethnicity of the audience singlehandedly, the editorial invention of the title most certainly creates the conditions of Jewishness within which the Pauline authorship of Hebrews was developed and would need to be perpetually engaged.[82] It is this material of Hebrews within the collection that provides the text with its earliest markers of Paulinity, markers that both constrain and enable subsequent discussion of the letter as

---

[80] Greek and Latin text found in Georg Strecker and Bernhard Rehm, *Die Pseudoklementinen I. Homilien*, 2nd ed., GCS 42 (Berlin: Akademie Verlag, 1992), 5: Κλήμης Ἰακώβῳ τῷ κυρίῳ καὶ ἐπισκόπων ἐπισκόπῳ, διέποντι δὲ τὴν Ἱερουσαλὴμ ἁγίαν Ἑβραίων ἐκκλησίαν. *Clemens Iacobo domino et episcopo Episcoporum, regent Hebraeorum sanctam ecclesiam Hierosolymis*. See also Pseudo-Clementine, *Recognitions*, 4.4.

[81] Gräßer, *An die Hebräer*, 41–42. So also James Moffatt, *The Epistle to the Hebrews*, ICC (Edinburgh: T&T Clark, 1924), xv; the title indicates that "all traces of the original destination of the writing had been lost."

[82] Wolfgang Kraus, "Zu Absicht und Zielsetzung des Hebräerbriefes," *KD* 60 (2014): 250–51; Kenneth Schenck, *A New Perspective on Hebrews: Rethinking the Parting of the Ways* (Minneapolis: Fortress, 2019).

Paul's. Again, Hebrews is less "accepted" as Pauline than it is encountered and explained.

3. The Earliest Discussions of Pauline Authorship

The earliest discussion of Hebrews as a Pauline letter we are able to "hear" was had by two second-century Christians affiliated with the Egyptian city of Alexandria; Clement of Alexandria and the "blessed elder," often thought to be one known elsewhere as Pantaenus, to whom Clement occasionally and cryptically refers.[83] This figure claimed that Paul, as the apostle to the Gentiles, wrote to the Hebrews out of an "abundance" and did not inscribe his name out of respect to the apostle to the Hebrews, Jesus (cf. Heb 3:1).[84] The elder's account of Hebrews is first and foremost an explanation of its anonymity. Clement's account of Hebrews is altogether different yet not actually contrastive with the earlier tale.

Clement positions Jesus as "the model of true philosophy" sent specifically "to the Hebrews" (*Paed.* 2.11.117).[85] But the blessed elder's emphasis on apostleship and respect is sidelined as Clement rachets up the Pauline biographical details of the origins of Hebrews through the narrative of

---

[83] Clement refers to "our Pantaenus" in *Eclogae Propheticae* 56.2. The famous reference to Clement's most revered teacher, a Hebrew from Palestine, in *Strom.* 1.11 has often been read as a reference to Pantaenus. Eusebius makes this connection in *Hist. eccl.* 5.11.2 and claims that Clement mentions Pantaenus elsewhere in the *Hypotyposes* (*Hist. eccl.* 6.13.2). Other pieces of evidence for Pantaenus include a fragment found in the *Scholia of Maximus* on Gregory the Divine, the reference to Pantaenus in the Letter of Alexander to Origen cited in *Hist. eccl.* 6.14.9, as well as Origen's letter in 6.19.13. Later references include Jerome, *Vir.* 36 and Photius, Bibl. cod. 118. On Pantaenus see Wolfgang Grünstäudl, "The Quest for Pantaenus: Paul Collomp, Wilhelm Bousset, and Johannes Munck on an Alexandrian Enigma," in *Alexandria: Hub of the Hellenistic World*, ed. Benjamin Schliesser, Jan Rüggemeier, Thomas J. Karus, and Jörg Frey, WUNT 460 (Tübingen: Mohr Siebeck, 2021), 413–39; Alfons Fürst, *Christentum als Intellektuellen-Religion: Die Anfänge des Christentums in Alexandria*, SBA 213 (Stuttgart: Katholisches Bibelwerk, 2007), 36–42; Martiniano Pellegrino Roncaglia, "Pantène et le Didascalée d'Alexandrie: Du Judéo-christianisme au christianisme hellénistique," in *A Tribute to Arthur Vööbus: Studies in Early Christian Literature and Its Environment, Primarily in the Syrian East*, ed. Robert H. Fischer (Chicago: Lutheran School of Theology, 1977), 211–33; Dietmar Wyrwa, "Religiöses Lernen im Zweiten Jahrhundert und die Anfänge der alexandrinischen Katechetenschule," in *Religiöses Lernen in der biblischen, frühjüdischen und frühchristlichen Überlieferung*, ed. Beate Ego and Helmut Merkel, WUNT 1/180 (Tübingen: Mohr Siebeck, 2005), 291–301.

[84] Eusebius, *Hist. eccl.* 6.14. "Then lower down he adds: 'But now, as the blessed presbyter used to say, since the Lord, being the apostle of the Almighty, was sent to the Hebrews, Paul, because of modesty, inasmuch as he had been sent to the Gentiles, did not inscribe himself as Apostle of the Hebrews both because of his respect for the Lord and because out of his abundance, he wrote to the Hebrews, being a preacher and apostle of Gentiles'" (trans. LCL Oulton, 265.47).

[85] *Clemens Alexandrinus I. Protrepticus und Paedagogus*, ed. Otto Stählin, GCS 12 (Leipzig, 1905), 227: ὁ τῆς ἀληθοῦς Ἑβραίοις φιλοσοφίας ὑποδεικνύμενος τὸν τύπον.

Acts 21, perhaps reflecting an increase or at least the consistency of dispute about Hebrews further into the second century.[86] Eusebius of Caesarea, writing later in the fourth century, claims to summarize a passage from Clement's (now-lost) *Hypotyposes* (Ὑποτυπώσεσιν) that features a discussion of the Pauline origins of Hebrews:[87]

> [Clement] says that the Epistle to the Hebrews is the work of Paul, and that it was written to the Hebrews in the Hebrew language (Ἑβραϊκῇ φωνῇ) but that Luke translated it carefully and published (ἐκδοῦναι) it for the Greeks, and hence the same style of expression is found (τὸν αὐτὸν χρῶτα εὑρίσκεσθαι κατὰ τὴν ἑρμηνείαν) in this epistle and in Acts. But he says that the words "Paul the Apostle" were naturally not prefixed because in sending it to the Hebrews, who were prejudiced and suspicious of him, he wisely did not wish to dissuade them from the very beginning by giving the name.

This description imaginatively locates the origins of Hebrews within the narrative of Acts 21, where Paul addresses fellow Jews in Jerusalem in the Ἑβραϊκῇ φωνῇ during what is described as a violent altercation.[88] In Acts

---

[86] Pace Rothschild, *Hebrews as Pseudepigraphon*, 37: "According to Eusebius, Clement received from Pantaenus, his predecessor in Alexandria, the tradition that Paul wrote Hebrews to Jews in Hebrew."

[87] *Hist. eccl.* 6.14.1–3; Greek text Eduard Schwartz and Theodore Mommsen, eds., *Eusebius Werke* II/II, *Die Kirchengeschichte*, ed. Friedhelm Winkelmann, 2nd ed., GCS N.F. 6.2 (Berlin: Akademie Verlag, 1999), 550: τὴν πρὸς Ἑβραίους δὲ ἐπιστολὴν Παύλου μὲν εἶναί φησιν, γεγράφθαι δὲ Ἑβραίοις Ἑβραϊκῇ φωνῇ, Λουκᾶν δὲ φιλοτίμως αὐτὴν μεθερμηνεύσαντα ἐκδοῦναι τοῖς Ἕλλησιν, ὅθεν τὸν αὐτὸν χρῶτα εὑρίσκεσθαι κατὰ τὴν ἑρμηνείαν ταύτης τε τῆς ἐπιστολῆς καὶ τῶν Πράξεων· μὴ προγεγράφθαι δὲ τὸ Παῦλος ἀπόστολος εἰκότως· Ἑβραίοις γάρ, φησίν, ἐπιστέλλων πρόληψιν εἰληφόσιν κατ' αὐτοῦ καὶ ὑποπτεύουσιν αὐτόν, συνετῶς πάνυ οὐκ ἐν ἀρχῇ ἀπέτρεψεν αὐτούς, τὸ ὄνομα θείς. εἶτα ὑποβὰς ἐπιλέγει. Eusebius here describes the *Hypotyposes* as an orderly abbreviation of the testamentary writings. On the fragments of the *Hypotyposes* see *Clement Alexandrinus, Dritter Band*, ed. Otto Stählin, GCS 17 (Leipzig: Hinrichs, 1909), 195–215; Jana Plátovaá, "Bemerkungen zu den Hypotyposen-Fragmenten des Clemens Alexandrianus," *SP* 46 (2010): 181–87; Adolf von Harnack, "Ein neues Fragment aus den Hypotyposen des Clemens," *Sitzungsberichte der Berliner Akademie der Wissenschaften* (1904): 901–8, reprinted in Harnack: *Kleine Schriften zur Alten Kirche: Berliner Akademieschriften 1890–1907* (Leipzig: Zentralantiquariat, 1980), 702–9.

[88] With these kinds of abbreviations and other *testimonia* found in the *Historia*, one must register the degree to which "Eusebius" is entangled in the report, shaping and otherwise editing these texts according to a larger set of aims. Eusebius never cites from the *Hypotyposes kata lexin*, although this is the case with Clement's *Stromata*, which receives a number of verbatim quotations in the *Historia*. The sixth-century Latin translation of Clement's lost *Hypotyposes*—commissioned by Cassiodorus and known as the *Adumbrations*—preserves a more modest account of the Pauline origins of Hebrews: "Luke is recognized as the pen that wrote the Acts of the Apostles and as the translator of the Letter of Paul to the Hebrews" (GCS 17:206: *sicut Lucas quoque Actus apostolorum stilo exsecutus agnoscitus et Pauli ad Hebraeos interpretatus epistolam*). See Luke J. Stevens, "The Evangelists in Clement's *Hypotyposes*," *JECS* 26.3 (2018): 354–55. The *Adumbrations* only refer to

21:18 Paul meets with James in Jerusalem, who encourages him to obey purity regulations because word has spread among other Jews that Paul teaches them to "turn away from Moses" (ἀποστασίαν διδάσκεις ἀπὸ Μωϋσέως, 21:21). James recommends that Paul reverse this report by participating in the Law (ἁγνίσθητι, "purify yourself"). Paul agrees, purifies himself alongside four Nazirites, goes to the temple to give notice of the days of purification, and pays for their offerings (21:26).[89] Despite keeping the νόμος, a group of "Jews from Asia" (οἱ ἀπὸ τῆς Ἀσίας Ἰουδαῖοι) see Paul at the Temple and seize him for the reasons previously outlined by James: "This is the man who teaches everyone everywhere against our people and our law and this place" (21:28).[90] A Roman commander intervenes to suppress the ensuing scuffle, and Paul is taken into custody in order to be investigated further (21:34). Paul evokes his Roman citizenship and is permitted to speak to the crowd, which he does in the Ἑβραΐδι διαλέκτῳ.

There are distinctive narrative correlates between Clement's account of the origins of Hebrews and this scene from Acts 21. Paul's speech in Ἑβραΐδι to Jews is the most overt linkage and may have been the initial point of entry for developing a narrative that accounts for an anonymous Pauline letter written to Ἑβραίους.[91] Clement weaves the idea of Luke as Paul's

Luke as the translator of the "letter of Paul to the Hebrews." The idea of "from Hebrew" seems to be implied.

[89] Tertullian refers to the Nazirites in this passage in *Marc.* 5.3.

[90] Acts 21:28: ἄνδρες Ἰσραηλῖται, βοηθεῖτε οὗτός ἐστιν ὁ ἄνθρωπος ὁ κατὰ τοῦ λαοῦ καὶ τοῦ νόμου καὶ τοῦ τόπου τούτου πάντας πανταχῇ διδάσκων. The accusation also includes that Paul brought Gentiles into the temple (ἔτι τε καὶ Ἕλληνας εἰσήγαγεν εἰς τὸ ἱερὸν καὶ κεκοίνωκεν τὸν ἅγιον τόπον τοῦτον). It is then explained in 21.29 that Paul had been seen with a Greek named Trophimus the Ephesian in Jerusalem and that it is only surmised that Paul brought this Triphimus into the temple (εἰς τὸ ἱερὸν εἰσήγαγεν ὁ Παῦλος).

[91] Acts 21 and Clement, decades later, are most likely referring to Aramaic when referring to the Ἑβραΐδι διαλέκτῳ or φωνῇ. The distinction between Aramaic and Hebrew is notoriously not clear cut. Aramaic was the lingua franca, though Hebrew is certainly more attested than some pockets of previous scholarship suggest. On Ἑβραΐδι as a reference to Hebrew see Randall Buth and Chad Pierce, "*Hebraisti* in Ancient Texts: Does Ἑβραϊστί Ever Mean 'Aramaic'?," in *The Language Environment of First Century Judaea*, ed. Randall Buth and R. Steven Notley (Leiden: Brill, 2014), 66–109. Daniel A. Machiela and Robert Jones have recently fortified the claim that there was a revival of Hebrew during the Hasmonean period, in "Was There a Revival of Hebrew during the Hasmonean Period? A Reassessment of the Evidence," *JAJ* 12 (2021): 217–80. For earlier iterations of the language as well as the varying political dynamics of Hebrew see William Schniedewind, "Aramaic, the Death of Written Hebrew, and Language Shift in the Persian Period," in *Margins of Writing, Origins of Cultures*, ed. Seth L. Sanders, OIS 2 (Chicago: Oriental Institute of the University of Chicago, 2006), 141–51; Seth Schwartz, "Language, Power and Identity in Ancient Palestine," *Past & Present* 148 (1995): 3–47; D. R. G. Beattie and P. R. Davies, "What Does Hebrew Mean?," *JSS* 56 (2011): 71–83; Nicholas de Lange, "The Revival of the Hebrew Language in the Third Century CE," *JSQ* 3 (1996): 342–58. Edmon Gallagher, *Hebrew Scripture in Patristic Biblical Theory: Canon, Language, Text*, VCSup 114 (Leiden: Brill, 2012), 123–31, notes that later

42 THE PAULINE HISTORY OF HEBREWS

Greek translator and the tensions between Paul and the Jews from Asia into an explanation for the painfully non-Pauline features of Hebrews, namely, that it does not have Paul's name and is not in Paul's "style of expression." Rather than actively ascribe Paulinity to Hebrews, Clement is confronted, backed into a corner by an anonymous letter circulating as a Pauline letter "to the Hebrews" but not written in a Pauline style. The story is Clement's way out of the tight spot, a way of accounting for non-Pauline stylistic features by reading the title through Acts 21. The process of collection gave Hebrews an audience and basic Paulinity, and in return, Clement gave Hebrews a narrative and a Paul, in this case, a Lucan Paul.[92]

Origen, too, was confronted with the same set of Pauline and non-Pauline features as Clement was, yet with increasing awareness of the growing discussion of the letter, not to mention his own literary and social context. Unlike Clement, Origen is primarily concerned with stylistic difference.[93] "As anyone who knows how to distinguish differences of phraseology would admit," Origen argues, "the Epistle entitled 'To the Hebrews' does not possess the apostle's idiom (τὸ ἐν λόγῳ ἰδιωτικὸν τοῦ ἀποστόλου)."[94] For Origen, the Greek of Hebrews is more technical than the Greek reflected in other Pauline letters.[95] Rather than position Hebrews as a translation, however, Origen frames Hebrews as a work of a follower of Paul who recalls to mind the teachings of the apostle. Accordingly, the "thoughts of the Epistle" are equal to those in the "acknowledged writings of the apostle."[96] Origen then offers his idea about the letter's generative context of production:[97]

> But if I were to give my opinion I would say that the thoughts are those of the apostle, but the phraseology and the composition are those of

---

Christians and Jews recognized the ambiguity of Aramaic and Hebrew; see Jerome, *Comm. Matt.* 6.24; *Praef. Tob.* 8–9; *Adv. Pelag.* 3.2 (the Gospel of the Hebrews written in "the Chaldean and Syrian language, but in Hebrew letters"); Epiphanius, *Pan.* 26.1.5 (referring to the "deep language" of Hebrew, not the "Syriac dialect"); m. Yad. 4.5 (the language is holy, not the script).

[92] Later in the fourth century, Epiphanius forwards the claim that Acts was translated from Greek to Hebrew as was the Gospel of John and housed in the treasuries of Tiberius (*Pan.* 30.3.8).

[93] Eusebius, *Hist. eccl.* 6.25.11. Eusebius claims this tradition came from Origen's no-longer extant *Homilies on Hebrews* (another fragment from these homilies is cited in *Eusebii et Pamphyli Apologia Origenis*, 49).

[94] Eusebius, *Hist. eccl.* 6.25.11.   [95] Eusebius, *Hist. eccl.* 6.25.11.

[96] Eusebius, *Hist. eccl.* 6.25.12.

[97] Eusebius, *Hist. eccl.* 6.25.13 (GCS N.F. 6.2, 578, 580): ἐγὼ δὲ ἀποφαινόμενος εἴποιμ᾽ ἂν ὅτι τὰ μὲν νοήματα τοῦ ἀποστόλου ἐστίν, ἡ δὲ φράσις καὶ ἡ σύνθεσις ἀπομνημονεύσαντός τινος τὰ ἀποστολικὰ καὶ ὥσπερ σχολιογραφήσαντός τινος τὰ εἰρημένα ὑπὸ τοῦ διδασκάλου.

someone who recalled to mind the teachings of the apostle and who, as it were, had made notes on what was said by the teacher.

The closest analog for this process of production and transmission is found in ancient philosophical approaches to writing. Anthony Grafton and Megan Williams locate Origen's bookishness and scholarly repertoire within the burgeoning second- and third-century philosophical tradition—featuring Philodemus, Plotinus, and Porphyry—with its patronage system and distinctive "bibliographic habits."[98] On note-taking, Williams points to Porphyry's *Life of Plotinus* and its lengthy quotation from the preface to a work called *On the End* written by Longinus in response to Plotinus and Gentilianus Amelius in the mid-third century CE. In this preface, Longinus comments on the varied approaches to writing among philosophers, with some inscribing their teachings in writing so that subsequent generations might benefit from them, whereas others constrain themselves to their immediate circles, leading the members of their school into an understanding of their philosophy.[99] Longinus knows of philosophers in both approaches (both Platonists and Stoics). Porphyry, in the preface to the *Life of Plotinus*, quotes from Longinus: "Among this group of writers, some write little more than compilations and transcriptions from the writings of their predecessors—so Euclides, Democritus, and Proclinus" (§20.55).[100] Elsewhere, Porphyry comments on editorial work as adjusting the clarity of the prose, fixing errors, and deleting material that detracts from the work's "purpose," but all of which preserves the "meaning" and leaves alone the "sense of what was spoken."[101] Origen's account of the production of Hebrews fits within this milieu and, consequentially, activates Hebrews as Pauline without grounding it in any explicit linguistic markers of Paulinity.

Some have claimed that Origen recognized the intrinsic stylistic features of Hebrews and knew that the text was not a translation from Hebrew into

---

[98] Anthony Grafton and Megan Williams, *Christianity and the Transformation of the Book: Origen, Eusebius, and the Library of Caesarea* (Cambridge, MA: Harvard University Press, 2006), 22–85, esp. 25, 56.

[99] Lloyd P. Gerson, *Plotinus: The Enneads*, trans. George Boys-Stones, John M. Dillon, R. A. H. King, Andrew Smith, and James Wilberding (Cambridge: Cambridge University Press, 2017), 32.

[100] Gerson, *Plotinus*, 32. Cf. Grafton and Williams, *Christianity and the Transformation*, 59, 30.

[101] See the Porphyry quotation in Eusebius, *Praep. evang.* 4.7.1.

Greek.¹⁰² But Origen takes the opposite argument in the case of Susanna in the *Letter to Africanus*.¹⁰³ Despite the linguistic arguments made by Africanus, Origen defends the view that Susanna was written in "Hebrew" and translated into Greek.¹⁰⁴ However, this process of production is directly tied to the authorization of Susanna since, in this context, a Hebrew original is a claim to *Jewish* antiquity, which is the focal point of contention with Africanus. In the case of the Letter to the Hebrews, Origen does not need Paul to be writing in Hebrew because he does not have a problem with the different style, he just needs the text connected to Paul in a meaningful way, and that connection is forged with the image of a student taking notes on the thoughts of the teacher.

For Origen, then, the Letter to the Hebrews contains the mind of Paul, and the process of production ensures the preservation of that Paulinity. With this framework, Origen is free to suspend judgment on which student of Paul transcribed the apostle's teaching: "Who the author of the epistle is truly God knows, but the account that has reached us from some is that Clement, who was bishop of the Romans, wrote the epistle; from others, that Luke, who wrote the Gospel and the Acts, is the author."¹⁰⁵ Origen's "God truly knows" (τὸ μὲν ἀληθὲς θεὸς οἶδεν) is typically read as though Origen was calmly and objectively suspending judgment on the Paulinity of Hebrews. However, Origen's suspension is only on the note-taking student, and the mind of the teacher is never in question. This is the same for all who provide a range of options on the translator of Hebrews (Jerome, Rufinus, Eusebius, and others). Still, the Luke-Paul connection continued into Origen's context, and Clement's earlier account of the origins of Hebrews was an open and developing tradition.

By the late second century, and certainly by the third, the parallel content in *1 Clement* 36 and Hebrews was recognized, and this point of connectivity was read into the narrative of origins developed by Clement of Alexandria.

---

¹⁰² For example, Karl Wieseler, *Eine Untersuchung über den Hebräerbrief namentlich seinen Verfasser und seine Leser. Erste Hälfte* (Kiel: C. F. Mohr, 1860), 11.

¹⁰³ Sextus Julius Africanus was a third-century Christian historian known for two extant letters, as well as a *Chronographiai* and *Kestoi* (Eusebius, *Hist. eccl.* 6.31), both of which are preserved only in fragments (e.g., P. Oxy. 3.412).

¹⁰⁴ See esp. Origen's argument on the Greek wordplay in *Ep. Afr.* 6.

¹⁰⁵ Eusebius, *Hist. eccl.* 6.25.14 (GCS N.F. 6.2, 580): τίς δὲ ὁ γράψαςτὴν ἐπιστολήν, τὸ μὲν ἀληθὲς θεὸς οἶδεν, ἡ δὲ εἰς ἡμᾶςφθάσασα ἱστορία ὑπὸ τινῶν μὲν λεγόντων ὅτι Κλήμης, ὁγενόμενος ἐπίσκοπος Ῥωμαίων, ἔγραψεν τὴν ἐπιστολήν, ὑπὸ τινῶν δὲ ὅτι Λουκᾶς, ὁ γράψας τὸ εὐαγγέλιον καὶ τὰς Πράξεις.

THE INVENTION OF PAUL'S LETTER TO THE HEBREWS   45

Clement of Rome was given a hand in the production of Hebrews.[106] Eusebius, for example, advances and prefers this updated version of Clement's testimony in *Hist. eccl.* 3.38.2–3:[107]

> Since Paul had conversed with the Hebrews in writing, in the language of the fathers (τῆς πατρίου γλώττης), some say it was Luke, but others that it was this very Clement who translated the writing. And that could be true, because of the fact that the Letter of Clement and the Letter of Hebrews maintain the same style of expression and that, throughout, both compositions include ideas that do not significantly differ.

1 Clement features heavily in discussions of the history of the Letter to the Hebrews and is often used as evidence for the anonymous circulation of Hebrews in Rome toward the end of the first century. There is, however, a lengthy debate whether the overlapping material indicates a reading of the text we call Hebrews or whether both texts reveal mutual use of shared (liturgical?) tradition.[108] The material in Hebrews 1 that also appears in *1 Clement* 36 is found in a context preceded by a litany of clauses beginning with διὰ τούτου (through whom), each of which mounts a description of "Jesus Christ the high priest of our offerings" (Ἰησοῦν Χριστόν τὸν ἀρχιερέα

---

[106] *1 Clement* is an epistle sent from "the Church of God dwelling in Rome" to Corinth around the turn of the second century and found in Codex Alexandrinus and Bryennios Codex Hierosolymitanus (1056 CE). Eusebius refers to the circulation of *1 Clement* in *Hist. eccl.* 3.16 and 3.38.

[107] GCS N.F. 6.1, 284: Ἑβραίοις γὰρ διὰ τῆς πατρίου γλώττης ἐγγράφως ὡμιληκότος τοῦ Παύλου, οἳ μὲν τὸν εὐαγγελιστὴν Λουκᾶν, οἳ δὲ τὸν Κλήμεντα τοῦτον αὐτὸν ἑρμηνεῦσαι λέγουσι τὴν γραφήν· ὃ καὶ μᾶλλον ἂν εἴη ἀληθὲς τῷ τὸν ὅμοιον τῆς φράσεως χαρακτῆρα τήν τε τοῦ Κλήμεντος ἐπιστολὴν καὶ τὴν πρὸς Ἑβραίους ἀποσῴζειν καὶ τῷ μὴ πόρρω τὰ ἐν ἑκατέροις τοῖς συγγράμμασι νοήματα καθεστάναι.

[108] The relationship between *1 Clement* and Hebrews is often considered within the larger question of the origins of the title "High Priest." If Hebrews and *1 Clement* evince mutual use of a liturgical source, then therein lies the context for the origin of the term. See Karlmann Beyschlag, *Clemens Romanus und der Frühkatholizismus*, BHT 35 (Tübingen: Mohr Siebeck, 1966), 29; Gerd Theißen, *Untersuchungen zum Hebräerbrief*, StNT 2 (Gütersloh: Mohn, 1969), 33–52, posits a common liturgical source used by both texts, though the form it takes in *1 Clement* is earlier than Hebrews; Donald A. Hagner, *The Use of the Old and New Testaments in Clement of Rome*, NovTSup 34 (Leiden: Brill, 1973), 79; Michael Mees, "Die Hohepriester-Theologie des Hebräerbriefes im Vergleich mit dem Ersten Clemensbrief," BZ 22 (1978): 115–24; G. L. Cockerill, "Heb 1:1–14, *1 Clem.* 36:1–6, and the High Priest Title," JBL 97 (1978): 437–40 (*1 Clement* paraphrases Hebrews); Paul Ellingworth, "Hebrews and *1 Clement*: Literary Dependence or Common Tradition?," BZ 23 (1979): 262–69 (a common liturgical source between the two without dependence); E. Lona, *Der erste Clemensbrief* (Göttingen: Vandenhoeck & Ruprecht, 1998), 52–55, 391–98, esp. 396–98. This discussion is also picked up by Andrew Gregory, "First Clement and the Writings that Later Formed the New Testament," in *The Reception of the New Testament in the Apostolic Fathers*, ed. Andrew Gregory and Christopher Tuckett (Oxford: Oxford University Press, 2005), 129–57.

46   THE PAULINE HISTORY OF HEBREWS

τῶν προσφορῶν ἡμῶν).[109] This repetitiveness, combined with the excerpted passages from the Psalms, is read as a sign of liturgical origins and led to the idea that *1 Clement* and Hebrews utilize a similar *Vorlage*. *1 Clement* 36.2–6 reads:[110]

> "He is the radiance of his magnificence, as superior to the angels as he has inherited a more excellent name." For so it is written, "The one who makes his angels spirits and his ministers a tongue of fire." But the Master says this about his son, "You are my son, today I have given you birth. Ask from me, and I will give you the nations as your inheritance, and the ends of the earth as your possession." And again, he says to him, "Sit at my right hand, until I make your enemies a footstool for your feet." Who then are the enemies? Those who are evil and oppose his will.

The passages from the Psalms are not "cited" from Hebrews in a clear order, and they are also given new introductory frames. The quotation of Psalm 2:7 in *1 Clement* 36.2 is not only more extended than it is in Hebrews, but framed with the theme of the Master and Son from earlier in *1 Clement* (διὰ τούτου ἠθέλησεν ὁ δεσπότης τῆς ἀθανάτου γνώσεως ἡμᾶς γεύσασθαι; "through this one the master has wished for us to taste the knowledge of immortality"). Rather than a reading or a citation of Hebrews, *1 Clement* is likely citing from shared or very similar material that is also found in Hebrews 1. Nevertheless, ancient and modern scholars seek to find in *1 Clement* evidence for the Paulinity of Hebrews.

Clare Rothschild claims that by evoking material from Hebrews between citations from the Pauline corpus, *1 Clement* implies that Hebrews is Pauline.[111] But where one finds implicit Paulinism, another might point out that "To the Hebrews" does not appear in *1 Clement* 36:2–6 as a *Pauline* letter or as anything at all. What appears is a list of quotations from the

---

[109] Greek text in *The Apostolic Fathers*, vol. 1, ed. Bart Ehrman, LCL 24 (Cambridge, MA: Harvard University Press, 2001), 98.

[110] Trans. Ehrman, *The Apostolic Fathers*, 101. Greek text LCL 24, 100: ὃς ὢν ἀπαύγασμα τῆς μεγαλωσύνης αὐτοῦ τοσούτῳ μείζων ἐστὶν ἀγγέλων, ὅσῳ διαφορώτερον ὄνομα κεκληρονόμηκεν. Γέγραπται γὰρ οὕτως· Ὁ ποιῶν τοὺς ἀγγέλους αὐτοῦ πνεύματα καὶ τοὺς λειτουργοὺς αὐτοῦ πυρὸς φλόγα. Ἐπὶ δὲ τῷ υἱῷ αὐτοῦ οὕτως εἶπεν ὁ δεσπότης· Υἱός μου εἶ σύ, ἐγὼ σήμερον γεγέννηκά σε· αἴτησαι παρ' ἐμοῦ, καὶ δώσω σοι ἔθνη τὴν κληρονομίαν σου καὶ τὴν κατάσχεσίν σου τὰ πέρατα τῆς γῆς. Καὶ πάλιν λέγει πρὸς αὐτόν· Κάθου ἐκ δεξιῶν μου, ἕως ἂν θῶ τοὺς ἐχθρούς σου ὑποπόδιον τῶν ποδῶν σου. Τίνες οὖν οἱ ἐχθροί; οἱ φαῦλοι καὶ ἀντιτασσόμενοι τῷ θελήματι αὐτοῦ.

[111] Rothschild, *Hebrews as Pseudepigraphon*, 6.

Psalms.¹¹² Even if this Psalms catena was taken from a copy of Hebrews, the reordering of passages (the order here is Heb 1:3, 1:4, 1:7, 1:5, 1:13) and recontextualization (extended quotation from Psalm 2, new introductory frames) stretches the notion of a "citation" to a breaking point. There is no Paulinity here, and *1 Clement* actively marks Pauline letters elsewhere. In *1 Clement* 47.1, for example, the Corinthian readers are told, "Take up the epistle of the blessed apostle Paul."¹¹³ To be sure, it is contextually fitting that this Pauline letter would be evoked in a later epistle also sent to Corinth (1 Cor is described as a letter "sent to you," *1 Clem.* 47.2), but the willingness to flag Pauline letters strains the claim that Hebrews is marked as "Pauline." If Hebrews appears at all, it is only as an anonymous and supplementary text, an approach that accords with the view espoused above, that Hebrews is an intentionally anonymous word of exhortation that has been forwarded to a secondary group of Christ-followers, perhaps to Rome.

As Eusebius of Caesarea considers *1 Clement*, he reads the relationship between Hebrews and *1 Clement* 36 through the prism of Pauline circulation. What *1 Clement* provides for Eusebius is a justification for collecting Hebrews within the *corpus Paulinum*:¹¹⁴

> [Clement] has included in this letter many ideas similar to the Letter to the Hebrews, and already uses some passages from it verbatim, which establishes most securely that this composition was not new, and consequently it seemed obvious to catalog it (ἐγκαταλεχθῆναι) with the rest of the Apostle's letters.

Eusebius uses the lexical affiliation between Hebrews and *1 Clement* to ground the inclusion of Hebrews within manuscripts of Pauline letters, commenting that Hebrews was rightly cataloged (ἐγκαταλεχθῆναι) with Paul's letters given the antiquity of the text. Eusebius too favors the idea that Clement was Paul's Greek translator rather than Luke. Both of these positions are interesting. Not only has the "East" read Rome, the epicenter of

---

¹¹² Perceptively, Gottlieb Lünemann, *Kritisch exegetisches Handbuch über den Hebräerbrief* (Göttingen: Vandenhoeck & Ruprecht, 1855), 7, notes how improbable the reputation of Rome's position on Hebrews would be if it is claimed to be Pauline so early in *1 Clement*.
¹¹³ Cf. *1 Clement* 5, where material about Paul is taken from 2 Corinthians 6.
¹¹⁴ Eusebius, *Hist. eccl.* 3.38.1. GCS N. F. 6.1 284: ἐν ᾗ τῆς πρὸς Ἑβραίους πολλὰ νοήματα παραθείς, ἤδη δὲ καὶ αὐτολεξεὶ ῥητοῖς τισιν ἐξ αὐτῆς χρησάμενος, σαφέστατα παρίστησιν ὅτι μὴ νέον ὑπάρχει τὸ σύγγραμμα, ὅθεν δὴ καὶ εἰκότως ἔδοξεν αὐτὸ τοῖς λοιποῖς ἐγκαταλεχθῆναι γράμμασι τοῦ ἀποστόλου.

48   THE PAULINE HISTORY OF HEBREWS

the "rejection" of Hebrews, in order to development the origin story, but the circulation of Hebrews as Pauline is driving the discussion for these figures.

Discussions of Pauline authorship in Clement, Origen, and Eusebius are, therefore, all conditioned by the circulation of Hebrews as Pauline. These readers are looking to account for the non-Pauline features of Hebrews in light of its material presence. Hebrews is "there" and needs to be explained. If we turn from Alexandria and Caesarea to Rome and Carthage, the "Western" reception of Hebrews also participates within this same dynamic, a negotiation with materiality.

4. East Versus West? A Shared Struggle for Paulinity

Clare Rothschild has recently challenged the idea of a "Western rejection" of Hebrews. Finding "rejection" to be a mischaracterization of the Latin afterlife of Hebrews, Rothschild intervenes by isolating the "what" of rejection more precisely and argues that by separating authorship from authority, resisting arguments from silence, and reading the conditions of agency underlying comments of "rejection," we are able to see that Hebrews was "accepted" in the West despite "empire-wide skepticism over the Pauline authorship of Hebrews."[115] Active "rejection" implies, and even requires, certain processes of authorization like circulation and ongoing use within reading communities. Censorship of the Pauline authorship of Hebrews took place across the Mediterranean and did not affect the letter's more functional authority.[116] What Rothschild unveils, then, is how conclusions drawn from the absence of Paulinity (that the letter was rejected) obscure the necessary levels of circulation and relative popularity for a text *to be* rejected.

Rothschild rightly emphasizes that descriptions of the "rejection" of Hebrews in ancient sources imply certain levels of circulation and use,

---

[115] Rothschild, *Hebrews as Pseudepigraphon*, 39. Rothschild finds that the absence of Hebrews in sources like the Muratorian fragment and Marcion is too often read as active rejection, amounting to a familiar *argumentum ex silencio* (32). Instances where Hebrews was likely known and yet not read as Pauline—Eusebius on Gaius of Rome, Epiphanius on Arians, Cyprian of Carthage—attest to the popularity and prominence of Hebrews as a circulating and authorized text.

[116] In fact, for Rothschild, as Clement and Origen register and absorb significant skepticism regarding Hebrews, their comments are not advancing and creating authorship but responding to the "high" status of Hebrews in Rome (!) (*Hebrews as Pseudepigraphon*, 38). As noted above, I argue that the pressure comes not from Rome but from the Egyptian circulation of Hebrews.

and that by looking beyond positive acceptance of the Pauline ascription in Greek sources, we can see these ulterior forms of agency in Latin contexts. But, in describing those forms of textual agency, Rothschild returns to the same categories of rejection and acceptance that positions readers as the arbiters of authenticity. The West, within this revamped frame, "never rejected Hebrews," shows "allegiance" to and "acceptance" of the letter, and reflects its ongoing Western "popularity."[117] In arriving at these conclusions, Rothschild moves from identifying verbal similarities to the "use" of Hebrews and, consequentially, its "authority" and "acceptance." For Rothschild, "Hebrews is cited by Polycarp, *Shepherd of Hermas*, Justin Martyr, Tertullian, Hippolytus and Irenaeus," when "to the Hebrews" is neither evoked, mentioned, cited, or otherwise noted in these sources, much less the Paulinity of Hebrews.[118] Even if verbal parallels indicate the possession and influence of Hebrews in these contexts, the text is formally absent in these sources, without authority, name, or Paulinity. The emergence of a *Pauline* Hebrews in Latin contexts remains obscured, and the language of acceptance masks its absence.

Further, the separation of Pauline authorship from the idea of acceptance, while rendering certain features of Hebrews visible, obscures the material processes by which the Paulinity of Hebrews emerges in Latin sources and the abiding centrality of (Pauline) authorship in providing the conditions of textual authority. The main evidence for the separation of authority and authorship is Tertullian, who, for Rothschild, "accepts the letter's authority while rejecting its Pauline authorship, attributing it, rather, to Barnabas."[119] But Tertullian's use of *ad Hebraeos* suggests that he neither rejects nor attributes authorship but attempts to strengthen an existing textual condition in which the question of authorship has been predetermined.

---

[117] Rothschild, *Hebrews as Pseudepigraphon*: "Hebrews was never 'rejected' in the West" (18); "The Western church maintained virtually uninterrupted allegiance to the text" (29); "The primary sources testify to widespread acceptance" (39). The Christian reception of Hebrews as Pauline is, for Rothschild, "a measured response to the text's pseudonymous claim" (119).

[118] Rothschild, *Hebrews as Pseudepigraphon*, 33. On Irenaeus see Eusebius, *Hist. eccl.* 5.26.1, where Irenaeus allegedly mentions Hebrews in a non-extant work but not as Pauline (similarly Stephanus Gobarus in Photius, *Bibliotheca*, Cod. 232). See here D. Jeffery Bingham, "Irenaeus and Hebrews," in *Christology, Hermeneutics, and Hebrews: Profiles from the History of Interpretation*, ed. Jon C. Laansma and Daniel J. Treier (London: T&T Clark, 2012), 71, who acknowledges the lack of citations in attempting to describe Irenaeus' use of the Hebrews. Photius, *Bibliotheca*, 121, also preserves a tradition that has Hippolytus of Rome denying that Hebrews was Pauline. On these sources see Spicq, *l'Epître aux Hébreux*, 177–83; Westcott, *Hebrews*, lxii–lxiii; Wieseler, *Eine Untersuchung über den Hebräerbrief*, 19–20; Lünemann, *Hebräerbrief*, 8; Hans Windisch, *Der Hebräerbrief* (Tübingen: Mohr Siebeck, 1913), 5.

[119] Rothschild, *Hebrews as Pseudepigraphon*, 20 n. 15.

In one of his later writings, *On Modesty*, Tertullian cites from a "Letter of Barnabas" (*epistola Barnabae*) that was written "To the Hebrews" (*ad Hebraeos*).[120] As noted by de Boer, the reference to a *titulus* with the name *Barnabae* suggests that Tertullian's manuscript contained a heading that named Hebrews as a letter from Barnabas.[121] In order to shore up the "Letter of Barnabas to the Hebrews" as an authorized source on the topic at hand, Tertullian Paulinizes Barnabas in order to confer authority to *ad Hebraeos* through apostolic lineage. Barnabas, according to Tertullian, is sufficiently accredited by God, as being one whom Paul has stationed next to himself in the uninterrupted observance of abstinence: "'Or else, I alone and Barnabas, have not we the power of working?'" (1 Cor. 9.6).[122] Tertullian uses the unique association between Paul and Barnabas ("I alone and Barnabas") to legitimize the authority of his apostolic source.[123] In doing so, Tertullian gives no indication that he knew *ad Hebraeos* also circulated as a Pauline letter elsewhere in the Roman Empire.[124] Hebrews, then, is neither rejected nor accepted here but encountered and engaged.

Returning to Tertullian's copy of *ad Hebraeos*, one finds reverberations of Hebrews circulating as a letter of Barnabas in later material contexts and literary contexts, and undoubtedly this had some impact on the non-Pauline tradition of Hebrews. In Codex Claromontanus (D 06), a fifth- or sixth-century Latin diglot codex, an "Epistle of Barnabas" is positioned between Jude and Revelation in the famed stichometric list on 467v–468v.[125] At 850 lines, this epistle is too short to be our *Epistle of Barnabas*, which has a stichometry of 1,360 in (Ps?) Nicephorus I of Constantinople.[126] In 𝔓⁴⁶

---

[120] *De pudicitia* 20.2: *Extat enim et Barnabae titulus ad Hebraeos* and later *Et utique receptior apud ecclesias epistola Barnabae illo apocrypho Pastore moechorum*. Latin text in *Tertullianus Opera II, Opera montanistica*, CCSL 2 (Turnhout: Brepols, 1954), 1324 (the text of *De pudicitia* is edited by E. Dekkers).

[121] E. A. de Boer, "Tertullian on 'Barnabas' Letter to the Hebrews' in *De pudicitia* 20.1–5," *VC* 68 (2014): 248: "The Latin *titulus* (Greek τίτλος) refers to a title, a heading, or a (library) tag. With the verbal form extant Tertullian states the fact that 'there remains a [work] by Barnabas, entitled To the Hebrews.'"

[122] Tertullian, *Pud.* 20.2. CCSL 2, 1324: *a Deo satis auctorati uiri, ut quem Paulus iuxta se constituerit in abstinentiae tenore,* "*Aut ego solus et Barnabas non habemus operandi potestatem?*"

[123] After all, the quotation from Hebrews 6 is framed as "a testimony from one of the companions of the Apostles, who can confirm with almost the same authority the discipline of the first masters" (*Pud.* 20.1). Clement of Alexandria too Paulinizes his copy of the *Epistle of Barnabas* in *Strom.* 2.20.116.

[124] Tertullian refers to thirteen Pauline letters in *Marc.* 5.20.

[125] Kelsie Rodenbiker, "The Claromontanus Stichometry and Its Canonical Implications," *JSNT* 44.2 (2021): 240–53.

[126] See *Nicephori archiepiscopi Constantinopolitam opuscula historica*, ed. C. Carl Gotthard de Boor (Leipzig: Teubner, 1880), 134.

the stichometry for Hebrews is 700. A description of New Testament texts in Codex Ambrosianus E 51 inf. mentions Barnabas as the sixth writer of the New Testament (*sextus Barnabas*) alongside Paul, Peter, James, and the writers of the Gospels.[127] Further, a quotation from 13:15 is attributed to "Barnabas" (*Santissimus Barnabas*) in a pseudonymous Origenian tractate now affiliated with Gregory of Elvira (late fourth century). The Barnabas attribution is also mentioned by Jerome (*Vir.* 5; *Ep.* 129 *ad Dardan*), Pelagius (*Expositiones XIII epistularum Pauli*), and Philastrius (*Haer.* 89).[128]

The origin of the *titulus* is unknown but is often affiliated with Montanist movements in Asia Minor, a conclusion, in part, born out of Tertullian's use of Hebrews 6:4–8 with its language of the "impossibility" ($\mathring{a}\delta\acute{v}v\alpha\tau ov$) of restoring certain people again $\epsilon\mathring{\iota}_S$ $\mu\epsilon\tau\acute{a}voιav$.[129] Tertullian's goal with this citation is to show that one who was intimately acquainted with the apostles did not know of a "second repentance."[130] Furthering this point, Tertullian claims that the *epistola Barnabae* is more received than the "apocryphal Shepherd of adulterers," which was known for its openness toward subsequent repentance.[131] The Letter of Barnabas to the Hebrews was primarily serviceable for Tertullian's late Montanist interests and, as other sources attest, Tertullian was not alone in reading Hebrews within a Montanist frame.

Eusebius too notices that Gaius of Rome, in writing against Proclus, a Montanist (Phrygian), only mentions thirteen Pauline letters, and from this

---

[127] See Donatien de Bruyne, "Un prologue inconnu des épitres catholiques," *RBén* 23 (1906): 82–87. Since Peter is first (*primus Petrus*), de Bruyne positioned the description within an Italian context.

[128] *Tractatus de libris sacrarum scripturarum*, 10, attributes a reference to Romans 12:1, to "the blessed apostle Paul," followed by a quotation of Hebrews 13:15 from Barnabas. This text is now affiliated with Gregory of Elvira. See Windisch, *Der Hebräerbrief*, 5; Otto, *Der Brief an die Hebräer*, 38 n. 2; de Boer, "Tertullian on 'Barnabas' Letter," 251.

[129] On the origins of the attribution of Barnabas, scholars invariably point out that in Acts 4:26, Joseph, a Levite, is nicknamed "Barnabas," which means "son of consolation" ($\upsilon\mathring{\iota}\grave{o}_S$ $\pi\alpha\rho\alpha\kappa\lambda\acute{\eta}\sigma\epsilon\omega_S$), which parallels the description of Hebrews as a "word of $\pi\alpha\rho\alpha\kappa\lambda\acute{\eta}\sigma\epsilon\omega_S$" (in Heb 13:22). Barnabas is also described as one *ex orientis partibus, natione Hebraeus, nominee Barnabas* in the Pseudo-Clementine *Recognitions* 1.7.7. Latin text in Bernhard Rehm, ed., *Die Pseudoklementinen II: Rekognitionen*, GCS 51 (Berlin: Akademie Verlag, 1965), 10. On Montanism and Barnabas see Zahn, *Introduction to the New Testament*, 303, who suggest the title derives from Montanist circles in Asia Minor, and Eduard Riggenbach, *Der Brief an die Hebräer*, KNT 14 (Leipzig: Deichert, 1913), xii, who provenances the title to Rome, which was later picked up by Montanists. On the origins, development, and historical dynamics of Montanism see esp. Paul McKechnie, *Christianizing Asia Minor: Conversion, Communities, and Social Change in the Pre-Constantinian Era* (Cambridge: Cambridge University Press, 2019), 96–146, and on the use of Hebrews in these movements see Patrick Gray, "The Early Reception of Hebrews 6:4-6," in *Scripture and Traditions: Essays on Early Judaism and Christianity in Honor of Carl R. Holladay* (Leiden: Brill, 2008), 321–39.

[130] *Pud.* 20.5.   [131] See Hermas, *Mand.* 4.3.3–6.

52 THE PAULINE HISTORY OF HEBREWS

Eusebius concludes that Gaius rejected Hebrews and did not reckon it as Pauline.[132] But this is only one reading of absence, as Gaius might not have rejected a Pauline Hebrews because of his anti-Montanism but rather did not know Hebrews to be Pauline at all, a condition that was likely fueled by the circulation as a letter from Barnabas.[133] There is no evidence that Hebrews circulated as a Pauline letter in Italy, Carthage, and much of Asia Minor throughout the second and third centuries. The earliest references to Pauline letters include Ignatius of Antioch (*Eph.* 13.2), Polycarp of Smyrna (*Phil.* 3.2, 11.3), and 2 Peter 3:16. These contexts give no indication that Hebrews was Pauline, let alone read at all.[134]

Tertullian's description of Marcion's early second-century collection of Paul—known as the *Apostolikon*—remains the earliest discussion of an order to Paul's letters.[135] According to Tertullian, Marcion's collection began with Galatians, as an opening cover letter of sorts, followed by nine Pauline letters ordered by descending length.[136] Marcion's *Apostolikon* was mostly likely a project of collection that modified earlier collections that were

---

[132] Eusebius, *Hist. eccl.* 6.20.3; Cf. Jerome, *Vir.* 59.

[133] Moreover, according to Philastrius of Brescia (*Haer.* 89.3), Ambrose (*De paenit.* 2.2), Epiphanius (*Pan.* 59.2.1), the Novatians appealed to Hebrews on the question of penance. Hebrews was also affiliated with Theodotus and the Theodotians (Ps.-Hippolytus, *Haer.* 7.36, 10.24, cf. Eusebius, *Hist. eccl.* 5.28.8–10), for its content on Melchizedek, a movement that purportedly influenced the third-century group known as the Melchizedekians, according to Epiphanius (*Pan.* 55.1.4, 55.5.1; cf. also Ps. Tertullian, *Adversus omnes haereses* 8). Other witnesses to Melchizedek's importance in ancient circles include 11QMelch, *2 Enoch* 71–72, *Pistis Sophia*, and the Nag Hammadi tractate Melchizedek (NHC IX, 1). See Eric Mason, "Melchizedek Traditions in Second Temple Judaism," in *"You Are a Priest Forever": Second Temple Jewish Messianism and the Priestly Christology of the Epistle to the Hebrews*, STDJ 74 (Leiden: Brill, 2008), 138–90.

[134] See esp. Andreas Lindemann, *Paulus im ältesten Christentum: Das Bild des Apostels und die Rezeption der paulinischen Theologie in der frühchristlichen Literatur bis Marcion*, BHT 58 (Tübingen: Mohr Siebeck, 1979); Andreas Lindemann, "Der Apostel Paulus im 2 Jahrhundert," in *The New Testament in Early Christianity, La reception des écrit néotestamentaires dans le christianisme primitif*, ed. Jean-Marie Sevrin, BETHhL 86 (Leuven: Leuven University Press, 1989), 39–67; Kurt Aland, "Methodische Bemerkungen zum Corpus Paulinum bei den Kirchenvätern des zweiten Jahrhunderts," in *Kerygma und Logos: Beiträge zu den geistesgeschichtlichen Beziehungen zwischen Antike und Christentum*, ed. Adolf Martin Ritter (Göttingen: Vandenhoeck & Ruprecht, 1979), 29–48; Enrico Norelli, "La tradition paulinienne dans les lettres d'Ignace," in Schröter et al., *Receptions of Paul*, 519–51.

[135] See esp. *Marc.* 5; Epiphanius, *Pan.* 42.12.1.

[136] According to Tertullian (*Marc.* 5), the order of this collection is Galatians, the Corinthian correspondence, Romans, the Thessalonian correspondence, "Laodiceans" (Ephesians), Colossians, Philippians, and Philemon. Epiphanius (*Pan.* 42.9.4, 42.11.10) has the same order but switches Philippians and Philemon, likely because of the connection between Philemon and Colossians. On Marcion's text of Galatians 1:1 (whether 'καὶ θεοῦ πατρὸς' was excised) as discussed by Tertullian and Jerome, see T. Baarda, "Marcion's Text of Gal 1:1: Concerning the Reconstruction of the First Verse of the Marcionite Corpus Paulinum," *VC* 42 (1988): 236–56. An anti-Marcionite corpus headed by the Letter to the Ephesians has been a notorious proposal over the years, but remains theoretical part from further evidence. See esp. Edgar J. Goodspeed, *The Formation of the New Testament* (Chicago: University of Chicago Press, 1926), 20–32.

already determined by a strategy of organization involving "seven" Pauline letters.[137]

Nils Dahl draws attention to the problem of the particularity of Pauline letters and the strategy of "the seven" as a theological path toward their universal applicability that determines the organization and structure of the developing *corpus Paulinum*.[138] The Muratorian fragment (Cod. Ambr. I 101 sup) also adopts this strategy.[139] This eighty-five-line Latin fragment describes the historical and theological occasions for Paul's letters.[140] The text contends that it is vital to grasp each of the occasions and purposes, for the seven churches represent Paul's ultimate audience; the one Church. The letters found in the Apocalypse of John, it is argued, similarly address seven churches and yet are clearly intended to be read by all. Paul's other, personal letters—to Philemon, Titus, and Timothy—were written out of affection and are used for the "regulation of ecclesiastical discipline" (ll. 58–63). The main point is that Paul wrote to *seven* churches, which makes the audience and the aims of these clear (even though only 1 Corinthians, Galatians, and Romans are described, ll. 42–46). The absence of Hebrews in the text is further evidence of the non-Pauline circulation of Hebrews,

---

[137] Gamble, *Books and Readers*, 59.

[138] Nils Dahl, "The *Particularity* of the Pauline Epistles as a Problem in the Ancient Church," in *Neotestamentica et Patristica: Eine Freundesgabe, Herrn Professor Dr. Oscar Cullmann zu seinem 60 Geburtstag überreicht* (Leiden: Brill, 1962), 261–71. Cf. Roy Gibson, "On the Nature of Ancient Letter Collections," *JRS* 102 (2012): 56–78, on other strategies for organizing letters collections. See also Krister Stendahl, "The Apocalypse of John and the Epistles of Paul in the Muratorian Fragment," in *Current Issues in New Testament Interpretation*, ed. W. Klassen and G. F. Snyder (New York: Harper and Row, 1962), 239–45.

[139] Christophe Guignard convincingly argues that the fragment is a fourth-century Latin translation of a Greek text from the late second century; see "The Original Language of the Muratorian Fragment," *JTS* 66.2 (2015): 596–624. Some voices argue that the text is a fourth-century fragment from the "East"; see Albert C. Sundberg Jr., "Canon Muratori: A Fourth Century List," *HTR* 66 (1973): 1–41; Geoffrey Mark Hahneman, *The Muratorian Fragment and the Development of the Canon* (Oxford: Clarendon Press, 1992); Geoffrey Mark Hahneman, "More on Redating the Muratorian Fragment," *StPatr* 19 (1988): 359–65. Responses to Sundberg and Hahneman include Joseph Verheyden, "The Canon Muratori: A Matter of Dispute," in *The Biblical Canons*, ed. J.-M. Auwers and H. J. De Jonge (Leuven: Leuven University Press, 2003), 500–550; Jean-Daniel Kaestli, "La place du fragment de Muratori dans l'histoire du canon: À propos de la thèse de Sundberg et Hahneman," *CrSt* 15.3 (1994): 609–34; P. Henne, "La datation du canon de Muratori," *RB* 100 (1993): 54–75; Evert Ferguson, "Canon Muratori: Date and Provenance," *SP* 17 (1982): 677–83. The proposal from Clare Rothschild, "The Muratorian Fragment as Roman Fake," *NovT* 60 (2018): 55–82, has been severely challenged by Christophe Guignard, "The Muratorian Fragment as a Late Antique Fake? An Answer to C. K. Rothschild," *RevSR* 93 (2019): 73–90. In general, see Eckhard J. Schnabel, "The Muratorian Fragment: The State of Research," *JETS* 57 (2014): 231–64.

[140] The order of epistles discussed is unique: Corinthians, Ephesians, Philippians, Colossians, Galatians, Thessalonians, and then Romans. The order might be unique to the fragment rather than reflect an order in a manuscript. The fragment also describes Luke, John, and the Johannine Epistles, the Revelation of John, the Apocalypse of Peter, the Shepherd of Hermas, and a Marcionite Psalter.

not to mention the subsequent mention of "forged" letters to the Laodiceans and Alexandrians that were designed to "[further] the heresy of Marcion" (ll. 64–65).[141] That the fragment does not mention a forged letter to the Hebrews is indictive of absence rather than something that was known but must be rejected.

Further into the third century, one observes the absence of Hebrews in the prologues developed for Pauline letters, often thought to be Marcionite in origin.[142] Meanwhile, conceptualizing Paul's letters according to the idea of "seven" (without additional reference to Hebrews) is mentioned by Cyprian (*Test*. 1.20, *Fort*. 11) and Victorinus of Pettua (*Comm. Rev.* 1.7).

As the universalizing seven-letter theory took shape, later Greek writers can be observed wrestling with this strategy of organization in light of their fourteen-letter corpus. Gregory of Nazianzus sidesteps the notion of seven letters and instead groups the two divisions of letters into "the ten and four epistles of Paul."[143] The "four" in this division are the letters to individuals (separating out 1 and 2 Timothy as two and including Philemon) and the ten are the letters to churches (the same principle of separation applies to the Corinthian and Thessalonian correspondences).[144] Gregory has placed Hebrews as the tenth letter. On the other hand, Amphilochius of Iconium comments that "the apostle Paul who wrote wisely to the churches twice seven epistles" (Παῦλον σοφῶς γράψαντα ταῖς ἐκκλησίαις ἐπιστολὰς δὶς

---

[141] Trans. Metzger, *Canon of the New Testament*, 307. Scholars like Adolf Hilgenfeld, *Historisch-kritische Einleitung in das Neue Testament* (Leipzig: R. Reisland, 1875), 105, suggest that Hebrews was also known as *ad Alexandrinos*, which, according to line 64, was fabricated like an epistle *ad Laodicenos*, under Paul's name in the spirit of Marcion. Lünemann, *Hebräerbrief*, 25, rightly notes that Hebrews does not fit the notion of a text forged "Pauli nomine" and "ad haeresem Marionis" (l.64–65).

[142] On the Marcionite prologues see Donatien de Bruyne, "Prologues bibliques d'origin Marcionite," *RBén* 24 (1907): 1–16. Nils Dahl, "The Origin of the Earliest Prologues to the Pauline Letters," *Semeia* 12 (1978): 233–77, continues a tradition of questioning the Marcionite origin of these prologues, following Wilhelm Mundle and Marie-Joseph Lagrange. A recent criticism of this view is found in Eric Scherbenske, "Evaluation of Nils Dahl's Argument against a Marcionite Origin of the OL Argumenta," in *Canonizing Paul: Ancient Editorial Practice and the Corpus Paulinum* (Oxford: Oxford University Press, 2013), 237–42, who argues that Marcion's *corpus Paulinum* was shaped by the *Antithesis* and *argumenta* (prologues), giving a hermeneutical justification for editorial practices (71–115).

[143] *Carmina Theologica* 1.1.12.(35) (PG 37:472–74), cited in Edmon L. Gallagher and John D. Meade, *The Biblical Canon Lists from Early Christianity: Texts and Analysis* (Oxford: Oxford University Press, 2017), 146. For a critical introduction to these texts see Claudio Moreschini and D. A. Sykes, eds., *St Gregory of Nazianzus: Poemata arcana*, Oxford Theological Monographs (Oxford: Clarendon Press, 1997).

[144] Cf. the *Primum Quaeritur* prologue to the Vulgate revision of the *corpus Paulinum* referring to the ten and four.

ἑπτά).[145] Here Amphilochius simply works a fourteen-letter corpus into the privileged system of "seven" through division, as there is no configuration through reduction or expansion that produces two even sets of seven letters. What Gregory and Amphilochius highlight is the ongoing struggle to stabilize the Paulinity of Hebrews within known strategies of organization. This same struggle is observed in the manuscript tradition itself, as Hebrews is subject to the most variance in terms of position within the collection.[146]

Hebrews occupies a place within letters addressed to churches. In addition to $\mathfrak{P}^{46}$, Hebrews is also placed between Romans and 1 Corinthians in six miniscule manuscripts (103, 455, 1961, 1964, 1977, and 1994), and a Syrian Canon from around the beginning of the fifth century (Cod. Syr. 10).[147] The fourth- or fifth-century Coptic (Oxyrhynchite) manuscript P.Mil.Vogl. V (LDAB. 107,795) and a number of Greek minuscules (1930, 1978, and 2248), as well as a Sahidic translation of Athanasius' thirty-ninth mid-fourth-century Festal epistle, push Hebrews into the next position after 2 Corinthians, before Galatians.[148] This might also be a principle of length but, in this instance, Hebrews appears on the other side of the Corinthian correspondence. Curiously, Hebrews is found in other positions within the church letters, yet not determined by length. Hebrews is

---

[145] *Iambi ad Seleucum* 300–301. Greek text in Eberhard Oberg, ed., *Amphilochii Iconiensis iambi ad Seleucum*, PTS 9 (Berlin: de Gruyter, 1969), 38. *Pace* Hans-Josef Klauck, *Die antike Briefliteratur und das Neue Testament: Ein Lehr und Arbeitsbuch* (Paderborn: Ferdinand Schöningh, 1998), trans. *Ancient Letters and the New Testament*, Daniel P. Bailey (Waco: Baylor University Press, 2006), 331: "The reason for increasing the number from thirteen to fourteen, in addition to the need to find a place for Hebrews, was probably the desire to arrive at the symbolic number seven (14…7)." Again, the direction of development and influence goes in the other direction. Figures like Amphilochius work from existing fourteen-letter collections together with known strategies for conceptualizing Paul's letters.

[146] There are many thorough treatments of the orders of Pauline letters, the most influential of which is William Hatch, "The Position of Hebrews in the Canon of the NT," *HTR* 29 (1936): 133–51. Hatch follows these stabilizing positions all the way up to the publication of critical editions in the seventeenth century. See also H. J. Frede, "Die Ordnung der Paulusbriefe und der Platz des Kolosserbriefs im Corpus Paulinum," *Vetus Latina: Die Reste der altlateinischen Bibel*, 24/2. Lief. 4 (Freiburg: Herder, 1969), 290–303; Aland, "Die Entstehung des Corpus Paulinum"; Metzger, *Textual Commentary*, 591–92.

[147] Hatch, "The Position of Hebrews," 133.

[148] Hatch, "The Position of Hebrews," 134, 138–42. In P.Mil.Vogl. V Hebrews is preceded by Romans and the Corinthians correspondence and is followed by Galatians, Philippians, Ephesians, 1–2 Thessalonians, and then Colossians. On this Coptic manuscript see Hans-Martin Schenke, "Mittelägyptischen 'Nachlese' I. Bermerkungen zum Adverb ϩⲓⲧⲣⲟⲩⲣ 'schnell' anlässlich der Edition von Restfragmenten in der Mailänder Handschrift der Paulusbriefe mit einem neuen Beleg," *ZÄS* 116 (1989): 160–74, reprinted in *Der Same Seths: Hans-Martin Schenkes Kleine Schriften Zu Gnosis, Koptologie und Neuem Testament*, ed. Gesine Schenke Robinson, Gesa Schenke, and Uwe-Karsten Plisch (Leiden: Brill, 2012), 637–58.

found between Galatians and Ephesians, for instance.[149] Hebrews quickly descends "down," as it were, and arrives between 2 Thessalonians and 1 Timothy in major uncials like Vaticanus, Sinaiticus, Alexandrinus, and Freerianus, as well as Ephraem's commentary on Pauline letters, and the Euthalian prologues (fifth to sixth century). The final position worth noting here has Hebrews at the end of the collection, decidedly out of the corporate letters and after the letters to individuals. This position is prominent in Syriac manuscripts, and since the *corpus Paulinum* often concludes the collection, Hebrews is sometimes the final letter, as in Codex Ephraemi Rescriptus, Fuldensis, and Jerome.[150]

In commenting on Marcion's placement of Philemon, Epiphanius comments on these two final positions of Hebrews in *Panarion* 41.12.1: "In some copies, however, it [Philemon] is placed thirteenth before Hebrews, which is fourteenth, but other copies have the Epistle to the Hebrews tenth, before the two Epistles to Timothy, the Epistle to Titus, and the Epistle to Philemon."[151] It is tempting to see here two competing views of Hebrews, one that has the letter as a final "church" letter and the other that relegates it to the end of the corpus, either as a letter to "individuals" or simply as a final Pauline text that defies both categorizations.[152] However, in his epistula *Ad Paulinum de studio Scripturarum* (53.9), Jerome comments that Paul wrote to seven churches and that Hebrews is the "eighth epistle" and "generally not counted in with the others" (*Paulus Apostolus ad septem Ecclesias scribit—octava enim ad Hebraeos a plerisque extra numerum ponitur*).[153] Jerome reads the position of Hebrews after 2 Thessalonians as a break from Paul's letters to churches, not as the final letter within this group. Thus,

---

[149] See here Ben Witherington III, "The Influence of Galatians on Hebrews," *NTS* 37 (1991): 146–52, who looks to register significance from the proximity of placement.

[150] British Library, Add. MS 14470; *Vat. Sir.* 470, 203, 275, 152, 150, 103 pt. 3, 16, 470; *Borg. Sir.* 117, 93; BNF Syr. 365, 402; Mardin, Turkey Chaldean Cathedral (CCM), 00058, 00473; Saint Mark's Monastery, Jerusalem (SMMJ) 00050, 00036, 00037, 00031 (Hebrews ends at 12:27), 00031; Sachau 311; Staatsbibliothek zu Berlin 81; Syriac 9; Biblioteca Medicea Laurenziana, Orientali 230. Hebrews can also be found in the ambiguous place between Paul and the catholic epistles in Ethiopic manuscripts (see, e.g., EMDA 00124, EMDA 00083) and the *Decretum Gelasianum*.

[151] Trans. Frank Williams, *The* Panarion *of Epiphanius of Salamis: Book 1 (Sects 1–46)*, NHMS 63 (Leiden: Brill, 2009), 360. Greek text Karl Holl, ed., *Epiphanius II: Panarion haer. 34–64*, GCS 31 (Berlin: Verlag, 1980), 181: ἔν τισιν δὲ ἀντιγράφοις τρισκαιδεκάτη πρὸ τῆς πρὸς Ἑβραίους τεσσαρεσκαιδεκάτης τέτακται, ἄλλα δὲ ἀντίγραφα ἔχει τὴν πρὸς Ἑβραίους δεκάτην πρὸ τῶν δύο πρὸς Τιμόθεον καὶ Τίτον καὶ Φιλήμονα.

[152] David Young, *The Concept of Canon in the Reception of the Epistle to the Hebrews* (London: T&T Clark, 2021), 99, argues that the shift to this fourteenth position constitutes an implicit rejection of the Pauline status of Hebrews or at least registers its status as a disputed letter.

[153] Latin text from *Patrologiae cursus completus. Series latina*, vol. 22 (Paris: Migne, 1845), 548 col. 280. Cf. also *Praef. in Tit*; *Ep.* 129.3 *ad Dardanum*.

both positions might be seen as the relegation of Hebrews outside of the "seven" and as the "East" accommodating the "West" in pushing Hebrews outside of the seven letters to churches by placing it after 2 Thessalonians.

Flexible practices of circulation are evident in Codex Vaticanus (B, Vat. gr. 1209)—a mid-fourth-century codex perhaps with a Roman provenance. Hebrews is positioned in Vaticanus after 2 Thessalonians; however, the remaining numbering system indicates that the exemplar for Vaticanus positioned Hebrews between Galatians and Ephesians, as the page numbers for Hebrews (59–69) run successively from Galatians (54–58) and Ephesians (70–75).[154] Vaticanus appears to accommodate a "Latin" order for Paul's letters by repositioning Hebrews from its place in the exemplar. On the other hand, Schlossnikel has confirmed what many have long suspected, that a later scribe added the text of Hebrews to the *corpus Paulinum* in Codex Claromontanus, the prominent Latin diglot codex mentioned earlier.[155] In Claromontanus, Hebrews does not have an incipit, whereas the preceding text, Philemon, ends with a large and prominent banner (fol. 467r) which is followed by a stichometry (fols. 467v–468v).

The placement of Hebrews in these codices does not indicate the softening of the "West's resistance to the East's arguments" but the flexible circulation practices in both Latin and Greek contexts that are emblematic of a common struggle to accommodate a growing collection of Paul's letters in light of an ever-evolving tradition of appropriation.[156] The absence of Hebrews continues to "appear" in various Latin texts and canons in the fourth century.[157] But Hebrews begins to emerge as a Pauline letter in various Latin writers as well as Greek and Syriac sources.[158] Undoubtedly, conciliary moments contributed to the increase of a Pauline Hebrews, the first of which was the Council of Laodicea (363), not to mention the canon of

---

[154] Metzger, *Textual Commentary*, 661 n. 2.

[155] R. F. Schlossnikel, *Der Brief an die Hebräer und das Corpus Paulinum: Eine linguistische "Bruchstelle" im Codex Claromontanus (Paris, Bibliothèque Nationale Grec 107 + 107A + 107B) und ihre Bedeutung im Rahmen von Text- und Kanongeschichte* (Freiburg: Herder, 1991).

[156] *Pace* Anderson, "Hebrews Among the Letters," 263.

[157] The list of usual absences includes the African Canon (c. 360), the synods of Hippo Regius in 393 and of Carthage (in 397 there are "tredecim" Pauline letter and in 419 there are "quattuordecim"), Optatus of Mileve, the Acts of the Donatist Controversy, Zeno of Verona, Foebadius of Agen, Phoebadius of Gaul, Ambrosiaster; Victorinus of Pettua. See Moffat, *Epistle tot he Hebrews*, xxi; Wieseler, *Eine Untersuchung über den Hebräerbrief*, 23; Windisch, *Der Hebräerbrief*, 6.

[158] Marius Victorinus of Rome (*Adversus Arium* 2.3); Innocent I (*Epistula* 6); Ambrose of Milan (*De paenit.* 2.2.6 and 10); Lucifer of Calaris (*De nonconveniendo cum haereticis* 10); Rufinus of Aquileia (*Commentarius in symbolum apostolorum* 35); Hilarius of Potiers (*Tractatus in Ps* 14, 5); Apollnarius of Laodicea (*Dial. de Santa Trin.* 922); Apostolic Constitution 8.47.85.

Pope Innocent 1 recognizing fourteen Pauline letters (*Ep. ad Exsuperium*). However, the continued rise of the circulation of Hebrews as Pauline coupled with the willingness to adjust its position to accommodate "Western" strategies for organizing the *corpus Paulinum* was likely more determinative for the success of Hebrews in the corpus.

5. Conclusion

Hebrews is encountered as a curated Pauline text within a collection of Pauline letters, and early readers "account" for this Paulinity in different ways as they triangulate between the Jewish valence of the title, its non-Pauline features, and their own literary interests. These encounters, in turn, left an imprint on the subsequent transmission of the letter, as its position within the collection shifts in ways that show deference to early theories for categorizing Paul's letters. A closer look at the Latin circulation of Hebrews shows less of an active "rejection" than a slow emergence of circulation. We know that Hebrews circulated as a letter of Barnabas in North Africa, and the omission of Hebrews in discussions of Paul is likely an additional sign of the limits of its Pauline circulation, rather than the discerning judgments of critical readers. The stabilization of Hebrews as Pauline across Latin and Greek contexts occurs, in part, because of the willingness to shift the position of Hebrews within the *corpus Paulinum* in order to accommodate strategies of organizing Paul's letters that assume a thirteen-letter collect. By pushing Hebrews to the edge of the Pauline corpus, readers allowed it to remain within. In the end, the "Pauline authorship of Hebrews" is caught in a continual process of creation in which readers respond to scribal configurations, and scribes, in turn, react to varying literary discussions.

While earlier stages of the Pauline history of Hebrews may show the power of readers to configure and adopt the letter as Paul's, this might have happened within some liturgical environment. But what remains *to us* is a certain material priority. Circulation provides the "data" that the narrative of origins interprets and so it is the text as configured as Pauline that facilitates discourse on the authorship of Hebrews. To note that Hebrews is simply "Pauline" in a given context or for a particular writer masks this material and readerly interface.

But how does the "Paulinity" of Hebrews actually work within the context of a reader's corpus? How is Hebrews read in concert with other Pauline letters, and what images of Paul emerge in the process of reading a Pauline letter to Hebrews? What views of Judaism condition the understanding of Paul and the Hebrews? It is to this more internal dynamic of Paulinity within the corpora of Clement and Origen that the subsequent two chapters turn.

The Pauline History of Hebrews. Warren Campbell, Oxford University Press. © Oxford University Press 2025.
DOI: 10.1093/9780197769287.003.0002

3

Clement of Alexandria's (Dis)engagement with Hebrews

Clement of Alexandria (Titus Flavius Clemens) was born in the mid-second century (c. 150 CE), perhaps in Athens and to pagan parentage, and his social and educational formation took place within the context of Greek παιδεία.[1] Clement produced lengthy philosophical and didactic texts while living and working in the Egyptian city of Alexandria as a Christian *didaskalos*.[2] A tenuous political environment during the reign of Septimius Severus forced Clement to leave Alexandria at the turn of early third century and venture north to Cappadocia, where he remained until his death around 215 CE.

Clement's position in Alexandria and the "catechetical school" of Alexandria as a whole—its origins, curriculum, purpose, coherence, leadership, and overarching institutional contour—has been one of the classic questions of scholarship on second-century Alexandria.[3] Rather than

---

[1] On the social, educational, and cultural context of Clement's context in Athens and Alexandria see E. J. Watts, *City and School in Late Antique Athens and Alexandria* (Berkeley: University of California Press, 2006). On Clement's biography and corpus see Alain Le Boulluec, "Clement d'Alexandrie," in *Dictionnaire des philosophes antiques*, vol. 2, *Babélyca d'Argos à Dyscolius*, ed. Richard Goulet (Paris: Brepols, 1994), 426–31.

[2] On Clement as a *didaskalos* see Oleh Kindiy, *Christos Didaskalos: The Christology of Clement of Alexandria* (Saarbrücken: Verlag Dr. Müller, 2008), 124–98.

[3] See primarily Gustav Bardy, "Aux origines de l'école d'Alexandrie," *Recherches de Science Religieuse* 27 (1937) 65–90; Manfred Hornschuh, "Das Leben des Origenes und die Entstehung der alexandrinischen Schule," *ZKG* 71 (1960): 1–25, 193–214; Adolf Knauber, "Katechetenschule oder Schulkatechumenat? Um die rechte Deutung des 'Unternehmens' der ersten grossen Alexandriner," *TThZ* 60 (1951): 243–66; Francesco Pericoli Ridolfini, "Le origini della scuoladi Alessandria," *RSO* 37 (1962): 211–30; Alain Le Boulluec, "L'école d'Alexandrie: De quelques aventures d'un concept historiographique," in *ΑΛΕΞΑΝΔΡΙΝΑ: Hellénisme, judaïsme et christianisme à Alexandrie: Mélanges offerts au P. Claude Mondésert* (Paris: Les Editions du Cerf, 1987), 403–17; Alain Le Boulluec, "Aux origins, encore, de l'école' d'Alexandrie," *Adamantius* 5 (1999): 7–36, reprinted in *Alexandrie antique et chrétienne: Clément et Origène*, 2nd ed. (Paris: Institut d'études augustiniennes, 2012), 13–28, 29–62; Clemens Scholten, "Die alexandrinische Katechetenschule," *JAC* 38 (1995): 16–37; Roelof van den Broek, "The Christian 'School' of Alexandria in the Second and Third Centuries," in *Centers of Learning: Learning and Location in Pre-Modern Europe and the Near East*, ed. J. W. Drijvers and A. A. McDonald (Leiden: Brill, 1995), 39–47; Annewies van den Hoek, "The 'Catechetical' School of Early Christian Alexandria and Its Philonic Heritage," *HTR*

telling Eusebius' story of a neat succession of teachers in a singular and unified Christian school, scholars delicately situate Clement within the shifting topography of Christian associations in Alexandria and within various patronage systems necessary to support centers of learning and the textual production. Clement himself refers to the ἐκκλησία as the best αἵρεσις ("school," Strom. 7.15.92) comprising "ordinary believers" (Strom. 7.11.67, 7.14.84, 7.16.95), and which, of course, excludes rival "heretics" and their αἱρέσεις (Strom. 7.15.92).[4]

Clement's bibliographic profile is well known, and his extant corpus is a mosaic of scriptural language, citation, and interpretation.[5] Referring to his own writing as "my notes," Clement enjoys an excerpting style, stringing texts and topics together that advance quickly in unpredictable directions. Jane Heath has recently isolated Clement's lengthy *Stromata* alongside Roman writers like Plutarch and Pliny, showing how Clement purposely shapes a shared "miscellanistic" genre of note-making, *designed* to be chaotic and enticing for further study.[6] Such literary style agrees with Clement's own self-presentation as a teacher of both common and specialized forms of Christian gnosis. For Clement, the advanced Christian is known as the "Gnostic," and the aim of knowledge is increased proximity to the *logos*, the source of knowledge.[7]

90.1 (1997): 59–87; Dietmar Wyrwa, "Religiöses Lernen im zweiten Jahrhundert und die Anfänge der alexandrinischen Katachetenschule," in *Religiöses Lernen in der biblischen, frühjüdischen und frühchristlichen Überlieferung*, ed. Beate Ego and Helmut Merkel, WUNT 180 (Tübingen: Mohr Siebeck, 2005), 271–305.

[4] On Clement's heresiological discourse in *Stromata* book 7 see Alain Le Boulluec, *La notion d'hérésie dans la littérature grecque IIe–IIIe siècles*, vol. 2 (Paris: Études Augustiniennes, 1985), 361–438. The predominance of Clement's ἐκκλησία language is found in the seventh book of the *Stromata*. See especially *Strom.* 7.16.103–6 for Clement's discussion of ecclesial judgment against Marcion. On the conceptual overlap between "school" and "church" see Oleh Kindiy, "Approximating Church and School in Clement of Alexandria's Stromateis VII," in *The Seventh Book of the Stromateis: Proceedings of the Colloquium on Clement of Alexandria, Olomouc, October 21–23, 2010*, VCSup. 117 (Leiden: Brill, 2012), 291–98, and more generally Benjamin Edsall, "Clement and the Catechumenate in the Late Second Century," in *The Rise of the Early Christian Intellectual*, ed. Lewis Ayers and H. Clifton Ward, AK 139 (Berlin: de Gruyter, 2020), 100–127.

[5] See Otto Stählin and Ursula Treu, eds., *Clemens Alexandrinus, Bd. 4, Register 1. Teil, Zitatenregister, Testimonienregister, Initienregister für die Fragmente, Eingennamenregister*, GCS 39.1 (Berlin: Akademie, 1980), xix–xxxiv, 1–66.

[6] Jane Heath, *Clement of Alexandria and the Shaping of Christian Literary Practice: Miscellany and the Transformation of Greco-Roman Writing* (Cambridge: Cambridge University Press, 2020). Cf. Louis Roberts, "The Literary Form of the Stromateis," *Second Century* 1.4 (1981): 211–22.

[7] See especially, W. Völker, *Der wahre Gnostiker nach Clemens Alexandrinus*, TU 57.2 (Berlin: Akademie, 1952); Mark Edwards, "Clement of Alexandria and his Doctrine of the Logos," *VC* 54 (2000): 159–77.

Clement's corpus has been traditionally divided into two.[8] On the one hand, there is the purported "trilogy" of texts that correlate to the three functions of the *logos* in *Paedagogus* 1.2.3 (persuader, educator, and teacher): the *Protrepticus* (an exhortation to the Greeks), the *Paedagogus* (a text on the rebirth and the growth of Christians from childhood into adult moral beings) and the *Stromata* (a seven-book collection of notes and topics strung together).[9] The "other corpus" of Clement, increasingly being brought in from the margins, includes three texts found in one eleventh-century manuscript, Codex Laurentianus V.3, later copied in BNF sup. gr. 250. Following the seven books of the *Stromata* in this manuscript is the *Eclogae Propheticae* (a series of comments on excerpted passages from Israel's prophets), an eighth book of the *Stromata* (differing in content and style from the other seven), and the *Excerpta ex Theodoto* (excerpts from a Valentinian source).[10]

Clement is the earliest extant writer to quote Hebrews as a Pauline letter.[11] As noted in the previous chapter, Clement was aware of the second-century dispute concerning the authorship of Hebrews, and his insistence on its Pauline status likely arose, in part, from prior tradition claiming this position and the pressure exerted by the inclusion of Hebrews within early collections of Pauline letters. Clement's use of Hebrews has been taken up and surveyed by James Thompson, who explores quotations from Hebrews in

---

[8] In the *Historia*, Eusebius notes a number of Clementine texts that are no longer extant— *Hypotheses, On the Pascha, On Fasting, On Slander, Against the Judaizers* (6.13.2–3)—and Clement himself refers to a treatise *On the Resurrection* (*Paed*. 1.47.1) and *On Continence* (*Paed*. 2.94.1).

[9] These texts are dates to the final years of the second century CE. Increasingly, the inclusion of the *Stromata* in the trilogy is questioned. On the question whether Clement's corpus forms a trilogy see Walter Wagner, "Another Look at the Literary Problem in Clement of Alexandria's Major Writings," *CH* 37.3 (1968): 251–60; Pierre Nautin, "La fin des *Stromates* et les *Hypotyposes* de Clément d'Alexandrie," *VC* 30 (1976): 268–302; Eric Osborn, *Clement of Alexandria* (Cambridge: Cambridge University Press, 2005), 5–15; Andrew Itter, *Esoteric Teaching in the "Stromateis" of Clement of Alexandria* (Leiden: Brill, 2009); Bogdan Gabriel Bucur, "The Place of the *Hypotyposeis* in the Clementine Corpus: An Apology for 'The Other Clement of Alexandria,'" *JECS* 17 (2009): 313–35; Marco Rizzi, "The Literary Problem in Clement of Alexandria: A Reconsideration," *Adamantius* 17 (2011): 154–63; Marco Rizzi, "The End of Stromateis VII and Clement's Literary Project," in Havrda et al., *Seventh Book*, 299–311.

[10] Robert Casey, *The excerpta ex Theodoto of Clement of Alexandria* (London: Christophers, 1934); F. Sagnard, *Clément d'Alexandrie: Extraits de Théodote*, SC 23 (Paris: Cerf, 1970). Matyáš Havrda, *The So-Called Eighth "Stromateus" by Clement of Alexandria: Early Christian Reception of Greek Scientific Methodology*, Philosophia antiqua, 144 (Leiden: Brill, 2016).

[11] The first time Hebrews becomes Pauline is in *Strom*. 2.2.8, which cites Hebrews 11:1–2 "according to the divine apostle" (κατὰ τὸν θεῖον ἀπόστολον). On Clement's text of Hebrews see Michael Mees, *Die Zitate aus dem Neuen Testament bei Clements von Alexandrien*, Quoaderni di "Vetera Christianorum" 2 (Rome: Istituto die Letteratura Cristiana Antica, 1970), 171–75, as well as the larger discussion of the "Western" character of Clement's text, of which Mees is skeptical. For critical interaction with Mees see Carl P. Cosaert, *The Text of the Gospels in Clement of Alexandria*, SBLNTGF 9 (Atlanta: Society of biblical Literature, 2008), 41–44.

concert with some of Clement's central interests. Thompson draws attention to Clement's use of the prologue from Hebrews 1:1, the possible influence of Hebrews 9 on Clement's understanding of the Levitical priesthood, and the citations from Hebrews 11 in the polemic against rival conceptions of faith.[12] Thompson's approach exposes the texts in Hebrews that piqued Clement's interest. But the way Clement uses Hebrews as a *Pauline* text and how Clement engages the Jewish aspect of this Pauline letter remains to be seen.

1. Anonymity and the Avoidance of Paul

Clement cites from Hebrews far less than from texts like 1 Corinthians, Colossians, and Romans but still shows evidence of a close reading. Clement repeatedly evokes "high priest" as a title for Jesus and refers to the figure of Melchizedek on many occasions.[13] Clement also uses a number of phrases from Hebrews throughout his corpus, principally "many times and in many ways" from Hebrews 1:1, and other verses.[14] Clement even fuses content from Hebrews and other Pauline texts, perhaps spontaneously from memory. For example, in *Stromata* 2.13.57, Clement combines the language of "repentance" from 2 Corinthians 7:10 with Hebrews 10:25 and its caution against transgression after accessing knowledge of truth, into a single, unmarked phrase.[15] Clement might also have quoted Hebrews 9:14 from

---

[12] James W. Thompson, "The Epistle to the Hebrews in the Works of Clement of Alexandria," in *Transmission and Reception: New Testament Text-Critical and Exegetical Studies*, ed. J. W. Childers and D. C. Parker, TS 3.4 (Piscataway: Gorgias Press, 2006), 239–54.

[13] On the use of "high priest" see *Strom.* 2.9.45, 2.22.134, 6.17.153, 7.2.9, 7.2.13, 7.7.45. References to Melchizedek are found in *Strom.* 2.5.21, 2.22.136, 4.25.161. On Clement's use of the title "high priest" see Piotr Ashwin-Siejkowski, *Clement of Alexandria: A Projection in Christian Perfection* (London: T&T Clark, 2008), 55–68.

[14] *Strom.* 1.4.27, 5.6.35, 6.7.58 (πολυμερῶς καὶ πολυτρόπως). *Strom.* 3.10.69 (GCS 52:227: ἄξιος ἤδη τοῦ ἀδελφὸς πρὸς τοῦ κυρίου ὀνομάζεσθαι) paraphrases the idea of being called a brother from Hebrews 2:11 (δι' ἣν αἰτίαν οὐκ ἐπαισχύνεται ἀδελφοὺς αὐτοὺς καλεῖν). *Strom.* 7.1.2, alludes to Hebrews 5.14 (GCS 17:4: "τῶν τὰ αἰσθητήρια" φησὶν ὁ ἀπόστολος "συγγεγυμνασμένων"; Heb 5.14: τὰ αἰσθητήρια γεγυμνασμένα); *Strom.* 1.27.173 (GCS 52:107: ἔπειτα δὲ πιστὸν γενέσθαι θεράποντα) and 7.2.5 (GCS 17:6: καὶ οἱ μὲν ὡς φίλοι, οἱ δὲ ὡς οἰκέται πιστοί, οἱ δὲ ὡς ἁπλῶς οἰκέται) might allude to Hebrews 3.5 (καὶ Μωϋσῆς μὲν πιστὸς ἐν ὅλῳ τῷ οἴκῳ αὐτοῦ ὡς θεράπων); *Strom.* 7.11.63 (GCS 17:45) refers to "fixing eyes" (ἀφορῶν) on the patriarchs (πατριάρχας) (cf. Heb 12:2: ἀφορῶντες εἰς τὸν τῆς πίστεως ἀρχηγὸν καὶ τελειωτὴν Ἰησοῦν). *Strom.* 7.13.83 (GCS 17:59) refers to the final transposition (τῆς μεταθέσεως), which is also used in Hebrews 11:5 to refer to Enoch (πρὸ γὰρ τῆς μεταθέσεως μεμαρτύρηται εὐαρεστηκέναι τῷ θεῷ). Moreover, *Paed.* 1.8.74 and Hebrews 13.21 have similar doxological formula (ᾧ ἡ δόξα εἰς τοὺς αἰῶνας τῶν αἰώνων, ἀμήν).

[15] In another instance, Clement fuses a phrase "fellow heirs" from Hebrews with one from Romans. *Strom.* 2.22.134 (GCS 52:187): "the great high priest who designed to call us brothers and

memory, "to purify the conscience from works of death to the service of the living God," fusing it with Matthew 19.12.[16]

Perhaps these citations speak to Clement's memory and spontaneity, but there is also a conspicuous anonymity surrounding Hebrews in Clement's corpus, as it is not marked as Pauline but voiced as Clement. A lack of "attribution" is not unusual for Clement, and Pauline letters are cited in diverse ways, sometimes by memory or as a stock phrase without markers of attribution (*Strom.* 4.7.46).[17] However, unmarked citations of Hebrews often appear in close proximity to marked citations from other Pauline letters, supplementing the "more explicit" Pauline material. When Clement does cite Hebrews as a Pauline letter, it functions as supplemental Pauline testimony in a chain of citations.[18]

In *Stromata* 1.11.53, Hebrews 5:13 appears unmarked beside a citation of 1 Thessalonians 5:1 from "the Apostle." In his discussion of marriage in *Stromata* 4.20.126, Clement cites Hebrews 10:22 without any markers of attribution, but in the following section Clement cites the description of the "elder woman" (πρεσβύτιδας) from "Epistle to Titus" (πρὸς Τίτον ἐπιστολῇ).[19] Clement then adds a reordered citation from Hebrews

---

fellow heirs" (γίνομαί σου συγκληρονόμος [Romans 8.17: συγκληρονόμοι], ἐπεὶ τὸν ἀδελφὸν οὐκ ἐπῃσχύνθης [Hebrews 2.12 ἐπαισχύνεται ἀδελφοὺς]).

[16] *Strom.* 3.7.59 (GCS 52:223): Ἡμεῖς μὲν οὖν δι᾽ ἀγάπην τὴν πρὸς τὸν κύριον καὶ δι᾽ αὐτὸ τὸ καλὸν ἐγκράτειαν ἀσπαζόμεθα, τὸν νεὼν τοῦ πνεύματος ἁγιάζοντες· καλὸν γὰρ 'διὰ τὴν βασιλείαν τῶν οὐρανῶν εὐνουχίζειν ἑαυτὸν' πάσης ἐπιθυμίας καὶ 'καθαρίζειν τὴν συνείδησιν ἀπὸ νεκρῶν ἔργων ("So we embrace self-control out of the love we bear the Lord and out of its honorable status, consecrating the temple of the Spirit. It is honorable 'to emasculate oneself' of all desire 'for the sake of the kingdom of heaven' and 'to purify the conscience from works of death to the service of the living God'").

[17] Clement often evokes Pauline passages as unattributed stock phrases, for example, *Strom.* 1.5.28, 2.18.91 (Gal 3:24); *Strom.* 3.18.109 (1 Tim 6:20); *Strom.* 1.7.38 (Rom 4:2–3); *Strom.* 1.24.150 (Phil. 2:10–11); *Strom.* 2.2.7 (1 Cor 2:10); *Strom.* 2.18.74–75 (Eph. 2:4 and 4:18); *Strom.* 3.18.106 (Eph. 2:3); *Strom.* 4.18.113 (Rom 13:9); *Strom.* 6.17.152 (1 Cor 3:12). Clement also cites Paul from memory, in clusters of catena lists (*Strom.* 3.6.51), in commentarial settings with extended focus on a particular Pauline passage (*Strom.* 4.14–16), and also paraphrastically (*Strom.* 7.14.84).

[18] Clement refers to ten Pauline letters by name, most often the Corinthian correspondence and Romans. Clement names the "first letter to the Corinthians" or just "to the Corinthians" (e.g., *Paed.* 1.5.18, 1.6.33, 1.7.38, 2.2.33; *Strom.* 2.22.136, 3.11.75, 3.12.99, 4.16.100, 4.17.105, 5.12.80, 6.18.164, 7.14.84). He refers to Romans in *Paed.* 1.5.19 and *Strom.* 2.6.29, 2.33.134, 3.4.39, 3.11.75–76, 4.3.9, 4.22.145, 5.4.26. Clement also refers to Galatians, Ephesians, Philippians, Colossians, 1 Timothy, Titus, and Hebrews. Clement was likely using a fourteen-letter *corpus Paulinum* (inclusive of the Pastoral Epistles and Hebrews, although Clement does not cite Philemon). Clement also appears to quote Pauline letters from memory, as evidenced by a few misquotations as well as general statements about the location of Pauline passage "in one of his letters" (*Strom.* 3.6.53 referring to 1 Corinthians). On the text of the Pauline epistles see James A. Brooks, "The Text of the Pauline Epistles in the Stromata of Clement of Alexandria" (ThD diss., Princeton University, 1966).

[19] GCS 52:304–5. See here J. P. Broudehoux, *Mariage et famille chez Clément d'Alexandrie*, Théologie historique 11 (Paris: Beauschesne et ses fils, 1970).

10:14–16 and finishes the discussion by evoking the comments on marriage found in Hebrews 13:4, both of which are marked as "he says" and "adds." There is Paulinity here but it is supplemental.

In other instances, Clement groups texts together thematically in lists of citations, and here Hebrews serves as added testimony. In *Stromata* 2.22.136 Clement supports a quotation from Galatians 5:5–6 with a much larger passage from Hebrews 6:11–20:[20]

> "We," according to the noble apostle, "receive from faith the hope of righteousness, for in Christ neither circumcision nor uncircumcision has any power, only faith working in love." "We earnestly desire each of you to show the same zeal for the full realization of hope," and so on to, "having become a high priest forever, after the order of Melchizedek." Similarly, with Paul the all-virtuous Wisdom says, "He that hears me will dwell trusting in hope."

Clement uses Hebrews 6 for its language of hope. While Hebrews is brought into the orbit of Paul, its role is to confirm the thrust of Galatians 5:5–6 and poses no distinct point of its own. Clement often uses the "down to" (ἕως or τὰ ἑξῆς ἕως) technique when citing larger blocks of material.[21] This strategy allows Clement to flag the beginning and end of a passage to confirm his point without sacrificing space.[22] Hebrews takes a supplementary role here, and, in other cases, the text serves this function without markers of citation and Paulinity.

In *Stromata* 1.11 Clement distinguishes between various philosophical positions on divine providence in contrast to his own Christian-Gnostic

---

[20] *Strom.* 4.20.128–29. GCS 52:188: ἡμεῖς' τοίνυν κατὰ τὸν γενναῖον ἀπόστολον "ἐκ πίστεως ἐλπίδα δικαιοσύνης ἀπεκδεχόμεθα. ἐν γὰρ Χριστῷ οὔτε περιτομή τι ἰσχύει οὔτε ἀκροβυστία, ἀλλὰ πίστις δι' ἀγάπης ἐνεργουμένη." "ἐπιθυμοῦμεν δὲ ἕκαστον ὑμῶν τὴν αὐτὴν ἐνδείκνυσθαι σπουδὴν πρὸς τὴν πληροφορίαν τῆς ἐλπίδος" ἕως "κατὰ τὴν τάξιν Μελχισεδὲκ ἀρχιερεὺς γενόμενος εἰς τὸν αἰῶνα." τὰ ὅμοια τῷ Παύλῳ καὶ ἡ πανάρετος σοφία λέγει· "ὁ δὲ ἐμοῦ ἀκούων κατασκηνώσει ἐπ' ἐλπίδι πεποιθώς.

[21] Clement uses this technique quite often, most often with Pauline material, but also with scriptural material, the *Wisdom of Solomon*, Plato, and a work associated with Valentinus. For citations using ἕως see *Strom.* 2.22.136 (Heb 11); *Strom.* 3.1.3 (2 Cor 11:13–15); *Strom.* 3.11.75 (Rom 6.2–13); *Strom.* 3.18.107 (1 Cor 5:9–6:13); *Strom.* 3.18.108 (1 Cor 7:10–14); *Strom.* 2.22.135 (Isa 55:6–9); *Strom.* 3.2.11 (Jude 8–16); *Strom.* 3.3.17 (Plato, *Phaedo* 65C-D); *Strom.* 3.4.29 (a text associated with Valentinus). The other variant of this technique, τὰ ἑξῆς ἕως is used in *Strom.* 2.4.12 (Heb 11); *Strom.* 3.4.28 (Eph 5:5–11); *Strom.* 2.9.42 (Rom 12:9–21); *Strom.* 2.15.69 (Ez 34:4–6); *Strom.* 2.2.5 (Wisd 7:17–20).

[22] For Clement's other methods of citation see Annewies van den Hoek, "Techniques of Quotation in Clement of Alexandria: A View of Ancient Literary Working Methods," *VC* 50 (1996): 223–43.

position. Here Clement paraphrases the warning from Colossians 2:8, that no one be led astray by "philosophy or vain deceit," "human tradition," "according to the elementary principles." He then cites the "apostle" and draws upon the positive exhortation from Philippians 1:8–9, namely, that love may abound into greater knowledge and so "approve the things that are exceptional." Then, rebounding back to the language of "elements," Clement shifts to Galatians 4: the "same apostle" notes that a child, even though an heir, is not different from a slave, being enslaved to the "elementary principles." This Pauline catena paves the way for Clement's citation of Hebrews 5:13–14:

> So the philosophers too are children, if they have not been brought to maturity by Christ. For if the son of the maidservant shall not inherit along with the son of the free woman, he is still the seed of Abraham, and his own blessing was not a result of the promise but was received as a free gift. Solid food is for grownups, for those who have their faculties trained and conditioned to distinguish good from evil. Everyone who takes milk is inexperienced in the word of righteousness. He is a child and does not yet have any real knowledge of the Word who is the basis of his faith and action, and is incapable in himself of giving an explanation. "Test everything," says the apostle, "and hold firmly onto that which is good."[23]

One of Clement's most abiding interests is to position the philosophical tradition as a παιδαγωγός leading to Christ. Philosophy is simultaneously a container of divine truth and inadequate, partial, and muddled. Clement's use of Hebrews helps establish this point; philosophy alone is childish, whereas Clement's Gnostic is trained to recognize the "real knowledge" of the *logos*. Clement then returns to the apostles' voice and quotes the advice from 1 Thessalonians 5:1: "test everything and hold firm to that which is good." Here "Hebrews" is an unmarked extension of Clement's voice. Moreover, the Letter to the Hebrews does not guide the interpretation of other Pauline letters and is most often drawn upon as further testimony, sometimes anonymously. From this perspective, Hebrews does very little as a Pauline letter. It is rarely integrated with our texts in Clement's *corpus Paulinum* and often used without Pauline markers.

---

[23] *Strom.* 1.11.53.

In a rare moment when Clement does evoke Hebrews alone and as Pauline, it is as a witness against rival teachers, Basilides and Valentinus.[24] Judith Kovacs has drawn attention to the Valentinian and otherwise "gnostic" context of Clement's reading of the *corpus Paulinum*.[25] Clement's reading of 1 Corinthians 3:1–3, for example, is conditioned by the need to refute the Valentinian distinction between two kinds of believers and their corresponding modes of salvation using the Pauline distinction between the *pneumatikoi* and *psychikoi* from 1 Corinthians 2:6–7, 13–14.[26] Similarly, Kovacs shows how the Valentinian mapping of "grace" and "works" onto a two-pronged road to salvation (one for the simple and one for the spiritual) influences Clement's reading of the Pauline contrast.[27] Again, Clement's lengthy engagement with Paul's discussion of lawsuits and fornication in 1 Corinthians 6 in *Stromata* 7.14.84–88 is conditioned by interpretations of rival radical ascetics and Valentinians.[28] So too, in discussions of faith,

---

[24] Hebrews 5:14 briefly appears as from "the apostle" in *Strom.* 7.1.2 (GCS 17:4: "τῶν τὰ αἰσθητήρια" φησὶν ὁ ἀπόστολος "συγγεγυμνασμένων": Heb 5.14 τὰ αἰσθητήρια γεγυμνασμένα).

[25] Clement repeatedly names Paul as a site of competition with these rivals. In *Strom.* 7.17.106, Clement identifies Valentinus as a student of Theudas, a follower of Paul. "Heretics" reject the letters of Timothy (*Strom.* 2.11.52: τὰς πρὸς Τιμόθεον ἀθετοῦσιν ἐπιστολάς) and otherwise do "violence" (βιάζεται) to Pauline passages like Romans 6:14 (*Strom.* 3.8.61), Romans 7 (3.11.76), 2 Cor 11:3 (3.14.94). See also *Strom.* 4.7.45, reading Romans 7–8 against Marcion, and *Strom.* 4.13.89–94 against Valentinus. Fritz Buri, *Clemens Alexandrinus und der Paulinische Freiheitsbegriff* (Zurich: Niehans, 1939), also positions Clement's reading of Paul in light of rival appropriations among the group called "Gnostics" and claims Clement accepts the basic Gnostic de-eschatologicalization of Paul as he attempts to recreate a Paulinism that touches primarily on moral and spiritual development. See also Heirich Seesemann, "Das Paulusverständnis des Clemens Alexandrinus," *Theologische Studien und Kritiken* 107 (1936): 312–46. In an interesting moment, Clement comments on one Epiphanes, the son of Carpocrates, whose writing he *actually* possesses (*Strom.* 3.2.5: οὗ καὶ τὰ συγγράμματα κομίζεται).

[26] "Echoes of Valentinian Exegesis in Clement of Alexandria and Origen: The Interpretation of 1 Cor 3.1–3," in *Origeniana Octava*, ed. Lorenzo Perrone (Leuven: Peeters, 2003), 317–29. Kovacs focuses on *Strom.* 2.3.10–11.1; *Paed.* 1.6.25–52; and *Strom.* 5.10.66 and 5.4.26.1–4.

[27] Judith Kovacs, "Grace and Works: Clement of Alexandria's Response to Valentinian Exegesis of Paul," in *Ancient Perspectives on Paul*, ed. Tobias Nicklas, Andreas Merkt, and Joseph Verheyden, NTOA/SUNT 102 (Göttingen: Vandenhoeck & Ruprecht, 2013), 191–210.

[28] Judith L. Kovacs, "Saint Paul as Apostle of Apatheia: Stromateis VII, Chapter 14," in Havrda et al., *Seventh Book*, 199–216. See also Judith L. Kovacs, "Reading the 'Divinely Inspired' Paul: Clement of Alexandria in Conversation with 'Heterodox' Christians, Simple Believers, and Greek Philosophers," in *Clement's Biblical Exegesis: Proceedings of the Second Colloquium on Clement of Alexandria (Olomouc, May 29–31, 2014)*, ed. Veronika Cernuskova, Judith L. Kovacs, and Jana Plátová (Leiden: Brill, 2017), 325–43; Judith L. Kovacs, "Was Paul an Antinomian, a Radical Ascetic, or a Sober Married Man? Exegetical Debates in Clement of Alexandria's *Stromateis* 3," in *Asceticism and Exegesis in Early Christianity: The Reception of New Testament Texts in Ancient Ascetic Discourses*, ed. Hans-Ulrich Weidemann, NTOA/SUNT 101 (Göttingen: Vandenhoeck & Ruprecht, 2013), 190–93; Judith L. Kovacs, "Clement of Alexandria and Valentinian Exegesis in the Excerpts from Theodotus," SP 41 (2006): 187–200; Judith L. Kovacs, "Concealment and Gnostic Exegesis: Clement of Alexandria's Interpretation of the Tabernacle," StPatr 31 (1997): 414–37. Kovacs is joined here by Robert G. T. Edwards, "Clement of Alexandria's Anti-Valentinian

Clement bucks against Basilides' determinism that faith is a natural quality of the elect, and Valentinus' relegation of faith as an inferior form of knowledge, using Hebrews 11:3-4 to show that not only do humans have the ability to exercise their will to assent, but also that faith requires perception that is a form of knowledge (*Strom.* 2.4.12).

In the two instances in which Clement cites Hebrews alone *and* "according to the divine apostle" (κατὰ τὸν θεῖον ἀπόστολον), he uses the description of πίστις from Hebrews 11 as Paul's statement on faith in order to challenge competing definitions among the Ἕλληνες, as well as Basilides and Valentinus.[29] Against Greek disparagement, Clement suggests that faith is "an intellectual preconception (διανοίας πρόληψίς) regarding what is said," or simply "comprehension" (σύνεσίς) (*Strom.* 2.4.17).[30] In *Stromata* 2.2.8, Clement cites Hebrews 11:1-2 and 11:6 to show that πίστις is a "voluntary preconception" (πρόληψις ἑκούσιός) and the approval of θεοσεβείας.[31] Clement mobilizes this description against Basilides' notion that faith is a natural disposition only attainable for the elect, and against Valentinus, who claims faith is inferior to knowledge.[32] If faith requires cognitive perception (νοέω), it cannot be natural or inferior to knowledge.[33]

Clement found in Hebrews 11 material suited for his polemical engagement in intra-Christian disputes, but it also provides material for the discussion of martyrdom. In *Stromata* 4.16.101-3, Clement quotes a large block of material from Hebrews: 10:32-39, 11:36-40, 12:1-2, and then 11:26-27. Earlier in *Stromata* 4.16 Clement similarly flags large blocks of Pauline material, citing from Romans 10 and 12 and then 2 Corinthians 1 and 3, followed by 1 John. Clement's aim is to show that faith in God leads to a form of martyrdom. After citing Paul's passage about contentment from Philippians 4:11-13, Clement moves into the material in Hebrews

---

Interpretation of Gen 1:26-27," *ZAC* 18 (2014): 365-89. Cf. also Mark Edwards, "Gnostics and Valentinians in the Church Fathers," *JTS* 40 (1989): 25-47.

[29] On Basilides see Winrich Löhr, *Basilides und seine Schule*, WUNT 83 (Tübingen: Mohr Siebeck, 1996), and on Valentinus see Christoph Markschies, "Valentinian Gnosticism: Towards the Anatomy of a School," in *The Nag Hammadi Library After Fifty Years*, ed. John D. Turner and Anne McGuire, NHMS 44 (Leiden: Brill, 1997), 401-38. On the philosophical orientation of the group of texts and figures that are referred to as Gnostic see Winrich Löhr, "Christian Gnostics and Greek Philosophy in the Second Century," *EC* 3 (2012): 349-77.

[30] GCS 52:121. See here Eric Osborn, "Arguments for Faith in Clement of Alexandria," *VC* 48.1 (1994): 3-7.

[31] GCS 52:117. Clement builds on the idea of expectation and evidence found in Hebrews 11:1 ("the subject of things hoped for, the evidence of things not seen"; ἐλπιζομένων ὑπόστασις, πραγμάτων ἔλεγχος οὐ βλεπομένων).

[32] *Strom.* 2.3.10.   [33] Osborne, "Arguments for Faith," 7.

10–11 and keys on the idea that the audience was *formerly* enlightened and *therefore* endured suffering. The material from Hebrews is introduced as Paul's discussion with "others" in order to "put them to shame."[34] But here Clement hides the Jewish occasion for the epistle, and fills in the "divine examples" from Hebrews 11 with more characters from *1 Clement* (*Strom.* 4.17).

For Clement, Hebrews functions as Pauline letter when it provides material well suited in his polemic against rival Christians and larger competition over Paul.[35] This is the context in which a *Pauline* Hebrews is valuable for Clement, but citing Hebrews in this way, verbatim and marked as a letter of Paul, is not a common practice. Hebrews does not guide the interpretation of other Pauline letters and is drawn upon as supplementary, often anonymous, testimony. This, however, does not exhaust Clement's engagement with, and even marginalization of, Hebrews. Given Clement's voluminous approach to scriptural citations and allusions, the rich mine of scriptural texts found in Hebrews was too much for Clement to ignore entirely.

2. Clement's Paul: The Apostle of Scriptural Mysteries

Alain Le Boulluec rightly notes that in Clement's usage, the idea of an old διαθήκη had accrued a textual valance (τῆς παλαιᾶς γραφῆς).[36] In *Protrepticus* 9 Clement refers to the "collected scriptures" that the apostles called θεοπνεύστους.[37] For Clement, the idea of the νέα διαθήκη (*Strom.*

---

[34] *Strom.* 4.16.101 (GCS 52:293): τοῦτο δὲ καὶ πρὸς ἐντροπὴν ἄλλοις διαλεγόμενος οὐκ ὀκνεῖ λέγειν.

[35] One exception here is *Strom.* 7.10.58, where Clement notes that "the apostle used the phrase 'imprint of his substance'" (χαρακτὴρ τῆς ὑποστάσεως αὐτοῦ), referencing Hebrews 1:3 (GCS 17:42–43).

[36] *Strom.* 6.15.119 (GCS 52:491). Alain Le Boulluec, "De l'usage de titres 'néotestamentaires' chez Clément," in *La formation des canons scripturaires*, ed. M. Tardieu (Paris: Cerf, 1993), 192 (reprinted in *Alexandrie antique et chrétienne*, 123); James Carleton Paget, "The Christian Exegesis of the Old Testament in the Alexandrian Tradition," in *Hebrew Bible / Old Testament*, vol. 1, part 1, *From the Beginnings to the Middle Ages (Until 1300)*, ed. M. Sæbø, C. Brekelmans, and M. Haran (Göttingen: Vandenhoeck & Ruprecht, 1996), 48, observe that this is the first use of "old daitheke" with a textual element. On Clement's Septuagintal text, Otto Stählin, *Clemens Alexandrinus und die Septuaginta* (Nürnberg, 1901) argues that Clement shows affinities with Theodotian revisers, particularly in the Prophets.

[37] *Protr.* 9.87. Greek text in *Clemens Alexandrinus, Erster Band, Protrepticus und Paedagogus*, 2nd ed., ed. Otto Stählin and Ursula Treu, GCS 12 (Berlin: Akademie, 1972), 65: ἐξ ὧν γραμμάτων καὶ συλλαβῶν τῶν ἱερῶν τὰς συγκειμένας γραφάς, τὰ συντάγματα, ὁ αὐτὸς ἀκολούθως ἀπόστολος θεοπνεύστους καλεῖ ("The writings composed from these sacred letters and syllables, namely, the

5.1.3) is grounded in the disclosure of gnosis by the *logos* to the apostles, constituting a new way of knowing God and a new way of reading scriptural texts now called τῆς παλαιᾶς γραφῆς.[38] Scriptural texts that comprise the "old covenant" are, in effect, the "new covenant written in the old letter" (ἡ νέα διαθήκη παλαιῷ κεχαραγμένη γράμματι), even though it is symbolically and enigmatically laden.[39] After the coming of the *logos*, a higher form of gnosis can be found within these scriptural writings. And yet this gnosis is intentionally obscure and requires a kind of reading that respects and assumes the enigmatic quality of the text and brings the moral fitness of the reader into view: "The holy mysteries of the prophecies are veiled in the parables ... for the style of the scriptures is parabolic (παραβολικὸς)."[40]

For Clement, the superiority of the new covenant is assumed, yet he stresses the separate and internal coherence of "old" and "new," claiming that progression does not jeopardize the ultimate harmony that presides over both.[41] David Dawson describes this conception as the "unification and

---

collected scriptures, are consequently called by the same apostles 'inspired of God'"). See also *Prot.* 8.77.

[38] See *Strom.* 4.21.134, 6.5.41–42. On the Marcionite origins of the "New Testament" see Wolfgang Kinzig, "Καινὴ διαθήκη: The Title of the New Testament in the Second and Third Centuries," *JTS* 45 (1994): 519–44.

[39] *Paed.* 1.7.53. Greek text in *Le Pédagogue*, vol. 1, ed. Henri-Irénée Marrou and Marguerite Harl, SC 70 (Paris: Éditions du Cerf, 1949), 206. Here Clement notes the covenantal disparity between the "older people" and the "new people." The former had the Law that disciplined with fear and angelic messengers giving them the word. The new people have seen fear turned to love, and the mystical angel born as Jesus. He then cites Deuteronomy 6:2 (fearing God) and Matthew 22:37 (loving God) as examples of this disparity. However, he claims that a number of scriptural texts are still "enjoined on us." Here he ripples off quotations ("Cease from your own works, from your old sins"; "Learn to do well"; "Depart from evil, and do good"; "Thou hast loved righteousness, and hated iniquity") and adds that these phrases are the new covenant written in the old letter.

[40] *Strom.* 6.15.126 (GCS 52:495: διὸ δὴ τοῖς ἐκλεκτοῖς τῶν ἀνθρώπων τοῖς τε ἐκ πίστεως εἰς γνῶσιν ἐγκρίτοις τηρούμενα τὰ ἅγια τῶν προφητειῶν μυστήρια ταῖς παραβολαῖς ἐγκαλύπτεται· παραβολικὸς γὰρ ὁ χαρακτὴρ ὑπάρχει τῶν γραφῶν). *Strom.* 6.15.130 (GCS 52:497: λέγεται δ' οὖν εἶδος τῆς προφητείας ἡ 'παροιμία' κατὰ τὴν βάρβαρον φιλοσοφίαν λέγεταί τε καὶ 'παραβολὴ' τό τε 'αἴνιγμα' ἐπὶ τούτοις; "The proverb, according to the Barbarian philosophy, is called a mode of prophecy, and the parable is so called, and the enigma in addition"). Cf also *Strom.* 5.9.58 (GCS 52:365: οὐχ ἁπλῶς κατὰ πάντα τὰ ὀνόματα ἀλληγορητέοι, ἀλλ' ὅσα τῆς διανοίας τῆς καθόλου σημαντικά, καὶ δὴ ταῦτα ἐξεύροιμεν ἂν διὰ συμβόλων ὑπὸ παρακαλύμματι τῇ ἀλληγορίᾳ μηνυόμενα; "Barbarian philosophy as well as the myths in Plato, are to be expounded allegorically, not absolutely in all their expressions but in those which express the general sense"). On the confluence of ethics (pure in heart) and epistemology (seeing the divine face to face) in Clement's project see Raoul Mortley, "The Mirror and I Cor 13, 12 in the epistemology of Clement of Alexandria," *VC* 30 (1976): 109–20.

[41] In *Strom.* 2.5.29, he notes that "the Testaments, chronologically two, granted in the divine economy with an eye to the stage of progress, are one in power, Old and New, being presented by the one and only God through his Son." In *Strom.* 7.16.100 Clement refers to truth that is in "agreement of the testament" (GCS 17:70: τὴν ἀλήθειαν διὰ τῆς ἀκολουθίας τῶν διαθηκῶν). Cf. also *Strom.* 6.13.106.

revisionary subordination" of Israel's textual tradition.[42] For Dawson, when the voice of the *logos* is allegorically uncovered from the Hebrew scriptures, "It brings together as a single entity the heterogeneous collection of texts that comprise Hebrew scripture, yet it subordinates those texts to its own deeper discourse and underlying logic."[43] While the controversies surrounding Marcion linger around some of these claims,[44] the unity of the testaments (τὰς διαθήκας) supports Clement's own conception of the "ecclesiastical rule" (κανὼν δὲ ἐκκλησιαστικὸς) that is "the concord and harmony of the Law and the prophets in the covenant delivered at the coming of the Lord."[45] The interpretation of scripture brought about by the *logos* and taught to the apostles is the grounds for Clement's "ecclesiastical rule" that explores the "new covenant written in the old letter."[46] Paul stands at the heart of this interpretive system, mediating the scriptural knowledge disclosed by the *logos* in this epistolary corpus and providing Clement with a model for imitation.

For Clement, the earliest generation of Christians had privileged access to gnosis taught to them by the *logos*. Illustrating this point, Clement points to Isaiah 8:1, where the prophet is told to take up a new book and write in it. Clement reads this passage as a prophetic pronouncement that, through exposition of scriptural texts, a certain "sacred knowledge" will come that at that time was only spoken and so left "unwritten." However, the "unwritten rendering" (ἡ τῆς ἐγγράφου ἄγραφος) was taught to the apostles and "handed down also to us" (καὶ εἰς ἡμᾶς διαδίδοται παράδοσις).[47] This "unwritten rendering" is also referred to as the γνῶσις that has "descended by transmission to a few" and was "imparted unwritten by the apostles" (*Strom.* 6.7.61).[48] Since the higher level of gnosis embedded within the "old"

---

[42] David Dawson, *Allegorical Readers and Cultural Revision in Ancient Alexandria* (Berkeley: University of California Press, 1991), 206.

[43] Dawson, *Allegorical Readers*, 206. Le Boulluec also notes that Clement's conception of the "new covenant" and the unity of the two testaments serves his hermeneutical interests ("De l'usage de titres 'néotestamentaires,'" 124–25).

[44] *Strom.* 2.6.29. Clement also claims unity between the testaments and between Law and Gospel against figures like Epiphanes (*Strom.* 3.2.7) and Tatian (*Strom.* 3.12.82).

[45] *Storm.* 6.15.12 (GCS 52:495: κανὼν δὲ ἐκκλησιαστικὸς ἡ συνῳδία καὶ ἡ συμφωνία νόμου τε καὶ προφητῶν τῇ κατὰ τὴν τοῦ κυρίου παρουσίαν παραδιδομένῃ διαθήκῃ).

[46] S. R. C. Lilla, *Clement of Alexandria: A Study in Christian Platonism and Gnosticism* (Oxford: Oxford University Press, 1971), 155.

[47] *Strom.* 6.15.131 (GCS 52:498: αὐτίκα διδάξαντος τοῦ σωτῆρος τοὺς ἀποστόλους ἡ τῆς ἐγγράφου ἄγραφος ἤδη καὶ εἰς ἡμᾶς διαδίδοται παράδοσις, καρδίαις καιναῖς κατὰ τὴν ἀνακαίνωσιν τοῦ βιβλίου τῇ δυνάμει τοῦ θεοῦ ἐγγεγραμμένη).

[48] GCS 52:462: ἡ γνῶσις δὲ αὕτη [ἡ] κατὰ διαδοχὰς εἰς ὀλίγους ἐκ τῶν ἀποστόλων ἀγράφως παραδοθεῖσα κατελή- λυθεν. Ἐντεῦθεν δὲ ἄρα γνῶσιν εἴτε σοφίαν συνασκηθῆναι χρὴ εἰς ἕξιν θεωρίας ἀίδιον καὶ ἀναλλοίωτον.

writings of the "foreign philosophy" is enigmatic, encoded with "symbols and enigmatic allusions" (*Strom.* 2.1.1), and the gnosis disclosed by the *logos* constituting a new covenant is equally obscure, the apostles become the gatekeepers of gnosis, preserving and overseeing its transmission.[49] Still, the gnosis disclosed by the *logos* to the apostles unveils the inner meaning of "old" writings. Prophecy is, in fact, full of "gnosis," "given by the Lord" and "explained to the apostles" (*Strom.* 6.8.68).[50]

Clement names several apostolic authorities: Peter, John, Matthew, Barnabas, Clement of Rome, Matthias, and, of course, Paul.[51] While others require added clarification, Paul is known simply as "the apostle," albeit "blessed,"[52] "divine,"[53] "holy,"[54] "admirable,"[55] and "noble."[56] Clement grounds the idea of gnosis delivered to and transmitted by the apostles in Paul's language of "mystery." In *Stromata* 5.10.60–61 Clement cites the Pauline language of "mystery" from Ephesians and Colossians. In Ephesians 3, "Paul" notes that "by revelation the mystery was made known to me" that "in other ages was not made known" yet has "now been revealed to his holy apostles." So too, in Colossians 1, the apostle describes a "mystery which has been hidden from the ages and generations." Clement reads this Pauline phrase according to the particulars of his own scheme: "The mysteries that were hid until the time of the apostles and were delivered by them as they received them from the Lord, and concealed in the Old Testament, were manifested to the saints."[57] The apostles are here again the recipients, and the Old Testament is the container of mysteries. As a result, Clement imagines the apostles unrolling scrolls and finding the enigmas that refer

---

[49] Accordingly, Dawson positions Clement as an Alexandrian allegorical reader specializing in a tradition of the "elders" whose esoteric tradition concerning the Christian gospel has been transmitted orally from the *logos* through the apostles (*Allegorical Readers*, 184).

[50] GCS 52:466: γνώσεως γὰρ πλήρης ἡ προφητεία, ὡς ἂν παρὰ κυρίου δοθεῖσα καὶ διὰ κυρίου πάλιν τοῖς ἀποστόλοις σαφηνισθεῖσα.

[51] Barnabas (*Strom.* 2.6.31; 2.7.35); John (*Strom.* 3.6.45; 5.12.81); Peter as apostle (he is an "admirable man" in *Strom.* 3.10.75 and "blessed" in *Strom.* 7.11.63, and only "apostle" by virtue of his place in the list of apostles in *Strom.* 6.8.63); James (*Strom.* 6.8.63); Clement of Rome (*Strom.* 4.17.105); Matthew (*Paed.* 2.1.16); Matthias (*Strom.* 7.13.82).

[52] *Protr.* 9.9; *Strom.* 1.10.50.

[53] For example, *Strom.* 1.1.10, 1.19.94; 2.2.8, 2.20.109, 3.3.18, 6.11.95.

[54] *Strom.* 1.1.11; *Protr.* 8.81.   [55] *Strom.* 1.8.40, 3.8.61.   [56] *Strom.* 2.22.136, 7.14.84.

[57] GCS 52:367: ὥστε ἄλλα μὲν τὰ μυστήρια τὰ ἀποκεκρυμμένα ἄχρι τῶν ἀποστόλων καὶ ὑπ' αὐτῶν παραδοθέντα ὡς ἀπὸ τοῦ κυρίου παρειλήφασιν (ἀποκεκρυμμένα δὲ ἐν τῇ παλαιᾷ διαθήκῃ), ἃ "νῦν ἐφανερώθη τοῖς ἁγίοις." This agrees with his idea that the *logos* "expounded" the "Old Testament" by his coming (*Strom.* 4.21.134: οὐ συνήσετε τὴν διαθήκην τὴν παλαιάν, ἣν αὐτὸς κατὰ τὴν ἰδίαν ἐξηγήσατο παρουσίαν [GCS 52:308]).

to events surrounding Jesus. He cites the *Kerygma Petri* (ὁ Πέτρος ἐν τῷ Κηρύγματι) on this point:[58]

> But we, unrolling the books (ἀναπτύξαντες τὰς βίβλους) of the prophets who name Jesus Christ partly in parables (παραβολῶν), partly in enigmas (αἰνιγμάτων), partly expressly (αὐθεντικῶς) and in so many words, find his coming and death, and cross, and all the rest of the tortures that the Jews inflicted on him, and his resurrection and assumption to heaven previous to the capture of Jerusalem.

In *Stromata* 4.21.134, Clement focuses specifically on Paul, noting that though he is "young" relative to the activity of the earliest apostles, "his writings depend on the Old Testament (ἐκ τῆς παλαιᾶς ἤρτηται διαθήκης), breathing and speaking from it (ἐκεῖθεν ἀναπνέουσα καὶ λαλοῦσα)."[59] Paul's writing breathes and speaks from out of τῆς παλαιᾶς διαθήκης. Clement's Paul was an expert reader of scriptural enigmas,[60] and the preeminent model for Clement's ideal Gnostic.[61]

---

[58] Strom. 6.15.128 (GCS 52:496: ἡμεῖς δὲ ἀναπτύξαντες τὰς βίβλους ἃς εἴχομεν τῶν προφητῶν, ἃ μὲν διὰ παραβολῶν, ἃ δὲ δι' αἰνιγμάτων, ἃ δὲ αὐθεντικῶς καὶ αὐτολεξεὶ τὸν Χριστὸν Ἰησοῦν ὀνομαζόντων, εὕρομεν καὶ τὴν παρουσίαν αὐτοῦ καὶ τὸν θάνατον καὶ τὸν σταυρὸν καὶ τὰς λοιπὰς κολάσεις πάσας ὅσας ἐποίησαν αὐτῷ οἱ Ἰουδαῖοι, καὶ τὴν ἔγερσιν καὶ τὴν εἰς οὐρανοὺς ἀνάληψιν πρὸ τοῦ Ἱεροσόλυμα κτισθῆναι, καθὼς ἐγέγραπτο ταῦτα). See also Pierre Nautin, "Les citations de la Prédication de Pierre dans Clément D'Alexandrie, Strom, VI. V. 39–41," *JTS* 25.1 (1974): 98–105; Ernst von Dobschütz, *Das Kerygma Petri kritisch untersucht*, TU 11.1 (Leipzig: Hinrichs, 1893), reprinted in *Kerygma Petri* (Piscataway: Gorgias Press, 2010).

[59] GCS 52:307.

[60] Strom. 3.12.86: "All of the apostles' letters preserve the connection between the Law and the Gospel". See also Strom. 2.6.25: "Do you see how he traces faith back through the act of hearing and the preaching of the apostles to the utterance of the Lord and to the Son of God?" (Trans. John Ferguson, *Clement of Alexandria: Stromateis Books One to Three*, FC 85 [Washington DC: Catholic University of America Press, 1991], 175).

[61] See Judith Kovacs, "Divine Pedagogy and the Gnostic Teacher According to Clement of Alexandria," *JECS* 9.1 (2001): 8 n. 18, who notes the cluster of Pauline texts used when describing the Christian teacher in Strom. 1.1.1–10 (namely, 1 Cor 8:7; 2 Tim 2:1–2; Gal 6:8–9; 2 Cor 11:27–28; 1 Cor 11:27–31; 1 Thess 2:5–7; 1 Cor 3:8–9; Gal 6:10). Moreover, Clement uses the image of the book from the second vision in the *Shepherd of Hermas* (*Vis.* 2.1.3–4) in order to illustrate the Gnostic (Pauline) approach to scripture. For Clement, Hermas transcribes the book letter by letter because he cannot locate the syllables. As observed by Dan Batovici, "Hermas in Clement of Alexandria," *StPatr* 66 (2013): 49, rather than suggest ancient difficulties reading *scriptio continua*, Clement reads this allegorically. The practice of following letter by letter reflects the clarity of the scriptures for all people when given a "bare reading." On the other hand, knowing the syllables refers to the "Gnostic unfolding of the scriptures." In Strom. 7.16.104 the Gnostic is "aided by the Lord to discover the proofs (τὰς ἀποδείξεις) he is in search of both from the Law and the prophets." For the life of the Gnostic, as it seems to me, is nothing else than deeds and words agreeable to the tradition of the Lord." The Gnostic is envisioned as an expert in the textual particularities of scripture in Strom. 1.9.44, distinguishing between "the ambiguities and nominally similar terms in accordance with the testaments" (GCS 52:29: τάς τε ἀμφιβόλους φωνὰς τάς τε ὁμωνύμως ἐ

74 THE PAULINE HISTORY OF HEBREWS

Clement models himself on Paul in a number of ways. Since the act of writing was a contested medium for communicating special forms of knowledge—a tradition that goes back to Plato (*Phaed.* 264C)—Clement grounds his commitment to writing in Paul's own career and practice at the outset of *Stromata* 1.[62] Clement also imagines Paul and the apostles as exemplary masters over their passions and describes the Gnostic in similar terms.[63] Paul, for example, outlines the "preparatory exercises of Gnostic discipline" in 2 Corinthians 7:1–11.[64] However, Clement shows particular affinity for Paul as expert reader of scripture, and the number of overlapping scriptural citations is suggestive of targeted excerpting.

Clement may, for example, have taken Isaiah 54:1 (cited in *Protr.* 1.9.4), from Galatians 4:27, although his text differs from Paul,[65] and the claim that Orpheus was influenced by Isaiah 40:13 might derive from its use in

---

κφερομένας κατὰ τὰς διαθήκας). Such descriptions recall Clement's original praise of one "Sicilian bee" who culls the "pure substance of true knowledge" from the flower of the meadow of the Prophets (*Strom.* 1.1.11).

[62] In the opening of the *Stromata*, Clement raises a number of arguments designed to justify the act of writing: it shares wisdom (which must be shared), it passes on tradition, it proclaims the word just as the voice, and it combats heresy (*Strom.* 1.1.1–18). On this passage see Eric Osborn, "Teaching and Writing in the First Chapter of the 'Stromateis' of Clement of Alexandria," *JTS* 10.2 (1959): 335–39. Writing was not universally valued as a means of communication and Clement suggests an inclusive approach. In *Strom.* 1.1.4 Clement encourages his audience to accept written and oral modes of communicating the 'word'. His primary *model* here is Paul, who exhorts that his teaching be passed on (2 Tim 2:1–2 in *Strom.* 1.1.3), commends himself for the enrichment of many (2 Cor 6:4, 10–11 in *Strom.* 1.1.4), and affirms that both the tongue and the hand are "one" (1 Cor 3:8–9 in *Strom.* 1.1.7). Clement has high praise for Paul's writing skills, noting that the Apostle never using flattering words (1 Thess 2:5–7 in *Strom.* 1.1.6), rather he writes "brilliantly" (*Strom.* 1. 1.4); "divinely" (*Strom.* 4.21.145); "mystically and sacredly" (*Strom.* 4.23.149). Clement claims to be the first to have written down the apostolic *paradosis* (*Strom.* 1.1.11–12, *Eclog.* 27.1).

[63] For Clement, those who are under the direction of their own passions are precluded from receiving knowledge of the divine (*Strom.* 3.5.43). The Apostles were exemplary in this regard. In *Strom.* 7.12.74 the apostles are proofs of perfection in order to establish churches. They apostles were selected not because of a distinctive nature (*Strom.* 6.13.105), but because they obtained mastery over all emotion (*Strom.* 7.12.70). Clement also describes Paul as a master of self-control (*Strom.* 3.16.101) and in *Strom.* 3.12.86 he claims that all of the Apostle's letters teach emotional control. See also *Strom.* 2.20.12; 2.20.125; 7.14.84; 7.16.104; Judith L. Kovacs, "Saint Paul as Apostle of Apatheia: Stromateis VII, chapter 14," in *The Seventh Book of the Stromateis*, 199–216; "Was Paul an Antinomian, an Ascetic, or a Sober Married Man? Exegetical debates in Clement of Alexandria's Stromateis III," in *Asceticism and Exegesis in Early Christianity*, ed. H.-U. Weidemann (Leuven: Brepols, 2013), 186–202.

[64] *Strom.* 4.21.132: Ταῦτα γνωστικῆς ἀσκήσεως προγυμνάσματα (GCS 52:306). Cf. Judith L. Kovacs, "Divine Pedagogy and the Gnostic Teacher According to Clement of Alexandria," *JECS* 9 (2001): 3–25.

[65] Clement's citation uses ἀκουσάτω against Paul and Isaiah (εὐφράνθητι), ῥηξάτω φωνὴν ἡ οὐκ ὠδίνουσα against ῥῆξον καὶ βόησον, ἡ οὐκ ὠδίνουσα (Gal 4.27 / Isa 54.1), and πλείονα τὰ τέκνα against πολλὰ τὰ τέκνα (Gal 4.27 / Isa 54.1). Cf. also 2 *Clement* 2, which also cites Isa 54:1 with exposition.

Romans 11:34.[66] However, the particular affinity for *Paul's* scriptural citations is clear. In *Stromata* 1.3.23, he cites Isaiah 29:14 from 1 Corinthians 1:19[67] as "God's scriptures," and he lifts the composite citation of Job 5:13 and Psalm 93:11 (LXX) from 1 Corinthians 3:19–20. Clement removes the divide between these citations from 1 Corinthians 3.19–20 (καὶ πάλιν) and forges a composite citation from the two. So too, Paul's scripturesque quotations in Ephesians 5.14 ("therefore it says 'Sleeper awake!'") and 1 Corinthians 2:9 are also reappropriated by Clement.[68] Clement was evidently interested in scriptural material found in Pauline letters and he consistently excerpts passages directly from the *corpus Paulinum*.

3. Excerpting Hebrews, Imitating Paul

When excising scriptural quotations from Pauline letters, particularly Romans, Clement reproduces the order of these citations by imitating Paul's sequence. Three examples are noted here. First, in *Stromata* 1.27.174, Clement cites Romans 2:17–20 in order to claim that despite Paul's language of rebuke to Jews, the Law holds forth light, guidance, correction, and instruction.[69] Clement then notes that "like Paul, prophecy criticizes people for not understanding the Law,"[70] which is supported with a chain citation of Isaiah 59:7–8 and Psalm 36:1, taken from Romans 3:16–18. Clement then links Romans 1:22 onto the end of this chain and then ends with a quotation from 1 Timothy attributed to "the apostle." Though Clement excises Paul's scriptural citations from their epistolary setting, he works with them sequentially as he moves through Romans 2–3.

---

[66] Both *Strom.* 5.14.129 (GCS 52:413–14) and Romans 11:34 (NA28) read ἢ τίς σύμβουλος αὐτοῦ ἐγένετο against Greek Isaiah (καὶ τίς αὐτοῦ σύμβουλος ἐγένετο ὃς συμβιβᾷ αὐτόν).

[67] Clement's text reads ἀθετήσω (reject) with Paul against Greek Isaiah's κρύψω (conceal).

[68] In *Propt.* 10.94 Clement cites a similar source that is found in 1 Corinthians 2.9 (which Paul introduces with καθὼς γέγραπται). Clement's citation is more extended than the one found in 1 Corinthians 2:9 and Origen claims that Paul's text comes from secret writings of Elijah (*Comm. ser. Matt.* 177). See here Joseph Verheyden, "Origen on the Origin of 1 Cor 2,9," in *The Corinthians Correspondence*, ed. R. Bieringer, BETL 125, (Leuven: Peeters, 1996), 491–511; Klaus Berger, "Zur diskussion über die Herkunft von 1 Kor. 2:9," *NTS* 24 (1978): 270–83.

[69] Both Runar M. Thorsteinsson, *Paul's Interlocutor in Romans 2: Function and Identity in the Context of Ancient Epistolography*, CBNTS 40 (Stockholm: Almqvist & Wiksell, 2003) and Matthew Thiessen, "Paul's Argument against Gentile Circumcision in Romans 2:17-29," *NovT* 56 (2014): 373-91 suggest that the 'one who calls himself a Jew' in Romans 2:17 is a circumcised Gentile.

[70] GCS 52:108: ὁμοίως δὲ τῷ Παύλῳ ἡ προφητεία ὀνειδίζει τὸν λαὸν ὡς μὴ συνιέντα τὸν νόμον.

Second, and more forcefully, in *Stromata* 4.7.47–48, Clement cites Psalm 44:22 from Romans 8:36–37 and then cites the quotation found in Romans 10:10–11 without any Pauline markers.[71] Clement's larger concern in *Stromata* 4.7 is to uphold the dignity of martyrdom against Greek disparagement, citing Plato, Aeschylus, Epicharmus, the Gospel of Matthew, and Paul as positive testimony. Here the "suffering" language in Romans 8 together with the hoped-for "glory" are used by Clement to indicate that "martyrdom is taught for love's sake." Then, having used the scriptural citations in Romans 8 and 10:10–11, Clement returns to "Paul," citing material from 1 Timothy and Romans. The secondary citations appear within a concerted effort to read Romans 8.

Third, in *Stromata* 2.9.42, Clement uses Romans 10:2–3 to name and criticize a "Jewish" understanding of the Law and then cites Romans 10:14 regarding the "telos" the Law. He then excises Deuteronomy 32.21 and Isaiah 65.1 and 65:2 from Romans 10:19–21 and cites them as separate scriptural testimony in *Stromata* 2.9.43:[72]

> This is the reason why he said to them through Moses, "I will make you jealous of those who are not a nation; I will make you angry against a people without understanding," [Deut. 32:21 from Romans 10:19] meaning of course a people who are ready to listen. Through Isaiah he says, "I have been found by those who did not look for me, I have appeared to those who did not ask for me," [Isaiah 65:1 from Romans 10:20] obviously dealing with the times before the Savior's coming, after which Israel today appropriately hears these prophetic words addressed to them as well: "All day long I have reached out my hand to a disobedient and contrary people." [Isaiah 65:2 from Romans 10:21]. Do you see the reason why the prophet calls them from the Gentiles? He says clearly that it is the disobedience and contrariness of the people. God's goodness is shown in regard

---

[71] GCS 52:269. Between these citations Clements cites an otherwise unattested tragedy, found in A. Nauck, *Tragicorum Graecorum fragmenta* (Leipzig: Teubner, 1889), 862–66, and Sophocles, *Antigone*, 450.

[72] Greek text in GCS 52:135–36: ὅθεν εἴρηται τούτοις παρὰ Μωυσέως· "ἐγὼ παραζηλώσω ὑμᾶς ἐπ' οὐκ ἔθνει, ἐπ' ἔθνει ἀσυνέτῳ παροργιῶ ὑμᾶς," τῷ εἰς ὑπακοὴν δηλονότι εὐτρεπεῖ γενομένῳ. καὶ διὰ Ἡσαΐου "εὑρέθην' λέγει 'τοῖς ἐμὲ μὴ ζητοῦσιν, ἐμφανὴς ἐγενόμην τοῖς ἐμὲ μὴ ἐπερωτῶσι," πρὸ τῆς τοῦ κυρίου παρουσίας δηλαδή, μεθ' ἣν καὶ τῷ Ἰσραὴλ ἐκεῖνα τὰ προφητευθέντα οἰκείως λέγεται νῦν· "ἐξεπέτασα τὰς χεῖράς μου ὅλην τὴν ἡμέραν ἐπὶ λαὸν ἀπειθοῦντα καὶ ἀντιλέγοντα." ὁρᾷς τὴν αἰτίαν τῆς ἐξ ἐθνῶν κλήσεως σαφῶς πρὸς τοῦ προφήτου ἀπείθειαν τοῦ λαοῦ καὶ ἀντιλογίαν εἰρημένην; εἶθ' ἡ ἀγαθότης καὶ ἐπὶ τούτοις δείκνυται τοῦ θεοῦ· φησὶ γὰρ ὁ ἀπόστολος· 'ἀλλὰ τῷ αὐτῶν παραπτώματι ἡ σωτηρία τοῖς ἔθνεσιν εἰς τὸ παραζηλῶσαι αὐτοὺς' καὶ μετανοῆσαι βουληθῆναι.

to them too. The apostle says, "Through their stumbling, salvation has come to the Gentiles so as to provoke Israel to jealousy" and the will to repentance.

Clement then returns to Paul and concludes the discussion with a citation of Romans 11:11. Clement's citations reveal a sequential reading of Romans, mixed with his tendency to excerpt scriptural passages as distinct citations. A similar strategy of scriptural separation while using the epistolary context of Paul is found in *Stromata* 2.6.25. Here Clement redesigns Romans 10:14–16 in ways that accent the scriptural passages not as direct quotations from Romans, yet the epistolary context of these citations remains:[73]

> "Lord, who has believed what we have heard?" says Isaiah. "Faith comes from hearing, hearing comes from the utterance of God," says the apostle. "How shall they call on one in whom they have not shown faith? How shall they hear without a preacher? How shall they preach unless they are sent as apostles?" As scripture has it, "How beautiful are the feet of those who bring a gospel of good news." Do you see how he traces faith back through the act of hearing and the preaching of the apostles to the utterance of the Lord and to the Son of God?

In this context, Clement cites Isaiah 53:1 from Romans 10:16, followed by Paul's voice in Romans 10:17, and then back to the scriptural voice in 10:14–15. Again, Romans is in some sense "recreated" as the citations are excised while the flow of Paul's letter is maintained.

Clement is consistent in reserving "scriptural" language for material found in the παλαιᾶς γραφῆς. In *Protrepticus*, the *corpus Paulinum* is first cited as an "apostolic writing,"[74] then as "the inspired apostle of the Lord,"[75] and later he is simply "the apostle," or "Paul." In *Protrepticus* 9.87, Paul is the "interpreter of the divine voice" (ἑρμηνεὺς γίνεται τῆς θείας φωνῆς)[76] and Clement never subordinates his agency to that of the Holy Spirit

---

[73] GCS 52:126: 'Κύριε, τίς ἐπίστευσεν τῇ ἀκοῇ ἡμῶν' Ἡσαΐας φησίν. 'ἡ μὲν γὰρ πίστις ἐξ ἀκοῆς, ἡ δὲ ἀκοὴ διὰ ῥήματος θεοῦ' φησὶν ὁ ἀπόστολος. 'πῶς οὖν ἐπικαλέσονται εἰς ὃν οὐκ ἐπίστευσαν; πῶς δὲ πιστεύσουσιν οὗ οὐκ ἤκουσαν; πῶς δὲ ἀκούσουσι χωρὶς κηρύσσοντος; πῶς δὲ κηρύξωσιν, ἐὰν μὴ ἀποσταλῶσι; καθὼς γέγραπται· ὡς ὡραῖοι οἱ πόδες τῶν εὐαγγελιζομένων τὰ ἀγαθά' ὁρᾷς πῶς ἀνάγει τὴν πίστιν δι' ἀκοῆς καὶ τῆς τῶν ἀποστόλων κηρύξεως ἐπὶ τὸ ῥῆμα κυρίου καὶ τὸν υἱὸν τοῦ θεοῦ.
[74] *Protr.* 1.4 citing Titus 3:3–5: ἡ ἀποστολικὴ γραφή (GCS 12:5).
[75] *Protr.* 1.7 citing Titus 2:11–13: τὸν θεσπέσιον ἐκεῖνον τοῦ κυρίου ἀπόστολον (GCS 12:7).
[76] GCS 12:65 (in this case the voice in Matthew 4:17).

(τὸ ἅγιον πνεῦμα) in the way he does with David and Jeremiah.[77] The particularity of Paul's epistles is noted with some regularity,[78] yet his teaching is "apostolic precept" (ἀποστολικῇ παραγγελίᾳ) and therefore given universal significance.[79] The apostle Paul was inspired, and his writing is called scripture on one occasion (*Paed.* 2.22), yet Barnabas and Clement of Roman are also apostles and their writings speak with seemingly equal authority, as with the *Kerygma Petri* and the *Shepherd of Hermas*.[80] For Clement, "gospel" functions as a large designation for material found in the four canonical Gospels, though he also refers to Matthew and John specifically.[81] Clement cites the "gospel" apart from "scripture" but also designates it as such in *Paedagogus* 3.11.74. Yet he also gleans logia of Jesus from a number of sources and quotes approvingly from the *Gospel to the Hebrews*.[82] Le Boulluec describes Clement's approach to apostolic writings that together comprise a new covenant as "assimilative," not restricted to a specific collection.[83] The character of Clement's "New Testament" is primarily an apostolic and so authorized collection of texts that explicate the mysteries of the *logos* disclosed in the old scriptures.[84] In this regard, Clement's image of Paul as an authorized reader of scripture is available for imitation.

Clement is focused on the scriptural passages found in Pauline letters and freely excerpts and repurposes them throughout his corpus. Clement's excerpting strategy for reading Pauline epistles likely finds its roots in Justin Martyr, who mined Paul (as well as Hebrews and *Barnabas*) for scriptural

---

[77] In fact, in *Paed.* 1.6.49, the Holy Spirit is the agent who puts Paul's words "on the lips of the Lord": "That is the reason the Holy Spirit mystically puts these words of the apostle on the lips of the Lord: 'I have given you milk to drink.'" Cf. *Protr.* 8.78: "Now Jeremiah, the all-wise Jeremiah prophet, or rather the Holy Spirit in Jeremiah, shows what God . . ." (GCS 12:50–60: Ἱερεμίας δὲ ὁ προφήτης ὁ πάνσοφος, μᾶλλον δὲ ἐν Ἱερεμίᾳ τὸ ἅγιον πνεῦμα ἐπιδείκνυσι τὸν θεόν). *Strom.* 6.6.49: "and again David, rather the Lord from the mouth of the said . . . openly says . . ." (GCS 52:456: πάλιν δὲ ἄντικρυς ὁ Δαβίδ μᾶλλον δὲ ὁ κύριος ἐκ προσώπου τοῦ ὁσίου...φησίν).

[78] *Strom.* 6.18.164; 4.13.92.; 4.15.97 (πρὸς πιστοὺς γὰρ ἐπέστελλεν); 6.8.62 (Hebrews and Greeks).

[79] *Protr.* 1.8 (GCS 12:8).

[80] Clement uses the biography of Paul to legitimize Barnabas (*Strom.* 2.2.116).

[81] *Paed.* 2.1.16, 'Matthew'; *Strom.* 5.12.81, 'John the apostles says'; *Paed.* 1.6.38, "He says in the Gospel according to John." Clement also cites approvingly from a *Gospel according to the Hebrews* (*Strom.* 2.9.45). See Carl P. Cosaert, "Clement's of Alexandria's Gospel Citations," in *The Early Text of the New Testament*, eds. Charles E. Hill and Michael J. Kruger (Oxford: Oxford University Press, 2012), 393–413; Carl P. Cosaert, *The Text of the Gospels in Clement of Alexandria*, SBLNTGF 9 (Atlanta: Society of biblical Literature, 2008).

[82] *Strom.* 2.9.45.

[83] Le Boulluec, "De l'usage de titres 'néotestamentaires,'" 198, 200 (reprint 129, 132).

[84] On this point see Hermann Kutter, *Clemens Alexandrinus und das Neue Testament: Eine Untersuchung* (Giessen: J. Richer Buchhandlung, 1897), 101–52.

citations.⁸⁵ Yet Clement is also interested in the epistolary logic of Romans and 1 Corinthians and often frames his excerpting within sequential discussions of Pauline letters.⁸⁶ When Clement applies this practice to Hebrews, however, there is a marked lack of attention to the "Pauline" epistolary setting of these citations.

Clement cites scriptural texts in ways that reveal they were excerpted from their context in Hebrews. For instance, on three occasions Clement cites Proverbs 3:11-12 ("My son, do not regard lightly the παιδείας of the Lord, nor loose heart when corrected by him"), which is also found in Hebrews 12:5-6.⁸⁷ In *Protrepticus* 9.82.1-3, Clement cites this passage with the added comment from Hebrews 12:21 (that Moses said, "I tremble with fear"). Clement modifies the opening of Proverbs 3:11 slightly, as he often flags a citation after the opening clause, and he switches the mood of εἰμί from the indicative to an infinitive:⁸⁸

Hebrews 12:5

υἱέ μου, μὴ ὀλιγώρει παιδείας κυρίου, μηδὲ ἐκλύου ὑπ' αὐτοῦ ἐλεγχόμενος·

Hebrews 12:21

καί, οὕτω φοβερὸν ἦν τὸ φανταζόμενον, Μωϋσῆς εἶπεν

Ἔκφοβός εἰμι καὶ ἔντρομος.

Protrepticus 9.82.1-3

"Μὴ τοίνυν μηκέτι," φησίν,

"υἱέ μου, ὀλιγώρει παιδείας κυρίου, μηδ' ἐκλύου ὑπ' αὐτοῦ ἐλεγχόμενος." Ὢ τῆς ὑπερβαλλούσης φιλανθρωπίας· οὐδ' ὡς μαθηταῖς ὁ διδάσκαλος οὐδ' ὡς οἰκέταις ὁ κύριος οὐδ' ὡς θεὸς ἀνθρώποις, πατὴρ δὲ ὡς ἤπιος» νουθετεῖ υἱούς. Εἶτα Μωυσῆς μὲν ὁμολογεῖ "ἔμφοβος εἶναι καὶ ἔντρομος," ἀκούων περὶ τοῦ λόγου, σὺ δὲ τοῦ λόγου ἀκροώμενος τοῦ θείου οὐ δέδιας;

---

⁸⁵ See overlapping scriptural citations in Romans 3:13-16 (*Dial.* 27.3), 4:3 (*Dial.* 92.3), 9:29 (*Dial.* 140.3, *1 Apol.* 53.7), 10:16 (*Dial.* 42.2, 13.3, 114.2, 118.4), 10:18 (*Dial.* 42.1, 64.8; *1 Apol.* 40.3), 10:19 (*Dial.* 119.2), 10:21 (*Dial.* 97.2; *1 Apol.* 35.3, 38.1, 49.3), 11:3-4 (*Dial.* 39.1), 11:34 (*Dial.* 50.5), 14:11 (*1 Apol.* 52.6), 15:21 (*Dial.* 13.3); 1 Cor 1:19 (*Dial.* 123.4, 35.5, 78.11); 2 Cor 6:2 (*Dial.* 122.5); Gal 3:6 (*Dial.* 92.3), 3:10 (*Dial.* 95.1), 3:13 (*Dial.* 96.1), 4:27 (*Dial.* 13.8; *1 Apol.* 53.5), 4:30 (*Dial.* 56.7); Eph 4:8 (*Dial.* 3.9.4, 87.6); Heb 1:6 (*Dial.* 130.1), 1:8-9 (*Dial.* 38.4, 56.14, 63.4), 1:9 (*Dial.* 86.3), 1:13 (*Dial.* 32.6, 56.14, 83.1-2, 127.5; *1 Apol.* 45.2), 2:12 (*Dial.* 98.5, 106.2), 5:5 (*Dial.* 88.8), 5:6 (*Dial.* 32.6, 33.1-2, 63.3, 83.2), 8:8 (*Dial.* 11.3, 28.3), 8:9 (*Dial.* 22.6). On Clement's interaction with and similarity to Justin, see Dawson, *Allegorical Readers*, 187-99. On Justin's own engagement with Paul see Rodney Werline, "The Transformation of Pauline Arguments in Justin Martyr's Dialogue with Trypho," *HTR* 92.1 (1999): 79-93.

⁸⁶ Relatedly, Clement also works through larger blocks of Pauline material, 1 Corinthians 7, throughout *Strom.* 3.12.79-80.

⁸⁷ In *Paed.* 1.9.78.4-5 Clement cites Proverbs 3.11 again, as an example of the Educator speaking through Solomon to "soften the severity of the correction and weaken its sting." In *Strom.* 1.5.32, he uses a fuller quotation of the passage (Prov 3.11-12) to justify Sarah's (wisdom) harsh treatment of Hagar (preliminary education) according to Philo's allegorical reading from *De congressu* 177. In this instance, Clement is channeling Philo's use of Proverbs 3.11-12, already embedded within the allegory from *De congressu*. See Annewies van den Hoek, *Clement of Alexandria and His Use of Philo in the Stromateis: An Early Christian Reshaping of a Jewish Mode* (Leiden: Brill, 1988), 23-47 esp. 42.

⁸⁸ GCS 12:62.

In other instances, Clement shows his textual dependence on Hebrews yet, again, without accenting the epistolary context for the citation nor registering the material as Pauline. For example, in *Protrepticus* 11.113.4 Clement cites Psalm 22:22. which is followed with language taken from Hebrews 2:12:[89]

Hebrews 2:11b-12	*Protrepticus* 11.113.4-5
δι' ἣν αἰτίαν <u>οὐκ ἐπαισχύνεται ἀδελφοὺς αὐτοὺς καλεῖν</u>, (12) λέγων, Ἀπαγγελῶ <u>τὸ ὄνομά σου τοῖς ἀδελφοῖς μου, ἐν μέσῳ ἐκκλησίας ὑμνήσω σε</u>·	Τοῦτό τοι καὶ ἐπήγγελται τῷ πατρὶ "διηγήσομαι <u>τὸ ὄνομά σου τοῖς ἀδελφοῖς μου· ἐν μέσῳ ἐκκλησίας ὑμνήσω σε</u>" Ὕμνησον καὶ διήγησαί μοι τὸν πατέρα σου τὸν θεόν· σώσει σου τὰ διηγήματα, παιδεύσει με ἡ ᾠδή. Ὡς μέχρι νῦν ἐπλανώμην ζητῶν τὸν θεόν, ἐπεὶ δέ με φωταγωγεῖς, κύριε, καὶ τὸν θεὸν εὑρίσκω διὰ σοῦ καὶ τὸν πατέρα ἀπολαμβάνω παρὰ σοῦ, γίνομαί σου συγκληρονόμος, ἐπεὶ <u>τὸν ἀδελφὸν οὐκ ἐπῃσχύνθης</u>

Clement links Psalm 22:22 with the idea that Jesus was not ashamed to call the "children for glory" his "brothers" (Heb 2:11). The reference is only in passing, and Clement fuses the idea with language from Romans 8:17 (fellow heirs). His reading of the scriptural passage is based in Hebrews, but he does not frame the material as Pauline.

There are more examples. In *Stromata* 4.11.80, Clement uses the introductory formula from Hebrews 13:6 (ὥστε θαρροῦντας ἡμᾶς λέγειν, "So we can confidently say"), which introduces a quotation from Psalm 118:6 (*Strom.* 4.11.80, ὥστε θαρροῦντα ἡμῶν). Earlier in *Stromata* 4.11 Clement responds to two objections arising from the reality of persecution: Why are Christians persecuted if God cares for them? On this second point, Clement cites Socrates: Though Anytus and Melitus may kill him, they will not hurt him. Similarly, those who may kill Clement's Christians do them no ultimate wrong in releasing them to "go to the Lord." Here Clement uses the secondary citation of Psalm 118:6 from Hebrews 13:6: "The Lord is my helper; I will not be afraid. What can anyone do to me?"

There is one passage excerpted from Hebrews in which Clement clearly mimics the epistolary logic containing the scriptural citation. In *Protrepticus* 9.84.3-4 Clement cites Psalm 95:7-11 in two parts, taken from Hebrews 3.7b-9a and 3.9b-11. While Hebrews introduces Psalm 95 as the direct speech of the τὸ πνεῦμα τὸ ἅγιον, Clement simply notes that "scripture says somewhere" (λέγει γάρ που ἡ γραφή). Yet, when Clement breaks up the

---

[89] GCS 12:80.

citation in order to rhetorically ask what is the "test" (δοκιμασίᾳ), he notes that "the Holy Spirit will show you" (τὸ ἅγιόν σοι πνεῦμα ἐξηγήσεται).[90] Building on the exhortation from Ephesians (Awake!), Clement continues and evokes the exhortative and warning context of Psalm 95. This secondary citation is the closest Clement gets to reading sequentially through Hebrews, as he mimics the repeated emphasis on "today" (σήμερον); a theme that Hebrews returns to in 3:13, 3:15, and 4:7. Further, Clement, together with Hebrews, draws the conclusion that the Israelites in the wilderness were not able to rest because of "unbelief" (Heb 3:19)—though Clement's aim is to exhort the Greeks to faith. However, as Clement uses this scriptural material from Hebrews, and even uses the thematic frame for Psalm 95 found in Hebrews, he does not reappropriate it as a way of modeling "Paul" explicitly.

While there are other possible secondary citations, the above texts show Clement's broad strategy for excerpting Hebrews.[91] Clement read Hebrews as a scriptural archive, excising these citations and reusing them within the context of his corpus. In some ways, Clement's excerpting of Hebrews is similar to his reading of the *Epistle of Barnabas*.[92] In *Paedagogus* 3.89.1–92.1 he notes that the Decalogue of Moses defines both sins and virtues in a manner conducive to salvation and attaches several scriptural passages that describe a variety of these practices: prayer, fasting, sacrifices, swearing, and lying. The cluster of scriptural passages that he assigns to these topics all appear in the early chapters of *Barnabas*:

Subject	Citation	Clement	Parallel in *Barnabas*
Manner of prayer	Isaiah 58:7–8	*Paed.* 3.89	*Barnabas* 3:4
Benefit of prayer	Isaiah 58:9	*Paed.* 3.89	*Barnabas* 3:5
Fasting	Isaiah 58:4–5	*Paed.* 3.90	*Barnabas* 3:1–3
Meaning of a fast	Isaiah 58:6–7	*Paed.* 3.90	*Barnabas* 3:1–3
Sacrifices	Isaiah 11:11–13	*Paed.* 3.90	*Barnabas* 2:5
Swearing	Jeremiah 7:22	*Paed.* 3.91	*Barnabas* 2:7–8
Liars / the proud	Isaiah 5:20	*Paed.* 3.92	*Barnabas* 4:11

[90] GCS 12:63.
[91] There are a number of other possibly secondary citations. *Protr.* 11.114 (Jer 31:33–34 / Heb 8:10–12); *Strom.* 2.20.126 (Heb 13.5 / Deut 31:6 / Josh 1:5); *Paed.* 2.8.65 (Psalm 45:7b / Heb 1:9); *Paed.* 1.7.2 (Psalm 45:7a / Heb 1:9).
[92] Clement, for example, uses the scriptural citation from *Barnabas* 3:16–19 in *Paed.* 2.3.36: "Divine scripture says aptly somewhere: 'Where are the princes of the nations, and they that rule over the beasts that are upon the earth? That take their diversion with the birds of the air? That hoard up silver and gold wherein men trust, and there is no end of their getting? Who work in silver and gold and are solicitous? And their works are unsearchable. They are cut off and gone down to hell.'" Cf. also *Strom.* 5.10.64, citing Isaiah 45:3 / *Barn.* 11.4. Eusebius describes Clement's open use of "disputed" texts, including Hebrews, *Barnabas*, Jude, *1 Clement*, and others (*Hist. eccl.* 6.13.4).

Scholars have noted the lack of uniform textual agreement between *Barnabas*, Clement, and the Old Greek of Isaiah, leading Martin Albl to posit the idea of a shared collection of *testimonia*.[93] Whether Clement is lifting from Barnabas in *Paedagogus* 3, Clement is elsewhere much more interested in the logic of Barnabas' scriptural citations than those found in Hebrews. In *Stromata* 2.7.35 Clement attributes the citation of Isaiah 5:21 to Barnabas (4:11), and then quotes the added comment on the scriptural passage:[94]

> The apostle Barnabas [after quoting], "Woe to those who have understanding in their own eyes and are shrewd in their own sight," adds (προτάξας ἐπήγαγεν), "Let us become spiritual, a perfect temple for God. So far as it rests with us, let us practice the fear of God, and let us strive to keep his commandments, so that we may find joy in his acts of justification." These are the grounds for the divine words: "The fear of the Lord is the beginning of wisdom."

Here Clement repeats the scriptural reasoning found in *Barnabas*. Rather than excerpt the passage out of *Barnabas* for his own purposes, the epistolary logic and interpretive direction is reused. Similarly, Clement cites Psalm 32.1–2 from *1 Clement* 50:6 but also includes the commentarial remark from *1 Clement* 50:7 that "this blessing comes to those who are chosen by God through Jesus Christ our Lord" (οὗτος ὁ μακαρισμὸς ἐγένετο ἐπὶ τοὺς ἐκλελεγμένους ὑπὸ τοῦ θεοῦ διὰ Ἰησοῦ Χριστοῦ τοῦ κυρίου ἡμῶν). Clement includes and authorizes this added interpretive aid from *1 Clement* as a way of framing Psalm 32.

Clement denounces some unnamed "worthless scoundrels" who "collect passages from extracts of the prophets, making an anthology and cobbling them together quite wrongly, taking literally what is meant allegorically" (*Strom.* 3.4.38).[95] However, Clement's complaint is ultimately with their

---

[93] *"And Scripture Cannot Be Broken": The Form and Function of Early Christian Testamonia Collections*, NovTSup 96 (Leiden: Brill, 1999), 152. Robert Kraft too notes the shared variant Barnabas and Clement's use of Isaiah 58:6, in "Barnabas' Isaiah Text and the 'Testimony Book' Hypothesis," *JBL* 79.4 (1960): 343. Cf. Pierre Prigent, *Les testimonia dans le christianisme primitive: L'Épître de Barnabé i–xvi et ses sources*, Études Bibliques (Paris: Lecoffre, 1961), who finds in *Barnabas* 2–3 the use of a distinctly anti-culture collection of *testimonia*.

[94] GCS 52:31: καὶ Βαρνάβας ὁ ἀπόστολος "οὐαὶ οἱ συνετοὶ παρ' ἑαυτοῖς καὶ ἐνώπιον αὐτῶν ἐπιστήμονες" προτάξας ἐπήγαγεν· "πνευματικοὶ γενώμεθα, ναὸς τέλειος τῷ θεῷ. ἐφ' ὅσον ἐστὶν ἐφ' ἡμῖν, μελετῶμεν τὸν φόβον τοῦ θεοῦ καὶ φυλάσσειν ἀγωνιζώμεθα τὰς ἐντολὰς αὐτοῦ, ἵνα ἐν τοῖς δικαιώμασιν αὐτοῦ εὐφρανθῶμεν" ὅθεν "ἀρχὴ σοφίας φόβος θεοῦ θείως λέλεκται."

[95] *Strom.* 3.4.38 (GCS 52:213: Ἀναλέγονται δὲ καὶ οὗτοι ἔκ τινων προφητικῶν περικοπῶν λέξεις ἀπανθισάμενοι καὶ συγκαττύσαντες κακῶς κατ' ἀλληγορίαν εἰρημένας ἐξ εὐθείας λαβόντες).

reading of these passages rather than the textual practice of creating scriptural anthologies itself; Clement's own *Excerpta ex Theodoto* attests this practice.[96] Clement goes on to challenge the text of one of these prophetic passages, claiming that it contains an erroneous variant. While Clement's use of Paul's scriptural quotations in Romans are repurposed in ways that mimic their Pauline epistolary context, he uses passages from Hebrews with less attention to their epistolary setting.[97] Clement clearly excerpted and repurposed scriptural passages found in Hebrews, but Clement does not model the epistolary setting of these passages in the way he does with Romans. Hebrews, then, is an apostolic scriptural archive for Clement and a resource with which Clement models his own image of Paul by mining these authorized testimonia.

Clement's reading of Hebrews is informed by his Paulinism but not in the way one might expect: The quotations and even excerpting practices on display speak to the marginality of Hebrews within Clement's *corpus Paulinum*. Clement does not ignore Hebrews, but it is not accented as Pauline. Perhaps this kind of marginalization is an indirect acknowledgment of the disputed status of Hebrews. Clement might be minimizing unnecessary exposure by resisting disputed texts. Yet Clement's distancing of Hebrews also extends to his reading of the letter's ethnic resonance, and so Clement's marginalization extends to the wider contextual features of Hebrews.

4. Clement's Formerly Jewish Paul and the Ethnic Valence of "To the Hebrews"

Together with other Christians in the second century, Clement accents the antiquity of the Jews: "Jewish people are the oldest" (*Strom.* 1.15.70). Though Clement wants to position Christians en masse as a symbolic crescendo of "Israel," he is also keen to establish a successive chain of influence from Moses to Greek philosophy to Christianity. The key for Clement here is the inclusion of Greek philosophy within the chain of influence. Indeed, Clement's

---

[96] See here André Méhat, "L'Hypothèse des 'Testimonia' à l'épreuve des Stromates: Remarques sur les citations de l'Ancien Testament chez Clément d'Alexandrie," in *La Bible et les Pères: Colloque de Strasbourg (1–3 octobre 1969)* (Paris: Presses universitaires de France, 1971), 229–42.

[97] Note also Clement's sequential reading of Philo in van den Hoek, "Techniques of Quotation," 211.

chronology in *Stromata* 1.21 connects Greek culture into a genealogy that flows back to Moses, who antedates the Greek philosophical tradition and whose Law lies behind the later appearance of (cultural, philosophical, and religious) heterogeneity.[98] Clement even reasons that since philosophy was to the Greek world what the Law was to the Hebrews, a tutor escorting them to Christ (*Strom*. 1.5.28), then it too must be a divinely bestowed covenant continually supported by providence. The two—Law and philosophy—are not equals, and the pedagogical value of the "Greek" tradition lies in its possession of a more ancient Barbarian "voice."[99] In Clement's corpus, barbarian is not a synonym for Israelites, but "ancient Jews" are considered part of the barbarians and the focus here.[100] Clement refers to the "scriptures of the barbarian philosophy" (αἱ τῆς βαρβάρου φιλοσοφίας γραφαί, *Strom*. 5.9.56) and remarks that the best of Greek philosophy is "Hebraic and enigmatic" (Ἑβραϊκὸς καὶ αἰνιγματώδης, *Strom*. 1.14.60) and has even stolen truths from the more ancient Jewish Law.[101]

---

[98] Raoul Mortley, "The Past in Clement of Alexandria: A Study of an Attempt to Define Christianity in Socio-Cultural Terms," in *Jewish and Christian Self-Definition*, vol. 1, *The Shaping of Christianity in the Second and Third Centuries*, ed. E. P. Sanders (Minneapolis: Fortress Press, 1980), 195. Mortley distinguishes Clement's conception from that found in the *Chronica* of Hippolytus, which attempts to create a "Jewish family tree" for each identifiable group within the known world (e.g., Cappadocians, Celts, and Galatians as the descendants of the sons of Noah). Mortley also notes the possible "goading" effect of contemporary Christian groups for developing Clement's historiographic vision, whether Valentinian anti-temporality or the radical rupture inherent within Marcionism (189–90).

[99] *Strom*. 6.8.67 (cf. *Strom*. 1.15–16).

[100] Similarly see Tatian's *Oration*, where "Barbarian" can refer to Christianity or to Jewish scripture (*Or*. 35.1–2, 29.2, 35.1, 41.2) but also refer to a variety of nations like the Babylonians, Egyptians, and Persians. See here Arthur J. Droge, *Homer or Moses? Early Christian Interpretations of the History of Culture* (Tübingen: Mohr Siebeck, 1989), 88–91; J. H. Waszink, "Some Observations on the Appreciation of 'the Philosophy of the Barbarians' in Early Christian Literature," in *Mélanges offerts à Mademoiselle Christine Mohrmann* (Utrecht: Spectrum, 1963), 41–56; Guy Stroumsa, *Barbarian Philosophy: The Religious Revolution of Early Christianity* (Tübingen: Mohr Siebeck, 1999), 70–78; Dietmar Wyrwa, *Die christliche Platonaneignung in den Stromateis des Clemens von Alexandrien* (Berlin: de Gruyter, 2011), 87–101. The use of "barbarians" is not universally negative, even in the Greek imagination; see, for example, Erich Gruen, *Ethnicity in the Ancient World—Did It Matter?* (Berlin: de Gruyter, 2020), 11–41; as well as Matthew R. Crawford, "Tatian, Celsus, and Christianity as 'Barbarian Philosophy' in the Late Second Century," in *The Rise of the Early Christian Intellectual*, ed. Lewis Ayres and H. Clifton Ward, AK 139 (Berlin: de Gruyter, 2020), 45–80.

[101] On the theme of Greek thievery of Hebrew philosophy see *Strom*. 1.23.153, 5.14, 6.1–4; Droge, *Homer Or Moses?*, 138–49; Alain Le Boulluec, "La rencontre de l'hellénisme et de la 'philosophie barbare' selon Clément d'Alexandrie," in *Alexandrie: Une mégapole cosmopolite*, ed. Jean Leclant (Paris: de Boccard, 1999), 186–88; Daniel Ridings, *The Attic Moses: The Dependency Theme in Some Early Christian Writers*, SGLG LIX (Göteborg: Acta Universitatis Gothoburgensis, 1995), 29–139; Stamenka E. Antonova, *Barbarian or Greek? The Charge of Barbarism and Early Christian Apologetics* (Leiden: Brill, 2019), 162–77. Moreover, the Greeks are indebted to the Jewish tradition for the very act of writing, and it is a given that Plato was a disciple of the barbarian philosophy. On the pre-Christian version of Plato's dependence on barbarian philosophy see

Clement works with formulaic dyads in which "Jewish-Law" and "Greek-philosophy" are positioned as the two preparatory-halves of the Christian whole: "Rightly, then, to the Jews belonged the Law, and to the Greeks philosophy, until the Advent."[102] The place that each half occupies in Clement's corpus is unequal.[103] The function of the Jewish tradition in this Clementine *Heilsgeschichte* is to fashion and sustain Greek philosophy as a divinely ordained preparation for Christian philosophy. The Jewish tradition then allows Clement to forge a new link in his assumed historical chain by inserting a Jewish "voice" into Greek philosophy. Accordingly, Clement invests the history of philosophy with the biblical language of covenant.[104] He concludes this discussion of covenants in *Stromata* 6.5.42:[105]

The same God that furnished both covenants was the giver of Greek philosophy to the Greeks, by which the Almighty is glorified among the Greeks. And it is clear from this. Accordingly, then, from the Hellenic training, and also from that of the Law are gathered into the one γένος of the saved λαοῦ, those who accept faith.

Here the "Law" is the default and assumed position that gains the addition of Hellenic training. Clement praises and critically evaluates these two covenants,[106] yet his interest in the philosophical covenant is evident: "Plato

---

Raoul Mortley, *The Idea of Universal History from Hellenistic Philosophy to Early Christian Historiography* (Lewiston: E. Mellen Press, 1996), 63–123.

[102] *Strom.* 6.17.159 (GCS 52:514: εἰκότως οὖν Ἰουδαίοις μὲν νόμος, Ἕλλησι δὲ φιλοσοφία μέχρι τῆς παρουσίας). *Strom.* 6.6.44 (GCS 52:453: Ἀλλ' ὡς κατὰ καιρὸν ἥκει τὸ κήρυγμα νῦν, οὕτως κατὰ καιρὸν ἐδόθη νόμος μὲν καὶ προφῆται βαρβάροις, φιλοσοφία δὲ Ἕλλησι, τὰς ἀκοὰς ἐθίζουσα πρὸς τὸ κήρυγμα). "But as the proclamation [of the Gospel] has come now at the fit time, so also at the fit time were the Law and the prophets given to the Barbarians, and philosophy to the Greeks, to fit their ears for the Gospel." *Strom.* 7.2.6: "He distributed his own bounty both to Greeks and to barbarians, and to the faithful and elect who were foreordained out of them and were called in their own season."

[103] See André Méhat, *Étude sur les "Stromates" de Clément d'Alexandrie*, Patristica Sorbonensia 7 (Paris: Éditions du Seuil, 1966), 395; Gedaliahu G. Stroumsa, *Hidden Wisdom: Esoteric Traditions and the Roots of Christian Mysticism*, SHR 70 (Leiden: Brill, 2005), 111.

[104] *Strom.* 6.8.67 (GCS 52:465: τὴν δὲ φιλοσοφίαν καὶ μᾶλλον Ἕλλησιν, οἷον διαθήκην οἰκείαν αὐτοῖς, δεδόσθαι, ὑποβάθραν οὖσαν τῆς κατὰ Χριστὸν φιλοσοφίας; "philosophy has been especially given to the Greeks, as a covenant proper to them, a stepping-stone to the philosophy of Christ").

[105] GCS 52:452: πρὸς δὲ καὶ ὅτι ὁ αὐτὸς θεὸς ἀμφοῖν ταῖν διαθήκαιν χορηγός, ὁ καὶ τῆς Ἑλληνικῆς φιλοσοφίας δοτὴρ τοῖς Ἕλλησιν, δι' ἧς ὁ παντοκράτωρ παρ' Ἕλλησι δοξάζεται, παρέστησεν. δῆλον δὲ κἀνθένδε. ἐκ γοῦν τῆς Ἑλληνικῆς παιδείας, ἀλλὰ καὶ ἐκ τῆς νομικῆς εἰς τὸ ἓν γένος τοῦ σῳζομένου συνάγονται λαοῦ οἱ τὴν πίστιν προσιέμενοι.

[106] The integrity of these covenants allows Clement to locate pockets of faith prior to the arrival of the Christian philosophy grounded in knowledge of the *logos*. He claims that the period of "unbelief" only describes the period of Christ's life and that, previously, both Jews and Greeks were led differently and through different covenants "to the perfection that is by faith" (*Strom.* 7.2.10).

gave new life to the dying ember of Hebrew philosophy."[107] Accordingly, Clement often frames Greek philosophy as the best foundation and preparation for Christianity.

In *Stromata* 7.3.19 Clement claims that Greek philosophy provides "preliminary cleansing" (προκαθαίρει) for the soul and the necessary training for "the reception of the faith, on which foundation the truth builds up the edifice of knowledge."[108] Elsewhere, Clement maintains that philosophy was given by "divine providence as a preparatory discipline (προπαιδεύουσαν) for the perfection that is by Christ."[109] Unsurprisingly, Clement defines Christians, in part, as philosophers,[110] and he designs parts of his corpus explicitly for Greeks (and Christian "heretics").[111] He notes that Paul addresses questions of philosophy throughout his corpus, and he repeatedly uses the depiction of Paul as a philosophically engaged apostle from Acts 17, where he addresses Greeks at the Areopagus in Athens. In *Stromata* 1.11.50, for instance, Clement reads the denunciation of philosophy in Colossians 2:9 through the lens of Acts 17:18, where Paul is critical of "the Epicurean variety" (specifically the denial of providence), not philosophy itself. In *Stromata* 1.19.91, he quotes the scene from Acts 17 at length (vv. 22–28); Paul explains the inscription found on the altar, "To the Unknown God," in part, by quoting from Aratus. Clement concludes, "From this it is clear that by using poetic examples from the *Phaenomena* of Aratus he approves the best statements of the Greeks."[112] Clement also uses

---

Accordingly, there were those who were "righteous according to the Law" and "righteous according to philosophy" (ἐν δικαιοσύνῃ τῇ κατὰ νόμον καὶ κατὰ φιλοσοφίαν; *Strom.* 6.6.45 [GCS 52:454]). Jesus' words in Matthew 9:22, "Your faith has saved you," do not mean that those who believe in any way are saved, for works must follow; rather Jesus was referring to Jews "who kept the Law and lived blamelessly, who wanted only faith in the Lord" (*Strom.* 6.14.108).

[107] *Paed.* 2.1.18.

[108] GCS 17:14: φιλοσοφία δὲ ἡ Ἑλληνικὴ οἷον προκαθαίρει καὶ προεθίζει τὴν ψυχὴν εἰς παραδοχὴν πίστεως, ἐφ᾽ ᾗ τὴν γνῶσιν ἐποικοδομεῖ ἡ ἀλήθεια.

[109] *Strom.* 6.17.153 (GCS 52:510: ὥστ᾽ οὐκ ἄτοπον καὶ τὴν φιλοσοφίαν ἐκ τῆς θείας προνοίας δεδόσθαι προπαιδεύουσαν εἰς τὴν διὰ Χριστοῦ τελείωσιν).

[110] The "Gnostic Christians" are a group of "philosophers" (*Strom.* 2.10.46); Clement describes those assembled in "ecclesia from on high" as the "philosophers of god" (οἱ φιλόσοφοι συνάγονται τοῦ θεοῦ; *Strom.* 6.14.108 [GCS 52:486]).

[111] The opening of book 7 is a good example of this: "Prove to the Greeks that the Gnostic alone is truly devout." Yet in *Strom.* 1.1.15, Clement claims that his notes "will not hesitate to use the highest examples from philosophy and all the other educational preliminaries." Clement also brings "heretics" into his direct view in *Strom.* 2.1.2.

[112] *Strom.* 1.19.91 (GCS 52:58–59: ἐξ ὧν δῆλον ὅτι καὶ ποιητικοῖς χρώμενος παραδείγμασιν ἐκ τῶν Ἀράτου Φαινομένων δοκιμάζει τὰ παρ᾽ Ἕλλησι καλῶς εἰρημένα).

this passage to show confluence between Paul and Plato, who appear together as a harmonious pair throughout the *Stromata*.[113]

In *Stromata* 6.15.117–19, Clement argues that the philosopher is the best candidate for becoming a Gnostic.[114] To illustrate this point, he uses the image of the wild olive branch grafted into the choice root of the olive tree from Romans 11:17 ("So also the philosopher, resembling the wild olive...").[115] He notes that there are four ways to engraft a branch, which each illustrate a way of receiving the word. The first graft, between the wood and the bark, reflects the simple and superficial reception of the *logos*. The second grafting comes by inserting the "cultivated branch into a cleft in the wood." This graft reflects those who have "studied philosophy" and have cut through their "dogmas" in order to perceive truth. Given the symbolic pair of Greek and Jew, Clement adds, "So also in the case of the Jews, by opening up the old writing" (ὣς δὲ καὶ Ἰουδαίοις διοιχθείσης τῆς παλαιᾶς γραφῆς).[116] The final graft is a form of "budding" that features the most careful insertion of the branch in the eye of the wood.[117] This regards the "Gnostic teaching" and is "of most service in the case of the cultivated trees." The discussion is framed as a focus on the place of Greek philosophers; they are the cultivated trees. The comment on Jewish reading of the old writings is a formulaic aside, one half of a symbolic pair that is decidedly not his main interest.[118]

---

[113] *Strom.* 5.11.75, "'For it was not from need that God made the world; that he might reap honors from men and the other gods and demons, winning a kind of revenue from creation, and from us, fumes, and from the gods and demons, their proper ministries,' says Plato. Most instructively, therefore, says Paul in the Acts of the Apostles: 'The God that made the world, and all things in it, being the Lord of heaven and earth, dwelleth not in temples made with hands; neither is worshiped by men's hands, as if he needed anything; seeing that it is he himself that giveth to all breath, and life, and all things.'" Paul and Plato are repeatedly cited in confirmation of each other (*Strom.* 1.1.10, 1.8.42, 4.7.44–46). On Clement's synthesis of Paul and Plato see Eric Osborn, "Paul and Plato in Second-Century Ethics," *StPatr* 15 (1984): 474–85; Lilla, *Clement of Alexandria*, 9–59; A. C. Outler, "The Platonism of Clement of Alexandria," *JR* 20 (1940): 217–40.

[114] Clement's interest in the Greek part of his symbolic pair is noticeable: "A camel will pass through a needle's eye sooner than a rich man will become a philosopher" (*Strom.* 2.5.22). Clement even switches out a "particularistic" Judaism for a "particularistic" Philosophy as the contrast for "universalistic" Christianity (*Strom.* 6.18.167). In *Strom.* 1, he divides the Torah up according to the three parts of the Platonic model (see Paget, "Christian Exegesis," 492), and in *Protr.* 1.9.1 Clement exchanges the questions from the Jewish priests and Levites for quotations from Homer (see Dawson, *Allegorical Readers*, 200).

[115] Romans 11:17 ("If some of the branches were broken off, and you the wild olive shoot had been grafted in their place and become partaker of the root and the fatness of the olive tree..." [Εἰ δέ τινες τῶν κλάδων ἐξεκλάσθησαν, σὺ δὲ ἀγριέλαιος ὢν ἐνεκεντρίσθης ἐν αὐτοῖς καὶ συγκοινωνὸς τῆς ῥίζης τῆς πιότητος τῆς ἐλαίας ἐγένου]).

[116] GCS 52:491.

[117] The third graft is forced in, reflecting the heretics who are made to return. On this aspect of the passage see Le Boulluec, *La notion d'hérésie*, 357.

[118] From this passage Robert Wilde concludes, "[Jews] are placed on the same rank and place as the Greek philosophers." *The Treatment of the Jews in the Greek Christian Writers of the First Three Centuries*, SP 81 (Washington, DC: Catholic University of America Press, 1949), 172. However,

4.1. Hebrews Thinking Jewishly

In *Stromata* book 5, Clement comments on the occasion prompting Paul's letter to the Hebrews. He cites Hebrews 5:12–14—a passage admonishing the implied readers that though they should be "teachers" (διδάσκαλοι), they need to be taught once again the "the basic elements of the oracles of God" (τὰ στοιχεῖα τῆς ἀρχῆς τῶν λογίων τοῦ θεοῦ).[119] The progression of the Gnostic is laborious and many remain "ordinary believers."[120] After all, there were certainly unwritten things delivered to "the Hebrews," and yet they consume "milk" when they should eat "meat."[121] Explaining the reason for their failure, he adds, "as if they had grown old in the old covenant" (ὡς ἂν ἐγγηράσαντες τῇ διαθήκῃ τῇ παλαιᾷ).[122]

For Clement, the Hebrews have become habituated in the wrong "thing," τῇ διαθήκῃ τῇ παλαιᾷ. Since Clement describes the true Gnostic as one who has "grown old in the study of the actual scriptures," the problem facing the Hebrews was not their aging, but the "location" of their aging.[123] The idea of the διαθήκῃ τῇ παλαιᾷ in *Stromata* 5.10.62 is likely a way of referring to the entire swath of ways of knowing and thinking that for Clement are prior to the emergence of Christianity. As though elaborating this phrase, Clement cites the same passage from Hebrews and notes that the Hebrew audience justly received Paul's admonishment in 5:12–14 because they were

---

Clement's context is driven by the philosopher and an isolated reading of passages juxtaposing Jews and Greeks misses the empty symbolism of the Jewish half.

[119] The admonishment in this passage confirms for Clement what others have called a leitmotiv in his corpus; the highest form of gnosis is purposefully enigmatic in order to prompt habitual study and prevent indiscriminate access. On this point see Lilla, *Clement of Alexandria*, 144–48 (citing *Strom.* 1.9.4, 5.19.2–3, 5.56.3, 6.15.126.), and H. Clifton Wards, "'Symbolic Interpretation Is Most Useful': Clement of Alexandria's Scriptural Imagination," *JECS* 25.4 (2017): 548–51.

[120] *Strom.* 7.7.79: τοῖς κοινότερον πεπιστευκόσι. In *Strom.* 5.9 Clement notes that limited attainment, even limited access, is appropriate, for there are advantages to "veiling" the truth. He reasons positively and negatively: light shining through a veil provides added reflections, but also reveals defects and keeps the benefits of wisdom from those who have not labored to obtain them. The philosophical tradition is once again exemplary for Clement. Hipparchus the Pythagorean was expelled from his philosophical school for writing in plain language, and Plato, the Epicureans, and the Stoics "concealed many things," keeping their disciples from reading their philosophical writings indiscriminately. They must first demonstrate that they are "genuine philosophers" (Clement goes on to discuss the mystery cults and that Platonic myths must be read allegorically).

[121] *Strom.* 5.10.62 citing Hebrews 5.12c–14. On the theme of milk (including 1 Cor 3:1–3) in Clement see Anneweis van de Bunt (Hoek), "Milk and Honey in the Theology of Clement of Alexandria," in *Fides Sacramenti—Sacramentum Fidei: Studies in Honour of Pieter Smulders*, ed. Hans Jorg Auf der Maur, L. Bakker, A. van de Bunt, and J. Waldram (Assen: Van Gorcum, 1981), 27–39; John David Penniman, *Raised on Christian Milk: Food and the Formation of the Soul in Early Christianity* (New Haven: Yale University Press, 2017), 102–5; Benjamin Edsall, *The Reception of Paul and Early Christian Initiation: History and Hermeneutics* (Cambridge: Cambridge University Press, 2019), 93–125.

[122] *Strom.* 5.10.62.   [123] *Strom.* 7.16.104.

"declining again from faith to the Law" (εἰς νόμον ἐκ πίστεως).[124] The terminology packed into these brief occasional descriptions is a dense constellation. These terms—νόμον, πίστεως, τῇ διαθήκῃ τῇ παλαιᾷ, and the unspoken but equally present "new covenant"—compress Clement's larger characterization of Jews and conception of the history of Judaism into this description of the occasion for Hebrews. For the Hebrews to "decline" (ἐπανακάμπτω) again from "faith" to the "Law" is to say that the Hebrews were acting like Jews.

Clement describes Jewish thinking as instinctively local and ethnically confined. When the rich man asks Jesus, "Who is a neighbor?" in Luke 10:29, Clement is careful to note that Jesus did not limit the idea of neighbor as the Jews do, namely, by blood, citizenship, proselytism, or some other measures of Law obedience such as circumcision.[125] Clement also claims that Jews are particularly prone to focus on quasi-divine and celestial objects. In *Stromata* 6.5.41, Clement cites a description of Greek and Jewish modes of worship from the *Kerygma Petri* as a means of describing the novel yet superior mode of Christian understanding. The Greeks lack the "perfect knowledge that was delivered by the Son," while the Jews, who claim exclusive knowledge of God, "adore" angelic beings and celestial objects.[126] Clement also focuses his criticism on Jewish reading. Citing Romans 10:2–3, Clement grabs hold of Paul's description of Jewish "zeal for God" (ζῆλον θεοῦ) and unpacks this zeal with a flurry of descriptions: They lack faith in the "prophetic power" of the Law, they follow the "bare letter" and "fear" (λόγῳ δὲ ψιλῷ καὶ φόβῳ), not the "inner meaning" and "faith" (οὐ διαθέσει καὶ πίστει).[127]

Clement provides an example of reading Jewishly (ἰουδαϊκῶς) in *Paedagogus* 1.6.34: Failing to identify that the particle in 1 Corinthians 3:2, "as," in "as little ones," indicates the presence of a metaphor that modifies "I fed you with milk" is a "ἰουδαϊκῶς" kind of reading. The specifics of this passage aside, the reading Clement wants to discard, the one that fails to recognize the presence of a metaphor, is "Jewish."[128] On the other hand,

---

[124] *Strom.* 6.8.62 (GCS 52:463: διὸ καὶ τοῖς Ἑβραίοις γράφων τοῖς ἐπανακάμπτουσιν εἰς νόμον ἐκ πίστεως).

[125] *Quis dives salvetur* 28.3–4 (GCS 17:178: τὸν πρὸς αἵματος οὐδὲ τὸν πολίτην οὐδὲ τὸν προσήλυτον οὐδὲ τὸν ὁμοίως περιτετμημένον οὐδὲ τῷ ἑνὶ καὶ ταὐτῷ νόμῳ χρώμενον).

[126] *Strom.* 6.5.41. Clement cites the example of the moon, which, if hidden, prevents Jews from holding the Sabbath and various festivals.

[127] *Strom.* 2.9.42.

[128] *Paed.* 1.6.34 (SC 70:172: 'Οὔ μοι γὰρ δοκεῖ ἰουδαϊκῶς ἐκδέχεσθαι; "For it does not seem to me that the expression is to be taken Jewishly").

Clement refers to Jewish ways of thinking in bodily terms, namely, as "fleshly" (σαρκικός), which similarly focus on the idea of "outwardly" and literal. In *Stromata* 6.15.124, Clement cites the placating power of Timothy's circumcision by the hand of Paul to keep the "Jews who believed" (τοὺς ἐξ Ἰουδαίων πιστεύοντας) from "revolting from the faith" (ἀποστῶσι τῆς πίστεως). It is this portion of the Law that Clement says was formerly understood in a "fleshly" way (σαρκικώτερον προειλημμένα).[129] A σαρκικός way of reading is what precludes Jews from understanding the true meaning of circumcision. Clement's criticism of thinking "fleshly" is an ethnically coded way of reading "Jewishly."[130]

Scholars have often noticed that Clement's description of Jews lacks some of the vitriol of texts written *adversus Judaeos*. Robert Wilde, for example, uses "impartial," "objective," "almost impersonal" to describe the way Clement describes and refers to Jews. For Wilde, Clement's Greek audience drives his concern, and the "notice that he takes of Jews, then, is only incidental to the end that he was pursuing."[131] James Carleton Paget pushes back against Wilde's claim that Clement's Greek audience informs his "impersonal" engagement with the Jewish tradition, noting that the criticisms leveled against Christians by Origen's Celsus are often Jewish, and that arguments *adversus Judaeos* have been used by Christians confronted by pagan criticism.[132] Clement's concern to address Greeks need not preclude engagement with Jews. Carleton Paget suggests that Clement's "disengaged" and "incidental" relation with Jews stems from a lack of historical interaction with contemporary Jews in a post-Jewish-revolt Alexandria.[133] To Carleton Paget's point, Clement's references to Jews reflect

---

[129] GCS 52:494.

[130] Heidi Wendt, *At the Temple Gates: The Religion of Freelance Experts in the Roman Empire* (Oxford: Oxford University Press, 2016), finds an increase of representations of foreigners in the late republic, especially in Rome, which gave rise to an increase in particular qualities and skills attributed to regions and ethnic groups (76–81). Certain skills and types of knowledge were given an ethnic coding: There is a certain astronomical expertise among the Chaldeans, and a magus is known to be a Persian expert endowed with particular skills and esoteric knowledge. Wendt notes how Josephus relishes the particular talents that Judeans have for exorcism, and he is ready to identify those Judeans who are impostors and false prophets (94). Those claiming expertise in ethnically coded skills may naturalize their proficiency on the basis of ancestry or provenance. Demarcating expertise also requires identifying charlatans and impostors. Accordingly, competition surrounds freelance experts, perhaps especially to capitalize on Roman interest in the exotic.

[131] Wilde, *Treatment of the Jew*, 180.

[132] James Carleton Paget, "Clement of Alexandria and the Jews," *SJT* 51.1 (1998): 94.

[133] Carleton Paget's larger aim in reframing the context for Clement's relation to Jews is to challenge Miriam Taylor, who, following in the tradition of Adolf von Harnack and pushing back against Marcel Simon, places Clement in the category of "symbolic anti-Judaism." See Paget, *Anti-Judaism and Early Christian Identity: A Critique of the Scholarly Consensus* (Leiden: Brill, 1995),

a kind of distance. In *Stromata* 1.15.70 Clement refers to Clearchus the Peripatetic, who claims he knew a Jew who studied with Aristotle. In *Stromata* 2.1.2, as Clement targets the Greeks, he notes that "it may turn out that the Jew in listening to us could experience an easy conversion." This posture, facing the Greeks and tangentially thinking about Jews, epitomizes Clement's interests.

Clement's comment on the occasion for Hebrews in *Stromata* 6.8.62, for example, is a supplemental and formulaic defense of Paul's interest in Greek philosophy:

> For Paul too, in the Epistles, plainly does not disparage philosophy, but deems it unworthy of the man who has attained to the elevation of the Gnostic any more to go back to the Hellenic "philosophy," figuratively calling it "the rudiments of this world," as being most rudimentary, and a preparatory training for the truth. Wherefore also, writing to the Hebrews, who were declining again from faith to the Law, he says, "Have you not need again of one to teach you which are the first principles of the oracles of God, and are become such as have need of milk, and not of strong

---

132; cf. also James Carleton Paget, "Anti-Judaism and Early Christian Identity," *ZAC* 1 (1997): 195–225. Taylor argues that early Christian anti-Judaism is preeminently an intra-Christian polemical strategy designed for the purposes of self-definition. Taylor's work generated a flurry of reaction, and scholars have typically settled in the space between Simon and Taylor. See, for example, Judith M. Lieu, *Image and Reality: The Jews in the World of the Christians in the Second Century* (Edinburgh: T&T Clark, 1996); Andrew Jacobs, "The Lion and the Lamb: Reconsidering 'Jewish-Christian Relations' in Antiquity," in *The Ways That Never Parted: Jews and Christians in Late Antiquity and the Early Middle Ages*, ed. A. H. Becker and A. Y. Reed (Tübingen: Mohr Siebeck, 2003), 95–118. On Jews and Jewish literature in Alexandria see Jan N. Bremmer, "The First Pogrom? Religious Violence in Alexandria in 38 CE?," in *Alexandria: Hub of the Hellenistic World*, ed. Benjamin Schliesser, Jan Rüggemeier, Thomas J. Kraus, and Jörg Frey, WUNT 460 (Tübingen: Mohr Siebeck, 2021), 245–59; Kimberley Czajkowski, "Jewish Associations in Alexandria?," in *Private Associations and Jewish Communities in the Hellenistic and Roman Cities*, ed. Benedikt Eckhardt, JSJSup 191 (Leiden: Brill, 2019), 76–96; Jan Dochhorn, "Jüdisch-alexandrinische Literatur? Eine Problemanzeige und ein Überblick über diejenige Literatur, die potentiell dem antiken Judentum entstammt," in *Alexandria*, ed. Tobias Georges, Felix Albrecht, and Reinhard Feldmeier, COMS 1 (Tübingen: Mohr Siebeck, 2013), 285–312; Tobias Nicklas, "Jews and Christians? Sketches from Second Century Alexandria," in *Jews and Christians—Parting Ways in the First Two Centuries CE? Reflections on the Gains and Losses of a Model*, ed. Matthias Konradt, Judith Lieu, Laura Nasrallah, Jens Schröter, and Gregory E. Sterling, BZNW 253 (Berlin: de Gruyter, 2021), 347–79; Roelof van den Broek, "Juden und Christen in Alexandrien im 2. und 3. Jahrhundert," in *Studies in Gnosticism and Alexandrian Christianity* (Leiden: Brill, 1996), 179–96; James Carleton Paget, "Jews and Christians in Ancient Alexandria from the Ptolemies to Caracalla," in *Alexandria, Real and Imagined*, ed. Anthony Hirst and Michael Silk (Aldershot: Ashgate, 2004), 143–66; M. B. Trapp, "Images of Alexandria in the Writings of the Second Sophistic," in Hirst and Silk, *Alexandria, Real and Imagined*, 113–32; A. F. J. Klijn, "Jewish Christianity in Egypt," in *The Roots of Egyptian Christianity*, ed. Birger A. Pearson and James E. Goehring, Studies in Antiquity and Christianity (Philadelphia: Fortress Press, 1986), 161–75; Aryeh Kasher, *The Jews in Hellenistic and Roman Egypt: The Struggle for Equal Rights*, TSAJ 7 (Tübingen: Mohr Siebeck, 1978).

meat?" So also to the Colossians, who were Greek converts, "Beware lest any man spoil you by philosophy and vain deceit, after the tradition of men, after the rudiments of this world, and not after Christ"—enticing them again to return to philosophy, the elementary doctrine.[134]

Philosophy and the Law are preparatory for the Gnostic, and Paul does not disparage either per se. Rather, as preparations, one must not slip back into the partial manifestation of knowledge contained in these two forms of "elementary doctrine." The passage, however, is designed to show Paul's criticism of the elementary form of philosophy and not a totalizing criticism of the philosophical tradition The occasion for Hebrews functions as a counterexample to affirm this claim.

4.2. When Paul Was a Ἰουδαῖος

In 1 Corinthians 13:11–12, Paul uses the metaphor of a child growing into an adult to illustrate a natural and fitting progression. Paul seeks to affirm the supremacy and abiding nature of love over prophetic powers, mysteries, and even selfless acts, which terminate in what he earlier calls τὸ τέλειον:

> ὅτε ἤμην νήπιος, ἐλάλουν ὡς νήπιος, ἐφρόνουν ὡς νήπιος, ἐλογιζόμην ὡς νήπιος· ὅτε γέγονα ἀνήρ, κατήργηκα τὰ τοῦ νηπίου. βλέπομεν γὰρ ἄρτι δι' ἐσόπτρου ἐν αἰνίγματι, τότε δὲ πρόσωπον πρὸς πρόσωπον.

> When I was a child, I spoke like a child, I thought like a child, I reasoned like a child; when I became an adult, I put an end to childish ways. For now, we see in a mirror, dimly, but then we will see face to face.

Clement quotes a modified version of this passage in the first book of the *Paedagogus* as he mounts an argument that Christians are best defined as

---

[134] *Strom.* 6.8.62–63 (GCS 52:463: ἐπεὶ καὶ Παῦλος ἐν ταῖς ἐπιστολαῖς οὐ φιλοσοφίαν διαβάλλων φαίνεται, τὸν δὲ τοῦ γνωστικοῦ μεταλαμβάνοντα ὕψους οὐκέτι παλινδρομεῖν ἀξιοῖ ἐπὶ τὴν Ἑλληνικὴν φιλοσοφίαν, "στοιχεῖα τοῦ κόσμου" ταύτην ἀλληγορῶν, στοιχειωτικήν τινα οὖσαν καὶ προπαιδείαν τῆς ἀληθείας. διὸ καὶ τοῖς Ἑβραίοις γράφων τοῖς ἐπανακάμπτουσιν εἰς νόμον ἐκ πίστεως" [ἢ] πάλιν φησί "χρείαν ἔχετε τοῦ διδάσκειν ὑμᾶς, τίνα τὰ στοιχεῖα τῆς ἀρχῆς τῶν λογίων τοῦ θεοῦ, καὶ γεγόνατε χρείαν ἔχοντες γάλακτος καὶ οὐ στερεᾶς τροφῆς." ὡσαύτως ἄρα καὶ τοῖς ἐξ Ἑλλήνων ἐπιστρέφουσι Κολοσσαεῦσι· "βλέπετε μή τις ὑμᾶς ἔσται ὁ συλαγωγῶν διὰ τῆς φιλοσοφίας καὶ κενῆς ἀπάτης κατὰ τὴν παράδοσιν τῶν ἀνθρώπων, κατὰ τὰ στοιχεῖα τοῦ τῆς κατὰ τὴν παράδοσιν τῶν ἀνθρώπων, κατὰ τὰ στοιχεῖα τοῦ κόσμου τούτου καὶ οὐ κατὰ Χριστόν," δελεάζων αὖθις εἰς φιλοσοφίαν ἀναδραμεῖν, τὴν στοιχειώδη διδασκαλίαν).

children. Clement then gathers the positive scriptural references regarding children while also acknowledging negative references to thinking and behaving like a child. Clement's harmonization is quite simple: "The word 'childish' can signify these two different things, one good and one bad" (*Paed*. 1.6.33). Still, having to account for Paul's self-description as a former child in 1 Corinthians 13:11, Clement chooses to read Paul's metaphor as a self-description of his own Jewishness in *Paedagogus* 1.6.34:[135]

> "ὅτε ἤμην νήπιος," τουτέστιν ὅτε ἤμην Ἰουδαῖος, Ἑβραῖος γὰρ ἄνωθεν ἦν, "ὡς νήπιος ἐφρόνουν," ἐπειδὴ εἱπόμην τῷ νόμῳ· "ἐπὶ δὲ γέγονα ἀνήρ," οὐκέτι τὰ τοῦ νηπίου, τουτέστι τὰ τοῦ νόμου, ἀλλὰ τὰ τοῦ ἀνδρὸς φρονῶ, τουτέστι τὰ τοῦ Χριστοῦ...

> "When I was a child," that is to say, "When I was a Jew" (for he was originally a Hebrew) "I thought as a child," since I followed the Law; "Now that I have become a man," no longer thinking the things of a child—that is, of the Law—but those of a man—that is, of Christ...

Clement reads "child" as a metaphor for being a Ἰουδαῖος, which is understood as a way of thinking. Clement describes Paul's "childhood," the period in which he was a Ἰουδαῖος, as the time he followed the Law.[136] However, given the cognitive language in 1 Corinthians 13:11 (thinking [ἐφρόνουν] and reasoning [ἐλογιζόμην] like a child), Clement uses Paul's Jewishness as the way he "thought." The Law itself is not a problem for Clement, as he stresses the essential integrity of the Law as a gift, a "measure of what is just," that which "leads to the divine."[137] It is an "old gift" given by the *logos* through Moses (*Paed*. 1.7.59) by which the *logos* educates (*Paed*. 1.11.96).[138] Nor is Clement critical of "following the Law" in the sense of obedience, as Christ came "to reveal what was possible to humanity by way of obedience

---

[135] SC 70:172.

[136] Just prior, Clement read Paul's childishness as a way of describing "his manner living under the Law," the point in Paul's life "when he persecuted the Word" (*Paed*. 1.6.33). Here Clement claims that Ἰουδαῖος is what Paul was as a child.

[137] *Strom*. 1.26.167. To be sure, Clement does not hesitate to employ the trope of Jewish hard-heartedness (*Paed*. 2.2.32), adopt the language of "transference" in reference to covenants, and suggest that Jews were particularly "prone" to certain social mores that resulted in their Egyptian slavery (*Strom*. 3.12.90; also *Paed*. 1.11.96–97, 2.1.17). But he does not use these tropes as reasons for giving the Law.

[138] Cf. also *Paed*. 2.1.17 and *Strom*. 3.6.36. Earlier in the second century, Justin Martyr claimed that the Law of Moses was a temporary response to curtail Jewish hard-heartedness; now obsolete save for its function to mark out Jews for divine judgment in the first and second centuries CE (*Dial*. 16.218.2–3, 46.5). Clement reverses the order of Justin's account.

to God's commandments."[139] Clement freely defines Christians in moral terms stemming from faith and the pursuit of moral perfection in accordance with the Law.[140] Rather, Clement reads Paul's metaphor as a juxtaposition of two ways of thinking. He does not key into the "naturalness" of the progression from child to adult, which is central in Paul's own metaphor. For Clement, thinking like a Jew by following the Law does not naturally lead to thinking the things of Christ. Rather, Clement simply judges different ways of thinking as being childish or mature. Paul's metaphorical "adulthood," read as the advanced capacity and quality of his thinking, is his Christianity.[141] In *Paedagogus* 1.6.34, what Clement wants erase from Paul is any indication that he still thinks like a Jew.

Clement's uses of Ἑβραῖος and Ἰουδαῖος lack rigid systemization, and, to some extent, the terms are interchangeable. Still, "Hebrew" in Clement's corpus carries an archaizing resonance and is often used to describe those aspects of ancient Israelite history that Clement considers laudatory and commendable, that is properly pre-Christian,[142] and when claiming Jewish influence on Greek philosophy.[143] Although these references have an air of neutrality, key negative descriptions of ancient Ἰουδαῖοι sharpens the positive edge to Ἑβραῖος considerably: Jews asked for a king under the prophetic career of Samuel and thereby "transgressed" (*Paed.* 3.4.27), Hebrews are recipients of the spiritually significant Manna (*Paed.* 1.6.41) and the

---

[139] *Strom.* 7.2.9.

[140] In *Strom.* 3.18.106, reading Galatians 2.19–20: "'Through the Law,' he says, 'I am dead to the Law in order to live to God. I am crucified with Christ. It is no longer I who am alive' in the way I used to live, lustfully, 'but Christ who is alive in me,' making me blessedly pure through obedience to the commandments." Similarly, *Strom.* 3.12.95: "So when the apostle says, 'Put on the new humanity created after God's way,' he is addressing us; we were shaped as we are by the Almighty's will. When he speaks of 'old' and 'new,' he is not referring to birth and rebirth, but to disobedient and obedient ways of living."

[141] In *Strom.* 7.1.1 Clement uses τὸν χριστιανισμὸν (GCS 17:3).

[142] For example, Hebrews in Egypt (*Strom.* 1.23.151, 1.23.157); the cloud followed Hebrews (*Protr.* 1.8); Hebrews receive manna in the wilderness (*Paed.* 1.6.41) and the rock flowing with water (*Paed.* 2.2.19); Susanna and the sister of Moses are superior to all the women among the Hebrews (*Strom.* 4.19.123); Hebrews built the temple/tabernacle (*Strom.* 5.5.28); Psalmist as Hebrew king (Psalm 33.1–3 in *Paed.* 2.4.41); ancient Hebrew kings wear crowns and jewels on their heads, symbolic for "Christ" (*Paed.* 2.8.61); Hebrew prophets (*Strom.* 1.17.87; 1.21.109); Hebrews during the period of Judges (*Strom.* 1. 21.109); also used for Jews in the early centuries BCE (Apion wrote *Against the Jews* against Hebrews; *Strom.* 1.21.101). Still, not every reference is positive; see *Paed.* 1.10.90 (on the golden calf); *Strom.* 2.18.8 (seduced by Midianite women); *Paed.* 2.13.126 (Hosea "reproaches the Hebrews").

[143] In *Protr.* 6.70 Clement claims that Greek beliefs about God derive from the Hebrew Sibyl (citing *Sib. Or.* 3.586–88, 590–94) and that Gyllus (Xenophon, *Memorabilia* 4.3.13–14) used the Sibyl as a source (*Protr.* 6.71). See also *Strom.* 1.21.101, where Clement claims that the Greeks plagiarized the *Hebrews*.

water from the rock (*Paed.* 2.2.19, cf. Exodus 17.6), Jews worship the golden calf (*Paed.* 1.8.90), Hebrews "live" by "doing" the Law (*Strom.* 2.10.46; Lev 18:5). For the most part, Clement maintains "Hebrew" as a protected space from "Jew," allowing him to praise and criticize ancient Israelites simultaneously.[144] Further, Clement positions Hebrews as the object of favor within the overarching divine plan for history.[145] He notes that there is "one salvation for the righteous" in the era prior to the coming of the *logos*.[146] On this point he cites the authority of the *Shepherd of Hermas*, who, when referring to the "dead" in *Similitudes*. 9.16.5-7 knows that there were "people of righteousness" before the time of Jesus and even before the giving of the Law.[147] Clement never explicitly connects the group of "righteous" within Israel who obeyed the Law and obtained salvation with the "Hebrews," but he does frame Hebrews as the group targeted by Christ, who arrived as "the model of true philosophy to the Hebrews" (*Paed.* 2.11.117).[148]

Despite these archaizing resonances, Hebrews are still Jews for Clement. The permeability between Ἑβραῖος and Ἰουδαῖος is evident in *Stromata* 6.15.124 and 7.9.53, where Clement moves freely between description of "ordinary Jews" (Ἰουδαίων τῶν χυδαίων)[149] and Hebrews. The apostle must be cautious when handling two understandings of circumcision, the one "of the heart" and the one that "means nothing." If presented untactfully, Paul would "drive out the Hebrews who were still hesitant to break off from the συναγωγῆς" (*Strom.* 7.9.53).[150] Clement's description of the occasion for Paul's letter to the Hebrews channels his criticism of Jews and reveals the instability of his ethnic reasoning. Clement configures the ethnicity of Paul as "Hebrew" and not "Jew," and yet he frames Paul's Hebrew audience as Hebrew but acting Jewishly. Clement conceptualizes Jewishness as both ephemeral and essential; the Hebrews are stuck between being non-Jewish and Jewish. Clement takes care to protect his image of Paul from anything too Jewish, yet the very category that releases Paul fixes the audience of

---

[144] A good example of this is his quotation of 1 Corinthians 9:20 in *Strom.* 1.1.15, "As the apostle puts it, it is reasonable to become a Jew by reason of the Hebrews and those subject to the Law; it is also reasonable to become Greek for the sake of the Greeks. We want to gain them all."

[145] But then again, in *Strom.* 6.15.124 "Jews" are those who believe.

[146] *Strom.* 4.15.125.   [147] *Strom.* 2.9.43–44. Cf. also *Strom.* 3.6.46, 5.6.38.

[148] Cf. *Strom.* 6.6.45 ("that he should bring to repentance those belonging to the Hebrews"). On early Christian identity as the restoration of Hebrews in the Pseudo-Clementines see Denise Kimber Buell, *Why This New Race? Ethnic Reasoning in Early Christianity* (New York: Columbia University Press, 2005), 70–72.

[149] See *Strom.* 7.18.109 (GCS 17:77).

[150] GCS 17:39: ἔτι τοὺς ἀκρωμένους τῶν Ἑβραίων ἀπορρῆξαι τῆς συναγωγῆς ἀναγκάσῃ.

Πρὸς Ἑβραίους. Such oscillation between ethnicity as fixed and as malleable places Clement within a larger tradition of early Christian ethnic reasoning, conceived as both fixed and fluid, which attempts to create and account for interpretive differences.[151]

For Clement, a "fleshly" reading fails to understand the symbolic, enigmatic, and hidden mysteries of scripture, which the *logos* has revealed to the apostles and interpreted according to the "ecclesiastical canon."[152] In *Stromata* 6.15.132, Clement compares those who "look at the body of the scriptures (τὸ σῶμα τῶν γραφῶν)" with those who "see through to the thoughts and what it is signified by the names."[153] These bodily descriptions are ethnically coded ways of referring to "reading Jewishly"; the inability to perceive the higher form of gnosis hidden within Israel's textual tradition. Further, Clement uses the illustration of the ritually clean animal from Leviticus 11:3 (chews the cud *and* parts the hoof) to describe Jews as less-than interpreters in *Stromata* 7.18.109.[154] Here Jews are the class of animal that chews the cud since they have the "oracles of God in their mouth" yet do not divide the hoof, not having "the firm footing of faith." Clement concludes that "these kinds of animals are liable to slip," not balanced by the "doubleness of faith."[155] The idea of an animal's "flawed" anatomy is used to create a hermeneutical criticism. The allegorical correspondence informing this criticism is rooted in ontology.

In the case of Paul's ethnicity in *Paedagogus* 1.6.34 noted above, Clement employs Ἰουδαῖος as a *non-ethnic* description of a way of thinking in order

---

[151] Buell, *Why This New Race?*, 1–35. Cf. also Denise Kimber Buell, "Race and Universalism in Early Christianity," *JECS* 10.4 (2002): 429–68.

[152] Cf. David Brakke, "Jewish Flesh and Christian Spirit in Athanasius of Alexandria," *JECS* 9.4 (2001): 453–81; Paget, "Christian Exegesis," 491–97. On Clement's "allegorical" terminology see W. den Boer, "De allegorese in het werk van Clemens Alexandrinus" (PhD diss., University of Leiden, 1940); H. Clifton Ward, "'Symbolic Interpretation Is Most Useful': Clement of Alexandria's Scriptural Imagination," *JECS* 25.4 (2017): 531–60; Andrew Dinan, "Αἴνιγμα and Αἰνίττομαι in the Works of Clement of Alexandria," *SP* 46 (2010): 175–80. On the idea of the "symbol" and the Egyptian hieroglyphic in Clement and Porphyry see Peter T. Struck, *The Birth of the Symbol: Ancient Readers at the Limits of Their Texts* (Princeton: Princeton University Press, 2004), 198–203. See also Heinz Ohme, *Kanon ekklesiastikos: Die Bedeutung des Altkirchlichen Kanonbegriffs*, Arbeiten zur Kirchengeschichte 67 (Berlin: de Gruyter, 1998), 122–55; Tomas Bokedal, "The Rule of Faith: Tracing Its Origins," *JTS* 7.2 (2013): 223–55.

[153] GCS 52:498. Cf. *Strom*. 3.4.38, "taking literally (εὐθείας) what was meant allegorically (ἀλληγορίαν)."

[154] Heretics divide the hoof but do not chew the cud (they "take their stand on the name of the Father and of the Son, but have no power to bring out the exact perspicuity of the oracles by subtle distinctions and by smoothing away of difficulties"). Clement's Gnostics chew the cud and divide the hoof.

[155] GCS 17:78: ὅθεν καὶ ὀλισθηρὸν τὸ γένος τῶν τοιούτων θρεμμάτων, ὡς ἂν μὴ σχιδανοπόδων ὄντων μηδὲ τῇ διπλόῃ τῆς πίστεως ἐπερειδομένων.

to distance Paul from his ethnically coded criticism of Jews as problematic thinkers. The category of "Hebrew" does the ethnic lifting Clement needs. However, the ethnic valence of this term was not lost on Clement. He immediately includes a parenthetical comment as soon as the logic of his reading of Paul's Jewishness takes shape. Paul can be temporarily Jewish because he was "originally" Hebrew (Ἑβραῖος γὰρ ἄνωθεν ἦν). Similarly, Clement describes Moses in *Stromata* 1.23.151; he was "originally Chaldean [ἄνωθεν τὸ γένος Χαλδαῖος] born in Egypt."[156]

Clement both fixes and untethers Jewishness in order to suit his aims. On the one hand, Clement's ethnically coded descriptions of Jewish thinking and reading are essentializing counter-descriptions of Clement's Christian Gnostic.[157] If Jews focus on things proximate to, yet ultimately lesser than, the Christian ideal, sidetracked into ethnic, fleshly, quasi-divine, and fearful ways of thinking and reading in accordance with a "natural" Jewish way of being, "The Gnostic alone is able to understand and explain the things spoken by the Spirit obscurely."[158] If the Greeks worship God Greekly (Ἑλλήνων ἐθνικῶς) and Jews Jewishly (Ἰουδαίων Ἰουδαϊκῶς), Christians do so in a new and spiritual way (καινῶς δὲ ὑφ' ἡμῶν καὶ πνευματικῶς γινωσκόμενον) as a third *genos* (τρίτῳ γένει σεβόμενοι Χριστιανοί).[159] On the other hand, given the ethnic valance of being Christian, Jewishness must be erasable and "Jew" must be a porous category, and Clement does position Jewishness in terms amenable to the kind of erasure he rhetorically describes.[160] Jennifer Otto rightly notes

---

[156] GCS 52:93.

[157] Christians are those who understand and comprehend the Law "as the Lord who gave the Covenants delivered it to the apostles" (*Strom.* 4.21.130). When Jesus described the Jews as a "wicked and adulterous generation" in Matthew 16:4, he meant, according to Clement, that they "do not know the Law in the way that the Law requires" (*Strom.* 3.12.90). In *Strom.* 1.27.174, Clement uses Romans 2:17–20 to demonstrate that the Law is without fault and the problem is thinking Jewishly.

[158] *Strom.* 6.15.115 (GCS 52:490: δηλῶν μόνον δύνασθαι τὸν γνωστικὸν τὰ ἐπικεκρυμμένως πρὸς τοῦ πνεύματος εἰρημένα νοήσειν τε καὶ διασαφήσειν).

[159] *Strom.* 6.5.41–42 (GCS 52:452). *Strom.* 6.13.107 (GCS 52:485): a third "particular people" (εἰς περιούσιον λαόν). Clement does not shy away from the rhetorical force of this conception: "The new people, in contrast to the older people, are young"; they have an "unaging youth," they are "ever at the prime of intelligence, ever young, ever childlike, ever new" (*Paed.* 1.5.21; SC 70:146, 148). Cf. Buell, *Why This New Race?* 73, 81. Eric S. Gruen, "Christians as a 'Third Race': Is Ethnicity at Issue?," in *Christianity in the Second Century: Themes and Developments*, ed. James Carleton Paget and Judith Lieu (Cambridge: Cambridge University Press, 2017), 241–42, argues against the idea that early Christian discourse surrounding a third *genos* should be read as references to a third "race"; rather, for Clement, the distinction in *Strom.* 6.5.41 is the mode of expressing devotion (242). However, there is undoubtedly an ethnic valance to worshiping Greekly and Jewishly.

[160] In *Strom.* 6.8.62 Paul warns the Colossians not to return to τὴν Ἑλληνικὴν φιλοσοφίαν. Elsewhere, Clement even refers to the "barbarian philosophy" (*Paed.* 2.1–2).

that Clement leaves no rhetorical space for a "Jewish Christian" in his Christian self-definition: "When one becomes a Christian, one ceases to be a *Ioudaios*."[161] But, while there is rhetorically neither Jew nor Greek, there are certainly Hebrew followers of Christ in Clement's world, and he claims they are acting like Jews.

Jewishness is malleable for Clement, and his primary use for Judaism is as one half alongside Greek philosophy, which together provide a Christian self-definition. Clement's interests, however, are squarely on the Greek side of this pair, and, as a result, Judaism remains a rather empty symbol, slotted in as a formulaic pair alongside Greeks or heretics, out of which Christians arise contrastively. This is the larger context in which Clement encountered and read the ethnic valence of Hebrews.

5. Conclusion

Clement's textual practices betray a marginalization of Hebrews as Pauline. It is often anonymous and it supplements other letters in the *corpus Paulinum*, evoked as Pauline primarily for its content regarding faith (Heb 11) against rival second-century teachers like Basilides and Valentinus. I suggest that this formal marginalization coheres with Clement's image of Paul as a former Jew turned Christian apostle who received special gnosis from the *logos* and reads scriptural passages in order to unearth the higher form of knowledge buried enigmatically within. Clement models himself on this image of Paul by excerpting scriptural passages from texts deemed apostolic and authoritative. As Clement excerpts Paul's scriptural citations from Romans, for example, he mimics the epistolary sequence of these citations, maintaining a Pauline logic. However, Clement excerpts Hebrews with little indication that he was attempting to recreate any "Pauline" epistolary setting. Rather, Hebrews is for Clement a scriptural archive providing material for him to model himself on his image of Paul as an apostle steeped in scriptural mysteries.

Further, since Clement imagines Paul's apostolic mission as the demonstration to the Greeks that Christianity provides a fully realized philosophical system of which Plato was preparatory, Clement has little need or room

---

[161] Jennifer Otto, *Philo of Alexandria and the Construction of Jewishness in Early Christian Writings* (Oxford: Oxford University Press, 2018), 59.

for Judaism apart from endowing Greek philosophy with a divine spark and existing as the caricatured antithesis of Clement's Gnostic Christian. Clement's imagined Jew is a fleshly and non-symbolic reader of sacred scripture. Clement uses the lexical distinction between "Hebrew" and "Jew" to distance his Paul from "Jewishness," yet Clement then situates Paul's "Hebrew" audience within his ethnically coded criticism of Jewish thinking. Again, Clement's larger interests and commitments inform how he engages with Hebrews as a Pauline text. Though Clement may champion the "Pauline authorship" of the letter, his engagement with it is marked by resistance rather than deep synthesis.

As Hebrews passes into the hands of Origen of Alexandria, a few decades later, this configuration of reading is entirely reconstituted, and the centrality of Hebrews as Pauline emerges with renewed force. Rather than a marginally Pauline letter, Hebrews becomes the Pauline statement of Jewish reading practices. For Origen, the description of Jewish reading in Hebrews provides the narrative axis of difference between Christianity and Judaism around which Paul and Jesus are reimagined and through which Origen engages with contemporary Jewish scholarship.

The Pauline History of Hebrews. Warren Campbell, Oxford University Press. © Oxford University Press 2025.
DOI: 10.1093/9780197769287.003.0003

4

Origen's Letter on the Nature of Jewish Reading

In book 6 of the *Historia ecclesiastica*, Eusebius of Caesarea offers the image of a young Origen "Adamantius," born in 185–86 CE in Alexandria to Christian parents, trained in sacred studies, and unsatisfied with reading sacred texts in a "literal" and "simple" manner.[1] Given the critical tools and control of Greek literature on display in Origen's corpus, scholars tend to agree with Eusebius' claim that Origen was trained in Greek scholarship and earned a living as a *grammatikos*—a teacher of Greek grammar, language, and literature.[2] Few, however, follow Eusebius' account that Origen was installed as the head of "the" catechetical school in Alexandria at the age of eighteen, himself having grown in prominence during violent political upheaval under Aquila, the governor of Alexandria (c. 206 CE).[3]

---

[1] The most influential account of Origen's life and corpus is found in Pierre Nautin, *Origène: Sa vie et son œuvre*, Christianisme Antique I (Paris: Bauchesne, 1977), esp. 363–414. Other notable accounts can be found in R. P. C. Hanson, *Origen's Doctrine of Tradition* (London: SPCK, 1954), 1–30; Ernst Redepenning, *Origenes: Eine Darstellung seines Lebens und seiner Lehre* (Bonn: Verlag, 1846), 3–268; Eugène de Faye, *Origène, sa vei, son oeuvre, sa pensée*, vol 1 (Paris: Ernest Leroux, 1923), esp. 1–65; René Cadiou *La jeunesse d'Origène: Histoire de l'École d'Alexandrie au début du IIIe siècle* (Paris: Bauschesne, 1936); Jean Daneliou, *Origène* (Paris: Table Ronde, 1948), 19–40.

[2] On the work of a *grammatikos* within the three levels of ancient education (*grammatodidaskalos*, *grammatikos*, and *rhetor*), the development of curriculum, localized variation in education, as well as the social, financial, and material dynamics of ancient education, see Martin Irvine, *The Making of Textual Culture: "Grammatica" and Literary Theory, 350–1100* (Cambridge: Cambridge University Press, 1994), 1–87; Raffaella Criboire, *Writing, Teachers, and Students in Graeco-Romans Egypt*, American Studies in Papyrology (Atlanta: Scholars Press, 1996), 13–26; as well as the influential work, H. I. Marrou, *Histoire de l'éducation dans l'antiquité* (Paris: Seuil, 1956), trans. George Lamd as *A History of Education in Antiquity* (New York: Mentor Books, 1964); on the *grammatikos* see 223–42 and on Origen see 428–38. In *Hist. eccl.* 6.4.1–6.5.7, Eusebius presents an image of Origen as a young scholar, disavowing the study of "letters," disposing all of his "volumes of ancient literature" for the price of four obols a day, living like a philosopher by removing all hindrances to "youthful lusts" and sleeping on the floor out of devotion to "the study of divine scripture" (cf. *Hist. eccl.* 6.3.9).

[3] *Hist. eccl.* 6.3.1. On Origen and the idea of an Alexandrian catechetical school see esp. Clemens Scholten, "Die alexandrinische Katechetenschule," *JAC* 38 (1995): 16–37; John McGuckin, "Origen as a Literary Critic in the Alexandrian Tradition," in *Origeniana Octava: Origen and the Alexandria Tradition; Papers of the 8th International Origen Congress, Pisa 27–31 August 2001*, ed. Lorenzo Perrone (Leuven: Peeters, 2003), 125: "The real Catechetical School of Alexandria needs to be looked for in the episcopal preparations for baptismal candidates, not in a supposed School of learned philosopher theologians whom Pantaenus is believed to inaugurate, followed by Clement

Origen had a complex relationship with(in) the still-emerging Alexandrian ἐκκλησία.⁴ His migration from Egypt to Palestine around 231–32 CE was likely the result of some "storm" with the Alexandrian bishop, Demetrius, and yet Origen's transition to Palestine came about under the auspices of Bishops Theoctistus of Caesarea and Alexander of Jerusalem.⁵ After leaving Alexandria, Origen continued to travel, yet Caesarea Maritima was the city of his later life, a life that, as tradition has it, ended in Tyre in the aftermath of the Decian edict around 254 CE.⁶

Behind the catechetical image of Origen shining through Eusebius many find a philosophical (and priestly) Christian *didaskolos*, whose curriculum was designed to advance a comprehensive Christian philosophy.⁷ Origen scholars are dispersed along a spectrum between "theologian" and "philosopher" as descriptors of what they see Origen attempting to accomplish, and the relationship between these two is far from settled.⁸ Origen was in larger part a biblical commentator and homilist.⁹ Origen produced

---

and then Origen. It is surely the case that all the learned teachers to whom Christian tradition has attached some kind of commonality as leaders of the Catechetical School were, in fact, individual professional *rhetor-didaskaloi*, who also happened to be Christian philosophers. It is only with Origen that the tension between what bishop Demetrius conceived as the proper role and function of the Christian *Didaskalos*, and what Origen understood to be his mission and vocation, becomes critically problematised."

⁴ Cf. Attila Jakab, *Ecclesia alexandrina: Evolution sociale et institutionelle du christianisme alexandrine (IIᵉ et IIIᵉ siècles)*, Christianismes anciens 1 (Bern: Peter Land, 2001).

⁵ *Comm. Jo.* 6.1.8 (cf. Eusebius, *Hist. eccl.* 6.19.15–19; Photius, *Bib.* 118); Jakab, *Ecclesia alexandrina*, 69–173.

⁶ Cf. John A. McGuckin, "Caesarea Maritima as Origen Knew It," *Origeniana Quinta, Origenism and Later Developments, Papers of the 5th International Origen Congress, Boston, 14–18 August 1989*, ed. R. J. Daly (Leuven: Leuven University Press, 1992), 3–25.

⁷ See (Ps.) Gregory Thaumaturgus' letter on Origen's curriculum in Henri Crouzel, ed., *Grégoire le thaumaturge: Remerciement a Origène suivi de la Lettre d'Origène a Grégoire*, Sources chrétiennes 148 (Paris: Cerf, 1969), 94–183; Henri Crouzel, "L'École d'Origène à Césarée: Postscriptum à une édition de Grégoire le Thaumaturge," *BLE* 71 (1970): 15–27; Adolf Knauber, "Das Anliegen der Schule des Origenes zu Cäsaraea," *Münchener Theologische Zeitschrift* 19 (1968): 182–203; McGuckin, "Origen as a Literary Critic," 121–35.

⁸ Scriptural texts, for Origen, contain ideas equal and even superior to those of Plato. See Arnold Von Johannes, "Mit Platon zur Erkenntnis Gottes? Der 'philosophische Exkurs' des Siebten Briefs bei Kelsos und Origenes," *ThPh* 95.3 (2020): 321–61. There is something of a scholarly spectrum between Origen the "philosopher" and the "theologian"; see de Faye, *Origène*; Hal Koch, *Pronoia und Paideusis: Studien über Origenes und sein Verhältnis zum Platonismus* (Berlin: de Gruyter, 1932); Charles Bigg, *Christian Platonists of Alexandria* (Oxford: Clarendon, 1913); Cadiou, *La jeunesse d"Origène*; Danéliou, *Origène*; Henri Crouzel, *Origène et la philosophie*, Théologie 52 (Paris: Aubier, 1962); Mark Edwards, *Origen against Plato* (Aldershot: Ashgate, 2002); Mark Edwards, "Christ or Plato? Origen on Revelation and Anthropology," in *Christian Origins: Theology Rhetoric and Community*, ed. Lewis Ayers and Gareth Jones (London: Routledge, 1998), 11–25; Ilaria Ramelli, "Origen, Patristic Philosophy, and Christian Platonism: Re-Thinking the Christianisation of Hellenism," *VC* 63 (2009): 217–63.

⁹ On the early context of the commentary (ὑπόμνημα) see Francesca Schironi, "Greek Commentaries," *DSD* 19 (2012): 399–441; Jan Assmann, "Text und Kommentar: Einführung," in

scriptural commentaries throughout his Alexandrian and Caesarean periods; however the homilies reflect the late, Caesarean Origen, and, as Nautin influentially argued, were produced in a three-year period between either 238–41 or 239–42 CE.[10] The size of Origen's literary corpus accents the importance of financial support and other forms of unrecognized, let alone enslaved, labor required for production.[11]

Among Origen's lost works are a commentary and a series of homilies on the epistle to the Hebrews. Despite the loss of these texts, the extant portions of Origen's corpus are furnished with quotations from Hebrews that quickly register the significance of "To the Hebrews" for Origen's theory of reading, a theory that conceptualizes Jewish reading practices as "literal."

Rowan Greer's monograph on the interpretation of Hebrews within the context of the Christological controversies of the fourth and fifth centuries is the only account of Origen's reading of the Letter to the Hebrews as a whole, that is, one that attempts to account for the totality of citations in relation to the driving thematic interests in Origen's corpus.[12] With a complex fourth- and

---

Text und Kommentar, ed. Jan Asmman and Burkhard Gladigow, Beiträge zur Archäologie der literarischen Kommunikation 4 (Munich: Fink, 1995), 9–33; Heinrich Dörrie and Matthias Batles, *Der Platonismus im 2. und 3. Jahrhundert nach Christus: Bausteine 73–100, Übersetzung, Kommentar* (Stuttgart: Bad Cannstatt, 1993), 28–54; R. F. MacLachlan, "The Context of Commentary: Non-Biblical Commentary in the Early Christian Period," in *Commentaries, Catenae and Biblical Tradition*, ed. H. A. G. Houghton, Texts and Studies 13 (Piscataway: Gorgias, 2016), 37–64; Alfons Fürst, "Origen: Exegesis and Philosophy in Early Christian Alexandria," in *Interpreting the Bible and Aristotle in Late Antiquity: The Alexandrian Commentary Tradition Between Rome and Baghdad*, ed. Josef Lössl and John W. Watt (Burlington: Ashgate, 2011), 13–32; Marcus Bockmuehl, "The Dead Sea Scrolls and the Origins of Biblical Commentary," in *Text, Thought, and Practice in Qumran and Early Christianity: Proceedings of the Ninth International Symposium of the Orion Center for the Study of the Dead Sea Scrolls and Associated Literature, Jointly Sponsored by the Hebrew University Center for the Study of Christianity, 11–13 January, 2004*, ed. Ruth A. Clements and Daniel R. Schwartz (Leiden: Brill, 2009), 3–29. On the early context of the homily see esp. Hartwig Thyen, *Der Stil der jüdisch-hellenistischen Homilie*, FRLANT 47 (Göttingen: Vandenhoeck & Ruprecht, 1955); Lawrence Wills, "The Form of the Sermon in Hellenistic Judaism and Early Christianity," *HTR* 77 (1984): 277–99; as well as Alistair Stewart Sykes, *From Prophesy to Preaching: A Search for the Origins of Christian Homily*, VCSup. 59 (Leiden: Brill, 2001).

[10] Nautin, *Origène*, 389–409. Cf. also Charles Renoux, "Origène dans la liturgie de l'Église de Jérusalem," *Adamantius* 5 (1999): 37–52, who finds in Origen's homilies on 1 Samuel an early pattern of the much later lectionary readings attested in Armenian and Georgian, which is discussed further in Harald Buchinger, "Origenes und die Quadragesima in Jerusalem ein Diskussionsbeitrag," *Adamantius* 13 (2007): 174–217. Renoux's dating has recently been challenged by Hugo Méndez, "Revising the Date of the Armenian Lectionary of Jerusalem," *JECS* 291 (2021): 61–92.

[11] On the intersection between financial support and the intellectual ascension among the social elite, see Jared Secord, "Julius Africanus, Origen, and the Politics of Intellectual life Under the Severans," *CW* 110.2 (2017): 211–35; Anthony Grafton and M. H. Williams, *Christianity and the Transformation of the Book: Origen, Eusebius, and the Library of Caesarea* (Cambridge, MA: Harvard University Press, 2006), 22–85.

[12] Rowan A. Greer, *The Captain of Our Salvation: A Study in the Patristic Exegesis of Hebrews*, BGBE 15 (Tübingen: Mohr Siebeck, 1973), 7–64.

fifth-century dispute as the guiding line of his project, Greer identifies passages from Hebrews that Origen employs to clarify the position of the *logos* within a "hierarchy of being" informed by Origen's participation within the Platonic tradition.[13] What Greer observes is that Origen's conception of the *logos* is driven by the question of revelation and is meted out through the description of two relationships: one, between the Word and the "invisible God,"[14] and the other, the Word and the human Jesus.[15] In both cases, Origen's *logos* is the key for his account of divine disclosure as an achievement.[16]

Greer's larger aim in this project was to advance scholarship on early Christian interpretive methods by scrutinizing the relationship between "theological principles" and "exegetical results" as they were typically configured with respect to the "schools" of interpretation in Antioch and Alexandria. Ultimately, Greer contends that differences between ancient Christian "schools" of interpretation derive from variance in basic theological principles not from the a priori selection of different interpretive methods. A distinctive

---

[13] For Greer, Origen's Christology requires a form of subordination of the *logos* to the Father that becomes an increasingly dangerous position for some to maintain in the fourth century (*Captain of Our Salvation*, 43). See also Robert M. Berchman, "The Categories of Being in Middle Platonism: Philo, Clement, and Origen of Alexandria," in *The School of Moses; From Philo to Origen: Middle Platonism in Transition*, ed. John Peter Kenney (Chico: Scholar's Press, 1984), 89–140; Anders-Christian Jacobsen, *Christ—the Teacher of Salvation: A Study on Origen's Christology and Soteriology* (Münster: Aschendorff Verlag, 2015).

[14] The idea of an "image," taken from Colossians 1:15, Hebrews 1:3, and Wisdom 7:25, is a central metaphor through which Origen expresses this relationship. Origen strings these texts together in *De princ.* 1.2.5 in order to claim that an image "preserves the unity of nature and substance" of the "imaged" thing (1.2.6; translation John Behr, ed. and trans., *Origen: On First Principles*, vol. 1 [Oxford: Oxford University Press, 2017], 49). What Hebrews 1:3 allows Origen to do specifically is articulate both distinction and unity in this relationship. For instance, Origen links the idea of "radiance" (ἀπαύγασμα) in Hebrews 1.3 with the description of God as "light" (φῶς) in 1 John 1:5 in order to claim that there can exist a form of inseparable proceeding (*De princ.* 1.2.7). Yet, as Greer emphasizes, the distinction in Origen serves the goal of revelation; it is "brightness" which makes known "light" and an incorporeal substance is not known if it were not for the existence of an "express image" (*Captain of Our Salvation*, 47; cf. also *Comm. Jo.* 13.25, where Origen links the idea of a "reflection" with "eternal light" for similar purposes). In *Comm. Rom.* 2.5.5 Origen associates the "glory of the Lord" filling the tabernacle in Exodus 40:43 with the "glory which the apostle is speaking when writing to the Hebrews concerning the Son." Here Hebrews 1:3 furnishes this connection for Origen, and reveals that "the source of glory is the Father himself, from whom the splendor of that glory, the Son, is generated" (trans. Thomas P. Scheck, *Origen: Commentary on the Epistle to the Romans, Books 1–5*, FC 103 [Washington, DC: Catholic University America Press, 2001], 115). In a fragment attributed to Origen's *Commentarii in Hebraeos* in Pamphilus of Caesarea's apology for Origen, which was translated by Rufinus in the late fourth century, Origen refers to "eternal light" in Wisdom 7.26 to argue, almost directly against Arius, that since light (Father) and radiance (Son) are linked eternally, "there was not a time when the Son was not" (*Eusebii et Pamphyli Apologia Origenis*, 49).

[15] Hebrews 1:1, 2:10–11, 4:15, 5:12, 12:2 are important texts for Origen in this regard. See *Comm. Jo.* 1.34.249–50; *Hom. Num.* 11.8; *Comm. Rom.* 3.8.1, 5.7.6, *Comm. Matt.* 15; *Cels.* 2.9.

[16] Greer, *Captain of Our Salvation*, 43, 45. See, for example, *Comm. Jo.* 2.10.72, 2.11.82; *De princ.* 4.4.1; *Cels.* 4.14–15, 4.18; *Comm. Rom.* 1.5.1, 4.7.5, 4.8.8; *Hom. Gen.* 1.13; *Hom. Jer.* 9.4.

Antiochene reading of Hebrews emerges out of an Antiochene theological tradition, not a distinctive method of reading.[17] What Origen's reading of Hebrews affords Greer, then, is not only a third-century vantage from which to observe fourth-century readers of the same letter, but a readerly encounter with Hebrews prior to those emerging debates in which a unique set of theological questions are at work in the complex process of reading. Greer sought to discern in what ways the questions of Origen's own intellectual context are apparent in his reading of Hebrews, and, on the other hand, what portions of Hebrews provide Origen with the language and concepts with which larger aspects of his thought are developed. While the sheer number of quotations from almost every portion of letter poses a challenge to identifying the "center" of Origen's reading of Hebrews,[18] Greer rightly discerns the importance of Hebrews 8:5 and 10:1 as vehicles through which Origen articulates some core dimensions of his interpretive theory.[19]

---

[17] Greer, *Captain of Our Salvation*, 4. See also Frances Young's chapter "Allēgoria *and* theōria" in *Biblical Exegesis and the Formation of Christian Culture* (Cambridge: Cambridge University Press, 1997), 161–85, and Miriam DeCock's more recent defense of meaningful methodological differences between Antioch and Alexandria in *Interpreting the Gospel of John in Antioch and Alexandria* (Atlanta: Society of Biblical Literature Press, 2020).

[18] Origen cites from Hebrews 1:1–9, 1:11–2:2, 2:4, 2:8–15, 2:17, 3:1–2, 3:5, 3:12, 3:14, 3:17, 4:1, 4:3, 4:6, 4:9, 4:11–15, 5:1–3, 5:5–6, 5:9–6:2, 6:4–8, 6:10, 6:13, 6:16–18, 6:20–7:3, 7:5, 7:7, 7:9–11, 7:14, 7:17, 7:19, 7:21, 7:25–8:3, 8:5, 8:8–9, 8:13, 9:2–7, 9:10–15, 9:19, 9:22–26, 9:28–10:2, 10:4, 10:7–8, 10:11–14, 10:18, 10:20, 10:23–24, 10:26–29, 10:32, 10:34, 10:36–37, 11:1–2, 11:5–6, 11:8–12, 11:16–17, 11:19, 11:24, 11:26, 11:28, 11:36–12:2, 12:4–9, 12:11–19, 12:22–23, 12:29, 13:2, 13:8, 13:11–13, 13:15–17, 13:20–21. Origen uses a number of passages from Hebrews as epitomizing descriptions and exhortations yet does not bring the *Pauline* valance of the text into view. For instance, Origen returns to the description of ὁ λόγος τοῦ θεοῦ as a "two-edged sword" (μάχαιραν δίστομον) from Hebrews 4:12 (*Comm. Jo.* 1.32.229; *Hom. Jer.* 2.2; *Hom. Jes. Nav.* 26.2; *Comm. Rom.* 3.4.3, 7.12.3, 9.3.9; *Hom. Gen.* 3.6, *Hom. Lev.* 16.7). Origen refers to Hebrews 1:14 for its description of angels as "ministering spirits" (λειτουργικὰ πνεύματα), highlighting the activity of these rational spirits as agents of divine providence (*Comm. Cant.* 4.14; *Cels.* 5.4; *De princ.* 1.5.1, 2.8.1, 3.3.6; *Comm. Jo.* 32.17.199; *Hom. Jes. Nav.* 8.6, 23.3; *Comm. Rom.* 1.18.6, 2.4.6, 7.1.2, 7.4.11, 7.5.3, 9.30.1; *Hom. Luc.* 13.2). Similarly, Origen uses the description of angels from Hebrews 1.7 as "spirits" and "flame of fire" (*De princ.* 2.8.3; *Hom. Luc.* 26.1; *Comm. Jo.* 1.13.75; *Comm. Rom.* 10.14.8; Pamphilus, *Apol. Orig.* 27). The language of repentance and punishment in Hebrews 6:4–6 and 10:26–29 provides Origen with exhortative material aimed at advancing proper Christian conduct (*Hom. Jer.* 13.2, 15.7, 16.7, 19.15; *Hom. Ezech.* 5.3, 12.1; *Comm. Jo.* 28.15.126, 28.7.55; *Comm. Rom.* 5.8.9; *Hom. Lev.* 11.2; *Hom. Jes. Nav.* 5.6; *Cels.* 8.10.5–7). Specifically, using Hebrews 6.7–8 allows Origen to focus on the moral freedom of human agents and necessity to respond to God's grace (see *Hom. Gen.* 1.3; *Hom. Lev.* 16.2; see Greer, *Captain of Our Salvation*, 31–34). While Origen draws the idea of a succession of ages out of Ephesians 2:7, Hebrews 3:13 ("Today if you hear his voice") and 9:26 ("he has appeared once for all at the end of the ages") also demarcate the uniqueness of the appearance of Christ in the present age (*De princ.* 2.3.5; *Hom. Josh.* 4.4). Origen mines Hebrews 11 for its description of faith (*Hom. Gen.* 8.1; *Comm. Rom.* 4.6.3), which is often applied to Abraham (*Comm. Rom.* 4.7.3; *Hom. Gen.* 8.1) but also to descriptions the "lives of the prophets" (Heb 11:37–38 in *Hom. Jer.* 14.14; *Comm. Rom.* 8.7.11).

[19] Greer claims that "it would be an exaggeration to say that the text [*both* Heb 8:5 and 10:1] is really an explanation for Origen's ideas, but it is perfectly possible to assert that it functions easily and convincingly as a vehicle for their expression" (*Captain of Our Salvation*, 23–24).

1. The Tabernacle and Origen's (Pauline) Theory of (Jewish) Reading

The description of the tabernacle in the Letter to the Hebrews is, for Origen, a unique instance of Pauline interpretation containing the underlying principle of reality that justifies and undergirds a method of reading *all* scriptural texts. In his homily on the tabernacle from Exodus 25, Origen approaches the Letter to the Hebrews with reverence:[20]

> The divine scriptures speak about this tabernacle in many places. They appear to indicate certain things of which human hearing can scarcely be capable. The apostle Paul especially, however, relates to us certain indications of a more excellent knowledge about the understanding of the tabernacle, but, for some unknown reason, perhaps considering the weakness of his hearers, closes, as it were, those very things that he opens.

What Paul "opens" and "closes" is a discussion of the significance of the elements housed within the tabernacle (Heb 9:2–4); they are "not to be spoken of now" (Heb 9:5: περὶ ὧν οὐκ ἔστιν νῦν λέγειν). Origen understands Paul's hesitancy not as a reference to the insufficiency of time and space at the moment when the apostle wrote Hebrews, but an indication of the sheer profundity of the mysteries (*magnitudine mysteriorum*) to which the elements housed within the tabernacle refer.[21] Though Paul "closes" this mystery, Origen summarizes what was "opened" by combining Hebrews 9:24 and 10:20: "Jesus has not entered into holy places made with hands, patterns (*exemplaria*) of the true, but into heaven itself, that he may appear now in the sight of God through the veil, that is his flesh."[22] Origen draws

---

[20] *Homiliae in Exodum* 9.1. Latin text in W. A. Baehrens, ed., *Origenes Werke Band 6, Homilien zum Hexateuch in Rufins Übersetzung, Erster Teil, Die Homilien zu Genesis, Exodus, und Leviticus*, GCS 29 (Berlin: de Gruyter, 1920), 235: *De quo tabernaculo multis quidem in locis memorant scripturae, divinae et indicare quaedam videntur, quorum vix capax esse possit humanus auditus; praecipue tamen Apostolus Paulus de intelligentia tabernaculi quaedam nobis prodit scientiae excelsioris indicia, sed, nescio quo pacto, fragilitatem fortassis intuens auditorum, claudit quodammodo ipsa, quae pandit.* Translation Ronald Heine, *Origen: Homilies on Genesis and Exodus*, FC 71 (Washington, DC: Catholic University of American Press, 1982), 334 (slightly modified). On the significance of Exodus 25:9 and the language of תַּבְנִית see Max Wilcox, "'According to the Pattern (TBNYT)...': Exodus 25, 40 in the New Testament and Early Jewish Thought," *Revue de Qumran* 13 (1988): 647–56.

[21] *Homiliae in Exodum* 9.1. GCS 29.235.

[22] *Homiliae in Exodum* 9.1. GCS 29.235. Translation, Heine, *Homilies on Genesis and Exodus*, 335.

attention to the interpretive associations at work here: Jesus is the ancient high priest, the physical veil separating the holy of holies is the *carnem Christi*, and the holy places made with hands actually refer to heaven itself, the location where this high priest has entered.[23] Here Origen pans out to consider the significance of these associations:[24]

> If anyone knows how to understand Paul's meaning, he can observe how great a sea of understanding he has disclosed to us. But they who love the letter of the Law of Moses too much, but flee its spirit hold the apostle Paul suspect when he brings forth interpretations of this kind.

Elsewhere, in *Homilies on Leviticus* 9.9, Origen returns to the idea of Jesus' entry into a celestial sanctuary to confirm the principle that the interior sanctuary of the physical tabernacle is but a "figure and image" (*figuram atque imaginem*) of a heavenly reality,[25] one instance in a more universal principle of correspondence. In the *Commentary on the Song of Songs*, for instance, Origen notes that "this visible world teaches us about that which is invisible, and...this earthly scene contains certain patterns of things heavenly" (*ostendens per haec quod visibilis hoc mundus de invisibili doceat et exemplaria quaedam caelestium contineat positio ista terrena*).[26] This universal correspondence is later invested with biblical imagery:[27]

---

[23] *Hom. Exod.* 9.1 (GCS 29.235). See David M. Moffit, "Jesus' Heavenly Sacrifice in Early Christian Reception of Hebrews: A Survey," *JTS* 68.1 (2017): 46–71, who identifies conceptions of heavenly ascension as a sacrificial act in later readings of Hebrews in Hippolytus, Origen, Theodore of Mopsuestia, and Theodoret, which Moffit positions in relation to his own monograph, which argues for a similar linkage in Hebrews. See *Atonement and the Logic of Resurrection in the Epistle to the Hebrews*, NovTSup. 141 (Leiden: Brill, 2011). See also Michael Kibbe, "Is it Finished? When Did It Start? Hebrews, Priesthood, and Atonement in Biblical, Systematic, and Historical Perspective," *JTS* 65 (2014): 25–61; Franz Laub, "'Ein für allemal hineingegangen in das Allerheiligste' (Hebr 9,12)—Zum Verständnis des Kreuzestodes im Hebräerbrief," *BZ* 35 (1991): 65–85.

[24] GCS 29.235: *ex his paucis sermonibus si quis intelligere novit Pauli sensum, potest advertere, quantum nobis intelligentiae pelagus patefecerit. Sed qui satis amant litteram legis Moysis, spiritum vero eius refugiunt, suspectum habent Apostolum Paulium interpretationes huiusmodi proferentem.*

[25] GCS 29.437. Cf. also *Hom. Lev.* 1.3.

[26] *Commentarius in Canticum* 3.13.9. Latin text in Luc Brésard and Henri Crouzel, with the collaboration of Marcel Borret, *Origène Commentaire sur le Cantique des Cantiques*, vol. 2, *Texte de la version latine de Rufin*, Sources chrétiennes 376 (Paris: Éditions du Cerf, 1992), 628. Translation R. P. Lawson, *Origen, The Song of Songs: Commentary and Homilies*, ACW 26 (Westminster: Newman Press, 1957), 218.

[27] *Comm. Cant.* 3.13.10. SC 376.630: *fortasse in tantum singula quaeque quae in terries sunt habent aliquid imaginis et similitudinis in caelestibus, ut etiam granum sinapis, quod minimum est in omnibus seminibuso, habeat aliquid imaginis et similitudinis in caelis* (trans. Lawson, *Origen, The Song of Songs*).

Perhaps the correspondence between all things on earth and their celestial prototypes goes so far, that even the grain of the mustard seed...which is the least of all seeds, has something in heaven whose image and likeness it bears.

Patricia Cox describes Origen's world as "an enigmatic bearer of the kingdom of heaven" that has "passed into the Book."[28] The principle of correspondence between heaven and earth describes the nature of the *written* Law. Scriptural texts are themselves a reflection of a platonic world of images and shadows. After all, Paul's interpretation of the tabernacle gives access to a greater depth of understanding and is contrasted with a kind of reading that privileges the "the letter of the Law." The sea of understanding available in Paul's treatment of the tabernacle is what grounds a method of reading in which one attends to the "spirit" of the text. The "sea of understanding" (*intelligentiae pelagus*) disclosed by Paul is, for Origen, a way of understanding the significance of Israel's scriptures, genealogy, and embodied rituals within a two-tiered Platonic world. As a compact expression that emphasizes the idea of correspondence between earthly and heavenly dimensions of reality most pointedly, Hebrews 8:5 provides the language with which Origen expresses this idea most often.

In Hebrews 8:5 the priests tasked with operating the Tent of Meeting are described as serving (λατρεύουσιν) a "shadowy exemplar" (ὑποδείγματι καὶ σκιᾷ) of a heavenly version.[29] Later, in Hebrews 10:1, the Law is described

---

[28] Patricia Cox, "Origen and the Bestial Soul: A Poetics of Nature," *VC* 36.2 (1982): 119, 129. Similarly, Daniel Boyarin, *Intertextuality and the Reading of Midrash* (Bloomington: Indiana University Press, 1994), 109: "perfect correspondence between the ontology of the world and that of the text."

[29] Hebrews 8:5: οἵτινες ὑποδείγματι καὶ σκιᾷ λατρεύουσιν τῶν ἐπουρανίων, καθὼς κεχρημάτισται Μωϋσῆς μέλλων ἐπιτελεῖν τὴν σκηνήν· ὅρα γάρ φησιν, ποιήσεις πάντα κατὰ τὸν τύπον τὸν δειχθέντα σοι ἐν τῷ ὄρει. I read ὑποδείγματι καὶ σκιᾷ τῶν ἐπουρανίων as a hendiadys, following Ceslas Spicq, *L'Épître aux Hébreux* (Paris: Libraire Lecoffre, 1953), 2:234; Herbert Braun, *An die Hebräer*, HNT 14 (Tübingen: Mohr Siebeck, 1984), 228; Harold Attridge, *Hebrews: A Commentary on the Epistle to the Hebrews* (Philadelphia: Fortress Press, 1989), 219. On the translation of ὑποδείγματι as "exemplar," capturing the double sense of model and example, see David T. Runia, "Ancient Philosophy and the New Testament: 'Exemplar' as Example," in *Method and Meaning: Essays on New Testament Interpretation in Honor of Harold W. Attridge*, ed. Andrew B. MacGowan and Kent Richards (Atlanta: SBL Press, 2011), 354–59. On the idea of a heavenly temple, whether fully formed or simply as a "pattern" (παράδειγμα; Exod. 25:9) see Ezekiel 40–48; *1 Enoch* 14; *Jubilees* 50.10–11; *Lives of the Prophets* 3.15; Songs of the Sabbath Sacrifice; Philo, *Mos.* 2.74–76; Ps.Philo, *LAB* 11.15; Wisdom 9.8; 2 Bar. 4.2–7; T. Levi 3.1–8, as discussed in Benjamin J. Ribbens, *Levitical Sacrifice and Heavenly Cult in Hebrews*, BZNW 222 (Berlin: de Gruyter, 2016), 52–81 (see also 102–13); cf. also Aelrod Cody, *Heavenly Sanctuary and Liturgy in the Epistle to the Hebrews* (St. Meinrad: Grail Publications, 1960). Otfried Hofius, *Der Vorhang vor dem Thron Gottes: Eine exegetish-religionsgeschichtliche Untersuchung zu Hebräer 6,19f. und 10,19ff.*, WUNT 14 (Tübingen:

as having a "shadow of the good things *to come*" (Σκιὰν γὰρ ἔχων ὁ νόμος τῶν μελλόντων ἀγαθῶν). Origen picks up on the temporal resonance of Hebrews 10:1; however, in *Commentary on the Epistle to the Romans* 5.1.39, he claims the text is *ambiguus*.[30] The good things "to come" may refer to the arrival of the *logos* in earthly time and space as Jesus Christ, who discloses the mystery of the heavenly realities by removing the "veil" laid over the old scriptures, or, on the other hand, to the further degrees of comprehension of which the body of knowledge disclosed by the *logos* still remains a shadow.[31] While Origen appreciates and preserves this variation between Hebrews 8:5 and 10:1, the temporal dimension of the shadow is ultimately eclipsed by Origen's emphasis on the mere fact of an earthly-heavenly correspondence as an indication of two "orders of reality."[32] In *Commentarium in Canticum Canticorum* 2.8 the "things to come" from Hebrews 10:1 refer to the interpretive results of Christian readers who advance through scriptural material on the presumption that all of scripture functions as a shadow of a heavenly "meaning." Similarly, in *Homilies on Leviticus* 8:5, the "good things to come" are the unbounded body of knowledge for those who read the "Old Testament" without the "veil" and follow the "path of understanding" of the principle of the shadow.[33]

Mohr Siebeck, 1971), 55–56, finds that Hebrews' conception of the heavenly tabernacle conforms seamlessly with earlier Jewish conceptions of a two-room heavenly building (4–37). See also Gregory E. Sterling, "Ontology versus Eschatology: Tensions Between Author and Community in Hebrews," *SPhilo* 13 (2001): 194, who suggests "sketchy copy" as a translation for ὑποδείγματι καὶ σκιᾷ, and that Hebrews channels both Platonic and temporal-eschatological concerns (208–11), a point of contention within scholarship on Hebrews.

[30] Latin text in Caroline P. Hammond Bammel, *Der Römerbriefkommentar des Origenes. Kritische Ausgabe der Übersetzung Rufins, Buch 4–6*, Vetus Latina 33 (Frieburg: Herder, 1998), 387.

[31] In *Comm. Rom.* 5.1.40–41, Origen reflects on this tension, noting that some read Hebrews 10:1 as a "past" fulfillment, and others consider these "types and shadows" to be future expectations. Origen even refers to *two* shadows, one advancing upon the other, but both falling short of "face-to-face apprehension" (see *Comm. Song.* 3.5; cf. also *Hom. Num.* 28:3; *Hom. Lev.* 1.1, 3.5, 7.2; *de Princ.* 3.6.8, 4.2.4; *Comm. Rom.* 5.1.41, 6.3.8). Origen often retains the ambiguity and refers to both possibilities in the same breath. See *De princ.* 4.3.13: "just as in his coming now he has fulfilled that Law which has a shadow of good things to come, so also by that glorious arrival the shadows of this arrival will be fulfilled and brought to perfect" (Behr, *Origen: On First Principles*, 555).

[32] See Greer, *Captain of Our Salvation*, 11–16 (citing *De orat.* 27.14; *De princ.* 4.3.13; *Hom. Lev.* 5.1; *Hom. Jes. Nav.* 17.1; *Hom Num.* 2.4.2). Greer's comments are instructive here: "The true issue is whether this typological view, no matter how it be expressed from the point of view of terminology, is merely a vestigial remnant of the Christian heritage upon which Origen builds, or whether it is seriously integrated into this thought.... The rather neat typological pattern tends to yield to a Platonising distinction between intelligible and perceptible realities, or, more Biblically, heavenly and earthly realities" (*Captain of Our Salvation*, 14). On the variety of ways that the heaven-temple relationship can be configured across a wide range of Jewish texts see Nicholas Moore, "Heaven and Temple in the Second Temple Period: A Taxonomy," *JSP* 33.1 (2023): 75–93.

[33] In *Cels.* 2.37 Origen regards an allegorical reading of Jesus drinking vinegar more valuable than understanding it as a proof of prophecy. See Greer, *Captain of Our Salvation*, 20–23.

Throughout his homilies, then, Origen defers to Hebrews 8:5 and 10:1 to confirm that what is "described in the Law that appears to concern earthly things is really a shadow of the good things of heaven."[34] Moses ascended Sinai to receive "divine mysteries" of which the written laws are shadows and copies, "as the apostle taught when he said, 'which serve as a copy and shadow of the heavenly sanctuary.'"[35] Elsewhere, "The Law has the shadow of heavenly things and speaks as a *hypodeigma*" (ὁ νόμος σκιὰν ἔχῃ τῶν ἐπουρανίων καὶ ὑπόδειγμα λέγηται).[36] Not only is the physical tabernacle a copy and shadow of a heavenly, but the host of characters, actions, and events throughout scriptural writings are "shadows" of a "higher" referent.[37]

As often as Origen employs the idea of the shadow from Hebrews in contexts concerning the art of interpretation, it is unsurprising that this passage is a prominent vehicle through which Origen famously outlines his view of "reading and understanding" (ἀναγνώσεως καὶ νοήσεως) the "spiritual" sense of scripture in book 4 of *De principiis* (4.2.1–3.15).[38] As

---

[34] *Homiliae in Numeros* 28.1. Latin text Wilhelm Adolf Baehrens, ed., *Origenes Werke Band 7, Homilien zum Hexateuch in Rufins Übersetzung. Teil 2: Die Homilien zu Numeri, Josua und Judices*, GCS 30 (Berlin: de Gruyter, 1921), 281: *Et si secundum ipsius nihilominus sententiam lex, cuius pars est haec lectio, quam habemus in manibus, umbram habet futurorum bonorum, consequens videtur et necessarium omnia, quae quasi de rebus terrenis describuntur in lege, umbras esse bonorum coelestium.* Translation Thomas P. Scheck, *Origen: Homilies on Numbers* (Downers Grove: IVP Academic, 2009), 184.

[35] *Hom. Jer.* 18.2: σκιὰ γὰρ καὶ ὑπόδειγμα ἐπουρανίων μυστηρίων ἐν τοῖς νόμοις τοῖς ἀναγεγραμμένοις, ὡς ἐδίδασκεν ὁ ἀπόστολος εἰπών· Οἵτινες ὑποδείγματι καὶ σκιᾷ λατρεύουσι τῶν ἐπουρανίων. Greek text in Erich Klostermann and Pierre Nautin, eds., *Origenes Werke Band 3, Jeremiahomilien. Klageliederkommentar. Erklärung der Samuel- und Königsbücher*, GCS 6 (Berlin: de Gruyter, 1983), 152. Cf. also *Hom Lev.* 13.1.

[36] *Hom. Ps.* 80.1.5. Greek text in Lorenzo Perrone, ed., with Marina Molin Pradel, Emanuela Prinzivalli, and Antonio Cacciari, *Origenes Werke*, vol. 13, *Die neuen Psalmenhomilien: Eine kritische Edition des Codex Monacensis Graecus 314*, GCS Neue Folge 19 (Berlin: de Gruyter, 2015), 489.

[37] In *Hom. Jes. Nav.* 12.1, Joshua's wars are a type and shadow of Jesus' wars with devil. The punishments enumerated in the Law are a shadow of the "true punishments" (see *Hom. Jer.* 7.1; *Comm. Rom.* 2.9.5).

[38] For discussions of this section of *De principiis* see Henri Lubac, *Histoire et esprit: L'intelligence de l'écriture d'après Origène* (Paris: Aubier, 1950), 92–125, 139–50; Marguerite Harl and Nicholas de Lange, eds., *Origène, Philocalie 1–20 Sur les Écritures et La Lettre à Africanus sur l'histoire de Suzanne*, Sources chrétiennes 302 (Paris: Cerf, 1983), 42–74; Rolf Gögler, *Zur Theologie des biblischen Wortes bei Origenes* (Düsseldorf: Patmos, 1963), 244–389; James Carleton Paget, "The Christian Exegesis of the Old Testament in the Alexandrian Tradition," in *Hebrew Bible / Old Testament: The History of Its Interpretation*, vol 1, *From the Beginnings to the Middle Ages (Until 1300)*, ed. Magne Sæbø with C. Brekelmans and M. Haran (Göttingen: Vandenhoeck & Ruprecht, 1996), 508–15; Karen Jo Torjesen, *Hermeneutical Procedure and Theological Method in Origen's Exegesis*, Patristische Texte und Studien 38 (Berlin: de Gruyter, 1986), 35–43. Origen's *De principiis* has been influentially associated with the ancient discussion of physics, understood as the relation between gods and the world; see B. Steidle, "Neue Untersuchungen zu Origenes's Περὶ ἀρχῶν," ZNW 40 (1941): 236–43; Marguerite Harl, "Structure et cohérence du Peri Archôn," in *Origeniana: Premier colloque international des études origéniennes (Montserrat, 18–21 septembre 1971)*, ed.

Origen advances a definition of Christian reading, he draws attention to the plight of the "most innocent" (οἱ ἀκεραιότατοι). These figures are described as adherents to the scriptural texts and have enough interpretive skill to recognize that the tabernacle is a τύπος, but the details enumerated for other types, such as accounts of marriage, childbearing, wars, and especially the sexual activity of Lot, Abraham, and Jacob are not clearly articulated (οὐ πάνυ σαφηνίζεται).[39] This picture of "simple" Christians whose quasi-successful interpretive process includes a basic understanding of the tabernacle reaffirms the importance of this passage in Origen's pedagogy. That Hebrews 8:5 bears the burden of defining the task of spiritual interpretation in *De principiis* 4.2.6 accents this point further:[40]

πνευματικὴ δὲ διήγησις τῷ δυναμένῳ ἀποδεῖξαι, ποίων ἐπουρανίων ὑποδείγματι καὶ σκιᾷ" οἱ "κατὰ σάρκα Ἰουδαῖοι ἐλάτρευον, καὶ τίνων μελλόντων ἀγαθῶν ὁ νόμος ἔχει σκιάν.

But spiritual interpretation is for the one who is able to show of what heavenly realities the Jews according to the flesh serve the pattern and shadow, and of what good things to come the Law has as a shadow.

The "spirit" understood as the higher part of the soul and preeminently immaterial likely informs Origen's use of the term to describe a form of interpretation that moves beyond the perceptible and "earthly" phenomenon.[41] Origen's approach to reading is grounded in the principle that physical instantiation (text) is always tethered to an immaterial form (meaning). Reading, then, is coordinate with the very nature of reality, in which scripture participates. Daniel Boyarin, following the celebrated work of Angus Fletcher, observes that "the very existence of allegory as a hermeneutical theory is made thus dependent on a Platonic universe."[42] Hebrews provides the idiom by which Origen's method is expressed: identifying the heavenly

---

Henri Crouzel, Gennaro Lomiento, and Josep Rius-Camps (Bari: Università di Bari, 1975), 11–32, esp. 20–24.

[39] *De princ.* 4.2.2. Greek text in Henri Crouzel and M. Simonetti, eds., *Origène: Traité des Principes*, Sources chrétiennes 268 (Paris: Cerf, 1980), 302, 304.

[40] Greek text in SC 268.320. The other Pauline texts that Origen uses here include 2 Corinthians 2:7–8, 1 Corinthians 10:4, 10:11.

[41] See esp. Richard Horsley, "Pneumatikos vs. Psychikos Distinctions of Spiritual Status Among the Corinthians," *HTR* 69 (1976): 269–88.

[42] Daniel Boyarin, "Philo, Origen, and the Rabbis on Divine Speech and Interpretation," in *The World of Early Egyptian Christianity: Language, Literature, and Social Context*, ed. James E. Goehring and Janet A. Timbie (Washington, DC: Catholic University of America Press, 2007),

images lying behind the earthly shadows. However, here, and elsewhere, the shadows are conspicuously Jewish.

What Greer rightly identified was the role Hebrews 8:5 occupied in Origen's description of the art of reading. Origen prefers the shadows of Plato's cave to a temporal progression of revelation and so emphasizes the vertical and static correspondence between earthly and heavenly phenomena over historical and temporal categories of fulfillment.[43] Yet the Pauline and Jewish valence of Hebrews shaping that articulation escaped Greer's account of Origen's appropriation of the letter.[44] Ruth Clements has drawn attention to the Pauline core of Origen's contrast between spiritual and literal readings in *De principiis* 4.2–4.3 and judiciously notes that the opposition evoked by Hebrews 8:5 contrasts "spiritual" with those things that "Jews according to the flesh served."[45] What Hebrews 8:5 unifies into a single narrative nexus is Origen's conception of reading, Jews, Paul, and Christian difference. It is at the core of his description of the spiritual sense and juxtaposed with Jewish reading. The Letter to the Hebrews is for Origen a demonstration of Christian reading built upon a negative description of "the circumcision." While these uses of Hebrews accent the text's importance for Origen's conception of Jewish and Christian reading, they do not detail how Origen conceptualized the wider Pauline context of the letter.

Since a significant amount of Origen's corpus was translated from Greek into Latin by the late fourth-century philologist Rufinus of Aquileia, who openly acknowledged his abridgment and loose rendering of Origen's Greek, scholars since Erasmus have discussed the extent to which the specter of Rufinus looms over the Origenian corpus.[46] Rufinus appears to shore

---

117; cf. Angus John Stewart Fletcher, *Allegory: The Theory of a Symbolic Mode* (Ithaca: Cornell University Press, 1964).

[43] See Greer, *Capitan of Our Salvation*, 14–18.   [44] Greer, *Captain of Our Salvation*, 9.

[45] Ruth Clements, "Origen's Readings of Romans in *Peri Archon*: (Re)Constructing Paul," in *Early Patristic Readings of Romans*, ed. Kathy L Gaca and L. L. Welborn (New York: T&T Clark, 2005), 165. Origen cites 1 Corinthians 9:9, 2 Corinthians 2.7–8, 1 Corinthians 10:4, 10:11, Galations 4:21–24, Colossians 2:16–17, and Romans 11.4 in *De princ.* 4.2.6.

[46] On Rufinus' life see Francis X. Murphy, *Rufinus of Aquileia (345–410): His Life and Works* (Washington, DC: Catholic University of America Press, 1945); Caroline P. Hammond, "The Last Ten Years of Rufinus's Life and the Date of His Move South from Aquileia," *JTS* n.s. 28 (1977): 327–429. Rufinus discusses the "abridgement" of Origen's larger fifteen-volume work in a preface to the *Commentarii in Romanos* (cf. Jerome, *Ep.* 33.4, 57.5). Rufinus was also convinced that Origen's corpus had been corrupted and so sought to correct misunderstandings through the process of translation (see esp. the preface to *De princ.*). All of *De princ.* 4.3.6–8 is missing from Rufinus' Latin translation, the reasons for which scholars differ (see John Behr, *Origen: On First Principles*, vol. 2 [Oxford: Oxford University Press, 2017], 533 n. 77). On Rufinus as a translator see

up the Pauline attribution of Hebrews in, at least, *De principiis* 3.1.10,[47] which is the kind of editorial intervention one might expect, given the mounting pressure to affirm the Pauline status of Hebrews in the fourth century and Rufinus' aim to defend the theological reputation of Origen.[48] Recalling the tradition preserved by Eusebius, Origen addressed the disputed authorial status of Hebrews in his no longer extant *Homiliae in Hebraeos*, where he claimed that despite a distinctively non-Pauline style,

Caroline P. Hammond Bammel, *Der Römerbrief des Rufin und seine Origenes-Übersetzung*, AGLB 10 (Freiburg: Hinrichs, 1985); Henry Chadwick, "Rufinus and the Tura Papyrus of Origen's Commentary on Romans," *JThS* n.s. 10 (1959): 10–42, esp. at 15: "a prolix but more or less faithful paraphrase"; J. E. L. Oulton, "Rufinus's Translation of the Church History of Eusebius," *JThS* 30 (1929): 150–74; R. P. C. Hanson, *Origen's Doctrine of Tradition*, 40–47; Monica Wagner, *Rufinus the Translator: A Study of His Theory and Practice as Illustrated in His Version of the Apologetica of St. Gregory Nazianzen* (Washington, DC: Catholic University of America Press, 1945); F. Winkelmann, "Einige Bemerkungen zu den Aussagen des Rufinus von Aquileia und des Hieronymus uber ihre Ubersetzungstheorie und Methode," in *Kyriakon: Festschrift Johannes Quasten*, vol. 2, ed. P. Granfield and J. Jungmann (Münster: Verlag Aschendorff, 1970), 532–47.

[47] Origen's citation of Hebrews 6:7–8 features a modest authorial attribution in the Greek fragments of *De principiis* derived from the fourth-century compilation of Origenian passages collected by Basil and Gregory Nazianzen known as the *Philocalia* (*Phil.* 21.9: ὁ ἀπόστολος ἐν τῇ πρὸς Ἑβραίους [SC 268.56]). Andrew Blaski, "The *Philocalia of Origen*: A Crude or Creative Composition?," *VC* 73 (2019): 174–89, suggests a unifying logic of this excerpted text centered around the "Word of God," understood as the critical relation between text and *logos*. At the same location (*De princ.* 3.1.10), Rufinus' Latin text wraps this quotation within a more explicit Pauline frame: "Let us take the illustration used by the apostle Paul in the Epistle to the Hebrews...[citation of Heb 6:7–8].... Therefore, from those words of Paul which we have quoted..." (*quo in epistola ad Hebraeos usus est apostolus Paulus dicens...Igitur ex his quos adsumpsimus Pauli semonibus euidenter ostenditur* [Paul Koetschau, ed., *Origenes Werke Band 5 De Principiis*, GCS 22 (Berlin: de Gruyter, 1913), 210]). Editorial interventions also appear in Origen's Greek text; see for example, *Cels.* 4.17.

[48] On Arius' supposed rejection of Hebrews see Theodoret, *Praef. in ep. ad Hebr* and Epiphanius, *Haer.* 69.37. In Origen's seventh homily on Joshua, one reads of "fourteen" epistles of Paul (*Hom. Jes. Nav.* 7.1). On Rufinus's defense of Origen see *Apologia adversus Hieronymum*, *De adulteratione librorum Origenis*, as well as Jerome, *Adversus Rufinum libri III*. Rufinus attributed the *Dialogue of Adamantius* to Origen, which is likely related its resonances with the Council of Nicaea. Vinzenz Buchheit suggests that the dialogue was falsified by Rufinus; see "Rufinus von Aquileia als Fälscher des Adamantiosdialogs," *ByzZ* 51 (1958): 314–28. The earliest critics of Origen include Peter of Alexandria and Methodius of Olympus, who were followed by Epiphanius, Eustathius of Antioch, and Jerome. See Thomas Graumann, "Origenes—ein Kirchenvater? Vom Umgang mit dem origeneischen Erbe im frühen 4. Jahrhundert," in Perrone, *Origeniana Octava*, 877–88; Elizabeth Clark, *The Origenist Controversy: The Cultural Construction of an Early Christian Debate* (Princeton: Princeton University Press, 1992), esp. 159–93; Krastu Banev, *Theophilus of Alexandria and the First Origenist Controversy: Rhetoric and Power* (Oxford: Oxford University Press, 2015); Henri Crouzel, "Les condemnations subies par Origène et sa doctrine," in *Origeniana Septima*, ed. W. A. Bienert and U. Kühnweg (Belgium: Leuven University Press, 1999), 311–15. On the "second" Origenist controversy see F. Diekamp, *Die origenistischen Streitigkeiten im sechsten Jahrhundert und das fünfte allgemeine Concil* (Münster: Aschendorff, 1899); Brian Daly, "What Did Origenism Mean in the Sixth Century?," in *Origene et la Bible / Origen and the Bible*, ed. G. Dorival and A. le Boulluec, BETL, 118 (Leuven: Leuven University Press, 1995), 627–38; Daniel Hombergen, *The Second Origenist Controversy: A New Perspective on Cyril of Scythopolis' Monastic Biographies as Historical Sources for Sixth-Century Origenism* (Rome: Pontificio Ateneo S. Anselmo, 2001). On the difference between Jerome and Rufinus as one between "author" and "library" see C. Michael Chin, "Rufinus of Aquileia and Alexandrian Afterlives: Translation as Origenism," *JECS* 18 (2010): 617–47.

the "thoughts" (τὰ νοήματα) of the epistle are of equal status with the "acknowledged writings" (τῶν ἀποστολικῶν ὁμολογουμένων γραμμάτων).[49] Origen's critical impulse is on display in the *Letter to Africanus*, where it is enough to refer to "the author" (ὁ γράψας) of the Epistle to the Hebrews even though a lengthy argument might be made that "it was Paul's" (τοῦ εἶναι Παύλου τὴν ἐπιστολήν).[50] In the context of Origen's homilies and commentaries, Hebrews is unquestionably "Pauline," in that passages from the letter are often linked with other Pauline letters[51] and the association between "Paul" and the Letter to the Hebrews forms part of the interpretive frame in which passages are quoted.[52] Origen even provides a Pauline context for Hebrews in the ninth homily on Leviticus:[53]

> But first of all let us show how the Apostle says these things which are listed about sacrifices are figures and forms of which the truth is shown in other forms, lest the hearers think we take the Law of God in a preconceived sense and pervert it violently, as if apostolic authority sets no precedent in these things which we affirm. Paul, therefore, writing to the Hebrews, those, of course, who were indeed reading the Law and had meditated on these things and were examining them well but lacked understanding as to how the sacrifices should be understood, says this...

Here Origen quotes Hebrews 9:24 and 7:27, which together refer to the heavenly locus of Jesus' sacrifice as high priest. Origen then pivots to consider the purpose of the letter as a whole:

---

[49] Eusebius, *Hist. eccl.* 6.25.11.   [50] Greek text in SC 302.542, 544.
[51] For example, *De princ.* 3.2.4 (with Ephesians); *Cels.* 3.53; *Hom. Lev.* 10.2 (with 1 Cor), *Comm. Rom.* 5.1.39; *Comm. Jo.* 10.14.84 (with Col); *de Princ.* 4.2.6 (with 1–2 Cor, Gal, Col).
[52] For example, *De princ. praef.* 1; *Comm. Rom.* 3.8.11, 4.6.3, 5.1.14; *Comm. Cant.* 1.4; See also *Comm. Rom.* 5.1.14; *Comm. Jo.* 10.14.84; *Hom. Jer.* 1.8. For a survey of some of this material see Matthew J. Thomas, "Origen on Paul's Authorship of Hebrews," *NTS* 65 (2019): 598–609.
[53] *Hom. Lev.* 9.2.(1): *Paulus ergo ad Hebraeos scribens, eos scilicet qui legem quidem legerent et haec meditate haberent, et bene nota, sed indigerent intellectu, qualiter sentiri de sacrificiis debeat, hoc modo dicit....Onnem epistolam ipsam ad Hebraeos scriptam si quis recenseat, et praecipua eum locum, ubi pontificem legis confert pontifici repromissionis, de quo scriptum est...inveniet quomodo omnis hic locus Apostoli, exemplaria et formas ostendit esse rerum vivarum et verarum, ill aquae in lege scripta sunt* (GCS 29.419). Translation, Gary Wayne Barkley, *Origen: Homilies on Leviticus: 1–16*, FC 83 (Washington, DC: Catholic University of America Press, 1992), 178. Origen occasionally adds descriptive commentary when referring to Pauline epistles by name. Those in Corinth, for example, "were Greeks and had not yet been purified in their habits" (*Cels.* 3.53: Ἕλλησι μέν, οὐ κεκαθαρμένοις δέ πω τὰ ἤθη [GCS 2.248]). Other examples of named Pauline epistles include *De princ.* 4.2.6; *Cels.* 2.63, 2.65, 8.24 (1 Cor); *Cels.* 6.19 (2 Cor); *Cels.* 4.44 (Gal); *Cels.* 2.50 (2 Thess); *Cels.* 3.20 (Eph, Col, 1–2 Thess, Phil, and Rom).

If anyone examines the entire epistle written to the Hebrews (and especially this place where he compares the high priest of the Law to the high priest of the promise, about whom it was written, "You are a priest forever after the order of Melchizedek,") he will find how this entire passage of the Apostle shows those things that were written in the Law are "copies" and "forms" of living and true things (*inveniet quomodo omnis hic locus Apostoli, exemplaria et formas ostendit esse rerum vivarum et verarum, ill aquae in lege scripta sunt*).

Once again Origen connects passages from Hebrews that refer to the heavenly sphere as the ultimate domain of the high priest's activities to support the principle compacted into Hebrews 8:5, namely, that all of the earthly and physical *realia* recorded in the Law—the precise *way* that all rituals, figures, and histories are described in this "body" of texts—are in fact mere "copies" of "true things."[54] The "entire epistle" points toward this idea. From this contextual frame, then, "To the Hebrews" emerges as a Pauline letter designed to communicate the interpretive principle of earthly-heavenly correspondence to Jewish Christians who lack the ability to discern the meaning of Levitical sacrifices.[55]

The quasi compliment that the Hebrews were "examining well" may suggest that Origen imagines the audience of the letter is "Jewish Christians." The lexical and rhetorical distinction between an archaizing "Hebrew" and a pernicious "Jew" is less clear cut in Origen than it is for Clement, but the dominant connotation behind "Hebrew" is still positive.[56] Still, Origen uses

---

[54] In *Comm. Jo.* 13.146, Origen connects the idea of Jesus as a high priest in the heavenly places with an interpretive principle: "We want to honor God in truth and no longer in types, shadows, and examples, even as the angels do not serve God in examples and the shadow of heavenly realities, but in realities that belong to the spiritual and heavenly order, having a high priest of the order of Melchizedech as leader of the saving worship for those who need both the mystical and secret contemplation" (translation Ronald Heine, *Origen Commentary on the Gospel According to John Books 13–32*, FC 89 [Washington, DC: Catholic University of America Press, 1993], 99). Origen often uses Hebrews to refer to Jesus as a "high priest," *Comm. Jo.* 1.2.11, 1.23.141; *Hom. Jer.* 1.12, 4.2; *Hom. Gen.* 14:1; *Hom. Jes. Nav.* 2.1, 16.2–3, 27.1; *Hom. Lev.* 1.2, 2.3, 4.6, 7.1, 7.6, 12.1; *Comm. Rom.* 1.9.2, 6.12.5; and often in connection to Melchizedek, *Comm. Jo.* 1.11; *Hom. Jes. Nav.* 5.6; *Hom. Gen.* 9.1, 14.2; *Hom. Lev.* 5.3; *Comm. Rom.* 5.1. On the place of Melchizedek in Origen's thought see Pamela Bright, "The Epistle to the Hebrews in Origen's Christology," in *Origeniana Sexta: Origène et la Bible / Origen and the Bible: Actes du Colloquium Origenianum Sextum Chantilly, 30 août–3 septembre 1993*, ed. Gilles Dorival and Alain Le Boulluec (Leuven: Peeters, 1995), 559–65.

[55] See esp. *Comm. Jo.* 6.51.266–67.

[56] See esp. Gilles Dorival and Ron Naiweld, "Les interlocuteurs hébreux et juifs d'Origène à Alexandrie et à Césarée," in *Caesarea Maritima: A Retrospective after Two Millenia*, ed. A. Raban and K. G. Holum (Leiden: Köln, 1998), 121–38, who identify three groups of "Hebrews" with

language of the Ἰουδαίων πιστεύοντας (*Cels.* 2.1), or as one *qui ex Hebraeis ad Christi fidem uenerunt* (*Comm. Rom.* 10.7.4).[57] However, more important than the precision of the imagined audience for the letter as a whole is the import of Hebrews 8:5 throughout Origen's corpus; it is a description of the way *non-Christian* Jews read scriptural texts. Quite simply, "The apostle used to say about the Jews, 'They serve a shadow and a copy.'"[58] In a similar fashion with Clement, the fundamental issue facing Paul's audience was that they were *Jewish* Christians.

What Hebrews names and corrects in Origen's imagination is the Jewish way of reading scripture—the inability to transcend the material dimension of reality for the immaterial, the earthly for the heavenly, letter for spirit. Since Origen invests the letter with a Pauline context that recognizes the Jewish context of the title as well as the primacy of reading as the central point of the letter, "To the Hebrews" ties "Paul," "Jews," and "reading" together within a nexus of narrative coherence. Given this nexus, Hebrews is uniquely poised to articulate the crucial difference between Christianity and Judaism as a distinction of reading.

2. The Hermeneutical Herald and the Jewish Allegorist

While in Caesarea, Origen produced a lengthy response to Celsus, a late second-century Platonist scholar whose treatise *True Doctrine* (Λόγος Ἀληθής) was written "against the Christians" (κατὰ Χριστιανῶν).[59] Celsus

---

whom Origen engages: Hebrews within the "Grande Eglise" in Alexandria, Hebrews in Caesarea who participate in Christian communities but who do not form a homogenous group, and Hebrews within the Jewish academy in Caesarea. Jennifer Otto rightly points to the positive refers to *Ioudaioi* and pushes back against a strong division in *Philo of Alexandria and the Construction of Jewishness* (Oxford: Oxford University Press, 2018), 105–9, 114–15. For uses of "Hebrew" in Origen see *Comm. Rom.* 6.6.9 (Hebrew slave), 7.19.6, 10.7.4 (Hebrew Christians); *Hom. Jes. Nav.* 10.3, 15.6, *Hom. Jer.* 1.2; *Hom. Ezech.* 10.3; *Frag. Ezech.* 3.5 (Hebrew prophet); *Hom. Jer.* 13.2, 20.2 (Hebrew tradition); *Hom. Gen.* 16.1–3 (Exodus generation); *Hom. Exod.* 2.1, 3.3, 4.1, 4.6; *Hom. Ezech.* 1.4 (Hebrew calendar); *Frag. Ezech.* 5.8, 8.1 (Exodus generation), 8.14; *Hom. Lev.* 15.2; *De princ.* 4.1.1, *Comm. Cant.* 2.2; *Cels.* 2.77, 4.31, 5.10, 5.50.

[57] Greek and Latin texts in GCS 2.126; Bammel, *Der Römerbrief des Rufin*, 806.

[58] *Hom. Lev.* 13.1 (GCS 29.467: *Huius mysterii Apostolus conscius dicebat die Iudaeis quia*).

[59] *Cels. praef.* 1; Greek text in Paul Koetschau, *Origenes Werke Band 1, Die Schrift vom Martyrium, Buch I–IV gegen Celsus*, GCS 2 (Berlin: de Gruyer, 1899), 51. Henry Chadwick, *Origen: Contra Celsum* (Cambridge: Cambridge University Press, 1953), xiv, follows the tradition preserved in Eusebius (*Hist. eccl.* 6.36.2), that *Contra Celsum* was written after 245 CE but before the edict of Decius on sacrifice to the gods in 259 CE (see J. B. Rives, "The Decree of Decius and the Religion of Empire," *JRS* 89 [1999]: 135–54). Origen locates Celsus during the reign of Hadrian and is not to be confused with another "Celsus" working under Nero (*Cels.* 1.8, 3.80, 4.36, 4.54, 4.75, 5.3).

initially framed his criticism of Christianity through the voice of a Jew who questions Christian claims of newness.[60] In book 2 of *Contra Celsum*, the Jew addresses "Jewish people who have believed in Jesus" and asks them, "What was wrong with you that you left the Law of our fathers?" (τί παθόντες κατελίπετε τὸν πάτριον νόμον).[61]

Origen wryly points out that Celsus is "technically" mistaken—there are "Israelites who believe in Jesus who have not left the Law of their fathers."[62] Not only do "Jewish believers in Jesus" (Ἰουδαίων εἰς τὸν Ἰησοῦν πιστεύοντες) such as the Ebionites (Ἐβιωναῖοι) still live according to the Law, but Peter the Jew also maintained the "Jewish customs according to the Mosaic Law" (τὰ κατὰ τὸν Μωϋσέως νόμον ἰουδαϊκὰ ἔθη) for quite some time.[63] Here Origen makes an interesting move and decides to provide Celsus with what would be a better argument. Celsus *should* have pointed out that when viewed from the outside, Christians appear deeply inconsistent when it comes to practicing Jewish customs, since there are those who have ceased these practices because they adopt "interpretations and allegories," while others accept a spiritual reading but still "observe the customs of [their] fathers as much as before."[64] Celsus' Jew should have argued that internal divisions among Christian groups regarding the place of Jewish Law call into question the legitimacy of Christian origins, thereby framing the emergence

---

See Silke-Petra Bergjan, "Celsus the Epicurean? The Interpretation of an Argument in Origen, Contra Celsum," *HTR* 94.2 (2001): 179–204; Michael Frede, "Celsus's Attack on the Christians," in *Philosophia Togata II: Plato and Aristotle at Rome*, ed. Jonathan Barnes and Miriam T. Griffin (Oxford: Clarendon, 1997), 232–40; Robert Louis Wilken, *The Christians as the Romans Saw Them*, 2nd ed. (New Haven: Yale University Press, 2003), 94–125.

[60] Cf. *Cels.* 1.71. Origen is adamant that Celsus's Jew is an "imaginary character" (*Cels.* 2.1). Ernst Bammel, "Die Zitate in Origenes' Schrift wider Celsus," in *Judaica et Paulina* 2, WUNT 91 (Tübingen: Mohr Siebeck, 1997), 57–61, wonders whether Origen would have recognized Celsus' Jew given his position in Caesarea. On the authenticity of Celsus' Jew and the nature of Jewish sources possibly involved see James Carleton Paget, "The Jew of Celsus and *adversus Judaeos* literature," *ZAC* 21.2 (2017): 201–42; Maren Niehoff, "A Jewish Critique of Christianity from the Second Century: Revisiting the Jew Mentioned in Contra Celsum," *JECS* 21 (2013): 151–75, esp. 154–59; Marc Lods, "Étude sur les sources juives de la polémique de Celse contre les chrétiens," *Revue d'Histoire et de Philosophie Religieuses* 21 (1941): 1–33. The text of *True Doctrine* is no longer extant, but Origen loosely structures *Contra Celsum* as a line-by-line response and so preserves at least a skeleton of Celsus' argument. Still, we know that Origen restructures Celsus' work to some extent, whether through omissions or reordering (see *Cels. praef.* 6).

[61] *Cels.* 2.3. GCS 2.129.

[62] *Cels.* 2.3 (GCS 2.130: Ἰσραηλίτας εἰς Ἰησοῦν πιστεύοντας καὶ οὐ καταλιπόντας τὸν πάτριον νόμον).

[63] *Cels.* 2.1. Prior to the vision of Gentile inclusion in Acts 10, Peter "was still a Jew and was still living according to the traditions of the Jews, despising those outside Judaism" (GCS 2.129: ἔτι Ἰουδαῖος καὶ κατὰ τὰς Ἰουδαίων παραδόσεις ζῶ).

[64] *Cels.* 2.3. There is even a third group who simply accepts that Jesus is one prophesied and also observes the Law of Moses.

of the movement as an illegitimate offshoot of Judaism. If Celsus had made this point, Origen would have responded that discrepancy among Christians such as the Ebionites is the lingering vestiges of a Jewish method of reading scriptural texts that Jesus corrected, albeit tactfully. From the beginning, Origen reasons, the Christian movement wrestled to be free of its Jewish past, and the separation is fundamentally rooted in the practice of reading.

Peter himself waivered on this point because he "had not yet learned from Jesus to ascend from the letter of the Law to its spiritual interpretation."[65] Origen refers the reader to Jesus' comments in John 16:12–13, where Jesus says that he has "many things" to say to the disciples, but they cannot bear them at the present time. In Origen's reading of the passage, Jesus sought to introduce a hermeneutic that was an affront to the Jewishness of the disciples. Origen explains:[66]

> This is my view. Perhaps because the apostles were Jews and had been brought up (συντραφεῖσι) according to the letter of the Mosaic law (τῷ κατὰ τὸ γράμμα Μωϋσέως νόμῳ), he had to tell them what was the true law, and of what heavenly things the Jewish worship was a pattern and shadow (ὑποδείγματι καὶ σκιᾷ), and what were the good things to come of which a shadow was provided by the law about meat and drink and feasts and new moons and sabbaths. These were the "many things" which he had to tell them. But he saw that it is very difficult to eradicate doctrines from a soul with which he was almost born and was brought up until he reached man's estate, and which persuade those who accept them that they are divine and that to overthrow them is impious.

Using the language of Hebrews 8:5 (and 10:1 and 9:11), Origen positions Jesus as the bearer of a new understanding of earthly, perceptible, and embodied Jewish phenomena, infusing these features with new meaning and significance, which, ultimately, entails the cessation of Jewish ritual and cultic practices. Later, Origen explains "many things" in a way that (re) emphasizes the centrality of non-Jewish reading as the marker of Christian newness. What Jesus taught was a method of interpretation and explanation (διηγήσεως καὶ σαφηνείας) of the Law according to the spiritual sense

---

[65] Cels. 2.1 (GCS 2.127 (ὡς μηδέπω ἀπὸ τοῦ Ἰησοῦ μαθὼν ἀναβαίνειν ἀπὸ τοῦ κατὰ τὸ γράμμα νόμου ἐπὶ τὸν κατὰ τὸ πνεῦμα).
[66] Cels. 2.2. GCS 2.128. Translation, Chadwick, Origen: Contra Celsum, 67–68, slightly modified.

that the disciples were not able to handle "because they had been born and brought up among the Jews."[67]

Origen's response is curiously circular; Celsus' Jew is wrong that Jews abandon the Law when becoming Christian, but ultimately, if consistent in following Jesus, that is precisely what they should have done, despite Origen's claim that abandoning its practices through spiritual reading is keeping the Law. The question posed by Celsus' Jews, therefore, remains: "What was wrong with you that you left the Law of your fathers?"[68] A fully Origenian response requires both connectivity and separation as Origen works within the well-established anti-Marcionite position that "Christianity has its origins in Judaism,"[69] yet also speaks of a definitive and punctiliar moment of "transfer" between two peoples.[70] Origen claims Jesus as the initiator of Christianity but does not evoke Jesus' Jewishness as a way of providing Christianity with a Jewish past. In fact, Origen consciously avoids the Jewishness of Jesus.[71] Indeed, Jesus was born of the "former people"

---

[67] *Cels.* 2.2 (GCS 2.128 πολλὰ γὰρ τὰ τῆς τοῦ νόμου κατὰ τὰ πνευματικὰ διηγήσεως καὶ σαφηνείας· καὶ οὐκ ἐδύναντο πως βαστάζειν αὐτὰ οἱ μαθηταί, ἐν Ἰουδαίοις γεγεννημένοι καὶ ἀνατεθραμμένοι τότε). Accordingly, Jesus found it difficult to show that the things written in the Law are "loss" (Phil 3:8) and so delayed this information "until a more suitable time after his passion and resurrection" Cf. also *Comm. Jo.* 10. 299.

[68] Origen returns to this question in *Cels.* 2.3.

[69] See *Cels.* 1.2 ("Judaism upon which Christianity depends"; GCS 2.57: τὸν ἰουδαϊσμόν, οὗ χριστιανισμὸς ἤρτηται); *Cels.* 1.22 ("He thinks he will more easily prove Christianity to be untrue if he can show its falsehood by attacking its origin in Judaism"; GCS 2.73: τῆς ἀρχῆς αὐτοῦ ἐν τοῖς ἰουδαϊκοῖς). One implication of this notion of connectedness is that Origen is quick to identify what he thinks are "misrepresentations" of Jews and frequently criticizes anti-Jewish tropes concerning the history of the Jews in Egypt (*Cels.* 1.26, 3.3, 4.31, 4.35). In fact, it is unusual to find Origen describe Jews as "bitter" (χολήν, *Cels.* 2.29 [GCS 2.157]), as "not well read in Greek literature" (Οὐ πάνυ μὲν οὖν Ἰουδαῖοι τὰ Ἑλλήνων φιλολογοῦσιν, *Cels.* 2.34 [GCS 2.160]), or as people who "spread rumours" (κατασκεδάσασι δυσφημίαν τοῦ λόγου *Cels.* 6.28 [GCS 3.97]). Origen is much more interested in defending Jews as a "holy and exceptional society" insofar as it legitimizes Christian claims to antiquity (τὰ τῆς σεμνῆς καὶ ἐξαιρέτου Ἰουδαίων πολιτείας, *Cels.* 5.42 [GCS 3.45]). Still, Hermann Josef Vogt, "Die Juden beim späten Origenes," in *Origenes als Exeget*, ed. Wilhelm Geerlings (Paderborn: Ferdinand Schöningh, 1999), 236, is right that Origen defends the Jews against these attacks only to point out the "valid approaches" (Origenes verteidigt die Juden also sozusagen nur deswegen gegen falsche Anschuldigungen, um die begründeten Vowürfe deutlich herauszustellen). On Marcion see *Comm. Rom.* 2.13.27; J. Rius-Camps, "Orígenes y Marción: Caracter preferentemente antimarcionita del Prefacio y del segundo ciclo del Peri archon," *Origeniana*, 297–313. On Origen's defense of the political and social life of Israel see Lorenzo Perrone, "Die 'Verfassung der Juden': Das biblische Judentum als politisches Modell in Origenes' *Contra Celsum*," *ZAC* 7 (2003): 310–28.

[70] The Jews were "loved" and had "favor with God" but Jesus "transferred the power at work among the Jews to those Gentiles who believed in him" (*Cels.* 5.50). GCS 3.54–55: ταύτην δὲ τὴν οἰκονομίαν μεταβεβηκέναι καὶ τὴν χάριν ἐφ' ἡμᾶς, μεταστήσαντος τὴν ἐν Ἰουδαίοις δύναμιν ἐπὶ τοὺς ἀπὸ τῶν ἐθνῶν πιστεύσαντας αὐτῷ Ἰησοῦ. In *Hom. Jer.* 4.1, the Jews have been handed a "bill of divorce" (similarly, *Cels.* 4.3). See also "transfer" in *Hom. Lev.* 12.5; *Comm. Cant.* 2.1; *Hom. Jer.* 11.6, 18.5; *Cels.* 2.8.

[71] For example, the Samaritan woman in John 4 incorrectly assumed that Jesus was a Jew when broaching the question of geography and worship (*De princ.* 1.1.4; cf. also *Cels.* 6.70). See here

according to the flesh, but his *anima* (soul) derives from "the *genere* and *substantia* of all human *animarum*."[72] Origen muses that Jesus came "to live among" the Jews and not some other nation because the former was especially conditioned to receive and experience "miracles" (*Cels.* 2.57). What Origen emphasizes is how Jesus "stopped" circumcision (*Cels.* 1.23)[73] and was able to convince others to "join him in abandoning the Law" (*Cels.* 1.30).[74] Within the context of *Contra Celsum*, what Origen needs is a Jew to embrace Jesus' way of finding new meaning in the earthly Jewish shadows and thereby replicate the larger vision of Jewish-Christian connectivity and parting simultaneously.

If Origen's Jesus directs the attention of the earliest Jewish disciples to the "heavenly things of which Jewish worship was a pattern and shadow," Origen's Paul is the Jew who grabbed hold of this conviction with unwavering certainty. "Our Paul," Origen notes, "was educated in those prophetic writings and desired the things of the other world and the region beyond the heavens."[75] Since Origen's Paul is a Jewish reader of scriptural texts who recognizes the heavenly significance of Israel's history and embraces allegory as a way of reading its sacred texts, Origen is able to frame the origins of Christianity as a legitimate development out of Judaism (τῆς ἀρχῆς αὐτοῦ ἐν τοῖς ἰουδαϊκοῖς).[76] Hence rather than dismiss or otherwise diminish

---

Barbara U. Meyer, *Jesus the Jew in Christian Memory* (Cambridge: Cambridge University Press, 2020), 66–98.

[72] *Hom. Lev.* 12.5, GCS 6.646: *ex genere et ex substantia fuerit hunianarum omnium animarum*. Cf. also Origen's discussion of the "seed of Abraham" in *Comm. Jo.* 21.1(5). Origen refers to the Jews as the "former people" (*prioris populi*, τοῦ προτέρου λαοῦ) in *De princ.* 4.1.4; *Hom. Jes. Nav.* 17.1; *Comm. Cant.* 2.1, 2.10; *Hom. Jer.* 14.12.

[73] Cf. also *Cels.* 1.29, where Origen responds to Celsus' account of an adulterous country woman named Mary who gave birth to Jesus in a poor Jewish village. Origen admits Jesus' humble beginnings, yet reasons that Jesus was able to devote himself to "teaching new doctrines and introduce to humanity a doctrine that did away with the customs of the Jews" while revering the prophets, because he was the recipient of serious education (GCS 2.80: ἐπεισάγων τῷ γένει τῶν ἀνθρώπων λόγον τά τε Ἰουδαίων ἔθη καταλύοντα μετὰ τοῦ σεμνοποιεῖν αὐτῶν τοὺς προφήτας).

[74] *Cels.* 2.52. Jesus introduced a new πολιτείαν (one according to τὸ εὐαγγέλιον) into one already existing but governed by "ancestral ethical codes and cultivation according to the established laws" (GCS 2.175: ἔθεσι πατρῴοις καὶ ἀνατροφαῖς ταῖς κατὰ τοὺς κειμένους νόμους). Cf. also *Cels.* 8.29, where Origen discusses eating meat and connects the idea of Jesus' renunciation of food laws (via Matt 15:11), with Paul's capacious comments (1 Cor 8:8) and the Jerusalem council's hesitation (Acts 15:22, 28–29).

[75] *Cels.* 6:19 (GCS 3.90: Καὶ ἀπ' ἐκείνων γε τῶν λόγων παιδευθεὶς ὁ Παῦλος ἡμῶν καὶ ποθῶν τὰ ὑπερκόσμια καὶ ὑπερουράνια καὶ δι' ἐκεῖνα πάντα πράττων, ἵν' αὐτῶν τύχῃ).

[76] *Hom. Gen.* 3.5: "For I do not permit you to take refuge in our allegories which Paul taught." *Hom. Gen.* 10.5: "I, following Paul the apostle, say that these things are 'allegories.'" This image of Paul the allegorist also refutes Celsus' dismissal of the allegorical potential of scriptural texts and that only later readers "take refuge" in allegory out of shame. Origen reasons that, since the very authors of the doctrines themselves and the writers interpreted these narratives allegorically, "what else can we suppose except that they were written with the primary intention that they should be

Paul's Jewishness, Origen celebrates that Paul is "the apostle from Israel" (*Hom. Jer.* 5.1), who "came to Christianity from the Jews" (*Cels.* 5.60).[77] While Paul provides Origen with a connection to Judaism, the apostle is also the one who embodies and performs the transition initiated theoretically by Jesus, by reading scriptural texts according to the principle of Hebrews 8:5.

What Hebrews 8:5 affords Origen in particular is a Pauline statement on the referent of scripture in explicit contrast to Jewish readers and so is programmatic for configuring Paul as a reader of scriptural texts in contrast to his own Jewish heritage. In *Homilies on Leviticus* 7.4.(2), for example, Origen notes that Paul was "a Hebrew of Hebrews according to the Law" and so "would never dare to speak of spiritual food and spiritual drink unless he had learned that this is the meaning of the Lawgiver through the knowledge of the truest doctrine handed down to him."[78] What Paul learned was that all these things are "a shadow of future things."[79] This Pauline conviction resurfaces in *Homilies on Numbers* 28, where Origen considers the land boundaries in Numbers 34–35 and asks how this passage should be read in the church, since to read "according to the sense of the Jews" (*Iudaeorum sensum*) will render the passages "superfluous" (*superflua*) and "pointless" (*inania*).[80] Origen reasons that "if we believe what Paul says in a mystery, that those who serve through the Law are serving "the shadow and image of heavenly things," then a new exegetical pursuit is opened up, as described in Sirach 4:22: "I went after [Wisdom] as a tracker."[81]

---

allegorized?" (*Cels.* 4.49). Three Pauline texts are especially important for Origen in this regard: Galatians 4:21–24 and 1 Corinthians 3:6, 9:9. Predictably, Paul's interpretation of Hagar and Sarah as an "allegory" is used by Origen as justification for his own promotion of an allegorical method (*Hom. Gen* 7.2; *Cels.* 4.44; *Comm. Cant.* 2.3; Alain Le Boulluec, "De Paul à Origène: Continuité ou divergence?," in *Allégorie des poètes, allégorie des philosophes: Études sur la poétique et l'herméneutique de l'allégorie de l'antiquité à la réforme*, ed. Gilbert Dahan and Richard Goulet, Fédération de recherche 33 du C.N.R.S., Textes et traditions 10 (Paris: Vrin, 2005), 113–32. The passage in 1 Corinthians 9:9 is similarly important for Origen. The law regarding the muzzling of an ox was, according to Paul, written "on our account." Both texts are "a few examples out of a great number" that deny Celsus' claim that scriptural texts "cannot be interpreted allegorically" (*Cels.* 4.49, cf. 4.44). The association between letter and death as well as a spirit and life in 2 Corinthians 3.6 fits well with Origen's largely twofold reading strategy which uses the same language.

[77] Paul is also "magnificent" (*Comm. Cant.* 2.2) and "divine" (*De princ.* 4.2.6).
[78] Throughout the *Commentarii in Romanos* Origen reconciles Paul's biographical claim in Romans 7:9, "once alive without the law" (ἔζων χωρὶς νόμου ποτέ), with another biographical claim in Philippians 3:5, "circumcised on the eighth day" (περιτομῇ ὀκταήμερος) and "a Hebrew born of Hebrews" (Ἑβραῖος ἐξ Ἑβραίων). For Origen, Paul was without the Law for a brief period as a child, that is, when unable to distinguish between good and evil (*Comm. Rom.* 3.2.7; 5.1.26, 6.8.7; cf. also *Comm. Rom.* 10.39.2; *Hom. Ezech.* 4.4).
[79] *Hom. Lev.* 7.4. GCS 29.382–83.   [80] *Hom. Num* 28.1. GCS 30.281.
[81] *Hom. Num* 28.1. GCS 30.281.

Origen uses Hebrews 8:5, then, to frame the relationship between Christianity and Judaism and represents Jesus and Paul as the figures who announce and enact that relationship. For Origen, the description of the physical tabernacle as a copy or shadow of a heavenly version is but one instance of a universal principle of correspondence in which the perceptible world and the book of scripture are both and together signifiers of a signified higher reality. So too, Paul is not only as an allegorical reader of a Jewish book but one who views the totality of "Judaism" as a shadow. The contrast between an "outward Jew" (τῷ φανερῷ Ἰουδαῖος) and a "secret Jew" (τῷ κρυπτῷ Ἰουδαῖος) in Paul's address (to what many think is a circumcised Gentile) in Romans 2:28–28 is a central Pauline distinction with which Origen builds an overarching contrast between Judaism and Christianity as distinct material and immaterial approaches.[82] The cacophony of dissimilarities is expressed most forcefully in *Commentary on the Epistle to the Romans* 9.1.(1):[83]

Cum per omnem textum epistulae in superioribus docuisset apostolus, quomodo a Iudaeis ad gentes, a circumcisione ad fidem, a littera ad spiritum, ab umbra ad veritatem, ab observantia carnali ad observantiam spiritalem religionis summa translata sit.

In the entire preceding text of the epistle [Romans 1–11] the Apostle had shown how the essence of *religionis* has been transferred from the Jews to the Gentiles, from circumcision to faith, from the letter to the Spirit, from shadow to truth, from fleshly observance to spiritual observance.

Since the physical, material, and otherwise perceptible features of the Jewish tradition are vessels of a higher and secondary meaning, Paul "did

---

[82] Given the context of Romans 2, Origen focalizes the contrast around circumcision. See, for example, *Comm. Jo.* 1.40–41; *Hom. Lev.* 6.3; *Hom. Gen.* 3.5. Origen refers to Jewish ethnicity in a variety of ways, for example, *sanguis* (*Hom. Lev.* 5.11 [GCS 29.353: τῷ γένει τῶν Ἑβραίων]; *Cels.* 2.77 [GCS 2.200]), κατὰ σάρκα Ἰσραηλίτῃ (*Cels.* 2.1 [GCS 2.127]), προγόνων Ἑβραίων (*Cels.* 3.8 [GCS 2.209]).

[83] Latin text in Caroline P. Hammond Bammel, *Der Römerbriefkommentar des Origenes: Kritische Ausgabe der Übersetzung Rufins, Buch 7–10*, Vetus Latina 34 (Frieburg: Herder, 1998), 710. Translation, Scheck, *Origen: Homilies on Numbers*, 191. Theresia Heither suggests that idea "transfer" as central to Origen's *Commentarii*, see *Translatio Religionis: Die Paulusdeutung des Origenes in seinem Kommentar zum Römerbrief*, Bonner Beiträge zur Kirchengeschichte 16 Cologne: Boehlau, 1990), esp. 57–67. Caroline P. Bammel argues that Rufinus minimized Origen's construal of the Jewish-Christian audience of Paul's Letter to the Romans, especially in the early books of the commentary, see "Origen's Pauline Prefaces and the Chronology of His Pauline Commentaries," in Dorival and Le Boulluec, *Origeniana Sexta*, 509–10.

not keep the tradition of the Jews" after receiving "the faith of Christ."[84] The totality of Judaism as fodder for Christian allegoresis is displayed forcefully in the *Commentarium in Canticum Canticorum*. In book 2, Origen comments on the Greek version of Song of Songs 1:11a, in which a group declares their intention to make "likeness of gold" for the "Bride" (ὁμοιώματα χρυσίου ποιήσομέν σοι).[85] "True gold" designates incorporeal, unseen, and spiritual things, not bodily and visible things, the "truth's shadow." Origen keys into the idea of "likeness" and reasons that since the Law is ordained by angels (Gal 3:19) and has "a shadow of the good things to come" (Heb 10.1), then "all the things that happened to those who are described as being under the Law happened in a figure, not in the truth."[86] Origen defers again to the tabernacle as an example of the "likeness of gold," since the apostles says that Jesus entered not into the "patterns of the truth, but into heaven itself" (Heb 9:24).[87] Origen concludes from this that "the whole of the *iudaicus cultus et religio*" is to be read as this "likeness of gold."[88] Elsewhere, Origen claims the beginner must learn to interpret (διηγήσει) and explain (σαφηνείᾳ) not only the prophetic writings but the "holy things of Moses" (τῶν ἱερῶν Μωϋσέως).[89]

Rufinus' translation, *religio et cultus*, suggests that the totality of Jewish history, genealogy, practice, and text is for Origen material infused with allegorical potential.[90] Since the written word, the physical world, and

---

[84] *Comm. Cant.* 2.3.
[85] See J. Christopher King, *Origen on the Song of Songs as the Spirit of Scripture: The Bridegroom's Perfect Marriage-Song* (Oxford: Oxford University Press, 2005).
[86] *Comm. Cant.* 2.8.
[87] Origen also includes as "likeness," the "Ark of the Testimony, the propitiatory, and the cherubim, and the altar of incense, and the table of proposition, and the loaves; likewise the veil, and the pillars, and the bars, and the altar of holocausts, and the Temple itself, and all the things that are written in the Law."
[88] *Comm. Cant.* 2.8.20. Latin text in L. Brésard and H. Crouzel, eds., *Origène: Commentaire sur le Cantique des Cantiques*, vol. 1, Sources chrétiennes 375 (Paris: Cerf, 1991), 418: *Omnis ergo iudaicus cultus et religio similitudines sunt auri.*
[89] *Cels.* 2.4 (GCS 2.130). See also *Hom. Jes. Nav.* 17.2: "Moses was a minister of the shadow and copy so that the Levitical order could not actually access the wisdom and knowledge of God." Daniel Schwartz, "Herodians and *Ioudaioi* in Flavian Rome," in *Flavius Josephus and Flavian Rome*, ed. Jonathan Edmondson, Steve Mason, and James Rivers (Oxford: Oxford University Press, 2005), 76, points out that Roman texts in Josephus (*AJ* 14. 228, 234, 237, 240, 258) refer to the ἱερὰ Ἰουδαϊκὰ that are observed by Jews living in the diaspora and that "we are basically in the realm of religion, not state" since the discussion regards whether they are to be permitted or not.
[90] Similarly see *Comm. Cant.* 3.5.13 (*et quomodo omnem Veterum culturam exemplar et umbram pronuntiet esse caelestium*, "all the rites of the ancients were an example and shadow of heavenly things"). Latin text in L. Brésard and H. Crouzel, eds., *Origène: Commentaire sur le Cantique des Cantiques*, vol. 1, Sources chrétiennes 376 (Paris: Cerf, 1992), 530, 532. Brent Nongbri, *Before Religion A History of a Modern Concept* (New Haven: Yale University Press, 2015), 25–28, points to Cicero (*On the Nature of the Gods*) and Lucretius (*On the Nature of Things*) as some of the earliest

(ethnic) Jews are all perceptible copies of heavenly, immaterial realities, Origen links Jewish ethnicity and scripture as ontologically analogous. In *Homilies on Leviticus* 5.1.(3) Origen connects these two ideas, moving seamlessly from "text" to "Jew." If the laws concerning grain and sin offerings in Leviticus 6 are read literally (*litterae textus*), says Origen, they will function as an "obstacle and ruin of the *Christianae religioni*."[91] However, if their proper sense is identified, then those who hear will becomes a "secret" Jew, not "in appearance."[92] So too, Origen wields the contrast between a fleshly, exterior Jew and a secret, interior Jew drawn from Romans 2:28 with the quality of scripture itself, with its bodily and "inner" sense. For Origen, to be a Jew is to be "outward," and thus to read "Jewishly" is to read texts "outwardly."[93]

In the wider context of Origen's response to Celsus, as well as his corpus as a whole, a conception of Judaism in relation to Christianity emerges in which the two relate to each other as the earthly phenomena and surface content of scripture relates to heavenly realities and spiritual meaning, as expressed in Hebrews 8:5.[94] Certainly, Origen often repudiates the "letter" as a means of ascending to the spiritual sense, whether it is deemed unprofitable, logically false, ahistorical, or otherwise inadequate, mirroring Origen's language of a transfer between people, but Origen also coordinates the senses as mutually informing, particularly in the *Commentarium in Canticum Canticorum*, where the "sequence of the narrative" is vital for spiritual interpretation.[95] In both instances, Origen's Christian allegoresis

examples (first century BCE) in which *religio* and "gods" are loosely associated. Nongbri finds that the early Christian use of *religio* in Minucius Felix, Tertullian, Arnobius, and Lactantius might suggest "rule," "worship practice," or "excessive concern about the gods," depending on context (28).

[91] GCS 6.332.
[92] Origen also connects the idea of a "secret Jew" with proper reading in *De princ.* 4.2.5, 4.3.6.
[93] *Hom. Jer.* 12.13 (GCS 6.99: Ὁ Ἰουδαῖος οὐκ ἀκούει κεκρυμμένως τοῦ νόμου· διὰ τοῦτο φανερῶς περιτέμνεται, οὐκ εἰδὼς ὅτι οὐχ "ὁ ἐν τῷ φανερῷ Ἰουδαῖός ἐστιν, οὐδὲ ἡ ἐν τῷ φανερῷ ἐν σαρκὶ περιτομή." Ὁ δὲ ἀκούων τῆς περιτομῆς κεκρυμμένως, "ἐν κρυπτῷ" περιτμηθήσεται; "The Jew does not hear the Law in a hidden way. Because of this he is circumcised outwardly, for he does not know that one is not a Jew who is one outwardly, nor is circumcision something outward in the flesh"). See also the ethnic-coded descriptions of reading as Jewish in *De princ.* 2.11.2 and *Comm. Jo.* 10.291.
[94] As John McGuckin observes, Origen advances a "conception of a Judaism interpreted through a Platonizing hermeneutic" ("Origen on the Jews," in *Christianity and Judaism: Papers Read at the 1991 Summer Meeting and the 1992 Winter Meeting of the Ecclesiastical History Society*, ed. D. Wood, Studies in Church History 29 [Oxford: Blackwell, 1992], 12).
[95] See esp. *Comm. Cant.* 3.8; 3.11: "We have anticipated these things and connected them with the preceding, so as not to leave the impression that we were disrupting the order of the play and the text of the narrative" (translation, Lawson, *Origen, The Song of Songs*, 208). When scriptural texts are rightly calibrated according to the letter and all the particularity accounted for, they provide a path through which to discern its reference and is therefore afforded its own integrity on

requires a Jewish *sensus literalis* since there is no image without the shadow.[96] For Origen, Christianity is continually produced by "reading" Judaism. Accordingly, it is the art of reading that uniquely legitimizes Christian newness while also preserving the Jewish heritage of Christianity, a schema that Jesus and Paul are made to narrate as the founders.

3. Hebrews or the Hebrew Tradition?

Origen's relocation in Caesarea Maritima marks an increase in references to Jews, Jewish practice, and, with that, the polemic against Jewish reading.[97] Throughout the twentieth century, a number of scholars explored Origen's literary interaction with contemporary Judaism in Caesarea, but the actual evidence of connection is far less concrete than the common image of Origen as a friendly colleague of contemporary rabbis. David Halperin claims that Origen drew upon a "complex of homiletical expositions" used in Caesarean synagogues on Shabuʻot (Feast of Weeks) in *Homiliae in*

---

more than one occasion. On the text "according to the letter" and its *historia*, see Torjesen, *Hermeneutical Procedure*, 138; Young, *Biblical Exegesis*, 79. Cf. also *Cels.* 4.47 and especially *Hom. Gen.* 2.2–3, where Origen defends the literal sense against Apelles.

[96] See A. Fürst and H. Strutwolf, *Der Kommentar zum Hohelied, Eingeleitet und übersetzt*, Origenes Werke mit deutscher Übersetzung, Bd. 9.1 (Berlin: de Gruyter, 2016), 12–15. Edwards, *Origen Against Plato*, 126: "Just as souls and bodies do not dwell in parallel worlds, but one is immanent in the other as the source and pilot of its vital functions, so the allegorical sense is not at war with the literal, but on the contrary endows it with the coherence and vitality of truth." At times, Origen moves from the "letter" to the "spiritual" sense without any justification or point of transition, simply moving on through the stages of exegesis. Some choice examples of this include *Hom. Gen.* 1.1; *Hom. Lev.* 9.9; *Hom. Jer.* 4.1, 19.14; *Comm. Cant.* 1.2. In other instances, critical tools like refutation are used to generate reasons for interpreting scriptural texts beyond the mere story or "letter." Other examples include any text that cannot "literally" be true, like an intoxicated person growing thorns in their hand (*Hom. Lev.* 16.5; *Hom. Gen.* 2.6) or directives that might be impossible to carry out (*De princ.* 4.3.2; *Comm. Rom.* 6.12). Origen often presses the value of a literal reading, texts that do not "edify" or "profit" the reader (*Comm. Song.* 4.14; *Hom. Exod.* 7.3) or God does not appear "proper" (*Hom. Jer.* 12.1).

[97] Vogt, "Die Juden beim späten Origenes," 255–39; A. Tzvetkova-Glaser, "Polemics Against Judeo Christian Practices in Origen's Homilies," *Studia Patristica* 46 (2010): 217–22; Heine, *Origen Commentary*, 158. On the political and social contours of Caesarea as well as the history of Jews in the ancient city see Lee Levine, *Caesarea under Romans Rule*, SJLA 7 (Leiden: Brill, 1975), esp. 46–106; Joseph Patrich, "Caesarea Maritima in the Time of Origen," in *Origeniana Duodecima: Origen's Legacy in the Holy Land—a Tale of Three Cities: Jerusalem, Caesarea and Bethlehem, Proceedings of the 12th International Origen Congress, Jerusalem, June 25–29, 2017*, ed. Brouria Bitton-Ashkelony, Oded Irshai, Aryeh Kofsky, Hillel Newman, and Lorenzo Perrone, BETL 302 (Leuven: Peeters, 2019), 375–409; Irving M. Levey, "Caesarea and the Jews," in *The Joint Expedition to Caesarea Maritima*, vol. 1, ed. C. T. Fritsch (Missoula: Scholars Press, 1975), 43–78; Michele Murray, "Jews and Judaism in Caesarea Maritima," in *Religious Rivalries and the Struggle for Success in Caesarea Maritima*, ed. Terence L. Donaldson, ESCJ 8 (Waterloo: Wilfrid Laurier University Press, 2000), 127–52.

Ezechielem 1, but dependency is inferred from opaque parallels and the rabbinic text might very well be post-Talmudic.[98] Origen's *Homiliae in Leviticum* has also been brought into comparison with relevant Mishnaic readings of Leviticus, although the juxtaposition reveals no direct interpretive overlap.[99] Origen's *Commentarium in Canticum Canticorum* has long received the most attention along these lines.

In an often-cited piece, Reuven Kimelman argues that Origen and Rabbi Yoḥanan were aware of each other's interpretive tendencies and that the rabbi waged an "exegetical battle" against Origen.[100] Kimelman focuses on the opening verses of the Song of Songs and finds certain antitheses between the two ancient exegetes that are understood as coordinate and directly combative. The parallels deduced are direct inversions framed as the vestiges of an exchange.[101] Further, Kimelman positions Rabbi Yoḥanan

---

[98] D. J. Halperin, "Origen, Ezekiel's Merkabah, and the Ascension of Moses," *CH* 50 (1981): 261-75. esp. 268; Abraham Wasserstein / אברהם וסרשטיין, "A Rabbinic Midrash as a Source of Origen's Homily on Ezekiel / מדרש יהודי אצל אוריגנס," *Tarbiz*/תרביץ 46 (1977): 317-18, who briefly considers *Hom. Ezech.* 4.8.

[99] Robert L. Wilken, "Origen's Homilies on Leviticus and Vayikra Rabbah," in Dorival and Le Boulluec, *Origeniana Sexta*, 81-91; Marc Hirshman, "Origen and the Rabbis on Leviticus," *Adamantius* 11 (2005): 93-100; R. Brooks, "Straw Dogs and Scholarly Ecumenism: The Appropriate Jewish Background for the Study of Origen," in *Origen of Alexandria: His World and His Legacy*, ed. by C. Kannengiesser and W. L. Petersen (Notre Dame: University of Notre Dame Press, 1988), 63-95. The overlapping material from Leviticus in the Mishnah and Origen's homilies include Leviticus 4:2-26 on sin offerings (*Hom. Lev.* 2.1; Horayot 1:3-5), 5:2-3 on corpse uncleanness (*Hom. Lev.* 3.2-6; Shebu'ot 2.5, 3.5), 12:1-7 on childbirth purification (*Hom. Lev.* 8.2-4; Keritot 6.9), 13:2 on leprosy (*Hom. Lev.* 8:5; Negaʿim 6.8, 9.2), and 25:29-31 on property redemption (*Hom. Lev.* 15.1-3; Arakhin 9.5-7). Brooks notes that Origen mentions Jewish interpretation only when discussing the issue of corpse-related ritual uncleanness ("Straw Dogs," 90) and misses key pieces of the rabbinic discussion (the spread of uncleanness, tent of uncleanness, the special dimension of uncleanness, degrees of uncleanness). Origen appears "ignorant" both of rabbinic details and as a whole.

[100] Reuven Kimelman, "Rabbi Yohanan and Origen on the Song of Songs: A Third-Century Jewish-Christian Disputation," *HTR* 73 (1980): 567-95.

[101] Throughout the commentary on Song of Songs 1:2-6, Origen stresses the mediation of the Law through angels, the superiority of the teaching of Christ to the Law, Christ as a pleasant fragrance, the heavenly Jerusalem as a mother, and the exile as repudiation. Drawing on Song Rab. (1.2.3) as well as *Pesiq. Rab. K.* (21.5), y. Ber. 1.7 3b (with parallels in Sanh. 11.6 30a, ʿAvod. Zar. 2.8 41c, Song. Rab. 1.2.2) and Genesis Rabbah, Kimmelman positions Rabbi Yoḥanan as a respondent to these claims: The Law is unmediated, Abraham is a pleasant fragrance, Jerusalem as a mother, and the aim of exile as reconciliation. See also Ephraim Urbach / אורבך א. אפרים, "Rabbinic Exegesis and Origen's Commentary on the Song of Songs and Jewish-Christian Polemics / דרשות חז״ל ופירושי אוריגנס לשיר השירים והוויכוח היהודי-נוצרי," *Tarbiz*/תרביץ 30 (1960): 148-70; later published as "Homiletical Interpretations of the Sages and the Expositions of Origen on the Canticles, and the Jewish-Christian Disputation," *Scripta Hierosolymitana* 22 (1971): 247-75. Urbach places a lot of weight on Origen's reading of Songs 1:2, which follows the Hebrew tradition ("wine") against the Greek ("breasts") (257). Frédéric Manns, "Une tradition juive dans les Commentaires du Cantique des Cantiques d 'Origène," *Antonianum* 65 (1990): 3-22, compares the treatment of biblical songs in Origen and two *Mekhiltot*, that of Rabbi Ishmael and Rabbi Shimon bar Yochai. Again,

as the respondent in this imagined disputation.[102] Early fervor for points of contact and exchange has now given way to other, less binary configurations of Jewish and Christian interpretation of the Song of Songs.[103]

To be sure, Origen names several interactions with Jews and frequently incorporates the "Hebrew tradition" (*Hebraicarum traditionum*, τῶν παρ' Ἑβραίοις ἐλλογίμων). In *Contra Celsum*, Origen refers to a "debate" (1.45; διαλέγομαι) and "meeting" (2.31; συμβάλλω) with Jews, which, as reported, centered on Isaiah 53, Psalm 44, and a comparison between Jesus and Moses.[104] In a fragment from his Caesarean *Commentary on the Psalms*, Origen refers to "Ioullos the patriarch" whom the "Jews considered wise" but whose identity remains a mystery.[105] Building on these explicit points of

---

there are parallels in the treatment of similar biblical texts, but none that requires or even suggests interaction as the basis for the parallel.

[102] For a consideration of Origenian impact on Rabbinic interpretation see Anna Tzvetkova-Glaser, *Pentateuchsauslegung bei Origenes und den frühen Rabbinen* (Frankfurt am Main: Peter Lang, 2010).

[103] See especially David Stern, "Ancient Jewish Interpretation of the Song of Songs in Comparative Context," in *Jewish Biblical Interpretation and Cultural Exchange*, ed. Natalie B. Dohrmann and David Stern (Philadelphia: University of Pennsylvania Press, 2013), 87–107, who points to Alon Goshen Gotshtein, "Polemomania—Methodological Reflection on the Study of the Judeo-Christian Controversy Between the Talmudic Sages and Origin [sic] over the interpretations of the Song of Songs / פולמוסומניה—הרהורים מיתודיים על חקר הוויכוח היהודי-נוצרי בעקבות פירושי חז"ל ואוריגנס לשיר-השירים", *JS* 42 (2003–4): 119–90. Similarly, rather than determine some form of exegetical overlap, Elizabeth Clark focuses on the internal logic of the commentary's conception of Jews, which stresses the eventual union of Jew and Gentile and the lengthy saga of both Judaism and Paganism to Christianity: "Origen, the Jews, and the Song of Songs: Allegory and Polemic in Christian Antiquity," in *Perspectives on the Song of Songs / Perspektiven der Hoheliedauslegung*, ed. John Barton, Reinhard G. Kratz, Choon-Leong Seow, and Markus Witte, Beihefte zur Zeitschrift für die alttestamentliche Wissenschaft 346 (Berlin: de Gruyter, 2005), 274–93.

[104] *Cels.* 1.45, 1.55–56, 2.31. In *Cels.* 2.38, 6.29 and *De orat.* 1.32–2.2, Origen refers to hypothetical disputes with Jews. It is not uncommon for larger inferences to be drawn from these meetings. For example, Ruth Clements, "τέλειος ἄμωμος: The Influence of Palestinian Jewish Exegesis on the Interpretation of Exodus 12.5 in Origen's Peri Pascha," in *The Function of Scripture in Early Jewish and Christian Tradition*, ed. Craig A. Evans and James A. Sanders (Sheffield: Sheffield Academic Press, 1998), 285–311, suggests that these public meetings "mark not only Origen's emergence as a champion for the Church, but more basically the emergence of Jewish-Christian public disputation as an institutional strategy of the Caesarean Christian and rabbinic Jewish communities" (294).

[105] See *Comm. in Ps.* (PG 12.1080 B–C). Cordula Bandt and Franz Xaver Risch attribute this work to Eusebius of Caesarea in "Das Hypomnema des Origenes zu den Psalmen—eine unerkannte Schrift des Eusebius," *Adamantius* 19 (2013): 395–410. Jerome refers to Origen's familiarity with a "Rabbis Huillus," a contemporary Jewish "patriarch" whose interpretations of the Psalms and Isaiah were appropriated by Origen (*Contra Rufinum* 1.13); however, Origen's work on Isaiah is not extant. On "Iollous" see Nicholas R. M. de Lange, *Origen and the Jews: Studies in Jewish-Christian Relations in Third-Century Palestine* (Cambridge: Cambridge University Press, 1976), 23–27; Ronald Heine, *Origen: Scholarship in the Service of the Church* (Oxford: Oxford University Press, 2010), 149; H. Graetz, "Hillel, der Patriarchensohn," *MGWJ* 25 (1881): 433–34. A "Ioullos," the "parnas" (supervisor), is named in a Greek inscription found in the Ḥammat Tiberius Synagogue; see Lee I. Levine, *The Ancient Synagogue: The First Thousand Years* (New Haven: Yale University Press, 2000), 434. Moshe Dothan, *Hammath Tiberias: Early Synagogues and the Hellenistic and Roman Remains* (Jerusalem: University of Haifa, 1983), 59–60, notes that the name is also written as הלל.

contact, others have suggested that Origen knew and interacted with Rabbi Hoshaya, the remembered founder of a rabbinic school in the mid-third century.[106] Lee Levine notes that "the paucity of our sources makes it idle to speculate whether there was any connection between the settlement of these two religious leaders in Caesarea at the same time."[107]

Gustave Bardy's seminal essay organizes passages where Origen defers to the "tradition of the Hebrews" as an exegetical resource but is careful to note the indeterminacy of its origin(s).[108] What Bardy notes is that Origen's "Hebrew tradition" is often mediated by "someone who was fleeing on account of the faith of Christ and on account of having advanced beyond the Law and who had come where we live."[109] In other instances, the tradition of the Hebrews is associated with "our old teachers."[110] In Origen's *Letter to Africanus* 11(7), Origen refers to a "learned Hebrew" (φιλομαθεῖ Ἑβραίῳ) who was the son of a "sage" (σοφοῦ υἱῷ) in support for the acceptance of *Susanna*.[111] It is difficult to parse which pieces of Jewish knowledge Origen discovered "on his own" and what is indebted to (what might be) a Jewish teacher held as authoritative within the Christian circles in Caesarea or other types of informants whose pieces of Jewish knowledge Origen collected or otherwise inherited.[112]

---

[106] For example, W. Bacher, "The Church Father Origen and Rabbi Hoshaya," *JQR* 3 (1891): 357–60; Philip Alexander, "'In the Beginning': Rabbinic and Patristic Exegesis of Genesis 1:1," in *The Exegetical Encounter Between Jews and Christians in Late Antiquity*, ed. Emmanouela Grypeou and Helen Spurling (Leiden: Brill, 2009), 26; Günter Stemberger, "Ebraismo a Caesarea Maritima: Personalità rabbinico a Caesarea Maritima," in *Caesarea Maritima e la Scuola Origeniana: Multiculturalità, forme di competizione culturale e identità Cristiana*, ed. Osvalda Andrei, Supplementi Adamantius 3 (Brescia: Morcelliana, 2013), 96–102; Marc Hirshman, "Reflections on the Aggada of Caesarea," in Raban and Holum, *Caesarea Maritima*, 469–75.

[107] Lee Levine, *Caesarea under Roman Rule*, SJLA 7 (Leiden: Brill, 1975), 88.

[108] Gustave Bardy, "Les traditions juives dans l'oeuvre d'Origène," *RB* 34 (1925): 217–52.

[109] *Hom. Jer.* 20.2. Cf. *De princ.* 1.3.4 (*Hebraeus magister*), 4.3.14 (*Hebraeus doctor*); *Hom. Num* 13.5; Heine, *Origen*, 30, 56; de Lange, *Origen and the Jews*, 21. See also Epiphanius' discussion of Joseph of Tiberius in Andrew Jacobs, *Remains of the Jews: The Holy Land and Christian Empire in Late Antiquity* (Stanford: Stanford University Press, 2004), 48.

[110] *Hom. Gen.* 2.2; *Hom. Jes. Nav.* 16.5. Bardy, "Les traditions juives," 219: "If we know that Clement himself had teachers and was content in a great number of cases to report traditions, it is almost impossible for us to make a precise distinction between what he received and what he added of his own making" (et si nous savons que Clément lui-même a eu des maîtres et s'est contenté en un grand nombre de cas de rapporter des traditions, il nous est à peu près impossible de faire le départ exact entre ce qu'il a reçu et ce qu'il a ajouté de son propre crû).

[111] SC 302.538. On Origen's engagement with Jewish tradition and triangulation of which books are accepted as scripture see Ronald Heine, "Origen and the Eternal Boundaries," in *Die Septuaginta und das frühe Christentum / The Septuagint and Christian Origins*, ed. Thomas Scott Caulley and Hermann Lichtenberger, WUNT 277 (Tübingen: Mohr Siebeck, 2011), 393–409.

[112] On Origen's informant(s) see Shaye J. D. Cohen, "Sabbath Law and Mishnah Shabbat in Origen De Principiis," *JSQ* 17.2 (2010): 160–89. Similarly, wielding postcolonial insights, particularly Bhabha's subversive notion of 'mimicry,' Andrew Jacobs positions this body of "real" Jewish knowledge as a disruption of Roman hegemony (*Remains of the Jews*, 60ff).

The significance and degree of Origen's interaction with contemporary Judaism is measured differently by scholars. We read that Origen "happily borrowed [Jewish] interpretations and hermeneutical principles"[113] or incorporated Jewish tradition "sporadically and without system."[114] One area in which Origen often defers to "Hebrew" tradition is in the discussion of the etymology of names.[115] Additionally, in *Commentarium in Canticum Canticorum praef.* 1 Origen relays that "the Hebrews" handle the Song of Songs with care, disallowing young hands from even holding the book, and in an oft-quoted comment from the *Philocalia*, Origen recalls the tradition that scripture is like a multiroom house with locked doors and mixed-up keys.[116] This image for sacred writing is for Origen "a very charming tradition transmitted to us by the Hebrews."[117] The hermeneutical significance of these examples is often overstated in contemporary description of Origen's polemic against Jewish "literalism."

Rather than mark the cross-fertilization of hermeneutical theory, these examples point to Origen's engagement with the *skopos* (aim) and the *lexis* (wording) of a text.[118] Bernhard Neuschäfer and Frances Young both find that Origen's textual practices reflect the principles found in Quintilian's *Institutio oratoria*, where proper μεθοδικός includes attending to "the letter" by establishing the correct text (διόρθωσις), determining the proper reading of the text (ἀνάγνωσις), and clarifying the language of the passage by parsing and defining archaic verbal forms.[119] For Quintilian, "Correct reading precedes interpretation."[120]

---

[113] Peter Martens, *Origen and Scripture: The Contours of the Exegetical Life* (Oxford: Oxford University Press, 2012), 139.

[114] McGuckin, "Origen on the Jews," 13. Cf. Nautin, *Origène*, 346–47; Brooks, "Straw Dogs," 92–94.

[115] *Hom. Exod.* 5.2; *Hom. Num.* 14.13; *Hom. Jes. Nav.* 15.6, *Hom. Ezech.* 4.8, *Cels.* 4.34; *Comm. Jo.* 1.34, 6.14 (84). On Origen's etymologies and the question of onomastic sources see primarily R. P. C. Hanson, "Interpretations of Hebrew Names in Origen," *VC* 10 (1956): 103–23.

[116] *Phil.* 2.3 (SC 302.244–45).

[117] Trans. de Lange, *Origen and the Jews*, 111.

[118] This is similarly exemplified by other ancient readers, such as Proclus, a fifth-century Neoplatonist. Mark Edwards, *Origen Against Plato*, 129, notes that *lexis* "signifies to Proclus not so much what we would call the literal meaning as the examination of particulars once the general import of the text has been established."

[119] Bernhard Neuschäfer, *Origenes als Philologe* (Basel: Friedrich Reinhardt Verlag, 1987); Young, *Biblical Exegesis*, 76–86. Quintilian, *Institutio Oratoria*, 4.1.1–2: "My words apply equally to Greek and Latin masters, though I prefer that a start should be made with a Greek: in either case the method is the same" (translation in H. E. Butler, ed., *Quintilian. Institutio Oratoria*, vol. 1, LCL 124 [Cambridge, MA: Harvard University Press, 1920], 63). On reading aloud as a way of determining the text according to Dionysius Thrax see Francesca Schironi, *The Best of the Grammarians: Aristarchus of Samothrace on the Iliad* (Ann Arbor: University of Michigan Press, 2018).

[120] Butler, *Quintilian. Institutio Oratoria*, 63.

Further, Quintilian describes the need to attend to the *historia* of a text, that is, all the particularities of the passage aside from its "historicity." In *Homiliae in Exodum* 5.5, for instance, Origen recalls that he heard "a tradition from the ancients" (*maioribus traditum*) that the Red Sea was divided according to the tribes, but this is used as a curious aside—"I thought that the careful student should not be silent about these things so observed by the ancients in the divine scriptures"—before Origen promptly returns to the "apostle's understanding."[121] Jewish knowledge is valuable insofar as it supports some understanding of the text, a piece of "philological analysis" according to Ruth Clements, from which to advance to a spiritual reading.[122] In *Homiliae in Exodum* 5.1 Origen refers to the alien quality of Jewish scripture in a way that invites this kind of interpretive aid:[123]

> "*Doctor gentium in fide et veritate*" *Apostolus Paulus tradidit ecclesiae, quam congregavit ex gentibus, quomodo libros legis susceptos ab aliis sibique ignotos prius et valde peregrinos deberet advertere, ne aliena instituta suscipiens et institutorum regulam nesciens in peregrino trepidaret instrumento. Propterea ergo ipse in nonnullis intelligentiae tradit exempla, ut et nos similia observemus in ceteris, ne forte pro similitudine lectionis et instrumenti Iudaeorum nos effectos esse discipulos crederemus.*

> The Apostle Paul "Teacher of the Gentiles in faith and truth" taught the Church that he gathered from the Gentiles how it ought to interpret the books of the Law. These books were received from others and were formerly unknown to the Gentiles and were very strange. He feared that the Church, receiving foreign instructions and not knowing the principle of the instructions, would be in a state of confusion about the foreign document. For that reason he gives some examples of interpretation that we also might note similar things in other passages, lest we believe that by imitation of the text and document of the Jews we be made disciples.

Origen is interested in as much detail as possible when it comes to these strange books of the Hebrews. When Origen confesses that he would have remained unaware of a particular aspect "had one of the Hebrews not called

---

[121] GCS 29.190. On the use of *maioribus traditum* see Cicero, *Pro Cluentio* 68; *De Domo Sua* 13.
[122] Ruth Clements, "Origen's *Hexapla* and Christian-Jewish Encounter in the Second and Third Centuries," in Donaldson, *Religious Rivalries*, 309.
[123] GCS 29.183. Heine, *Homilies on Genesis and Exodus*, 275.

our attention to what is in the passages,"[124] or that he once "heard a *Hebraeo* who was explaining this passage,"[125] it is not an admission of Jewish "spiritual" interpretation, but the work of a literary critic attending to the text. The hermeneutical significance of these examples is often overstated in contemporary description of Origen's polemic against Jewish "literalism."[126]

4. Origen, Philo, and the Intent of Sacred Writings

Nicholas R. M. de Lange's work *Origen and the Jews* features a careful account of Origen's social and literary engagement with Jewish texts, traditions, and people.[127] In contemporary Origen scholarship de Lange's self-proclaimed "beginnings" of an investigation of this complex question is often cited as the foundation of an Origen who was an irenic Christian scholar deeply familiar with antecedent and contemporary Jewish tradition.[128] Many follow de Lange's view that Origen's polemic against Jewish reading is deeply inconsistent with his appropriation of Philo the Jewish allegorist and robust familiarity with contemporary Jewish scholarship emerging in Caesarea at the turn of the third century.[129] In de Lange's

---

[124] *Comm. Matt.* 11.1 (εἰ μὴ τῶν Ἑβραίων τις ἐπιδέδωκεν ἡμῖν τὰ κατὰ τὸν τόπον οὕτως ἔχοντα). Greek text in Erich Klostermann, *Origenes Werke Band 10, Matthäuserklärung I*, GCS 40 (Berlin: de Gryuter, 1935), 48.

[125] *Hom. Ezech.* 4.8 (PG 13.703). See also *Hom. Ezech.* 5.10 and 10.3.

[126] That is not to say that these pieces of information in no way reflect Jewish views from third-century Greek-speaking Caesarea. See Maren R. Niehoff, "Auf den Spuren des hellenistischen Judentums in Caesarea: Ein Jüischer Psalmenforscher in Origenes' Glosse im Kontext Rabbinischer Literatur," ZAC 27.1 (2023): 31–76.

[127] De Lange, *Origen and the Jews*; Nicholas de Lange, "Origen and the Jewish Bible Exegesis," *JJS* 22 (1971): 31–52; Nicholas de Lange, "Origen and the Rabbis on the Hebrew Bible," *Studia Patristica* 14 (1976): 117–21. Early works on this question include Samuel Krauss, "The Jews in the Works of the Church Fathers," *JQR* o.s. 5 (1893): 122–57; A. Marmorstein, "Deux renseignements d'Origène concernant les juifs," *REJ* 71 (1920): 190–99; Henri Crouzel, *Origène et la "Connaissance Mystique"* (Paris: Desclée de Brouwer, 1961), 312–22; A. J. Philippou, "Origen and the Early Jewish-Christian Debate," *GOTR* 15 (1970): 140–52; and especially H. Bietenhard, *Caesarea, Origenes und die Juden* (Stuttgart: Kohlhammer, 1974), which is a slimmer complement to de Lange's work.

[128] De Lange, *Origen and the Jews*, ix. Cf. Young, *Biblical Exegesis*, 93–94. See also the reflections in William Horbury, "Origen and the Jews: Jewish-Greek and Jewish-Christian Relations," in *The Jewish-Greek Tradition in Antiquity and the Byzantine Empire*, ed. James K. Aitken and James Carleton Paget (Cambridge: Cambridge University Press, 2014), 79–90.

[129] De Lange, *Origen and the Jews*, 83, summarizes this sentiment: "It may be thought remarkable that Origen, of all people, who was well acquainted with Jewish exegesis in all its aspects, should have perpetuated this myth of 'Jewish literalism,' but perpetuate it he certainly does." Subsequent scholarship on the critical intersection between Origen and Jewish interpretation often evokes de Lange's work as a way of suggesting the extensiveness and sophistication of Origen's participation with Jewish tradition. See Kimelman, "Rabbi Yohanan and Origen," 572 n. 27;

account, since Origen's polemic against Jewish reading claims that Jews do not read in any "nonliteral" way, that is, beyond the mere words, his knowledge and appropriation of Jewish allegory or other "nonliteral" and symbolic readings of scripture highlights the obvious inconsistency of the theologically driven polemic. For de Lange, Origen's criticism of Jewish reading reflects his "dilemma." As a "theologian," the Jew must be discounted, but, as a "scholar," Origen remains indebted to the very tradition he dismisses.[130]

More recently, Peter Martens rejects the final picture in de Lange's configuration and seeks to absolve the dissonance lingering in the account by identifying the interpretive contexts giving rise to Origen's criticism.[131] Martens suggests we read Origen's polemic as a critique aimed at the threatening potential of particular "literalistic" readings of scripture, which, if accepted, would be an affront to the defining features of Christianity.[132] Origen's criticism is not a "universal dismissal of all Jewish exegesis," as though there were a universal procedural flaw in Jewish scholarship, but a polemical engagement with the literal understanding of a "a very particular set of passages within the Law," namely, any "ceremonial customs" or prophetic texts that Christians understood as prophecies of Christ.[133] For Martens, if we appreciate the specificity of Origen's objection then the "selective retrieval and integration" of Jewish allegory is not such an overt signal of hypocrisy, and the cogency of Origen's project is preserved.[134] Thus, where de Lange sees a universal dismissal of Jewish reading distinct from Origen's scholarly work, Martens finds a particularistic polemic.

P. M. Blowers, "Origen, the Rabbis, and the Bible: Toward a Picture of Judaism and Christianity in Third-Century Caesarea," in Kannengiesser and Petersen, *Origen of Alexandria*, 112; John H. C. Neeb, "Origen's Interpretation of Genesis 28:12 and the Rabbis," in Dorival and Le Boulluec, *Origeniana Sexta*, 71–80.

[130] De Lange, *Origen and the Jews*, 31: "It was Origen's dilemma that as a theologian he must condemn the Jews while as a scholar and exegete he depended on them."

[131] Martens, *Origen and Scripture*, 134: "We understand his critique poorly if we think it identifies a procedural flaw that runs throughout all Jewish exegesis—that is, as if the fundamental exegetical deficiency among the Jews was their singular insistence upon discovering the literal referents of scripture. If this is how Origen understood Jewish literalism, then we will indeed face intractable difficulties in our attempts to make sense of this critique."

[132] Martens, *Origen and Scripture*, 134; Peter Martens, "Why Does Origen Accuse the Jews of 'Literalism'? A Case Study of Christian Identity and Biblical Exegesis in Antiquity," *Adamantius* 13 (2007): 218–30.

[133] Martens, *Origen and Scripture*, 143. Similarly, Otto, *Philo of Alexandria*, 115: "Jewish literalism ought to be understood as a denunciation of *Jewish legal observance* and not of rigidly literal interpretations of the scriptures as a whole."

[134] Martens, *Origen and Scripture*, 147.

Martens and de Lange find an Origen who is deeply familiar with Jewish nonliteral exegesis and relied on this Jewish interpretation as he developed his own allegorical reading of scripture. They then read Origen's criticism that Jews cannot read beyond the "letter" of the text as an unfortunate theological dismissal of a tradition he was otherwise open to engage, *precisely for* its nonliteral, symbolic, and allegorical readings.[135] Origen's engagement with Jewish tradition (lived conversations, and perhaps various personal relationships for sharing textual expertise) is then read as a "scholarly activity" set apart from the tensions of a "religious" or "theological" conflict. Instead, Martens and de Lange's position Origen as hermeneutically dependent upon (nonliteral) Jewish tradition.[136]

John McGuckin poses another image of Origen for consideration, one whose polemic against Jews is so thoroughly shaped by a reading of Paul that he works within a "relatively enclosed system" than a "form of converging dialogue."[137] As noted above, Origen leverages the uniquely "Pauline" and "Jewish" context of "To the Hebrews" in order to mobilize a Platonist ontology toward a hermeneutical account of Jewish-Christian difference and, consequently, the letter becomes the vehicle through which Origen describes the core of Jewish reading practices. Both Martens and de Lange minimize the Paulist features of Origen's criticism of Jewish reading through the appropriation of Hebrews. Origen's appropriation of Hebrews is conspicuously absent throughout Martens' account, one that maintains that Origen rarely refers to "Jewish literalism in abstraction."[138]

Following McGuckin, I question whether we can separate Origen's scholarship and theology in the way de Lange describes, and whether we can avoid Origen's universal characterization of Jewish reading. Rather, Origen's engagement with Jewish scholarship reinforces the Paulinist contour of his criticism of Jewish reading and theological context in which he uses Greek

---

[135] John McGuckin, "Origen on the Jews," 10, describes the image of Origen at work in this scholarship pointedly, "an Origen who was personally interested in Jewish scholarship, but who presented a more official face, as Christian presbyter in Caesarea, as both a theological and a practical critic of the rival system."

[136] This conception of Origen's relationship to Jewish interpretation has been increasingly criticized; see Perrone, "Die 'Verfassung der Juden,'" 310–12; J. S. O'Leary, "The Recuperation of Judaism," in Dorival and Le Boulluec, *Origeniana Sexta*, 373–79; Brooks, "Straw Dogs"; John McGuckin, "Origen on the Jews," in *Christianity and Judaism: Papers Read at the 1991 Summer Meeting and the 1992 Winter Meeting of the Ecclesiastical History Society*, ed. D. Wood, Studies in Church History 29 (Oxford: Blackwell, 1992), 1–13.

[137] McGuckin, "Origen on the Jews," 10; together with John McGuckin, "Origen on the Glory of God," *StPatr* 21 (1989): 316–24.

[138] Martens, *Origen and Scripture*, 141.

literary criticism. Origen's conflict with Jews emerges out of the theological narrative of Christian origins rather than a robust lived experience informed by a Philonic heritage. Further, Origen's concept of Jewish literalism is not simply the failure to advance metaphors, symbols, and other "nonliteral" readings of scripture but the failure to ascend into the heavenly, that is, Christological context of scriptural meaning. A closer look at Origen and Philo further supports this point.

There are three well-known references to Philo in Origen's corpus: *Contra Celsum* 4.51, 6.21, and *Commentarium in evangelium Matthaei* 15.3.[139] David Runia estimates that there are roughly thirteen anonymous quotations from the Philonic corpus, in which Philo is referred to cryptically as one "before us" (τῶν πρὸ ἡμῶν τις).[140] In *Commentarium in evangelium Matthaei* 15.3, Origen cites Sextus Empiricus (*Sentences* 13 and 273) and Philo (*Det.* 176) as twin witnesses to radical asceticism. Here Philo is described as "highly esteemed among intelligent people for many of his treatises on the Law of Moses." Yet, as Jennifer Otto points out, Origen criticizes Philo within the context of the citation: "But one should not believe them, for they have not understood the intent of the Holy Scriptures in these things."[141] On the question of Philonic borrowings, Christoph Blönnigen observes that very few motifs are appropriated by Origen as guides for interpretation, and, when parallels do arise, Origen mostly defers to interpretive material drawn from the Pauline corpus.[142] Origen and Philo

---

[139] See David Runia, *Philo in Early Christian Literature* (Assen: Van Gorcum, 1993), 57–83; Otto, *Philo of Alexandria*, 91–135.

[140] See *Cels.* 5.55, 7.20; *Sel. Gen.* 44; *Hom. Exod.* 2.2; *Hom. Lev.* 8.6; *Hom. Nom.* 9.5; *Hom. Jes. Nev.* 16.1; *Hom. Jer.* 14.5; *Comm. Matt.* 10.22, 17.17; *Comm. Matt. fr. ad* 23:30; *Comm. Jo.* 6.25; David T. Runia, "Philo and Origen: A Preliminary Survey," in Daly, *Origeniana Quinta*, 333–39; Runia, *Philo in Early Christian Literature*, 160–63. In *Cels.* 6.21 Origen describes Philo as "worthy of intelligent and wise study" and "highly esteemed among intelligent people for many of his treatises on the Law of Moses" (GCS 11.91.26). Runia also contends that Origen most likely preserved Philo's writings by bringing the collection from the library in Alexandria to the one established in Caesarea, which then passed through Pamphilus and Eusebius. See David T. Runia, "Caesarea Maritima and Hellenistic-Jewish Literature," in Raban and Holum, *Caesarea Maritima*, 492. On the early preservation of Philo in Alexandria see Annewies van den Hoek, "The 'Catechetical' School of Early Christian Alexandria and Its Philonic Heritage," *HTR* 90.1 (1997): 79–85. However, our vision of institutional continuity between Alexandrian figures is more obscure than Eusebius suggests. See, for example, Otto, *Philo of Alexandria*, 27–47.

[141] GCS 10.354: Ἀλλ' οὐ πιστευτέον αὐτοῖς μὴ τὸ βούλημα τῶν ἱερῶν γραμμάτων περὶ τούτων ἐξειληφόσιν.

[142] See Christoph Blönnigen, *Der griechische Ursprung der jüdisch-hellenistischen Allegorese und ihre Rezeption in der alexandrinischen Patristik*, Europäische Hochschulschriften XV, Klassische Sprachen und Literaturen 59 (Frankfurt am Main: Peter Lang, 1992), 263–65. The five core principles shared by the two Alexandrians suggested by Daniélou, *Origen*, 178–91, are not problematic, but they are quite general (the body of scriptures is inspired and can never be meaningless or

are, at the very least, two Alexandrian scholars who appropriated methods of ancient criticism as a means of engaging their sacred texts in such a way as to converse actively and critically with the Platonic tradition while also preserving the unique contour of their own intellectual projects.[143]

As an "allegorical" reader of Jewish scripture who engages the Platonic tradition in the process of interpretation while also integrating concepts of *logos* and Wisdom as means of divine mediation, Philo of Alexandria is naturally considered a major influence on Origen.[144] One way of framing indebtedness between Origen and Philo is to say that both interpret "scripture in light of philosophy" and that Philo was Origen's "main inspirer for the very technique of philosophical allegoresis of scripture."[145] But Origen's project is far less derivative than this suggests.

By the third century CE, readings that by modern convention are called "figural" or "allegorical" but in practice are referred to by a cluster of terms like τροπικός, ἀλληγορικός, and ἀλλήγορος, had become a familiar, though debated, practice.[146] These readings spring out of the perceived metaphorical quality of a text, which may be designed as an "allegory" or is simply receptive to an allegorical reading. As allegorical readers began to emerge at the turn of the first millennium, Plato's metaphor of text as a human body and soul was an important way of conceptualizing unity between the "letter" and the "intention" (*skopos*) of a text, to which allegory was understood

---

useless, every portion of scripture has a "figurative" meaning, they share numerical and symbolic treatments of certain texts, allegorical readings have moral implications, and that share a threefold metaphor for scripture as a body, soul, and spirit).

[143] Hans Georg Thümmel, "Philon und Origenes," reprinted in in *Karpoi: Ausgewählte Aufsätze. Patristik—Philosophie—christliche Kunst (1966–2004)*, ed. Christfried Böttrich, Greifswalder theologische Forschungen 14 (Frankfurt am Main: Peter Lang, 2007), 78–91, points to the different contours of Origen and Philo's larger project conceived as the soul's return to the heavenly realm and the guiding tradition of Torah.

[144] On the *logos* in Philo see Harry Austryn Wolfson, *Philo: Foundations of Religious Philosophy in Judaism, Christianity, and Islam*, vol. 1 (Cambridge, MA: Harvard University Press, 1962), 201–94; Peter Schäfer, *Two Gods in Heaven: Jewish Concepts of God in Antiquity*, trans. Allison Brown (Princeton: Princeton University Press, 2020), 62–64; Maren Niehoff, *Philo of Alexandria: An Intellectual Biography* (New Haven: Yale University Press, 2018), esp. 209–24.

[145] Ilaria Ramelli, "Philo as Origen's Declared Model: Allegorical and Historical Exegesis of Scripture," *Studies in Christian-Jewish Relations* 7 (2012): 5–6. See de Lange, *Origen and the Jews*, 16.

[146] See Robert D. Lamberton, *Homer the Theologian: Neoplatonist Allegorical Reading and the Growth of the Epic Tradition* (Berkeley: University of California Press, 1986); Ilaria Ramelli and Giulio Lucchetta, *Allegoria*, vol. 1, *L'età classica* (Milan: Vita e Pensiero, 2004); Peter T. Struck, *Birth of Symbol: Ancient Readers at the Limits of Their Texts* (Princeton: Princeton University Press, 2004), esp. 162–203; Jean Pépin, *Mythe et allegorie: Les origines grecques et les contestations judéochrétiennes* (Paris: Etudes Augustiniennes, 1976); Hans-Josef Klauck, *Allegorie und Allegorese in synoptischen Gleichnistexten*, NA 13 (Münster: Aschendorff 1978), 32–66.

to grant access.¹⁴⁷ The adoption of this metaphor was not uncritical. As David Dawson notes, Philo, Origen, and the Neoplatonists Porphyry and Proclus reverse Plato's negative assessment of writing and narrative as media of communication,¹⁴⁸ and instead "re-narrativize" the Platonic tradition by defending allegorical reading as a means of accessing the "soul" of a text.¹⁴⁹ On this point Origen and Philo are agreed: Scriptural texts are a body and a soul and thus invite the use of an allegorical method.¹⁵⁰ However, for Origen, the underlying meaning of scripture is so determined

---

[147] Young, *Biblical Exegesis*, 94; Edwards, *Origen Against Plato*, 128; Annewies van den Hoek, "The Concept of *soma tōn graphōn* in Alexandrian Theology," *StPatr* 19 (1989): 250–54. Origen's conceptual similarity to Porphyry on this point relates to the ongoing question of Origen's relationship to one of the founders of Neoplatonism, Ammonius Saccas, the teacher of Plotinus. Ilaria Ramelli argues for the viability and possibility of the identification between the "Origen Adamantius" and "Origen the Neoplatonist" mentioned by Porphyry, Hierocles of Alexandria, and Proclus; see "Origen the Christian Middle/Neoplatonist: New Arguments for a Possible Identification," *JECH* 1.1 (2011): 98–130, and "Origen's Allegoresis of Plato's and Scriptures' 'Myths,'" in *Religious Competition in the Greco-Roman World*, ed. Nathaniel DesRosiers and Lily C. Vuong, WGRWSupp. 10 (Atlanta: SBL Press, 2016), 85–107. However, the issue is unsettled. See H. Dörrie, "Ammonios der Lehrer Plotins," *Hermes* 83 (1955): 439–77; Mark Edwards, "Ammonius, Teacher of Origen," *JEH* 44 (1993): 169–81; F. H. Kettler, "War Origenes Schüler des Ammonios Sakkas?," in *Epektasis: Mélanges patristiques offerts au Cardinal Jean Daniélou*, ed. J. Fontaine and C. Kannengiesser (Paris: Beauchesne, 1972), 327–35. See also P. F. Beatrice, "Porphyry at Origen's School at Caesarea," in Bitton-Ashkelony et al., *Origeniana Duodecima*, 267–83.

[148] David Dawson, "Plato's Soul and the Body of the Text in Philo and Origen," in *Interpretation and Allegory: Antiquity to the Modern Period*, ed. Jon Whitman (Leiden: Brill, 2000), 89–107. Dawson draws attention to the body-soul distinction found in Plato's dialogues as a means of criticizing the effectiveness of writing for conveying the internal thought of the author (*Phaed.* 264C). Since writing is an external expression of the thoughts of the author, it is akin to a painting, which, unlike a dialogue, remains silent when questioned (*Phaed.* 275D). The most effective writing is when the subject achieves knowledge of its object, when it is "written in the soul of the learner" (95, citing *Phaed.* 276A). The "soul" of the author is the ultimate locus of meaning, and the "body" of piece of writing is only ever a limited conduit and may even indicate the lack of a "soul." Dawson then notes that Plato rejected allegorical readings of poetic narratives; since the outward form of the narrative imposes a questionable morality and since the meaning achieved by allegory accesses a truth arrived at by the author prior to writing, the philosopher can discover that truth without the aid of the poem (*Rep.* 378). See also John Dawson, "Allegorical Reading and the Embodiment of the Soul in Origen," in Ayres and Jones, *Christian Origins*, 26–43.

[149] Dawson notes that Philo moves from the interaction between body and soul (see *QG* 4.117) to suggest that the reader's own soul is tethered to the text *as written* since the narrative details of the text are brought to the mind through sense perception. Philo famously defends an embodied application of the laws of the text *together with* spiritual and philosophical reflection precisely because of the connection between body and soul (*Mig.* 89–93). Dawson concludes that "both Philo and Origen used the analogy of the body of the text as part of a progressive scheme in which the allegorical reader moves toward greater spiritual and ethical perfection" ("Plato's Soul," 107).

[150] See Philo, *Migr.* 93; *Contempl.* 78. However, Lubac rightly points out that Origen's threefold metaphor—body, soul, and spirit—draws upon a complex of scriptural metaphors, Pauline terminology, and an emerging tradition of anthropological divisions within both Christian and Greek scholarship, even though this point is used as a defense and revival of Origen's method as uniquely theological in problematic ways, namely, that Origen, who relied on Philo only tangentially, still used Philo "too much" (*Histoire et esprit*, 150–66, esp. 162: "Il lui en emprunte même beaucoup trop à notre gré").

by the *logos*, that the spiritual sense of any passage is Christological. Hence, scripture is analogous to a Christological body in *Homilies on Leviticus* 1.1:[151]

> *carnis namque adspectus in eo patebat oiunibus, paucis vero et electis dabatur divinitatis agnitio...nam sicut ibi carnis, ita hic litterae velamine tegitur, ut littera quideni adspiciatur tamquam caro, latens vero intrinsecus spiritalis sensus taiuquam divinitas sentiatur. Tale ergo est quod et nunc invenimus Ii brum Levitici revolventes, in quo sacrificiorum ritus et hostiarum diversitas ac sacerdotum ministeria describuntur.*

> The sight of his flesh was open for all to see, but the knowledge of his divinity was given to the few... it was covered with the veil of flesh, so here with the veil of the letter, so that indeed the letter is seen as flesh but the spiritual sense hiding within is perceived as divinity. Such, therefore, is what we now find as we go through the book of Leviticus, in which the sacrificial rites, the diversity of offerings, and even the ministries of the priests are described.

Karen Torjesen and Ruth Clements both accent the Christological contour of Origen's understanding of textual and interpretive unity vis-à-vis the spiritual sense. "Literal interpretation," notes Clements, "may be functionally defined as any interpretation, however figurative, which does not reveal the voice of the Logos."[152] Similarly, Torjesen finds in Origen a threefold pedagogical conception of the *logos* whose activity results in the production of scripture, its varying forms of communication, and who is disclosed in the contemporary interpretation of the spiritual sense.[153] Accordingly,

---

[151] GCS 29.280; transation Barkley, *Origen: Homilies on Leviticus*, 29. Hom. Lev. 5.5: "Holy Scripture results from the visible and the invisible just as from a body the letter, which is certainly something seen, and the soul, the understanding of which is understood within, and of the Spirit, according to that which some also hold in 'heaven' as the apostle said, 'They serve as models and shadows of the celestial things'" (Barkley, 89). See also Annewies van den Hoek, "Mistress and Servant: An Allegorical Theme in Philo, Clement, and Origen," in *Origeniana Quarta: Die Referate des 4. Internationalen Origeneskongresses (Innsbruck, 2.–6. September 1985)*, ed. Lothar Lies, Innsbrucker theologische Studien, Bd. 19 (Innsbruck: Tyrolia, 1987), 344–48.

[152] Ruth A. Clements, "Peri Pascha: Passover and the Displacement of Jewish Interpretation within Origen's Exegesis" (ThD diss., Harvard Divinity School, 1997), 35; Cohen, "Sabbath Law," 166: "'Literally' for Origen means 'not informed by a belief in Christ.' His 'literal' is not necessarily what we call 'literal,' and is not necessarily what the medieval Jewish exegetes called peshat." See also Menahem Kister, "Allegorical Interpretations of Biblical Narratives in Rabbinic Literature, Philo, and Origen: Some Case Studies," in *New Approaches to the Study of Biblical Interpretation in Judaism of the Second Temple Period and in Early Christianity*, ed. Gary Anderson, Ruth Clements, and David Satran (Leiden: Brill, 2013), 133–83.

[153] Torjesen, *Hermeneutical Procedure*, 113–21.

"The Logos is the guiding principle of Origen's spiritual exegesis."[154] Daniel Boyarin pushes this further, claiming that the "Logos incarnate" provides Origen with the theoretical answer to the question of allegorical knowing.[155] Boyarin suggests that Philo lacked a way of accounting for the fact that Moses was uniquely endowed with capabilities of understanding but was unable to record such knowledge plainly, which is precisely what the allegorical reader is able to do through contemplation and reading.[156] Origen, Boyarin reasons, grounds his interpretive method in the earthly arrival of the *logos* who instructs in the art of reading directly.[157] For Boyarin, "Origen himself finds a hermeneutics ungrounded in the *logos* to be the source of disagreement within 'Judaism' and the context is interestingly not polemic in nature."[158] Indeed, Origen states disagreement quite passively in *Contra Celsum* 5.60:[159]

> [Celsus] thinks that we hold the same opinions as the Jews about the stories he quotes. We will say that we both confess that the books were written by divine inspiration, but concerning the interpretation of the contents of the books we no longer speak alike. In fact, the reason why we do not live like the Jews is that we think the literal interpretation (κατὰ τὸ ῥητόν) of the laws does not contain the intention (τὸ βούλημα) of the legislation.

---

[154] Torjesen, *Hermeneutical Procedure*, 108. See also Origen's exegetical prayer in *Comm. Jo.* 20.1.

[155] Daniel Boyarin, "Philo, Origen, and the Rabbis," 113–29, which reappears as "Origen as Theorist of Allegory in Alexandria," in *The Cambridge Companion to Allegory*, ed. Rita Copeland and Peter T. Struck (Cambridge: Cambridge University Press, 2010), 39–54. Subsequent citations are to the original.

[156] Boyarin, "Philo, Origen, and the Rabbis," 116.

[157] Boyarin, "Philo, Origen, and the Rabbis," 123: "Incarnational Christology was to reveal itself as the ma(r)ker of difference between 'Judaism' and 'Christianity.'"

[158] Boyarin, "Philo, Origen, and the Rabbis," 113. Cf. Robert Wilken, "Creating a Context: 'Anti-Judaism' and Scholarship on Origen," in Perrone, *Origeniana Octava*, 55–59. Riemer Roukema's conclusion is relevant here, that Origen often universalizes (New Testament) texts that are directly critical of Jews as (critical) references to all people: "Origen, the Jews, and the New Testament," in *The "New Testament" as a Polemical Tool: Studies in Ancient Christian Anti-Jewish Rhetoric and Beliefs*, ed. Rimer Roukema and Hagit Amirav, NTOA 118 (Göttingen: Vandenhoeck & Ruprecht, 2018), 253.

[159] GCS 2.63: τὴν κατὰ τὸ ῥητὸν ἐκδοχὴν τῶν νόμων εἶναι τὴν περιέχουσαν τὸ βούλημα τῆς νομοθεσίας. See also *Hom. Exod.* 5.1: *Hoc ergo differre vult discipulos Christi a discipulis synagogae, quod legem, quam illi male intelligendo Christum non receperunt, nos spiritaliter intelligendo ostendamus eam ad ecclesiae instructionem merito datam* (GCS 29.183). "He wishes, therefore, to distinguish disciples of Christ from disciples of the Synagogue by the way they understand the Law. The Jews, by misunderstanding it, rejected Christ. We, by understanding the Law spiritually, show that it was justly given for the instruction of the Church" (Heine, *Homilies on Genesis and Exodus*, 275).

The "meaning" (βούλημα) of scripture was locked up until the advent of the *logos*, after which every constituent part of the texts relates back to the significance of this advent when understood according to the spiritual sense. In the *Commentarium in Canticum Canticorum*, Origen often returns to the idea that "the letter of the Law" was "closed and bound up and covered over with a sort of overlying carnal interpretation."[160] But, Origen continues, "As a result of his presence and coming, a bud of spiritual understanding has been put forth from it, and the fresh and living meaning that was concealed in it, has now appeared."[161] For Origen, Christology produces a coherence of meaning across the totality of scriptural texts.

In book 4 of *Contra Celsum*, Origen sidesteps Celsus mockery of Genesis by defending allegorical reading and challenges Celsus' blanket criticism of Jewish and Christian allegoresis by referring to the success of Philo:[162]

> [Celsus] seems to me to have heard also that there are treatises containing allegories of the Law.... He appears by this to mean the works of Philo or even writers still earlier such as the writings of Aristobulus. But I hazard the guess that Celsus has not read the books, for I think that in many places they are so successful that even Greek philosophers would have been won over by what they say.

---

[160] *Comm. Cant.* 4.14; cf. also 2.8, 3.9, 3.13. Especially, *Hom Jer.* 9.1 (GCS 6.63: Κατὰ μὲν τὴν ἱστορουμένην παρουσίαν τοῦ κυρίου ἡμῶν Ἰησοῦ Χριστοῦ γέγονεν αὐτοῦ ἡ ἐπιδημία σωματικῶς καθολική τις καὶ ἐπιλάμψασα ὅλῳ τῷ κόσμῳ, ὅτε ὁ λόγος σὰρξ ἐγένετο καὶ ἐσκήνωσεν ἐν ἡμῖν; "His dwelling was in a body and a kind of universal event that illuminated the whole world, when the Word was made flesh and dwelt among us").

[161] *Comm. Cant.* 4.14. See also *Hom. Lev.* 4.7: "For unless the gospel shall have taken the veil from the face of Moses, it is not possible for his face to be seen nor his meaning to be understood." Andrew Blaski, "Jews, Christians, and the Conditions of Christological Interpretation in Origen's Work," in Bitton-Ashkelony et al., *Origeniana Duodecima*, 505–17, draws attention to the tension in Origen between the emergence of genuinely new knowledge at the arrival of the *logos* and the lineage of privileged Israelites, priest, patriarchs, and Moses, for example, who were able to grasp the spiritual significance of which the Law was a shadow (see Origen's vacillation in *Comm. Jo.* 6.22–23 and 13.310; as well as *Cels.* 4.6; 5.44; *Comm. Cant. praef.* 3, 2.5; *Comm. Rom.* 1.10.3, 6.7.6; *Hom. Lev.* 13.1). Blaski suggests that knowledge of the mere mystery of the Law is one way Origen eases out of this tension and maintains the *logos* in history as a privileged event.

[162] *Cels.* 4.51 (GCS 1.324.11). Throughout the context in *Contra Celsum* book 4 Origen continually points to the arbitrariness of Celsus' criticism against Christian attempts at allegoresis. Celsus is simply inconsistent, Origen argues, when he concedes that "the more reasonable Jews and Christians allegorize these things" (*Cels.* 4.48), but in the end maintains that scriptural texts are "stupid fables" that cannot be "explained in this way" (*Cels.* 4.50). Origen asks, "Are the Greeks allowed to explain and allegorize this story [Dionysus/Zeus] as referring to the soul?" (*Cels.* 4.17 [GCS 2.286: Ἡ Ἕλλησι μὲν ἔξεστι τὰ τοιαῦτα εἰς τὸν περὶ ψυχῆς ἀνάγειν λόγον καὶ τροπολογεῖν]).

Origen's admission of Philo's success is the epitome of inconsistency when "allegory" is univocal for Origen's "spiritual" or "higher" sense.[163] But Origen recognized that allegory was a convention practiced within Greek literary criticism and not a Christian discipline. Accordingly, not every allegorical reading is successful,[164] and to read allegorically does not guarantee the discovery of the spiritual sense.[165] Allegory is a tool within Origen's larger system for conceptualizing the referent of scriptural texts and closely affiliated with the "spiritual sense." However, the spiritual sense, as Torjesen observes, is not always obtained through "allegorical transposition."[166] In the context of *Contra Celsum* Origen is arguing for the *right* to read scriptural texts allegorically in order to position Christian and Greek scholarship as at least equals, and Philo helps establish the integrity and depth of the tradition of allegorical reading among Jews, from whom Christians emerge.

The heuristic value of "literal" and "allegorical" as descriptions of Origen's method are increasingly questioned among Origen scholarship, even though the basic framework of this twofold method is drawn from ancient criticism in which attending "to the letter" and reading "allegorically" had emerged within Alexandrian and Homeric scholarship.[167] Indeed, while Origen famously describes a "threefold" interpretive schema in *De principiis* 4.2.4, in which the meaning of scriptural texts is analogous to a body, soul, and spirit, and a threefold frame for reading technically makes an appearance in unimaginative and iterative ways across his corpus,[168]

---

[163] Martens, *Origen and Scripture*, 140, for example, notes that "Jewish allegorical reading of Scripture flourished in Alexandria prior to Origen's own exegetical activity."

[164] *Cels.* 3.23: "If, however, those who compose a defense of these stories take refuge in allegories, we must examine the allegories one by one to see if they are sound" (GCS 2.219: Ἐὰν δὲ καὶ οἱ περὶ τούτων ἀπολογούμενοι ἐπὶ ἀλληγορίας καταφεύγωσιν, ἰδίᾳ μὲν ἐξεταστέον τὰς ἀλληγορίας, εἰ τὸ ὑγιὲς ἔχουσιν); *Cels.* 4.38: "whether one's allegory is successful or not" (GCS 2.310: εἴτ' ἐπιτυγχάνοντα ἐν τῇ ἀλληγορίᾳ εἴτε καὶ μή).

[165] *Hom. Gen.* 10.1: "The words that have been read are mystical. They must be explained in allegorical secrets" (*Quae leguntur mystica sunt, in allegoriis exponenda sunt sacramentis*; Peter Habermehl, *Origenes Werke, Band 6 Homilien zum Hexateuch in Rufins Übersetzung, Teil 1: Die Homilien zu Genesis*, GCS Neue Folge 17 [Berlin: de Gruyter, 2012], 148).

[166] Torjesen, *Hermeneutical Procedure*, 143.

[167] Clement and Origen, for example, both appropriate Homeric criticism in the tradition of Porphyry, in which any tensions and problems internal to Homer's text are to be resolved with other Homeric texts. See, for example, *Hom. Lev.* 5.8; Miyako Demura, "Origen's Allegorical Interpretation and the Philological Tradition of Alexandria," in *Origeniana Nona: Origen and the Religious Practice of His Time; Papers of the 9th International Origen Congress, Pécs, Hungary, 29 August–2 September 2005*, ed. György Heidl and Róbert Somos (Leuven: Peeters, 2009), 149–58.

[168] Origen refers to three senses in, for example, *Hom. Lev.* 5.5; 9.1; *Hom. Gen.* 2.6. See Elizabeth Ann Dively Lauro, *The Soul and the Spirit of Scripture Within Origen's Exegesis* (Leiden: Brill, 2005); K. J. Torjesen, "'Body,' 'Soul,' and 'Spirit' in Origen's Theory of Exegesis," *ATR* 67 (1985):

he predominantly reads texts in a twofold way—"one literal and the other spiritual."[169] In practice, Origen has quite a large lexicon available to describe both of senses. The first sense is, for instance, according to the letter (τὸ ῥητὸν / τὸ γράμμα) and the wording (την λέξιν) of a passage (*Hom Jer.* 19.11; *Cels.* 2.4); it is bodily or carnal (*corporaliter*, *Comm. Rom.* 3.7.7; *Hom. Gen.* 5.5), historical (*historia*, *Hom. Lev.* 9.9), and concerned with the "earthly" (*terrenis*, *Comm. Cant.* 3.12). Origen's "higher" sense is principally spiritual, but it is also mystical (μυστικῶς, *Cels.* 4.95), inward (*interiorem sensum*, *Comm. Rom.* 2.5.2), secret (*secreti*, *Comm. Cant.* 2.8), something hinted at (τι ἠνίσσετο, *Cels.* 1.38), and, indeed, allegorical.[170]

Origen caricatures Jewish reading as the inability to ascend beyond the literal reference of a text, and this stands in tension with Origen's acknowledgment of Jewish reading that moves beyond the "letter" in some way, even if these readings are sometimes rejected as "meaningless Jewish myths" (*Comm. ser. Matt.* 13.17 GCS 38.28), "Jewish fables" (*Hom. Lev.* 4.7; *Hom. Gen.* 3.6, 6.3), "Jewish mythological interpretation" (*De princ.* 4.3.2), or the "superstitions of the Jews" (*Hom. Lev.* 12.5). However, while Origen does criticize Jewish reading as an attachment to the plain language of a text, there are many configurations: Jews do not hear in a "hidden way"

17-30; Edwards, *Origen Against Plato*, 135-36; Marguerite Harl, *Origène et la fonction révélatrice du Verbe Incarné*, Patristica Sorbonensia 2 (Paris: Éditions du Seuil, 1958), 103-18.

[169] In a well-known passage, Origen summarizes: "We maintain that the Law has a twofold interpretation, one literal and the other spiritual" (*Cels.* 7:20). For Origen, "Both meanings lie in the same text for the one who knows how to understand it (*Cels.* 4.71: πολλάκις ἐν τῇ αὐτῇ λέξει ἑκατέρων τῷ εἰδότι ἀκούειν αὐτῆς κειμένων). Origen's description of the ideal interpreter often includes identifying two meanings (e.g., *Hom. Jer.* 18.4; *Hom. Lev.* 5.1). How exactly Origen conceives of and relates these two "meanings" gets at the heart of Origen's exegesis and one of the more dominant threads of Origen scholarship since the mid-twentieth century. See Theresia Heither, "Origenes als xeget: Ein Forschungsüberblick," in *Stimuli: Exegese und ihre Hermeneutik in Antike und Christentum, Festschrift für Ernst Dassmann*, ed. Georg Schöllgen and Clements Scholten (Münster: Aschendorff, 1996), 141-53; Peter Martens, "The Modern Receptions of Origen's Biblical Scholarship: A Bibliographic Essay," in *Origeniana Undecima: Origen and Origenism in the History of Western Thought*, ed. Ander-Christian Jacobsen (Leuven: Peeters, 2016), 67-86. Origen's theory of reading has been variously evaluated and revived as a normative guide for contemporary readers. Most importantly see Lubac, *Histoire et esprit*; Daniélou, *Origen*; Hanson, *Allegory and Event*; David Dawson, *Christian Figural Reading and the Fashioning of Identity* (Berkeley: University of California Press, 2001). Martens's emphasis on the biographical description of the scriptural interpreter in *Origen and Scripture* joins Torjesen, *Hermeneutical Procedure*, in accenting the social and transformational aspects of Origen's conception of reading.

[170] See Paget, "Christian Exegesis," 522. The distinction used by E. Auerbach, "Figura," in *Scenes from the Drama of European Literature*, ed. W. Godzich and J. Schulte-Sasse, trans. R. Manheim (Minneapolis: University of Minnesota Press, 1984), between "typology" and "allegory' as a way of describing acceptable and unacceptable forms of "nonliteral" has long been influential yet also heavily criticized in Origen scholarship; see Peter Martens, "Revisiting the Allegory/Typology Distinction: The Case of Origen," *JECS* 16.3 (2008): 283-317. Origen describes the Jewish approach to the Law in *Cels.* 6.70 as both a σωματιχῶς and a τυπικῶς way of reading (GCS 3:140).

(*Hom. Jer.* 12.13.1), they "follow the letter" (*Hom. Lev.* 4.7), they "do not see the intention of scripture" (*Comm. Matt.* 11.14, 16.10), they understand texts "simply and carnally" (*simpliciter vel corporaliter*, *Hom. Lev.* 16.2), they fulfill the commands of the Law "$σωματικῶς$ $καὶ$ $τυπικῶς$" (*Cels.* 6.70).[171] Origen means to claim that Jews do not read in a way that attains to the higher meaning of scriptural texts, or, more faithfully to Origen's idiom, the heavenly images of earthly copies. Framing Origen's criticism of Jewish reading as a failure to read "allegorically" does not register the Paulinist frame within which he exercises his training in Greek criticism.

5. Conclusion

Origen invests Hebrews with a Pauline context that recognizes the Jewish context of the title as well as the primacy of reading as the central point of the letter. The interpretation of the tabernacle in Hebrews 8 in which the physical structure is a shadow coordinate with a heavenly image forms the center of Origen's own reading of the letter and provided the language with which to describe a Christian version of the Platonic correspondence between the earthly and the heavenly spheres of reality. As a comment equally applicable to the book of scripture, Hebrews 8:5 provided Origen with a biblical idiom with which to describe the nature of scriptural texts, identify the locus of textual meaning, and ground a strategy of reading. While technically a comment about the tabernacle, Hebrews 8:5 is seen to have a universalizing potential, a "path of understanding" (*Hom. Lev.* 8.5). This Platonic principle applies to the entirety of the written text of scripture, in which the description of all "earthy" phenomena, whether objects, figures, or narratives, are mere shadows, patterns, or copies of a "higher" meaning. Accordingly, Origen expresses a Christian theory of reading with the language of Hebrews 8:5. To read "spiritually" is to discover these higher references.

Given the importance of this exemplum of scriptural interpretation, the ethnic valance of Hebrews, and the appropriation of the text as Pauline, Hebrews emerges as the vehicle through which Origen organizes the difference between Judaism and Christianity as one of reading. Origen's Jesus introduces a new hermeneutic according to the principle of reading in Hebrews 8:5

---

[171] See Martens, *Origen and Scripture*, 135–38.

and thereby initiates the beginnings of Christianity. Since Origen conceptualizes Paul's Jewishness and subsequent "conversion" to "Christianity" around this principle of interpretation, the apostle becomes the embodiment of transition while also grounding Christianity within Judaism. In other words, the image of Paul as the Jewish apostle who was able to assent to Jesus' new hermeneutic is what allows Origen to position Christianity's interpretive tradition within and beyond Judaism simultaneously.

The typical configuration of Origen's criticism of "Jewish literalism" as a theological inconsistency that contrasts with his otherwise capacious engagement with and adoption of Jewish exegetical tradition undervalues the Paulinist context of Origen's theory of reading and conception of Judaism. Origen's appropriation of Hebrews as Pauline allows us to see that his engagement with Jewish tradition was primarily filtered through his reading of Paul, with Hebrews as a central epistle. In this way, Origen's appropriation of Hebrews is an amplification of the emphases of Clement; the letter is now the *definitive* Pauline description of Jewish reading and is given a *privileged* place within Origen's corpus.

The Pauline History of Hebrews. Warren Campbell, Oxford University Press. © Oxford University Press 2025.
DOI: 10.1093/9780197769287.003.0004

5

Prefacing Hebrews and the Institutionalization of Paulinity

Clement and Origen have rather contrastive evaluations and priorities for the Letter to the Hebrews. The images of Paul, histories of Judaism, and assumptions about Jewishness at work in each of these thinkers inform how they encounter and activate the letter. Since these distinctive features condition engagement with this unique letter, what the Pauline ascription means for a given figure and what the ascription affords within the context of a particular corpus is far from predetermined. As Hebrews is copied and transmitted as Pauline, migrating to contexts beyond second- and third-century Egypt, it is brought again and again into such complex readerly moments, encountered as a Pauline letter, variously clashing and melding with other Pauline epistles in ways determined by a reader's unique and complex set of interpretive assumptions and interests.[1]

In the fourth and fifth centuries, however, Hebrews is ushered into the complexities of burgeoning Christological controversies and these discourses undoubtedly condition the questions asked of Hebrews and which passages are the focus of contention. As attempts to reconcile commitment to a singular divine figure as $\dot{α}γέννητος$ (unborn, un-begun) with liturgical practices that treat Jesus as "a god," according to Pliny (*Ep*. X. 96)—attempts that generate

---

[1] While such moments of confrontation include these kinds of readerly moments, other systems that defer to Pauline texts as scriptural authorities also highlight this interpretive coalescence. Hebrews is featured extensively in the Priscillian canons, a fourth-century system of *canones* with accompanying Pauline proof texts. Matthew Crawford and T. J. Lang note the precedent for these *Canones* in Cyprian's *Ad Quirinum testimoniorum Libri III*—a collection of proof texts organized under various headings that address questions of ethics, Christology, and Judaism—but rightly note that the Priscillian canons are exclusively concerned with Pauline texts as the source of *testimonia* and should be thought of as a "Pauline theology". See T. J. Lang and Matthew Crawford, "The Origins of Pauline Theology: Paratexts and Priscillian of Avila's Canons on the Letters of the Apostle Paul," *NTS* 63 (2017): 139 n. 57. Vincent Déroche has also identified a list of *kephalaia* directed against the Jews that often integrates Hebrews into the headings as a kind of proof text; see "La politique anti-judaïque au VIe et au VIIe siècle un memento inédit, les kephalaia," *Travaux et Mémoires* 11 (1991): 275–311. Still, other ordering technologies do not include Hebrews, such as Adrian's *Introduction to the Divine Scriptures* and the Ps.-Pelagian *Concordia Epistularum*.

the language of ὁμοούσιος and ὁμοιούσιος—the Letter to the Hebrews provides a number of passages ripe for exegetical competition.[2] By the late fourth and the fifth centuries, Hebrews is remembered in connection with its fraught reception among those categorized as "the" Arians.[3] In Panarion 69.37.2, Epiphanius of Salamis forwards what seems to be a familiar point, that these Arians take the letter "away from the apostle" (ἀπό τοῦ ἀποστόλου).[4] Later in the fifth century, Theodoret of Cyrrhus takes aim at the lack of Arian reception of Hebrews in his summary of the letter: "They who suffer from the Arian disease do not act admirably, raging against the apostolic letters, separating the Letter to the Hebrews from the rest, and calling it spurious (νόθον)."[5]

While these fourth-century theological debates churn, there were notable advances in the production of commentaries on books now bounded by labels like νέα διαθήκη (e.g., Clement in *Strom.* 5.1.3). As Pauline letters ascend into the "New Testament," they are read and engaged as a "corpus"

---

[2] Especially Hebrews 1:1–3, 2:9–10, 3:1, 4:12, 5:7–9, and 13:8. As noted in the previous chapter, Rowan Greer's engagement with Origen as a reader of Hebrews is the earliest piece in a much larger project on the interpretation of Hebrews in these Christological controversies. Greer focuses on Athanasius, Eustace, Diodore, Gregory of Nazianzus, Gregory of Nyssa, Basil the Great, Theodore Mopsuestia, Cyril of Alexandria, Theodoret of Cyr, and John Chrysostom. See also Frances M. Young, "Christological Ideas in the Greek Commentaries on the Epistle to the Hebrews," *JTS* 20 (1969): 150–63; P. M. Parvis, "The Commentary on Hebrews and the Contra Theodorum of Cyril of Alexandria," *JTS* 26 (1975): 415–19; D. Gonnet, "L'utilisation christologique de l'Épître aux Hébreux dans les orations contra Arianos d'Athanase d'Alexandrie," *StPatr* 32 (1997): 19–24; Jean-Noël Guinot, "La christologie de Théodoret de Cyr dans son commentaire sur le Cantique," *VC* 39 (1985): 256–72; Joseph M. Hallman, "The Communication of Idioms in Theodoret's Commentary on Hebrews," in *In Dominico Eloquio = In Lordly Eloquence: Essays on Patristic Exegesis in Honour of Robert Louis Wilken*, ed. Paul M. Blowers, Angela Russell Christman, David G. Hunter, and Robin Darling Young (Grand Rapids: Eerdmans, 2002), 369–79; Jean-Claude Dhôtel, "La 'sanctification' du Christ d'après Hébreux, II, 11: Interprétations des Pères et des scolastiques médiévaux," *RSR* 47 (1959): 515–43; "La 'sanctification' du Christ d'après Hébreux II,11. Seconde partie: L'exégèse de Heb. II,11 dans les commentaires de l'épître aux Hébreux de saint Jean Chrysostome à saint Thomas," *RSR* 48 (1960): 420–52; S. Haidacher, "Rede des Nestorius über Hebr. 2,1 überliefert unter dem Namen des hl. Chrysostomus," *ZKT* 29 (1905): 192–95.

[3] Scholars often note the polemical hue painted over the extant sources for Arian controversies. See primarily Hanns Christof Brennecke, Uta Heil, Annette von Stockhausen, and Angelika Wintjes, eds., *Athanasius Werke*, III/1, *Dokumente zur Geschichte des arianischen Streites*, vols. 1–5 (Berlin: de Gruyter, 1934, 2007, 2014, 2021). Others rightly emphasize the rhetorical power and function of a singular "Arianism" in Athanasius works. See Maurice Wiles, *Archetypal Heresy: Arianism Through the Centuries* (Oxford: Oxford University Press, 2001), 1–26; David M. Gwynn, *The Eusebians: The Polemic of Athanasius and the Construction of the "Arian Controversy"* (Oxford: Oxford University Press, 2006).

[4] Greek text in Karl Holl, ed., *Epiphanius Dritter Band: Panarion haer. 65–80*, GCS 37 (Leipzig: Hinrichs, 1933), 185.

[5] J. L. Schluze, ed., *Interpretatio Epistolae Ad Hebraeos*, Patrologia Graecae 82 (Paris: J.-P. Migne, 1859), 647C: Θαυμαστὸν οὐδὲν δρῶσιν οἱ τὴν Ἀρειανικὴν εἰσδεξάμενοι νόσον, κατὰ τῶν ἀποστολικῶν λυττῶντες γραμμάτων, καὶ τὴν πρὸς τῶν λοιπῶν Ἑβραίους Ἐπιστολὴν ἀποκρίνοντες, καὶ νόθον ταύτην ἀποκαλοῦντες.

and increasingly the object of commentary and homily. Explicit discussions *about* the Paulinity or Pauline authorship of Hebrews are most often isolated in certain prefatory practices that in Greek contexts are referred to as the ὑπόθεσις (*hypóthesis*).

The term ὑπόθεσις has a long history. David Wolfsdorf draws attention to the use of ὑπόθεσις in fourth-century BCE Attic contexts and points to the basic semantic sense of "something laid down."[6] Wolfsdorf points out that a ὑπόθεσις in Demosthenes, Xenophon, and Isocrates is "something underlying" that includes a proposition, a subject matter, a topic, or some "point of departure" that acts as a "foundation."[7] The language of the ὑπόθεσις would come to describe the preliminary statements regarding literary materials, especially plays, a practice that might go back as far as Aristophanes of Byzantium in the second century BCE and is certainly part of scholarship in Hellenistic Alexandria more broadly.[8] In the same century, Polybius uses τὰς ὑποθέσεις to refer to initial statements (*Hist.* 1.15.11) or to the "starting point" of a literary text (*Hist.* 1.5.3).[9]

By the fifth century, one finds prefatory texts that do not use the language of *hypóthesis* or *argumentum* but assume similar aims for matters to be said "before" the text begins. Servius' commentary on Virgil's *Aeneid* claims that in expounding an author (*exponendis auctoribus*), the life (*vita*) and title of

---

[6] David Wolfsdorf argues that the method described by Plato as ἐξ ὑποθέσεως in *Meno* 86e1–87d8 is not "hypothetical" in the colloquial sense of a tentative idea yet to be "proven," but a method derived from geometry that seeks to reduce the difficulty of a problem. See "The Method ἐξ ὑποθέσεως at *Meno* 86e1–87d8," *Phronesis* 53 (2008): 35–64, esp. 37–41. Wolfsdorf points to Carl Huffman's work on the use of ὑπόθεσις and the verb ὑποτίθεσθαι in the Hippocratic corpus and finds an equivalence between establishing a ὑπόθεσις and positing an ἀρχή (39, citing Carl Huffman, *Philolaus of Croton: Pythagorean and Presocratic. A Commentary on the Fragments and Testimonia with Interpretive Essays* [Cambridge: Cambridge University Press, 1993], 78–92). See also J. T. Bedu-Addo, "Recollection and the Argument 'from a Hypothesis' in Plato's *Meno*," *Journal of Hellenic Studies* 54 (1984): 6–7, who finds two senses to "hypothetical" in the passage from *Meno*: one that is traditionally "hypothetical," that is, to be determined with further consideration, and another that is more concrete and determined. Aristotle too uses ὑπόθεσις to describe the "beginning" of subsequent demonstrations (*Metaphysics* 1013a), as does Xenophon, *Oec.* 21.1.

[7] Wolsdorf, "The Method ἐξ ὑποθέσεως," 37–38.

[8] For a hypothesis on Meander's *Dyskolos* see *Aspis. Georgos. Dis Exapaton. Dyskolos. Encheiridion. Epitrepontes*, ed. and trans. W. G. Arnott, LCL 132 (Cambridge, MA: Harvard University Press, 1979), 181–84; Penelope J. Photiades, "Pan's Prologue to the 'Dyskolos' of Menander," *Greece & Rome* 5.2 (1958): 108–22; William J. Slater, ed., *Aristophanis Byzantii Fragmenta post A. Nauck collegit, testimoniis ornavit, brevi commentario instruxit* (Berlin: de Gruyter, 1986).

[9] In the first century CE, Asconius' *Commentaries on Speeches of Cicero* includes the Latin equivalent, *argumenta*. On the range of this "isagogic" literature see esp. Jaap Mansfeld, *Prolegomena: Questions to be settled before the study of an author or a Text*, PhA 61 (Leiden: Brill, 1994), who notes Porphyry's "erotapocritic" commentary on Aristotle's *Categories* and use of ὑπόθεσις (20–21) as well as Proclus' introduction to Plato in *In Platonis Rempublicam* (31). See also I. Hadot, "Les introductions aux commentaires exégétiques chez les auteurs néoplatoniciens et les auteurs chrétiens," in *Les règles de l'interprétation*, ed. M. Tardieu (Paris: Cerf, 1987), 99–122.

the work, together with its quality, design, number of books and their order, must be considered.¹⁰ Also in the fifth century, Theodoret's hypothesis to Hebrews begins with confrontational comments against the Arians and only later shifts focus to what the ὑπόθεσις τῆς ἐπιστολῆς actually is. At this turn, Theodoret formulates an appropriate background for the letter—persecution of the Hebrew congregations—and how the apostle responds effectively to this context. So, while the entire prefatory text is the "hypothesis" to Hebrews, this internal shift tightens the function of the hypothesis as a literary site for occasional or contextual descriptions that facilitate the reader's comprehension of the text.

As with κεφάλαια or *capita*, which come to structure legal texts like the third-century *libri Ad Sabinum*, *hypothéseis* are affiliated with a wide range of texts.¹¹ In the late second century, Sextus Empiricus (*Math* 3.3.) notes that there are different kinds of *hypothéseis* and that Dicaearchus wrote them for Euripides and Sophocles, summarizing the salient plot points.¹² In ancient Christian use, hypotheses are a feature of homilies, commentaries, and, importantly, editions of the *text itself*. By isolating this kind of prefatory material, the boundaries between these literary forms become blurry, and it is more apparent that the material copies of commentaries, homilies, and of Hebrews "itself" with various commentarial marginalia are all "editions" of Hebrews with various supplements. Each of these textual contexts has some kind of text-paratext relationship and incorporates prefatory comments as a way of instantiating the text as Pauline by negotiating this authorial status with an ever-increasing history of interpretation.

What hypotheses allow us to see is how the Letter to the Hebrews is Paulinized across these various literary forms. Far from cryptic and subtle suggestions of ways of reading with minimal intervention, hypotheses are quite explicit in their hermeneutical force and even fronted as the "first things" to be said about a text, its logic, purpose, origins, and contours.

---

[10] Maurus Servius Honoratus, *In Vergilii carmina comentarii. Servii Grammatici qui feruntur in Vergilii carmina commentarii*, ed. Georgius Thilo (Leipzig: Teubner, 1881), 1: *In exponendis auctoribus haec consideranda sunt: poetae vita, titulus operis, qualitas carminis, scribentis intentio, numerus librorum, ordo librorum, explanatio*.

[11] Dario Mantovani, *Les juristes écrivains de la Rome antique: Les oeuvres des juristes comme litterature. Docet omnia* (Paris: Les Belles Lettres, 2018), 241–84.

[12] See here Gertjan Verhasselt, "The Hypotheses of Euripides and Sophocles by 'Dicaearchus,'" *GRBS* 55 (2015): 609. See also Eleanor Dickey, *Ancient Greek Scholarship: A Guide to Finding, Reading, and Understanding Scholia, Commentaries, Lexica, and Grammatical Treatises, from Their Beginnings to the Byzantine Period* (New York: Oxford University Press, 2007), 32, on the types of these Euripidian hypotheses.

This chapter traces the history of "hypothesizing" Hebrews from the fourth century to the sixteenth, when Hebrews was first de-Paulinized by Erasmus. How do these hypotheses to Hebrews configure the letter as Pauline, and what traditions of reading do they enshrine?

1. The Fourth-Century ὑποθέσεις to Hebrews and the Gatekeeping of Eusebius

The fourth century witnessed a marked increase in commentaries and homilies on the Pauline corpus, particularly in Greek, Latin, and Syriac contexts.[13] Given that Greek and Syriac sources are the earliest to engage and encounter Hebrews as a Pauline letter in the second and third centuries and that Hebrews is only later reckoned as Pauline in Latin texts, it is fairly unsurprising that Hebrews would first become an object of commentary and the basis of a homily in Greek and Syriac sources much earlier than in Latin. The earliest Pauline commentaries in the Latin tradition are found in Victorinus[14] in the late third century and the one called "Ambrosiaster"[15] in the mid-fourth, followed by Jerome, Augustine, and Pelagius.[16] While Hebrews emerges as Pauline in Latin sources, it is not the object of

---

[13] Pierre Boucaud, "The *Corpus Paulinum*: Greek and Latin Exegesis of the Epistles in the First Millennium," *Revue de l'Histoire des Religions* 230 (2013): 299–332. Of course, Clement of Alexandria, Origen, Hippolytus of Rome, and other figures mentioned secondarily, such as Basilides, Heracleon, Theodore of Heraclea, and Theophilus of Antioch, comprised earlier iterations of this commentary tradition, but the fourth-century increase in production is notable. See here Gilles Dorival, "Les formes et modèles littéraires," in *Histoire de le littérature grecque chrétienne: Introduction*, ed. Bernard Pouderon and Enrico Norelli (Paris: Cerf, 2008), 139–88; Gilles Dorival, "The Bible, Commentaries, Scholia, and Other Literary Forms," in *On the Fringe of Commentary: Metatextuality in Ancient Near Eastern and Ancient Mediterranean Cultures*, ed. S. H. Aufrère, P. S. Alexander, and Z. Pleše (Peeters: Leuven, 2014), 163–74.

[14] Bernhard Lohse, "Beobachtungen zum Paulus-Kommentar des Marius Victorinus und zur Wiederentdeckung des Paulus in der lateinischen Theologie des vierten Jahrhunderts," in *Kerygma and Logos: Beiträge zu den geistesgeschichtlichen Beziehungen zwischen Antike und Christentum. Festschrift für Carl Andresen zum 80. Geburtstag*, ed. Adolf Martin Ritter (Göttingen: Vanderhoeck & Ruprecht, 1979), 351–66; Karl T. Schäfer, "Marius Victorinus und die Marcionitischen Prologe zu den Paulusbriefen," *RBén* 80 (1970): 7–16; Wolfgang Karl Wischmeyer, "Bemerkungen zu den Paulusbriefkommentaren des G. Marius Victorinus," *ZNW* 63 (1972): 108–20.

[15] Ambrosiaster, *Commentarius in xii epistulas Paulinas*, ed Heinricus Iosephus Vogels, CSEL 81/1–3 (Vindobonae: Hoelder, 1966–69).

[16] For Jerome's four commentaries on Pauline letters (Galatians, Ephesians, Titus, Philemon) see F. Bucchi, ed., *Commentarii in epistulas Pauli apostoli ad Titum et ad Philemonem*, CCSL 77C (Turnhout: Brepols, 2003); G. Raspanti, ed., *Commentarii in epistulam Pauli apostoli ad Galatas*, CCSL 77A (Turnhout: Brepols, 2006); as well as Andrew Cain, *Jerome's Commentaries on the Pauline Epistles and the Architecture of Exegetical Authority* (Oxford: Oxford University Press, 2022).

commentarial and homiletical activity in these works.[17] Not until the ninth and tenth centuries do we find Latin commentaries on Hebrews in authors like Alcuin, Claudius of Turin, Haimo of Auxerre, and Atto of Vercelli.[18] The staggered emergence of commentaries on Hebrews in Latin and Greek sources mirrors the evidence discussed in Chapter 2, that Hebrews first appeared as a circulating Pauline "letter" in Greek and Syrian contexts and was slower to appear as Pauline in Latin, perhaps even *because* it circulated as a letter from Barnabas.

The earliest *hypothéseis* for Hebrews can be found in Chrysostom's preface to the *Homilies on Hebrews*, Ephrem the Syrian's commentary on the Pauline corpus, and the prefatory comments of Rufinus in the Vulgate prologue known as the *Primum Quaeritur*.[19] Each of these different literary settings (homily, commentary, and text edition) features preliminary statements which are designed to contextualize the text for proper reading.

Chrysostom's preface to the *Homilies on Hebrews* is certainly the most expansive and influential of these three, fully extant prefatory comments from the fourth century.[20] Chrysostom's preface begins with a basic question

---

[17] See here Alexander Souter, *The Earliest Latin Commentaries on the Epistles of St. Paul* (Oxford: Clarendon, 1999); H. A. G. Houghton, "The Layout of Early Latin Commentaries on the Pauline Epistles and Their Oldest Manuscripts," StPatr 91 (2017): 71–112.

[18] See especially Eduard Riggenbach, *Historische Studien zum Hebräerbrief*, vol. 1, *Die ältesten lateinischen Kommentare zum Hebräerbrief*, vol. 8.1 of *Forschungen zur Geschichte des neutestamentlichen Kanons und der altkirchlichen Literatur*, ed. Theodor Zahn (Leipzig: Deichert, 1907); Karl Theodor Schäfer, *Untersuchungen zur Geschichte der lateinischen Übersetzung des Hebräerbriefs*, Römische Quartalschrift 23, Supplementheft (Freiburg: Herder, 1929). On Alcuin in particular see Michael Fox, "Alcuin's Expositio in epistolam ad Hebraeos," *JML* 18 (2008): 326–45.

[19] In addition to Chrysostom's thirty-four homilies, Hermann Josef Sieben, *Kirchenväterhomilien zum Neuen Testament: Ein Repertorium der Textausgaben und Übersetzungen. Mit einem Anhang der Kirchenväterkommentare*, Instrumenta Patristica 11 (The Hague: Martinus Nijhoff International, 1991), 174–78, adds one homily from Gregory the Illuminator (PL 39, 1969–71), two from Caesarius of Arles (CCL 104, 744–49 and 749–53), one homily from Nestorius (PG 63, 53–60 on Heb 3.1), and a pseudonymous homily attributed to Augustine (PL 39, 1971–72).

[20] Pauline Allen and Wendy Mayer draw attention to the work of I. Opelt, who argues that this series was preached at Antioch, not Constantinople, between 396 and 398, which departs from the traditional date of the homilies to the final year of John's episcopate in Constantinople, ca. 402–3. See I. Opelt, "Das Ende von Olympia: Zur Entstehungszeit der Predigten zum Hebräerbrief des Johannes Chrysostomos," ZKG 81 (1970): 64–69. Allen and Mayer, however, argue that it is more likely that the homilies derive from both Constantinople and Antioch, "The Thirty-Four Homilies on Hebrews: The Last Series Delivered by Chrysostom in Constantinople?," *Byzantion* 65 (1995): 309–48. See also Pauline Allen and Wendy Mayer, "The Homilist and the Congregation: A Case-Study of Chrysostom's Homilies on Hebrews," *Augustinianum* 36 (1996): 397–421. See also Wendy Mayer, "Les homélies de Jean Chrysostome: Problèmes concernant la provenance, l'ordre et la datation," *REAug* 52 (2006): 329–53, who emphasizes the importance of provenance prior to considerations of chronology. On Chrysostom's homilies more broadly see James D. Cook, *Preaching and Popular Christianity: Reading the Sermons of John Chrysostom*, Oxford Theology and Religion Monographs (Oxford: Oxford University Press, 2018); Wendy Mayer, *The Homilies of St John Chrysostom—Provenance: Reshaping the Foundations*, Orientalia Christiana Analecta 273

that has gripped most ancient readers—Why would Paul write to Hebrews? For Chrysostom, if Paul is the self-proclaimed apostle of the ἔθνη (Rom 11:13, citing also Acts 22:21) and Peter is an apostle of the "circumcision" (Gal 2:18), Chrysostom asks, "What did [Paul] have in common with the Hebrews? and why did he also write an epistle to them?"[21] This question leads Chrysostom into an excursus detailing the kinds of hostility between Paul and other Jews.[22] When returning to this initial "why," Chrysostom records that the Letter to the Hebrews was sent to "Jerusalem and Palestine," which might indicate that Jerusalem was the particular destination and yet Palestine was the larger region that the letter was addressing. Chrysostom defends Paul's expansive epistolary activity, that is, moving into Peter's "territory" beyond the horizon of the Gentiles, by noting the lack of an explicit prohibition against contact with the Hebrews. Just as Paul might baptize without being commanded to baptize (1 Cor 1:13–17), so Paul may also write to the Hebrews. The absence of a command is not the same as active forbiddance. Moreover, and more simply, Chrysostom asks how Paul could be willing to be accursed for his "brothers according to the flesh" (Rom 9.3) and yet not write a letter to them. After all, in Hebrews 13:23, Paul writes, "I will see you."[23]

The second half of this lengthy preface emphasizes the political context of the audience, especially the violence that they previously endured. Chrysostom cites 1 Thessalonians 2:14, where Paul tells the Thessalonians that in what they have suffered they have joined "the churches of God

---

(Rome: Pontificium Institutum Orientalium Studiorum, 2005); Jaclyn L. Maxwell, *Christianization and Communication in Late Antiquity: John Chrysostom and His Congregation in Antioch* (Cambridge: Cambridge University Press, 2009).

[21] Greek text in J.-P. Migne, *Patrologiae cursus completus*, 63 (Paris: Migne, 1862), 9: τί κοινὸν πρὸς Ἑβραίους εἶχε; τίδὲ αὐτοῖς ἐπέστελλεν.

[22] In this excursus, Chrysostom claims that when someone "distinguished and earnest" like Paul leaves an *ethnos* it especially vexes the larger group, especially with Paul because of his subsequent public disputes. Second, Chrysostom claims that Paul's turn toward Christ-following was particularly noteworthy for Jews because Paul was not an eyewitness of any great signs or wonders, as were Peter and the other disciples. Paul, however, by merely hearing a voice was moved to leave "the Jews." This, for Chrysostom, explains the animosity between Paul and fellow Jews (perhaps not "fellow" for Chrysostom), but it is also pointed out that Jewish believers were hostile toward Paul. For Chrysostom, Paul preached Christianity "purely" to the Gentiles and, if he happened to be traveling through Judaea, he had no problem making the same proclamation to Jews. Here Chrysostom cites the comment from James to Paul in Acts 21:20–21 regarding the "thousands of Jews" who are believers and under the impression that Paul teaches fellow Jews to forsake the Law. For this reason, whether Christ-followers or not, Jews were hostile to Paul.

[23] Here Chrysostom evokes the postscript's language of seeing Timothy "soon" (Heb 13.23). The reference to Timothy's release and Paul's travels allows Chrysostom to date Hebrews before 1 Timothy.

which are throughout Judaea." Chrysostom connects this theme to Hebrews 13:34, where the audience is praised for welcoming the "spoiling of [their] goods" with joy. Given Chrysostom's focus on the poor and almsgiving, he takes time to develop Paul's interest in the Hebrews' financial situation, finding references to support of Jerusalem in Romans 15:25, 1 Corinthians 16:3–4, and Galatians 2:9–10, which are quoted in succession.[24] Chrysostom then reasons that many of the Hebrews would be "fainthearted" from this series of political misfortunes, since "they were Jews and learned from the fathers that they must expect both their good and their evil immediately and must live accordingly."[25] Contrasting this "Jewish" mode of conceptualizing the timing of reward, for Chrysostom, is the hope of reward after death. Correcting this overarching misperception is foundational to the purpose of Hebrews and the way Chrysostom concludes the preface:[26]

> [Paul] speaks much of both the New and the Old Covenant, since this was useful to him as proof of the resurrection. In case [the Jews] should disbelieve that [Christ] rose on account of the things that he suffered, [Paul] confirms it from the prophets, and shows that not the Jewish, but ours are the sacred [institutions]. Since the temple still stood and the sacrificial rites, he says, "Let us go forth therefore bearing his reproach." But this also was made an argument against him: "If these things are a shadow, if these things are an image, how is it that they have not passed away or given place when the truth was manifested, but these things still flourish?" This also [Paul] quietly intimates will happen, and that at a time close at hand.

Chrysostom concludes by tying together his idea of Jewish immediacy with Paul's purposes in Hebrews; to confirm the overarching transfer from one

---

[24] On issues of poverty see Homily 24. See also Blake Leyerle, "John Chrysostom on Almsgiving and the Use of Money," *HTR* 87 (1994): 29–47; Elizabeth Clark, "Comment: Chrysostom and Pauline Social Ethics," in *Paul and the Legacies of Paul*, ed. W. S. Babcock (Dallas: Southern Methodist University Press, 1990), 193–99. See also Bronwen Neil Allen and Wendy Mayer, eds., *Preaching Poverty in Late Antiquity: Perceptions and Realities*, Arbeiten zur Kirchen- und Theologiegeschichte 28 (Leipzig: Evangelische Verlagsanstalt, 2009).

[25] PG 63.12: Ἐπειδὴ γὰρ καὶ Ἰουδαῖοι ἦσαν, καὶ αὐτοὶ παρὰ τῶν πατέρων ἐμάνθανον, ὅτι καὶ τὰ ἀγαθὰ καὶ τὰ κακὰ παρὰ πόδας ἐχρῆν προσδοκᾶν, καὶ οὕτω βιῶναι.

[26] PG 63.14: Ποιεῖται δὲ πολὺν λόγον καὶ περὶ τῆς Καινῆς καὶ Παλαιᾶς Διαθήκης· καὶ γὰρ πρὸς τὴν τῆς ἀναστάσεως πίστιν σφόδρα αὐτῷ τοῦτο ἐχρησίμευεν. Ἵνα γὰρ μὴ ἐξ ὧν ἔπαθε διαπιστῶσιν ὅτι ἀνέστη, ἀπὸ προφητῶν αὐτὸ ἰσχυροποιεῖ· καὶ δείκνυσιν οὐκ ὄντα σεμνὰ τὰ Ἰουδαϊκά, ἀλλὰ τὰ ἡμέτερα· ἔτι γὰρ καὶ ὁ ναὸς εἱστήκει, καὶ τὰ τῶν θυσιῶν· διὸ καὶ ἔλεγε, Τοίνυν ἐξερχώμεθα ἔξω, τὸν ὀνειδισμὸν αὐτοῦ φέροντες. Ἠναντιοῦτο δὲ αὐτῷ καὶ τοῦτο· εἰκὸς γὰρ ἦν εἰπεῖν τινας, ὅτι Εἰ ταῦτα σκιά, εἰ ταῦτα εἰκών, πῶς οὐ παρεχώρησεν, οὐδὲ ὑπεξέστη τῆς ἀληθείας φανείσης, ἀλλ' ἔτι ταῦτα ἀνθεῖ; Καὶ τοῦτο δὲ ἠρέμα ἠνίξατο ἐσόμενον καὶ αὐτὸ εἰς καιρὸν τὸν προσήκοντα.

set of sacred institutions to another and to impress the importance of the *delay* of heavenly rewards.

Chrysostom's preface is joined by Rufinus' prologue to the Pauline corpus and Ephrem the Syrian's *Commentary on Hebrews*. While both Rufinus and Ephrem share elements with Chrysostom, they are much more overt in their indebtedness to Eusebius. Rufinus is credited with revising the Vulgate edition of the *corpus Paulinum*, and in the vast majority of Vulgate manuscripts there is an introductory prologue known as the *Primum quaeritur* that, again, is increasingly attributed to Rufinus in scholarship despite some manuscript attributions to Pelagius.[27] In this prologue, Rufinus takes up the Letter to the Hebrews, and his framing of the problem and the solution are decidedly Origenian, mediated by Eusebius. After noting the two problems for Paulinity, that is, anonymity and style, Rufinus advances various solutions: Barnabas is the author according to Tertullian, Luke according to "others," or even Clement, that *episcopi Romanae ecclesiae*.[28] Rufinus then forwards his Origenian perspective on the letter via Eusebius:[29]

> To these it is necessary to respond: now then, if it is not Paul's because it does not have his name, it is nobody's because it is entitled with no name. But if this is absurd, that which shines with such eloquence of his own doctrine, ought all the more to be believed to be his.
>
> *Quibus respondendum est: si propterea Pauli non erit quia eius non habet nomen, ergo nec alicuius erit quia nullius nomine titulatur; quod si absurdum est, ipsius magis esse credenda est quae tanto doctrinae suae fulget eloquio.*

With Origen, Rufinus embraces anonymity and its obfuscation of authorship and instead situates the doctrine of the letter as the seat of its Paulinity. From here, Rufinus advances the point from Clement of Alexandria, that since the Hebrew audience is suspicious of Paul—due to the circulating idea

---

[27] On this point see Eric W. Scherbenske, *Canonizing Paul: Ancient Editorial Practice and the Corpus Paulinum* (New York: Oxford University Press, 2013), 183–84, esp. n. 37, as well as Timothy W. Dooley, "Marcionite Influences in the Primum Quaeritur Preface to Vulgate Paul," *StPatr* 99 (2018): 139–56.

[28] Latin text in Johannes Wordsworth and Henricus Julianus White, eds., *Novum Testamentum Domini Nostri Iesu Christi Latine*, with Alexandro Ramsbotham, Hedley Friderico Davis Sparks, and Claudio Jenkins, *Pars Secunda—Epistulae Paulinae* (Oxford: Clarendon, 1913–41), 2.

[29] Latin text in Wordsworth and White, *Novum Testamentum Domini*, 2–3. Translation, Scherbenske, *Canonizing Paul*, 187.

that Paul advocates the abolishment of the Law in Acts 21—the name of Paul and the authority of his apostolic status are not mentioned in the letter:[30]

> But since [Paul] was thought of as a destroyer of the law among the assemblies of the Hebrews by false suspicion, he wished to narrate the relationship of the example of the law and the truth of Christ without mentioning his name in case the hatred of his name displayed at the front [would] exclude the utility of reading. It is certainly not surprising, if he seems more eloquent in his own [language], i.e., Hebrew, than in a foreign one, i.e., Greek, the language in which the other letters are written.
>
> *Sed quoniam apud Hebraeorum ecclesias quasi destructor legis falsa suspicione habebatur, uoluit tacito nomine de figuris legis et ueritate Christi reddere rationem, ne odium nominis fronte praelati utilitatem excluderet lectionis. Non est sane mirum si eloquentior uideatur in proprio id est hebraeo quam in peregrino id est graeco, quo ceterae epistulae sunt scriptae sermone.*

Rufinus stays fairly close to the Clementine evidence mediated by Eusebius: hostility between Paul and Jewish-Christians in Acts 21, anonymity as humility, Hebrews as a translated text. Ephrem the Syrian likewise writes from within the Eusebian line, opening his preface to Hebrews by acknowledging the two perennial obstacles to Pauline authorship: anonymity and stylistic difference. According to Ephrem, those who advance these two arguments against Pauline authorship also claim that the Letter to the Hebrews was written directly by Clement of Rome—that is, without a Pauline urtext—given its similarity to the Clementine corpus (*Clementinae*).[31] This, to be sure, is an alternative version of the data preserved in Eusebius. Ephrem goes on to note *another* group who claim the more familiar origin story associated with Clement of Alexandria—a Hebrew original translated into Greek by Clement of Rome, left anonymous in order to not upset the Hebrew audience.

---

[30] Latin text in Wordsworth and White, *Novum Testamentum Domini*, 3. Translation, Scherbenske, *Canonizing Paul*, 187, slightly modified.

[31] Ephrem's commentary is only preserved in Armenian. See Ephrem Armenius, Սրբոյն Եփրեմի մատենագրութիւնք (Venice: Tparani Srboyn Ghazaru, 1836), 1.194. Ephrem's Armenian commentaries are also translated into Latin. See Patres Mekitharistes, *S. Ephræm Syri commentarii in epistolas D. Pauli nunc primum ex armenio in Latinum sermonem a patribus Mekitharistis translate* (Venice: Ex Typographia Sancti Lazari, 1893).

For Ephrem, Paul's closing remarks in Hebrews 13:23 concerning the sending of Timothy to the audience of Hebrews—as well as the language in Hebrews 10:32 and 10:34 that is later cited as supplemental evidence—reveal that he is writing to a known group. The Hebrews are, for Ephrem, the disciples of the "Hebrew leaders," James and Peter. Ephrem wonders if the apostles Peter and James were still in Jerusalem since they received an "apostleship of circumcision" and still engaged in a "great struggle" and "agony" for the gospel since the temple in Jerusalem was still intact with its "adorned and ordered" sacrificial system and these "Hebrew hearers" have faced political hardship as the text of Hebrews indicates (citing Heb 10:32, 10:34). The Letter to the Hebrews is Paul's intervention, designed to disrupt the appeal of participation in the temple by voiding the priesthood, sacrifices, and Jewish offices of service. Yet, in intervening in this way, and even knowing that he was more powerful than other apostles, Paul suppressed his name so that his humility and concern for direct instruction would appear.

Taking these three prefatory texts as a whole, there are certain commonalities. Chrysostom's citation of Hebrews 10:34 ("welcomed with joy the spoiling of your goods") is also quoted by Ephrem. Rufinus, too, comments on the suffering of the audience and their commendation to the Thessalonians.[32] Eusebius is certainly the gatekeeper for Rufinus and Ephrem, but less so for Chrysostom, whose preface breaks from the core points of the discourse, namely, style and anonymity. Despite Chrysostom's uniqueness—which

---

[32] An *incipit argumentum* noted by White and Wordsworth also emphasizes persecution as the primarily historical context for the letter, together with the Origenian emphasis on dispelling the shadows of the Law. The argumentum refers to "whipping" (*uerbera*), all kinds of injuries (*omni paene iniuriam*), and how they endured the robbery of their property (*rapinam bonorum suorum cum gaudio sustinuerunt*). Latin text in Wordsworth and White, *Novum Testamentum Domini*, 681. There are two other argumenta in the Latin tradition. The main argumentum forwards the familiar point that Paul writes to the Hebrews, believers from the circumcision, out of humility and in recognition of their pride, but adds that John approaches writing analogously (commenting on the anonymity of 1 John). The argumentum also mentions that Paul sent the letter in Hebrew and that Luke retains the meaning and order (*sensum et ordinem*) of the epistle in Greek. There is no mention of Clement of Rome as the translator. The third, "Explicit Argumentum," likewise identifies the Hebrews as the name of the "nation" and the proper name of "Jews who had believed in Christ' (*qui in christum crediderant ex iudaeis*) and uniquely adds that these Hebrews occupy congregations throughout the land of Judaea that Paul refers to in Galatians 1:21–22. The postscript in Hebrews 13 is also read as an indication that Paul was writing *from* Italy "by Timothy." See also the argumentum in White and Wordsworth, *Novum Testamentum Domini*, 9, which is found in H (Codex Hubertianus) and Θ (Codex Theodulphianus) and certainly related to the *Primum quaeritur*: *Ad ultimum hebraeos qui in christum crediderant et postmodum persequutionibus iudaicis territi a fide recesserant confortat atque ad gratiam euangelii reuocat* (Finally, he comforts the Hebrews who had believed in Christ and, afterward, terrified by the Jewish persecutions that had departed from the faith, he comforts and calls them back to the grace of the Gospel).

may in turn contribute to the popularity of this preface in subsequent transmission—Eusebius does drive much of the subsequent discourse regarding Hebrews as a Pauline. Two examples from the fifth century bear this point out. In responding to the rejection of Hebrews among the "Arians," Theodoret evokes Eusebius as a principal witness:[33]

> Εἰ δὲ μηδὲ τοῦτο ἱκανὸν πεῖσαι αὐτούς, Εὐσεβίῳ γοῦν ἔχρην πεισθῆναι τῷ Παλαιστινῷ, ὃν τῶν οἰκείων δογμάτων ἀποκαλοῦσι συνήγορον.
>
> If this is not enough to persuade them, they should certainly be persuaded by Eusebius the Palestinian, whom they call a defender of their own doctrines.

Another late fifth-century fragment from Severian of Gabala also registers the importance of Eusebius as a gatekeeper of the Pauline authorship of Hebrews:[34]

> Εὐσέβιος ὁ Παμφίλου ἱστορικώτερος γεγονὼς τῶν πρὸ αὐτοῦ καὶ μετ' αὐτοῦ, ἐμνημόνευσε τῆς ζητήσεως, καὶ ὅτι τοῖς πατράσιν ἡμῶν τοῖς παλαιοῖς τῶν ἐπισκόπων ἔδοξε Παύλου τὴν Ἐπιστολὴν εἶναι.
>
> Eusebius Pamphilus, the foremost historian of the things before and with him, remembered the investigation, and that the epistle appeared to be from Paul to our fathers, the old bishops.

The deference shown to Eusebius in these fifth-century contexts is matched by the subsequent recycling of the Eusebian plot points used to explain the unique origins of this Pauline letter. The same ideas regarding anonymity, stylistic difference, hostilities in Acts 21, and Paul's humility continue as the necessary prefatory comments, from Īshoʻdād of Merv in the ninth century to Aquinas in the thirteenth.[35] However, as noted earlier, hypotheses become

---

[33] Greek text in J.-P. Migne, *Patrologiae Cursus Completus*, Series Graeca, vol. 82 (Paris, 1864), 673, 675.

[34] Greek text from Karl Staab, *Pauluskommentare aus der griechischen Kirche aus Katenenhandschriften gesammelt und herausgegeben*, NTA 15 (Münster: Aschendorff, 1933), 345–46.

[35] Īshoʻdād of Merv, *The Commentaries of Ishoʻdad of Merv: Bishop of Hadatha (c. 850 A.D.) in Syriac and English*, ed. Margaret Dunlop Gibson and J. Rendel Harris, vol. 5, part 2 (Cambridge: Cambridge University Press, 1916), 101–2; Richard Larcher, trans., *Aquinas, Commentary on the Letter of Saint Paul to the Hebrews*, ed. J. Mortensen (Lander: Aquinas Institute for the Study of Sacred Doctrine, 2012).

a feature of the "text itself" and not just derived from the commentarial tradition. Joining these readers of Hebrews are other hypotheses for the letter that reside not in the lengthy tradition of commentaries and homilies but within editions of the text of Paul.

2. Origen's Shadow in the "Euthalian" ὑπόθεσις to Hebrews

The "Euthalian apparatus" refers to an evolving constellation of ordering and prefatory systems for a fourteen-letter collection of Paul, which was later expanded to include the Catholic epistles and Acts as a larger, perhaps two-volume, project.[36] The fullest manifestation of this apparatus features a lengthy prologue for the Pauline collection that describes Paul's life, letters, wondrous deeds, and death, followed by chapter titles designed to partition and interpret the epistles, lists of lections and scriptural citations (*martyria*), as well as hypotheses with their summarizing and contextualizing work. Complexities and lingering mysteries surround the figure "Euthalius" as well as the possible dates and relationships between the various parts of the apparatus.

The apparatus has long been associated with Caesarea, most notably through the famed colophon after the Letter to Titus in Codex Coislinianus 202 (Hᵖ); a sixth-century fragmentary codex and the earliest example of Euthaliana. The colophon reads:

> I wrote and edited this volume of Paul the apostle, arranging it in verses according to my abilities, so that the text of our brothers may be clearly written and easy to understand, and I ask all of them for forgiveness for my audacity, that I may receive acceptance through prayer for my [work (?)]. The book was compared with a copy in the library of Caesarea, written with the hand of the holy Pamphilus (Ἀντεβλήθη δὲ ἡ βίβλος. πρὸς τὸ ἐν Καισαρίᾳ ἀντίγραφον· τῆς βιβλιοθήκης τοῦ ἁγίου Παμφίλου· χειρὶ γεγραμμένον).[37]

---

[36] The two monographs driving much of contemporary scholarship on Euthaliana are Vemund Blomkvist, *Euthalian Traditions: Text, Translation and Commentary*, TU 17 (Berlin: de Gruyter, 2012), and Louis Charles Willard, *A Critical Study of the Euthalian Apparatus*, ANTF 41 (Berlin: de Gruyter, 2009).

[37] Henri Omont, "Notice sur un très ancien manuscrit grec en onciales des épîtres de Saint Paul conservé à la Bibliothèque Nationale (H ad epistulas Pauli) par H.O.," *NEMBM* 33 (1890): 189.

Pamphilus was a contemporary of Eusebius in Caesarea who lived to see the turn of the fourth century and is remembered primarily as a defender of Origen as well as a caretaker of the long-romanticized library at Caesarea. The colophon has been a pivotal text in discussions of the origins of the Euthalian apparatus, yet, as a rule, claims to the Caesarean library are often tapping into the cultural cache of such bibliographic ties rather than a bare description of textual origins. Since this colophon is copied and found in a number of other contexts, one must resist thinking that Codex H[p], though the earliest witness, preserves an unmediated, historically descriptive colophon.[38] And yet references to Eusebius are found throughout the Euthalian material, most notably in the prologue, where indebtedness to "the chronological tables of Eusebius, the disciple of Pamphilus" is explicit.[39] Euthalius describes Eusebius as a painstaking accountant of the martyrdom of Paul and urges the reader to move beyond Acts of the Apostles and to "trust for the rest to Eusebius the Chronicler and accept the narrative with a reasonable spirit as a friend" (709C).

The "I" in this colophon has always been mysterious, as the line in Codex H[p] is notoriously opaque; the first line has been erased and the second line is partially overwritten (fol. 14r). Albert Ehrhard pointed to other copies of this colophon in other Euthalian manuscripts that interestingly name an "Evagrius" as the "I" (GA 88 and GA 915, for example).[40] This tantalizing yet complex scenario led Ehrhard to posit that Evagrius, not "Euthalius," lies behind the colophon in Codex H[p], which others have attempted to find with UV light.[41] Since one of the late pieces of the apparatus refers to the year 396 CE in a discussion of the date of Paul's death, and Evagrius of

---

[38] Similar colophons are found in GA 88 (Biblioteca Nazionale Ms. II. A. 7), BML Add 19, 730 (in Armenian), and the Philoxenian edition of the Syriac NT (Cambridge Add. 1700). See esp. H. S. Murphy, "On the Text of Codices H and 93," *JBL* 78 (1959): 228–37; Fred C. Conybeare, "On the Codex Pamphili and the Date of Euthalius," *Journal of Philology* 23 (1895): 241–59, who takes up this Armenian codex and claims that it reflects the best representative of this apparent Pamphilus codex; as well as Fred C. Conybeare, "The Date of Euthalius," *ZNW* 5 (1904): 39–52; Günther Zuntz, *The Ancestry of the Harklean New Testament*, British Academy, Supplemental Papers 7 (London: Oxford University Press, 1945).

[39] Other references to Eusebius are found in 708B and 712 C. See especially James Rendel Harris, "Euthalius and Eusebius," in *Hermas in Arcadia and Other Essays*, ed. Harris (Cambridge: Cambridge University Press, 1896), 60–83.

[40] Albert Ehrhard, "Der Codex H ad epistulas Pauli und 'Euthalius diaconos,'" *Centralblatt für Bibliothekwesen* 8.9 (1891): 385–411. Bertrand Hemmerdinger, "Euthaliana," *JTS* 11 (1960): 349, points to Evagrius of Antioch as another, more obscure, option from the late fourth century.

[41] Willard, *Euthalian Apparatus*, 114, notes this from Bertrand Hemmerdinger, "L'auteur de l'édition 'Euthalienne,'" in *Acten des XI. Internationalen Byzantinistenkongresses, München 1958*, ed. Franz Dölger and Hans-Georg Beck (Munich: C. H. Beck, 1960), 227.

Pontus was operating in late fourth century and later condemned as an Origenist, there is quite a bit of fuel for this reconstruction.[42]

While Euthalius is sometimes called a διάκονος, as in the prologue to the epistles of Paul, other variants refer to one Euthalius ἐπισκόπου Σούλκης.[43] The identification of Σούλκης is still fraught, however, though parallels are noted by Vacher Burch, such as the Sardinian township Σούλκης noted by George of Cyrus, and the town Σόλκοι mentioned by Stephanus Byzantinus.[44] Some reconstructions identify Euthalius as a late fourth-century Egyptian deacon who later became bishop of a city in Sardinia and was commissioned to produce an edition of Paul that included previously developed *kephalaia* while adding lections and scriptural testimonies, not to mention an extended prologue describing Paul and his letters. But again, the system is far from uniform; there is source material going back to the third century and subsequent additions, infused at various stages in textual transmission and reproduction.

The prologue to the Pauline epistles is typically read as one of the earliest elements, in which a deacon named Euthalius (Πρόλογος Ἐυθαλίου διακόνου) writes to an anonymous "most honored father" (πάτερ τιμιώτατε) about the creation of an edition of Paul.[45] In the prologue, "Euthalius" takes credit for cataloging scriptural citations in the letters—"We have systematically summarized the most precise divisions of the readings (τῶν ἀναγνώσεων) and the acceptable list of the divine testimonies (τῶν θείων μαρτυριῶν) by reading through the text" (708A)—whereas the chapter headings are attributed to "one of the wisest of our fathers, a lover of Christ" (ἐνὶ τῶν σοφωτάτων τινὶ καὶ φιλοχρίστῳ πατέρων).[46]

---

[42] See also Ernst von Dobschütz, "Ein Beitrag zur Euthaliusfrage," *Zentralblatt für Bibliothekswesen* 10 (1893): 49–70, who tones down Ehrhard's theory and claims that Evagrius was simply the scribe; and Joseph Armitage Robinson, *Euthaliana*, Texts and Studies 3.3 (Cambridge: Cambridge University Press, 1895), 100, who is favorable to the idea that Evagrius of Pontus as a contributor to an *editio minor* of the apparatus.

[43] For variants see Hermann Freiherr von Soden, *Die Schriften des Neuen Testaments in ihrer ältesten erreichbaren Textgestalt hergestellt auf Grund ihrer Textgeschichte, I. Teil: Untersuchungen, I. Abteilung: Die Textseugen* (Göttingen: Vandenhoeck and Ruprecht, 1911), 649–50.

[44] Vacher Burch, "Two Notes on Euthalius of Sulci," *JTS* 17, no. 66 (1916): 179, who also adds the reference to Σελεύκεια, μεγάλη πόλις in Strabo, *Geographica* 16.1.18, which was the location of a fifth-century council.

[45] On the prologue see Blomkvist, *Euthalian Traditions*, 194–217; Willard, *Euthalian Apparatus*, 11–21; and Nils Dahl, "The 'Euthalian Apparatus' and 'Affiliated Argumenta,'" in *Studies in Ephesians: Introductory Questions, Text- & Edition-Critical Issues, Interpretation of Texts and Themes*, ed. D. Hellholm, V. Blomkvist, and T. Fornberg (Tübingen: Mohr Siebeck, 2000), 234–40.

[46] Greek text and translation in Blomkvist, *Euthalian Traditions*, 107.

Copying Euthalian material creates alternative configurations, and, as it stands, all or various parts of the apparatus are found in a number Greek manuscripts. Greg Fewster rightly cautions us to resist idealizing reconstructed editions of full paratextual systems and thereby overlook their somewhat messy growth as ordering technologies within variegated manuscript records.[47] With this in mind, scholars have noted that the hypotheses are a later addition to the apparatus, as they are not mentioned in the prologue, and, more importantly, the hypotheses and the superscriptions to the Pauline letters differ on the destination of the letters.[48] The Euthalian hypotheses also appear in the Ps.-Athanasian *Synopsis Scripturae Sacrae*, which is a defensive list of canonical (κεκανονισμένα) books, with the names of each book as well as the opening line, before hypotheses for each book.[49] Little is known about this *Synopsis*, and there is confusion on the direction of influence.[50] Zahn is likely right that the synopsis reflects dependence on a number of fourth- and fifth-century literary texts and might derive from the early sixth century.[51] Tentatively, we might conclude that the hypotheses were added toward end of the fourth century and perhaps in the early fifth

---

[47] Gregory P. Fewster, "Finding Your Place: Developing Cross-Reference Systems in Late Antique Biblical Codices," in *The Future of New Testament Textual Scholarship: From H. C. Hoskier to the Editio Critica Maior and Beyond*, ed. Garrick V. Allen (Tübingen: Mohr Siebeck, 2019), 159. The first edition of the Euthalian apparatus in 1698 might be guilty of exactly this, as it was based on a particular manuscript with an especially full apparatus (ms. 181). Lorenzo Alessandro Zacagni, *Collectanea monumentorum veterum Ecclesiae graecae ac latinae quae hactenus in Vaticana bibliotheca delituerunt. Tomus primus* (Rome: Sacred Congregation for the Propagation of the Faith, 1698). Untangling the "messy growth" of the *Euthaliana* was the focus of the late nineteenth century, which saw a flurry of scholarship on the apparatus before a relatively quiet twentieth. As one might expect, this generation focused on the gritty questions of textual development, the relation between the constituent parts, their date and location of production.

[48] Willard, *Euthalian Apparatus*, 70–71, and the literature cited in 70 n. 8. Nils A. Dahl also finds that the hypotheses differ from the *kephalaia* in that the latter describe what each part of a letter is about, while the former describe what the author does in each letter ("Euthalian Apparatus," 234. Dahl goes on to note the illocutionary aspect of these Pauline argumenta and their affiliation with the epistolary handbooks of Ps.-Demetrius, Ps.-Libanius, and Proclus (258–59).

[49] See Gilles Dorival, "L'apport des Synopses transmises sous le nom d'Athanase et de Jean Chrysostome à la question du corpus littéraire de la Bible?," in *Qu'est-ce qu'un corpus littéraire? Recherches sur le corpus biblique et les corpus patristiques*, ed. Gilles Dorival, Christian Boudignon, Florence Bouet, and Claudine Cavalier (Leuven: Peeters, 2005), 53–93.

[50] C. H. Turner, "Greek Patristic Commentaries on the Pauline Epistles," in *A Dictionary of the Bible*, vol 5, Supplement, ed. James Hastings (Edinburgh: Clark, 1898), 527, suggests Euthalius borrowed from the synopsis, and J. Wettstein, *Novum Testamentum Graecum* (Amsterdam: Dommeriana, 1752), 2.76, suggests the opposite direction of influence.

[51] Theodor Zahn, *Geschichte des neutestamentlichen Kanons, Zwieter Band: Urkunden und Belege zum ersten und dritten Band, Erste Hälfte* (Leipzig: Deichert, 1890), 315: "Die Abhängigkeit unserer Synopsis von derjenigen des Chrysostomus, vom 39. Festbrief des Athanasius, ferner von einem palästinensischen Kanon vielleicht des 5. Jahrhunderts und wahrscheinlich auch von Epiphanius versetzt uns in eine Kloster- oder Kirchenbibliothek, in welcher diese verschiedenartigen Geister als gleich ehrwürdige Autoritäten vereinigt waren. Vor dem 6. Jahrhundert ist die Compilation gewiß nicht entstanden, vielleicht noch später."

century.[52] This range coheres with Louis Willard's important point that the surviving Greek tradition of the apparatus is subsequent to the inclusion of the argumenta.[53]

The hypothesis to Hebrews imagines Paul writing to Hebrew Christians about the "abolishment" (πέπαυσθαι) of the Law's shadow:[54]

> ἡ δὲ πρόφασις τῆς ἐπιστολῆς αὕτη· ἐπειδὴ οἱ Ἰουδαῖοι ἐνίσταντο τῷ νόμῳ, <u>καὶ ταῖς σκιαῖς</u>, διὰ τοῦτο ὁ ἀπόστολος Παῦλος διδάσκαλος ἐθνῶν γενόμενος, καὶ εἰς τὰ ἔθνη ἀποσταλεὶς, κηρύττει τὸ εὐαγγέλιον, γράψας τε πᾶσι τοῖς ἔθνεσι, γράφει λοιπὸν καὶ πᾶσι τοῖς ἐκ περιτομῆς πιστεύσασιν Ἑβραίοις ἀποδεικτικὴν ταύτην τὴν ἐπιστολὴν περὶ τῆς τοῦ Χριστοῦ παρουσίας, καὶ τοῦ πέπαυσθαι τὴν σκιὰν τοῦ νόμου.

> The occasion for the letter is this: Since the Jews adhered to the Law and the shadows, for this reason Paul the apostle proclaimed the gospel, having become the teacher of the Gentiles and having been sent to the Gentiles. Having written to all the Gentiles, now he writes also to all Hebrew believers of the circumcision this letter as a demonstrative letter about the coming of Christ and the abolishment of the shadow of the Law.

This is the occasion (πρόφασις) of Paul's Letter to the Hebrews. The rest of the hypothesis contains a summary of the letter's content that moves from the proclamation of the prophets to the importance of Christ as Son becoming a human in order to destroy death. Moving through Hebrews 9–10, the summary notes the importance placed on types of blood and then doubles down on the content in Hebrews 10:1 (via 8:5):[55]

> ἀποδείκνυσι δὲ, ὅτι ὁ νόμος οὐδένα ἐτελείωσεν, ἀλλὰ σκιὰν εἶχεν τῶν μελλόντων ἀγαθῶν· καὶ οὐ κατέπαυσεν ὁ λαός, ἀλλὰ κοινὴ πᾶσιν ἡμῖν ἀπολείπεται ἡ ἡμέρα τῆς καταπαύσεως.

> And [Paul] shows that the Law has not made anyone perfect, but has a shadow of the good things to come. Nor did the people find rest, but the day of rest, common to all of us, remains.

---

[52] See Willard, *Euthalian Apparatus*, 72. Willard notes that GA 81 (BL Add. 20003, 1044 CE) is the only Greek manuscript with Euthalian material that is not a byproduct of the expanded edition of the Euthalian apparatus that saw the addition of hypotheses (72). Vemund Blomkvist notes that the language of the *hypotheses* is rather homogenous and thus perhaps the product of a single editorial figure (*Euthalian Traditions*, 193).
[53] Willard, *Euthalian Apparatus*, 70.
[54] Greek text found in von Soden, *Die Schriften des Neuen Testaments*, 346.
[55] von Soden, *Die Schriften des Neuen Testaments*, 346.

As seen in the previous chapter, the physical tabernacle from the book of Exodus is called a "shadow" of a heavenly copy in Hebrews 8. The unavoidable Platonic contrast between a shadow and a body or image—going back to the cave itself (*Rep.* 7.515c) and later filtered through so-called Middle Platonism in which Hebrews participates alongside Philo of Alexandria (*Conf.* 190; *Migr.* 12; cf. Josephus, *Bell.* 2.28) and other Pauline imitations, like Colossians (2:17 refers to the "shadow")—is fronted in the hypothesis as a central characterization of letter as a whole.

Rather than an isolated description of Hebrews, the notion of the Law as a shadow structures the configuration of Paul and the Jewish Law in the hypotheses to Romans, Galatians, and Philippians. In each of these hypotheses, circumcision is a synecdoche for the Law, and both are described as a shadow that has passed away. In each hypothesis, Paul's epistolary activity is motivated by the cessation of the shadow and of minimizing its influence upon his audience. Paul writes in "To the Romans" that "circumcision lasted until a certain time, but now it has been abolished . . . the shadow of the Law passed away (ἡ σκιὰ τοῦ νόμου παρῆλθε)."[56] In writing to the Galatians, Paul interprets the wives of Abraham allegorically in order to show that "the shadow and the circumcision were given until a certain time" (μέχρι καιροῦ δεδόσθαι τὴν σκιὰν καὶ τὴν περιτομὴν), and that they are (now) useless after the coming of Christ.[57] To the Philippians, Paul attempts to disrupt the burgeoning influence of some who corrupt the "ears of the pure" with "the shadow of the Law and circumcision" (τῆς σκιᾶς τοῦ νόμου καὶ τῆς περιτομῆς).[58] The language of the shadow has rippled out from Hebrews into the hypotheses for other Pauline letters and provides the apparatus with a holistic description of Jewish Law and its purported erasure. Paul's epistolary career is imagined as announcing this erasure and minimizing its lingering influence.[59]

---

[56] von Soden, *Die Schriften des Neuen Testaments*, 346.
[57] von Soden, *Die Schriften des Neuen Testaments*, 343.
[58] von Soden, *Die Schriften des Neuen Testaments*, 346.
[59] I think we can add to this Caesarean association the Origenian matrix for the hypotheses to Paul, at least insofar as they channel and extend Origen's strategy for reading of Hebrews within the corpus. Of course, Origen's influence does not determine the location of production, but it does provide further and not insignificant Caesarean context for the growth of the *Euthaliana*. While resisting added hypothetical reconstructions, we can note that scholars have long seen an incipient Origenism as the context for the rather opaque and shifting authorial attribution of the apparatus. Günther Zuntz, for example, claimed that the textual editor of this apparatus was one Euzoius, who suppressed his own name in order to limit any association with Origen since Caesarea was the not-so-subtle context for the development of apparatus (Günther Zuntz, "Euthalius = Euzoius?" *VC* 7.1 [1953]: 16–22). Other systems for organizing and structuring textual material are quickly affiliated

We see here that the Euthalian hypotheses to the Pauline letters channel an earlier, third-century reading of Paul, which synthesizes Hebrews within the corpus with this very language of the shadow. Origen's third-century reading of Hebrews as a Pauline description of the nature of Jewish Law and Jewish reading practices structures and informs the Euthalian configuration of Paul, Jews, and the Law throughout the hypotheses to the Pauline letters. This example of reading and writing Hebrews as Pauline reminds us that material editions of Paul's letters not only create traditions of interpretation but are also marked by them.

Origen's influence on the reception of Hebrews is also registered, even if subtly, in the prefaces of Rufinus, Cyril, and Chrysostom. Rufinus gravitates toward Eusebius' quotation from Origen that emphasizes how the content within Hebrews is reflective of a Pauline mind. For Rufinus, the epistle "shines with the eloquence of [Paul's] own teaching" (*quae tanto doctrinae suae fulget eloquio*).[60] Cyril of Alexandria uses the language of "the shadow of the Law" when describing the ongoing practice of circumcision among the Hebrews; language that might derive from his own reading of Hebrews, from Origen, or from Chrysostom, who likewise ends his preface by making the point that the Jewish temple and the sacrificial system are shadows.[61] Material contexts of Hebrews are also marked by Origen. In a well-known tenth-century manuscript containing Acts and the Catholic and Pauline epistles—Codex Athos Laura 184, also known as Codex von der Goltz (GA 1739)—the opening folio (fol. 87v) for the Letter to the Hebrews features a marginal quotation taken from Eusebius containing Origen's reflections on the authorship and style of Hebrews.[62] The comment begins with the

---

with less mysterious figures; Athanasius and Chrysostom, for example, are both linked to scriptural *Synopses*. The apparatus is clearly unabashed in its desire to link itself to the tradition of Caesarea through Pamphilus and Eusebius. Might we see Origen's shadow lying across the hypotheses and the increasing tenuousness of Origen in the fourth century as further contextual reasons for the shifting and unclear authorial attribution of the apparatus?

[60] Latin text in Wordsworth and White, *Novum Testamentum Latine, Secundum Editionem Sancti Hieronymi* (London: Simon Wallenerg, 1911), 1.

[61] Other citations of the "shadow of the law" from Hebrews 8:5, 10:1 are found in Epiphanius (*Pan.* 69.37, 42.260), Methodius (*Banquet of the Ten Virgins* 7); Eusebius (*Praeparatio evangelica* 4.16.5, 12.19.1); Basil of Caesarea (*Enarratio in prophetam Isaiam*, 6.187).

[62] Kirsopp Lake and Silva Lake, explore the named scribe "Ephraim" in 1739, and suggest that Marc. Cod. 788 also goes back to the same figure, "The Scribe Ephraim," *JBL* 62.4 (1943): 263–68. Codex von der Goltz has become important for its connection with Origen's text of Pauline letters; see Otto Bauernfeind, *Der Römerbrieftext des Origenes nach dem Codex von der Goltz (cod. 184, B64 des Athosklosters Lawra)*, TUGAL 3 Reihe, Bd. 14, Heft 3 (Leipzig: Hinrichs, 1923); K. W. Kim, "Codices 1582, 1739, and Origen," *JBL* 69.2 (1950): 167–75; J. Neville Birdsall, "The Text and Scholia of the Codex von der Goltz and Its Allies, and Their Bearing upon the Texts of the Works of Origen, Especially the Commentary on Romans," in *Origeniana: Premier colloque international des*

abbreviation ωργ (for ωριγενης) before a verbatim citation from *Historia Ecclesiastica* 6.25.11–14, including Eusebius' intermediate sentence connecting the two Origenian fragments.[63] At the end of the comment is a siglum for Origen—an interlaced "ω" and "ρ"—which von der Goltz records finding throughout the manuscript.[64] But these sprinkles of Origenian voices are punctiliar when compared to the Euthalian hypothesis that becomes the most frequently copied hypothesis throughout the history of transmission.

3. The Sixth-Century Turn to Catenae and the Remains of the *patéres*

Miriam DeCock draws attention to the ways in which Theodoret's prefaces curate earlier traditions of interpretation and how this fifth-century commentator frames his own "late" historical position relative to the third and the fourth centuries as the mark of interpretive virtue.[65] As DeCock observes, Theodoret's image of the exemplary commentator is one who properly curates an inherited exegetical cache, and he himself valorizes "previous scholars" (ἄλλοι φιλομαθεῖς ἄνδρες) as an authorized resource of exegesis.[66] In the hypothesis for Hebrews, Theodoret follows Chrysostom in citing

---

etudes origéniennes, Montserrat, 18–21 septembre 1973, ed. Henri Crouzel, Gennaro Lomiento, and Josep Rius-Camps (Bari: Instituto di Letteratura Christiana Antica, 1975), 215–22; Caroline P. Bammel, "A New Witness to the Scholia from Origen in the Codex von der Goltz," in *Origeniana Quinta: Papers of the 5th International Origen Congress, Boston College, 14–18 August 1989*, ed. Robert Daly, BETL 105 (Leuven: Peeters, 1992), 137–41; Georg Gäbel, "The Text of Hebrews in GA 1739, in Selected Other Greek Manuscripts, and in Works of Origen: Preliminary Quantitative Assessments," in *The New Testament in Antiquity and Byzantium: Traditional and Digital Approaches to Its Texts and Editing. A Festschrift for Klaus Wachtel*, ed. H. A. G. Houghton, D. C. Parker, and H. Strutwolf, ANTF 52 (Berlin: de Gruyter, 2019), 147–63.

[63] Transcriptions are found in Eduard von der Goltz, *Eine textkritische Arbeit des zehnten bezw. sechsten Jahrhunderts*, TU 17.4 (Leipzig: Hinrichs, 1899), 85–86; Kirsopp Lake, Johannes de Zwaan, and Morton S. Enslin, "Athos, Laura 184 [B'64] (Greg. 1739; von Soden α78), Acts, Catholic Epistles, Paul," in *Six Collations of New Testament Manuscripts*, ed. Kirsopp Lake and Silva New, HTS 17 (Cambridge, MA: Harvard University Press, 1932), 216–17.

[64] See von der Goltz, *Eine textkritische*, 55–56. Von der Goltz also claims that Athos Iviron 648 contains similar content, Eusebius' quotations from Clement and Origen. A quotation from Clement via Eusebius appears in the margins in GA 1424 (ninth-tenth c., formerly: Lutheran School of Theology at Chicago, Gruber 152).

[65] Miriam DeCock, "Theodoret of Cyrus and His Exegetical Predecessors: A Study of His Biblical Commentary Prefaces," *Open Theology* 7 (2021): 445–60.

[66] DeCock, "Exegetical Predecessors," 456. DeCock focuses on the prefaces found in Theodoret's *Commentary on the Song of Songs*, *Commentary on Daniel*, *Commentary on the Twelve Prophets*, *Commentary on the Psalms*, and *Questions on the Octateuch*.

Hebrews 10:34 regarding the spoiling of goods endured by the Hebrews, and, toward the end, he notes that "they say" (φασιν) the letter was translated from Hebrew into Greek by Clement of Rome. Theodoret's fifth-century concern for previous scholars is shared by the sixth-century development of a new form of commentary and textual production, one that self-consciously depends upon the history of interpretation as its primary authority.

The earliest manifestations of what is now known as "chain" (Latin, *catena*) commentary—a form of exegesis that organizes excerpts from favorable interpreters of the third, fourth, and fifth centuries, now elevated into "tradition," as marginal comments around the sacred text—are found in the work of Procopius (465–528 CE), a sixth-century scholar and leader of a rhetorical school in Gaza.[67] Reynolds and Wilson point to the second century CE return to Attic Greek pronunciation and grammar and the study of rhetoric as the effective precursors for the development of scholia commentaries and, later, the Byzantine catena form.[68] Reynolds and Wilson join others in locating the development of scholia on the rhetor Demosthenes in Gaza in the fourth and fifth centuries.[69] Certainly, Gregory Nazianzus and Basil of Caesarea's *Philokalia* of Origen and Clement of Alexandria's *Excerpta ex Theodoto* provide some pre-fifth-century precedent for these later collections of excerpts, but it is the work of Procopius and his commentary on the

---

[67] On catena see esp. Robert Devreesse, "Chaines exégétiques grecques," in *Dictionnaire de la Bible: Supplément*, ed. Louis Pirot (Paris: Letouzey et Ané, 1928), coll. 1084–233; E. Mühlenberg, "Katenen," in *Theologische Realenzyclopädie* 18, ed. Gerhard Krause and Gerhard Müller (Berlin: de Gruyter, 1989), 14–20; Gilles Dorival, "Des commentaires de l'écriture aux chaînes," in *Le monde grec ancien et la Bible*, ed. Claude L. Mondésert, Bible de tous les temps I (Paris: Beauchesne, 1984), 361–86; Gilles Dorival, "Biblical Catenae: Between Philology and History," in *Commentaries, Catenae and Biblical Tradition*, ed. H. A. G. Houghton (Piscataway: Gorgias, 2016), 65–81; *The Septuagint from Alexandria to Constantinople: Canon, New Testament, Church Fathers, Catenae* (Oxford: Oxford University Press, 2021), 135–54; Richard A. Layton, "Catenae," in *The Oxford Handbook of Early Christian Biblical Interpretation*, ed. Paul M. Blowers and Peter M. Martens (Oxford: Oxford University Press, 2019), 220–28. On Procopius' literary context see Bas ter Haar Romeny, "Procopius of Gaza and His Library," in *From Rome to Constantinople: Studies in Honour of Averil Cameron*, ed. Hagit Amirav and Bas ter Haar Romeny, Late Antique History and Religion 1 (Leuven: Peeters, 2007), 173–90.

[68] Leighton Durham Reynolds and Nigel Guy Wilson, *Scribes and Scholars: A Guide to the Transmission of Greek and Latin Literature*, 4th ed. (Oxford: Oxford University Press, 2013), 52–53. Cf. Carlo Vessella, *Sophisticated Speakers: Atticistic Pronunciation in the Atticist Lexica*, Trends in Classics—Supplementary Volume 55 (Berlin: de Gruyter, 2018); Timothy Whitmarsh, *The Second Sophistic*, New Surveys in the Classics, no. 35 (Cambridge: Cambridge University Press, 2005); and Graham Anderson, *The Second Sophistic: A Cultural Phenomenon in the Roman Empire* (London: Routledge, 1993).

[69] Reynolds and Wilson, *Scribes and Scholars*, 53. Cf. also N. G. Wilson, "A Chapter in the History of Scholia," *Classical Quarterly* 17 (1967): 244–56 (on the scholia to Aristophanes' *Birds*, Apollonius Rhodius, and Pindar). Another important figure includes Olympiodorus of Alexandria, a fifth-century Neoplatonist who developed scholia for Aristotle.

Octateuch that is the first catena commentary to emerge together with the language and procedure of the catena form.[70]

In the introductory preface to the *Commentary on Genesis*, Procopius describes his work as an assemblage (συνελεξάμεθα) of extracts from commentaries (ὑπομνημάτων) and discourses (διαφόρων λόγων) on the Octateuch that are from the πατέρες.[71] Gilles Dorival notes that the latter half of the seventh century marks an increase in catenae on New Testament books and an increase in new authorial figures in the marginal comments (Diodore, Theodore, and Zigabenus).[72] Codex Zacynthius, a palimpsest with uncial script containing fragments on Luke 1:1–11:33, is the oldest catena manuscript (circa 700 CE, +/− 50); however the majority of manuscripts derive from the tenth through fourteenth centuries.[73] Scholarship on the Pauline catenae manuscripts in particular began with the sixteenth-century publication of the entire catenae attributed to Oecumenius by Bernardus Dontatus.[74] John Cramer's massive eight-volume project published from 1842 to 1844 brought the study of catena to the attention of English scholarship, though these volumes have been regularly criticized for errors in transcription and other editorial choices.[75] For the Letter to the

---

[70] See here Karl-Heinz Uthemann, "Was verraten die Katenen über die Exegese ihre Zeit?," in *Stimuli: Exegese und ihre Hermeneutik in Antike und Christentum. Festschrift für Ernst Dassmann*, ed. Georg Schöllgen and Clemens Scholten (Münster: Aschendorff, 1996), 284–96; René Cadiou, "La bibliothèque de Césarée et la formation des chaînes," *RevScRel* 16.4 (1936): 474–83, who attempts to isolate stages in the development of catenae.

[71] Greek text in Prokop von Gaza, *Eclogarum in libros historicos Veteris Testamenti epitome, Teil I: des Genesiskommentar*, ed. Karin Metzler, GCS N.F. 22 (Berlin: de Grutyer, 2015), 1. See also Ernest Lindl, *Die Oktateuchcatene des Prokop von Gaza und die Septuagintaforschung* (Munich: Hermann Lukaschik, 1902), 17–22. The title given for Procopius' work is an "epitome of exegetical extracts." See Dorival, "Des commentaires de l'Écriture aux chaînes," 362, for other titles found in manuscripts. On stages of catena prior to Procopius see Dorival, "Biblical Catenae," 73; as well as Cadiou, "La bibliothèque de Césarée," 474–83.

[72] Dorival, "Biblical Catenae," 77.

[73] D. C. Parker and J. N. Birdsall, "The Date of Codex Zacynthius (Ξ): A New Proposal," *JTS* 55 (2004): 117–31, argue that W. H. P. Hatch, "A Redating of Two Important Uncial Manuscripts of the Gospels—Codex Zacynthius and Codex Cyprius," in *Quantulacumque: Studies Presented to Kirsopp Lake*, ed. R. P. Casey, S. Lake, and A. K. Lake (London: Christophers, 1937), 333–38, places it too early, while the eighth-century date proposed by S. P. Tregelles, *Codex Zacynthius E or Greek Palimpsest Fragments of the Gospel of St. Luke, Deciphered, Transcribed, and Edited* (London: Samuel Bagster and Sons, 1861), is too late.

[74] *Expositiones antiquae ex diversis sanctorum patrum commentariis ab Oecumenio et Aretha collectae in hosce Novi Testamenti tractatus. Oecumenii quidem in Acta Apostolorum. In septem Epistolas quae Catholicae dicuntur. In Pauli omnes. Arethae vero in Ioannis Apocalypsim* (Verona: Apud Staphanum & fratres Sabios, 1532).

[75] John A. Cramer, *Catenae Graecorum patrum in Novum Testamentum*, vols. 1–7 (Oxford: Oxford University Press, 1842–44). For criticism of Cramer's transcription work and editorial additions see Karl Staab, *Die Pauluskatenen nach den handschriftlichen Quellen untersucht* (Rome: Verlag des Päpstlichen Bibelinstituts, 1926), 45–46, 56–60, 76–77.

Hebrews, Cramer published a transcription of Coislin 204 and Paris grec. 328.[76] However, the real advance in the study of Pauline catena manuscripts was made by Karl Staab.

One of Staab's main contributions was the development of a sixfold typology of Pauline catena manuscripts.[77] Three of these types are labeled according to the holding locations of their principal manuscripts—Vaticanus, Monacensis, and Parisinus—and the other three types are named after their authorial attributions—Nicetas, Theophylact, and Oecumenius—which emerge around the turn of the tenth and eleventh centuries. The Letter to the Hebrews is attested in four of these text-types: Parisinus, Nicetas, Oecumenius, and Theophylact.

The Parisinus type of catena is only attested in one manuscript, Coislin 204. This eleventh-century, double-columned parchment manuscript contains catena on eleven Pauline epistles (Galatians, Ephesians, Philippians, Colossians, 1–2 Thessalonians, 1–2 Timothy, Philemon, and Hebrews).[78] The text of these Paulines is semi-uncial, while the comments are minuscule and the format is that of an alternating type. The transition between prefatory comments and the text of Hebrews is indicated with marginal stroke, but, as Karl Staab has observed, this is far from consistent for the manuscript as a whole, and quotations from other biblical texts included within the commentary are also marked with the same strokes.[79] Figure 1 shows the transition between the prefatory content and the opening verses of Hebrews, together with the different script types in the bottom half of the leftmost column (the text of Hebrews 1:1 is marked with marginalia).

---

[76] Cramer, *Catenae Graecorum*, 112–278 (Coislin 204) and 279–598 (Paris gr. 238). Cramer also published a transcription of the hypothesis for Hebrews found in Paris gr. 224 (iv–v). This hypothesis is from Theophylact's catena commentary on Paul but is presented by Cramer as an anonymous and *ineditum commentarium*.

[77] Staab builds upon the earlier typological work of Georg Karo and Hans Lietzmann, *Catenarum Graecarum Catalogus*, Nachrichten der Akademie der Wissenschaften zu Göttingen, Philologisch-historische Klasse (Göttingen: Lüder Horstmann, 1902), 1–66, 299–350, 559–620; Hans Lietzmann, *Catenen*, Mitteilungen über ihre Geschichte in handschriftlicher Überlieferung (Freiburg: Mohr Siebeck, 1897). Staab has also done extensive work on the Catholic epistles; see "Die griechischen Katenenkommentare zur den katholischen Briefe," *Biblica* 5 (1924): 296–353.

[78] Coislin 204 is an important ancestor of BAV, Vat. gr. 762 (GA 1915), which is the exemplar of the Vaticanus type. See Konrad Zawadzki, "Der verlorene Schluss des Codex Vaticanus Graecus 762: Eine Rekonstruktion anhand der Codices Pantokratoros 28 und Vaticanus Graecus 692," *Museum Helveticum* 77 (2020): 277–96; Agnès Lorrain, "Autour du Vaticanus gr. 762: Notes pour l'étude des chaînes à présentation alternante," *Byz* 90 (2020): 67–95.

[79] Staab, *Pauluskatenen*, 54.

Figure 1 Folia 236v, the transition between the preface and Hebrews 1:1 in Coislin 204. Courtesy of the Bibliothèque nationale de France (Archives et Manuscrits)

The hypothesis for Hebrews is an extensive preface comprised of excerpts from interpreters, headed by an edited version of Chrysostom's hypothesis to Hebrews. In fact, Chrysostom's preface is abbreviated, and the lengthy excursus is excised and filled with content from Severian of Gabala and Theodore Mopsuestia, before returning again to Chrysostom, who is followed by Severian and Cyril of Alexandria. The order of the prologue runs as follows:

Chrysostom I	(50 lines)
Severian Gabala I	(20 lines)
Theodore Mopsuestia	(57 lines)
Chrysostom II	(56 lines)
Severian of Gabala II	(14 lines)
Cyril of Alexandria	(44 lines)
Hebrews 1:1	

The transitions between these figures are marked with a marginal symbol and a brief citation formula, as for example with the fragment from Cyril of Alexandria on folio 236r, shown in Figure 2.

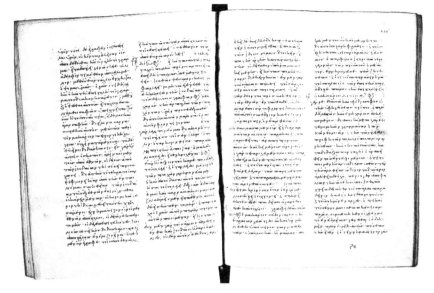

Figure 2 Folia f.236r in Coislin 204, the fragment from Chrysostom marked in margin and in the text (third line from top in the second column from the left, followed by Severian and Cyril in the subsequent columns). Courtesy of the Bibliothèque nationale de France (Archives et Manuscrits)

The opening excerpt from Chrysostom's hypothesis sets the stage, asking how Paul could send a letter to the Hebrews as apostle to the *Gentiles* especially when the Hebrews were hostile to the apostle. Cutting out the excursus that details that hostility, this hypothesis moves right into Chrysostom's statement about the Jerusalem destination of the letter and that Paul's appointment to the Gentiles is not a prohibition against contact with the Hebrews. The excerpt closes with Chrysostom's remarks about Hebrews being written after 1 Timothy. This kind of editorial work transforms Chrysostom's lengthy prose hypothesis into a fast-moving statement about the context of the letter.

The following two fragments from Severian Gabala and Theodore Mopsuestia are rather short and reflect the core ideas found in the evidence preserved in Eusebius.[80] Severian uses the established context for thinking

---

[80] Staab, *Pauluskommentare*, 345: οἱ αἱρετικοί φασιν μὴ εἶναι Παύλου τὴν Ἐπιστολήν, καὶ τούτου πρώτην ἀπόδειξιν προφέρουσι τὸ μὴ προτετάχθαι αὐτοῦ τὸ ὄνομα ὡς ἐν ταῖς ἄλλαις Ἐπιστολῖς· δεύτερον τὸ τὴν φράσιν ἄλλην εἶναι, τουτέστι ξένην παρὰ τὴν Παύλου, καὶ τὴν κατασκευήν. δεῖ τοίνυν εἰδέναι, ὅτι Παῦλος ἐμισεῖτο ὑπὸ Ἰουδαίων, ὡς ἀποστασίαν νόμου διδάσκων· διά τοι τοῦτο καὶ κινδυνεύσας ἐν Ἱεροσολύμοις καὶ μόλις διαφυγών, ἐπέμφθη εἰς Ῥώμην. ὠφέλιμα τοίνυν γράφων Ἑβραίοις, οὐ προτίθησι τὸ ὄνομα τὸ ἑαυτοῦ· ἵνα μὴ τῷ μίσει τῷ πρὸς αὐτὸν, ζημιωθῶσι τὴν ὠφέλειαν τὴν ἀπὸ τῆς Ἐπιστολῆς.

about Hebrews, namely, Acts 21. Since Severian claims that Paul was persecuted by Ἰουδαίων while in Jerusalem and yet sent a letter from Rome back to the Ἑβραίοις, he likely follows the predominant reading that the Hebrews are Christ-followers in Jerusalem and reserving Ἰουδαῖος as essentially non-Christian. Severian then notes the two defeaters to Pauline authorship—anonymity and style—but attributes the defeaters to the αἱρετικοί. The "heretics" here are the "Arians," who are increasingly concretized, however rhetorically, as principal rejectors of the Pauline status of Hebrews. The fragment from Theodore, on the other hand, focuses on the audience and the anonymity of the letter.[81] Theodore argues that Hebrews was written to those who believe (τοῖς πιστεύουσιν) and that the conclusion of the letter demonstrates the mutual familiarity between Paul and this group of Hebrews.[82] Paul's anonymity is attributed to the limits of his authority as apostle to the Gentiles.[83]

The preface then returns to Chrysostom and features his comments about the persecution(s) experienced by the audience. The final two fragments come from Severian and Cyril of Alexandria. In the second and very terse Severian fragment, it is mentioned how Hebrews was written in Hebrew and translated (ἡρμηνεύθη) by a disciple, whether Luke or Clement.[84] The final fragment is excerpted from Cyril of Alexandria's lost Greek commentary on Hebrews. Since we now have an Armenian translation of Cyril's commentary, despite differences between the Greek fragments and this Armenian work, it is apparent that this fragment is the conclusion of Cyril's hypothesis and functions as such in Coislin 204. Cyril's contribution focuses on the absence of Paul's name as a sign of wisdom, as is the opening emphasis on the "fathers, patriarchs and holy prophets" (զհարսն եւ զնահապետսն եւ զսուրբ զմարգարէսն).[85] These are the means by which the anonymous Paul desires to convince the Hebrews that, compared to the truth, the writings of Moses are images.

The production of this unique preface requires several editorial decisions. The material from Chrysostom, for example, is abbreviated in order

---

[81] Greek text found in Staab, *Pauluskommentare*, 200–201. Theodore's commentaries on Galatians, Ephesians, Philippians, Colossians, 1–2 Thessalonians, 1–2 Timothy, Titus, and Philemon are all extant. There are also Latin fragments of Theodore. Eligius Dekkers has found other fragments of Theodore in a Latin manuscript, "Un nouveau manuscrit du commentaire de Théodore de Mopsueste aux épîtres de S. Paul," *SacEr* 6 (1954): 429–33.

[82] Staab, *Pauluskommentare*, 200.   [83] Staab, *Pauluskommentare*, 200–201.

[84] Staab, *Pauluskommentare*, 345.

[85] Armenian text in Cyril of Alexandria, *Commentary on the Letter to the Hebrews: Armenian Critical Text*, ed. Xač'ik Grigoryan (Yerevan: Ankyunacar, 2020), 26.

to bring out his most direct contextual statements about the letter. The longer excursus about hostility between Paul and fellow Jews in Jerusalem is cut out, and this editorial choice was likely guided by the desire for readability. Yet the entirety of these fragments now assembled creates less of a wholly new, coherent, and connected preface than a repetitive, somewhat choppy, and derivative mosaic of prefatory comments. Still, such overlap might be the point behind this assembly: to instill a sense of coherence by accenting the unity of voices across the tradition of interpretation. If Procopius assembles extracts from previous writers in such a way that the text appears as though it is from *one* voice (φωνάς), that is, with unmarked extracts, perhaps this preface in Coislin 204 has similar aims but with a different method, to project the singularity of interpretation from the various named interpreters. In any case, the importance of Chrysostom's hypothesis is registered in Coislin 204 from its position as the first comment about Hebrews as well as the overall length of the two fragments.[86]

Preference for Chrysostom's preface is also apparent in other catena contexts, such as the catena on Paul by Nicetas, an eleventh-century cleric and who became bishop of Heraclea by 1117 CE. In GA 1938 (Paris grec. 238), the Letter to the Hebrews is prefaced by three figures, Theodoret, Origen, and Clement.[87] The lengths of these comments are significantly lopsided, as the material marked as Theodoret stretches from folios 1r to 9r, while the comments from Origen (fol. 9r–v) and Clement (fol. 9v bottom half) are brief—given the limitations of the material preserved by Eusebius. The reason for this discrepancy is that whoever was responsible for this preface has included the entirety of Chrysostom's rather lengthy hypothesis "within" the Theodoret section.[88] Chrysostom's preface is stitched into Theodoret's seamlessly in the sense that there are no intentional authorial flags or markings to indicate the insertion or transition. Since the opening and closing seams of this insertion are unmarked, Chrysostom's hypothesis rests

---

[86] Karl Staab describes Coislin 204 as essentially an expanded form of Chrysostom's homilies (*Pauluskatenen*, 60, 64).

[87] Paris, gr. 238 is an incomplete copy of Athos, Vatopedi 38 (Heb 1:1–2, 4:12–13), as is GA 2890 (Ambrosiana, Milan A. 241 inf.). On Nicetas' other catenae projects see Joseph Sickenberger, *Die Lukaskatene des Niketas von Herakleia*, TUGAL, 22.4 (Leipzig: Hinrichs, 1902); von Soden, *Die Schriften des Neuen Testaments*, 613–24; and, on his corpus as a whole, Bram Roosen, "The Works of Nicetas of Heracleensis (ὁ) τοῦ Σερρῶ," *Byz* 69.1 (1999): 119–44.

[88] The opening εἰ of Chrysostom's preface is marked with a larger epsilon, and when the text switches back to Theodoret, the opening ὅτι is likewise marked; however, these markings are not authorial signals so much as sense divisions. It is understandable that these two might happen to align at the literary seam. Cramer's edition creates new sense divisions, some of which align with Paris grec. 238 and many of which do not.

anonymously within the confines of Theodoret. Whatever Nicetas' relationship was to the production of this creative preface, Paris grec. 238 is another indication of the enduring utility of Chrysostom's hypothesis while also highlighting the close proximity between Theodoret and Chrysostom in catena contexts.[89]

These two hypotheses for Hebrews are connected by their emphasis on Chrysostom and their larger editorial impulse to arrange multiple voices within a single prefatory text. While Paris gr. 238 does not add otherwise non-attested fragments from the commentarial tradition on Hebrews, Coislin 204 is incredibly important in this regard. With this one witness added, the hypotheses of the fourth century are significantly expanded, as shown in Table 1.

But the medium through which these prefaces survive is important for thinking about their significance. After all, Coislin 204 is the lone Greek witness for three writers commenting on Hebrews at the turn of the fifth century, not to mention the sole exemplar for the Parisinus type of Pauline catenae.[90] Excising these prefaces out of their final resting place within catena manuscripts risks overstating their significance in the history of

Table 1 Author and means of preservation of the fourth-century hypotheses to Hebrews

Author	Preservation
Ephrem of Edessa 306–76	Armenian translation
Rufinus 340–411	Vulgate mss.
Chrysostom 347–407	Greek mss.
Theodore of Mopsuestia 350–428	Coislin 204
Cyril of Alexandria 376–444	Coislin 204 + Armenian translation
Severian of Gabala 380–425	Coislin 204
Theodoret 393–458	9 Greek mss.

[89] Cf. Marcel Richard, "Les citations de Théodoret conservées dans la chaîne de Nicétas sur l'Évangile selon Saint Luc," *RB* 43.1 (1934): 88–96.

[90] Karl Staab has also canvassed Greek catena manuscripts for fragments of now-lost commentaries on Pauline letters. Staab's efforts yield a number of fragments: from Didymus the Blind (Heb 1:6), Severian of Gabala, Gennadius of Constantinople, Oecumenius, and Photius (in order of appearance, see *Pauluskommentare*, 44–45, 354–51, 420–22, 462–69, 637–52). Others have also published fragments; see Otto Fridolin Fritzsche, *Theodori episcopi Mopuesteni In novum testamentum commentariorum quae reperiri potuerunt* (Turici: Meyer et Zeller, 1847), 121–59; H. B. Swete, *Theodori Episcopi Mopsuesteni in epistolas B. Pauli Commentarii: The Latin Version with the Greek Fragment*, 2 vols. (Cambridge: Cambridge University Press, 1880, 1882); P. E. Pusey, *Sancti patris nostri Cyrilli archiepiscopi Alexandrini in D. Joannis evangelium*, vol. 3 (Oxford: Clarendon, 1872). For additional fragments from Theodore and Gennadius in a catena

Paulinizing Hebrews. Of course, the prefaces to Hebrews from Cyril of Alexandria, Theodore Mopsuestia, and Severian of Gabala may have exerted unique influence upon their own circles of readers, but from the vantage of the material remains, their exegetical influence is limited by a lack of preservation. The Euthalian hypothesis, on the other hand, far outmatches the kinds of "patristic" prefaces found in Coislin 204 and Paris gr. 238. In fact, the Euthalian hypothesis with Origen's reading of Hebrews migrates into the most popular and far-reaching catenae for the Pauline epistles.

4. The Oecumenian Catenae and Origen's Hidden Legacy

Prior to the discovery of a commentary on the Apocalypse of John attributed to one Oecumenius, bishop of Trikka, it was standard practice to locate the Oecumenian catena in the tenth century.[91] Scholars are now willing to isolate some stages of the famed catenae to this sixth-century Oecumenius, as indeed extracts from Oecumenius appear in the catena itself, even if the attribution is likely pseudonymous.[92] That fact that the Oecumenian commentary uses the Euthalian hypotheses for the Pauline letters, provides a *terminus post quem* at around the fourth and fifth centuries. Moreover, some of the manuscripts of the Oecumenian commentary are dated to the ninth and tenth centuries, some of which are already identified as expansions, and thus round out the *ante quem*.[93] A late sixth-century or early seventh-century date for the preliminary stages of this catena commentary aligns with these basic boundaries.

---

commentary on Romans in GA 2966 see Georgi Parpulov, "An Unknown Catena on the Pauline Epistles," *Byzantine Review* 2 (2020): 9–16.

[91] J. C. Lamoreaux, "The Provenance of Ecumenius' Commentary on the Apocalypse," *VC* 52 (1998): 88–108; Franz Diekamp, "Mittheilungen über den neuaufgefundenen Commentar des Oekumenius zu Apokalypse," *Sitzungsberichte der Königlichen Preussischen Akademie der Wissenschaften zu Berlin* (1901): 1046–58; H. C. Hoskier, "The Lost Commentary of Oecumenius on the Apocalypse," *AJP* 34.3 (1913): 300–314; H. C. Hoskier, ed., *The Complete Commentary of Oecumenius on the Apocalypse* (Ann Arbor: University of Michigan, 1928); J. Suggit, trans., *Oecumenius, Commentary on the Apocalypse* (Washington, DC: Catholic University of America Press, 2006).

[92] See Staab, *Pauluskommentare*, xxxvii–xl. Staab wonders whether Oecumenius' own marginal comments on Chrysostom were later "lemmatized" in catenae. Relevant here is Marc de Groote, "Die Kirchenväter in Oecumenius' *Scholia in Iohannem Chrysostomum*," *VC* 55.2 (2001): 191–200.

[93] GA 605, for example, is a tenth-century manuscript of Oecumenian catena, as is GA 619 (d. 984 CE).

The Oecumenian catena on the Pauline epistles is a complex and widely edited tradition with nonlinear permutations into distinct text-types. Staab finds five "types" within this large Oecumenian tradition: a "normal type" within which four groups are distinguished, a "special type" attested by GA 622 (Vat gr. 1430), an "expanded type" of the normal, a "secondary expansion," and a type that collects extracts from the Oecumenian catenae.[94] Part of the task of untangling the growth of this tradition is identifying late additions such as the *Scholia Photiana* (additions from Photius in the ninth century) and the *Corpus Extravagantium* (a set of unnumbered comments added to the number system of Oecumenius).[95] But the earliest stages of this commentary are inaccessible to us, despite some indications of textual development and adaptation.

The Oecumenian catena commentary includes hypotheses for the Pauline letters. These hypotheses are taken from the Euthalian apparatus and supplemented with additional hypotheses attributed pseudonymously to Theodoret. Most Pauline letters have these two hypotheses; however, the Ps.-Theodoret hypotheses are oddly missing from Romans and 1 Thessalonians. For the Letter to the Hebrews, however, there are three distinct prefatory hypotheses. A notable example of the full prefatory content for Hebrews is found in GA 1906 (Coislin 28, d. 1058). Figure 3 shows the verso of folio 232 and the recto of folio 233. On folio 232v is the Euthalian hypothesis in the first position, followed by the ἕτερα hypothesis in the second position, both marked with titles—ὑπόθεcιc τῆc πρὸc ἑβραίουc ἐπιcτολῆc and ὑπόθεcιc ἑτέρα. This second hypothesis is sometimes called ἄλλωc[96] and, less frequently, a πόλογοc.[97] The hypothesis of Theodoret is shown on folio 233v and continues to the recto of folio 233, as shown in Figure 4. The text of Hebrews with marginal comments keyed by rubricated Greek letters appears on the verso of folio 234.

---

[94] For the witnesses for each type see the table of contents in Staab, *Pauluskatenen*, v–vii. Staab's typology, while pioneering, is still "open" for recategorization. Theodora Panella, "The Pseudo-Oecumenian Catena on Galatians" (PhD diss., University of Birmingham, 2017), 72–78, finds that Staab's "Specialtypus" is a quilt-like text comprised of the normal, the expanded, and the secondary expansion. Moreover, the "sekundärer" expansion, for Panella, is an entirely new catena commentary rather than an extension of the Oecumenian tradition (81).

[95] Cf. Panella, "Pseudo-Oecumenian Catena," 54.

[96] GA 35, GA 1100, GA 1879, GA 1971, GA 1761.

[97] GA 203 (British Library Add 28816, fol. 115r); contrasted with the Euthalian ὑπόθεcιc on the verso fol. 115v (this is also a rare instance where the ἕτερα precedes the Euthalian). It is a πόλογοc in GA 69 (fol. 150r), where it appears alone. The Ps.-Theodoret hypothesis noted below is also called a πόλογοc in GA 075 (fol. 322v).

HEBREWS AND THE INSTITUTIONALIZATION OF PAULINITY 173

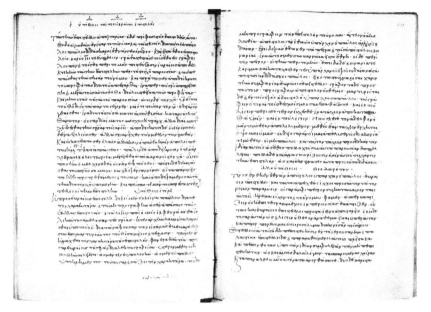

Figure 3 Folia 232v and 233r in Coislin 28. Courtesy of the Bibliothèque nationale de France (Archives et Manuscrits)

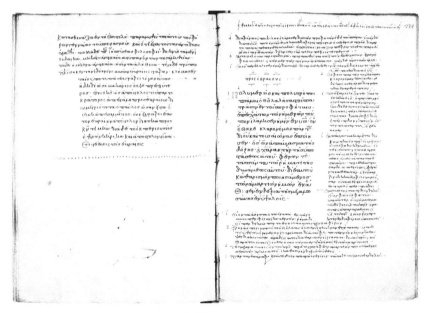

Figure 4 Folia 233v and 234r in Coislin 28. Courtesy of the Bibliothèque nationale de France (Archives et Manuscrits)

The ἕτερα hypothesis features many of the explanatory reconstructions of the letter from Eusebius' collection of Clementine testimonies. The hypothesis begins with the recognition that the epistle seems (δοκέω) not to be from Paul because of its anonymity and style (τὸν χαρακτῆρα).[98] Explaining stylistic difference is the predictable account of translation from Hebrew, and the absence of Paul's name is attributed to his apostolic mission to the Gentiles as well as the rumor circulating among the Hebrews that Paul teaches the abolishment of the Law (Acts 21). One unique element that appears in this hypothesis is a quotation of Hebrews 2:3-4 in which the authorial voice, unlike Paul, admits a certain distance from the earliest generation of eyewitnesses ("It was declared at first by the Lord, and it was attested to us by those who heard"). In the tradition of Chrysostom and Ephrem, the ἕτερα hypothesis also evokes Hebrews 13 as evidence of Pauline authorship.[99] The final line adds that many others know of the letter as is shown by the history of reading (ἡ ἀνάγνωσις αὐτή).[100]

The Ps.-Theodoret preface is often marked with an authorial attribution such as θεοδωρίτου (GA 1921, fol. 231r) or ὑποθεcι ετέρα θεοδωρήτου (GA 641, fol. 266v).[101] In other instances, the opening word, τινο(s), is accented by *ekthesis* (GA 911, Add MS 39599), sometimes with an additional Δω in the margin (GA 1970, Coislin 30). In at least two manuscripts—GA 641 and GA 1919—the ἕτερα hypothesis has been cut out, leaving Euthalius and Ps.-Theodoret, although in GA 1919 the Ps.-Theodoret preface appears in the margins.[102]

Shedding some much-needed light on these pseudonymous hypotheses attributed to Theodoret, Agnès Lorrain considers their sources, varying positions, and textual history.[103] Lorrain rightly observes that these hypotheses

---

[98] Greek text in von Soden, *Die Schriften des Neuen Testaments*, 347. Von Soden's text of the hypothesis takes note of the many variants throughout the manuscript tradition.

[99] Citing Hebrews 10:34 and 13:23.

[100] Von Soden, *Die Schriften des Neuen Testaments*, 347.

[101] Some manuscripts contain a shorter version of this hypothesis that ends at αληθειαν (line 12 in von Soden, *Die Schriften des Neuen Testaments*, 353). Von Soden notes this shorter version in GA 1871. I have also identified the shorter version in GA 454 (tenth c.v Biblioteca Medicea Laurenziana, Plut. 04.01, which seems to be a practice copy of Ps.-Theodoret), GA 327 (thirteenth c., New College 59), GA 075 (tenth c., Athens, National Library, grec. 100), and GA 2011 (eleventh c., Paris, Suppl. grec. 1264).

[102] The ἕτερα hypothesis also appears in the margins of GA 91 (Paris, grec. 91, fol. 223v [917v]).

[103] Agnès Lorrain, "Des prologues bibliques d'origine chrysostomienne: Les arguments attribués à Théodoret et à Théophylacte sur les épîtres pauliniennes," *ZAC* 19 (2015): 481–501. The typical position of this hypothesis after Euthalius (and after the ἕτερα) is rightly noticed by Lorrain (483), but two witnesses are also identified in which the Ps.-Theodoret hypothesis functions as the sole prefatory text, namely GA 075 (Athens, National Library, gr. 100) and GA 622 (Vat. gr. 1430).

attributed to Theodoret are summaries of Chrysostom's prefaces to the Pauline letters.[104] This pseudonymous preface shares with Chrysostom an emphasis on Paul's apostleship to the Gentiles, the same "baptizing" argument from 1 Corinthians, the same line that the letter was sent to Jerusalem and Palestine, and also shares the same quotations from Hebrews 12:1 and Acts 20:22 that are found in Chrysostom's preface.[105] Again, as noted by Lorrain, this kind of Chrysostomian epitomizing dependence is paralleled by Theophylact of Ohrid (1050–1108 CE), whose catena commentary on the fourteen letters of Paul receives widespread use, reflected in a sizable manuscript tradition particularly from the fourteenth century.[106] That Theophylact's hypotheses to Paul are abbreviations of Chrysostom is widely recognized, and the hypothesis to Hebrews reflects this practice quite clearly.[107]

With these three hypotheses bounded in succession, the Oecumenian tradition brings together various lines of interpretation in the framing of Hebrews as Pauline. The Euthalian hypothesis channels Origen's interpretive emphases, the ἕτερα hypothesis stands in the tradition of Eusebius and Clement, and the final hypothesis attributed to Theodoret brings Chrysostom's voice into the fold.[108] Chrysostom's importance within this

---

I have also found this hypothesis as the sole prefatory texts in GA 2011 (eleventh c., Paris, Suppl. gr. 1264, fol. 183r–v), GA 1922 (thirteenth c., Florence, Biblioteca Medicea Laurenziana, Pluteo X. 19, fol. 219v). In GA 607 (thirteenth c., Paris, gr. 218) Theodoret's hypothesis is written on fol. 271r–v before the addition the Ps.-Theodoret hypothesis on folio 272r. Lorrain also notes that in Sinaiticus gr. 274 all of the Ps.-Theodoret hypotheses are collected at the end of the codex (483).

[104] Lorrain, "Des prologues bibliques," 485.
[105] Greek text in von Soden, *Die Schriften des Neuen Testaments*, 352–53.
[106] Picking up on these interconnected epitomizing practices, Lorrain suggests that the hypotheses of Theophylact (longer summaries) and Ps. Theodoret (shorter summaries) have a complex literary relationship. Since Theophylact abbreviates elements from Chrysostom that are not found in the Ps.-Theodoret hypotheses, and yet these two epitomizers share similar reorganizations of Chrysostom (as is the case with the hypothesis to Colossians), *and* the shorter summaries have material not found in the longer Theophylact summaries, Lorrain wonders whether these short summaries attributed to Theodoret in the Oecumenian catenae are based on a textual tradition of Theophylact no longer available to us (490), but, then again, they are attested earlier than Theophylact.
[107] Theophylact copies Chrysostom's opening point that Paul was apostle to the Gentiles and that there was a hatred for Paul among the non-Christian Hebrews because he was such a vehement persecutor and yet still became a follower of Christ. Theophylact uses the same logic concerning baptism to explain why Paul wrote to the Hebrews and also cites the example from Romans 11 about Paul's love for his brothers. Theophylact briefly notes Chrysostom's point about Jerusalem as the destination, the persecution of the Hebrews (citing, like Chrysostom, Hebrews 10:34). The quirky point made by Chrysostom that Jews learned to receive benefits within their lifetime is copied by Theophylact, as is the claim that Paul responds to this tendency in two ways. From beginning to end, then, Theophylact has abbreviated Chrysostom. This preface is also published by Cramer, although it is unclear whether Cramer knows that it is Theophylact and not another anonymous preface.
[108] The attribution of this Chrysostom-inspired hypothesis to Theodoret may stem from the larger inclination within catenae traditions to pair these two interpreters. Dorival, "Biblical

intertwining is notable, as seen already in Coislin 204 and Paris, grec. 238. And yet the Oecumenian catenae, as with the Euthalian apparatus, is a fluid constellation, and the most common combination of hypotheses within this tradition is the one from Euthalius together with the ἕτερα (see the Appendix, Figure 5).

This combination accents Origen's reading of Hebrews and the shadow of the Law, which is supplemented with the recycled details from Eusebius. Perhaps the ἑτέρα hypothesis was added to the Euthalian hypothesis as a way of attending to the expected discussions about the letter's origins. But as it stands, the Euthalian hypothesis does the hermeneutical heavy lifting, and does not mention anything about the apparent non-Pauline features of the texts (anonymity and stylistic difference). Rather, the hypothesis focuses on the occasion (πρόφασις) for the letter and what it demonstrates (ἀποδείκνυμι), namely, the παρουσία of Christ and the abolishment of the shadow of the Law (τοῦ πέπαυσθαι τὴν σκιὰν τοῦ νόμου). Table 2 gives a growing sense of the importance of the Euthalian hypothesis:[109]

In addition to the predominance of this combination of two hypotheses for Hebrews, the Euthalian hypothesis is also observed *migrating into other traditions of commentary and catena*. In GA 2007 (Biblioteca Medicea Laurenziana, Pluteo IX 10), the Nicetas catena appears with Euthalian hypotheses for the Pauline letters (GA 2007).[110] Theophylact's commentary is similarly found with the Euthalian hypothesis in GA 1947 (Ottob. gr. 61, fol. 121r–v).[111] In GA 245 (Athens, National Library 490, 14th) the Euthalian hypothesis is written on folio 713r, followed by the Euthalian *kephalaia* on folio 714r–v. After the *kephalaia*, the hypothesis of Theophylact is written in full on folios 714v–715r, which transitions into a fragment from the hypothesis in Theodoret's commentary (fol. 715r).[112]

Catenae," 78, finds a certain transition from Palestine to Constantinople regarding catena production and strategy that, in part, featured an increase in the dominance of Chrysostom and Theodoret as authorities within the catena around the turn of the eighth century.

[109] Willard, *Euthalian Apparatus*, 160–69.

[110] These hypotheses appear on fols. 247r to 246v to 246r. The manuscript suddenly flips and runs backward, which is the cause for the reverse order of folios.

[111] In GA 1947 the Euthalian hypothesis is written in black and Theophylact's hypothesis in red. According to *Pinakes*, GA 242 (Moscow, Sinod. gr. 407/Vlad. 25), and GA 1995 (Vat grec. 2180) also combined Euthaliana with Theophylact.

[112] This fragment from Theodoret cuts out at τῷ προοιμίῳ, and the final five lines of text are taken from the end of the Ps.-Theodoret hypothesis in the Oecumenian tradition, starting at τίνι. At both of these switches there is a notation in the margin.

Table 2 Preliminary checklist of the Euthalian and ἕτερα hypotheses

Aland #	Century or date	Contents	Folios	Institution and self-mark
GA 1998	10th	Euthalius + ἕτερα	158r–v	Vat. Pal. grec. 204
GA 457	10th	Euthalius + ἕτερα	269v–272r	Laurentian Library, Plut.04.29
GA 250	10th	Euthalius + ἕτερα	306r–308r	Paris, Coislin 224
GA 1845	10th	Euthalius + ἕτερα	215v–216v	Vat. gr. 1971
GA 1932	10th	Euthalius + ἕτερα	197r–v	Paris, grec. 222
GA 314	11th	Euthalius + ἕτερα	219v–221r	Bodleian Library, Ms. Barocci 3
GA 35	11th	Euthalius + ἕτερα	296r–297r	Paris, Coislin 199
GA 1934	11th	Euthalius + ἕτερα	188v	Paris, grec. 224
GA 424	11th	Euthalius + ἕτερα	292r–293r	Vienna, ÖNB, Theol. gr. 302
GA 133	11th	Euthalius + ἕτερα	216v–218v	Vat gr. 363
GA 1847	11th	Euthalius + ἕτερα	324r–326v	Palat. grec. 38
GA 1770	11th	Euthalius + ἕτερα	65v–67r	Athos, Lavra, Γ΄ 63
GA 1888	11th	Euthalius + ἕτερα	222r–223r	Patriarchate of Jerusalem, Taphos, 38
GA 1828	11th	Euthalius + ἕτερα	257v–259r	NLG 91
GA 1879	11th	Euthalius + ἄλλος	267r–269v	Saint Catherine, Monastery, Gr. 282
GA 1971	12th	Euthalius + ἄλλος	302r–v	Coislin, grec 95
GA 88	12th	Euthalius + ἕτερα	107r–v	National Library, Naples Ms. II. A. 7
GA 1855	13th	Euthalius + ἕτερα	171v–172v	Monastery of Iviron 404
GA 1956	13th	Euthalius + ἕτερα	170v–172r	BL Add MS 7142
GA 1864	13th	Euthalius + ἕτερα	114v–115v	Stavronikita, Athos, MS 52
GA 1852	13th	Euthalius + ἕτερα	146v–147v	Uppsala MS grec. 11
GA 1780	13th	Euthalius + ἕτερα	174r–v	Duke, Greek MS 001
GA 1827	13th	Euthalius + ἕτερα	131v–133r	NLG 131
GA 18	14th	Euthalius + ἕτερα	306v–307v	Paris, grec. 47 (dated 1364)
GA 1100	14th	Euthalius + ἄλλος	220v–221r	Athos, Dionysiu 8 (old 75)
GA 5	14th	Euthalius + ἕτερα	165v–166v	Paris, grec. 106
GA 62	14th	Euthalius + ἕτερα	101v–102v	Paris, grec. 60
GA 76	14th	Euthalius + ἕτερα	336v–337v	Austrian National Library, gr. 300
GA 1761	14th	Euthalius + ἕτερα	182v–183v	NGL 2521
GA 1948	15th	Euthalius + ἕτερα	100v–101v	Otto.gr.176
GA 61	16th	Euthalius + ἕτερα	224v–235v	Trinity College, MS 30
GA 1768	1519	Euthalius + ἕτερα	205v–206r	Monastery of Iviron 771

Spanning out from this lengthy history of transmission, the Euthalian hypothesis emerges above other prefatory texts as the most frequent and flexible hypothesis for the Letter to the Hebrews. Even beyond the Oecumenian catena and these kinds of fusions with other catenae traditions, the Euthalian material circulates widely in late antiquity Syriac, Armenian, Latin, Georgian, and Gothic, each of which advances Origen's Paul on the framing of Hebrews.

5. Conclusion

As Hebrews cascades through the second, third, and fourth centuries, it continually cycles back and forth from material configuration and readerly interaction, both of which work to produce and sustain its Paulinity. Following the Letter to the Hebrews over the course of the following millennia are hypotheses that distill the core themes and context of this text and are the literary containers for the discourse about Pauline authorship. Even though this discourse is institutionalized and repetitive, the transmission history of these hypotheses reveals a complex network of prefatory systems that crisscross, unite, and morph traditions of reading, which, in turn, function as interpretive grids for subsequent readers. Within this process we see interpretive questions manifest themselves in the material transmission of Hebrews as the hypotheses configure the letter as Pauline in distinctly Clementine and Origenian ways. Given their privileged place across the tradition, it is perhaps unsurprising to find that Chrysostom, Oecumenius, and Theodoret are depicted together as a consortium of Pauline interpreters in Paris grec. 224 (Appendix, Figure 6).

On this illuminated page, Chrysostom is given the most prominent position, supplemented with the two adjacent readers. Though Chrysostom's influence is great, the transmission of Hebrews reveals the subtle dominance of Oecumenius, positioned off to the side, whose commentary transmits the Euthalian hypothesis for Hebrews that values and configures the letter according to Origen's interpretive frame. This Euthalian hypothesis emerges as a highly attested and by extension, influential and significant prefatory text that preserves Origen's interpretive lens for Hebrews as a statement about the shadow of the Law. When Desiderius Erasmus and Johann Froben published the first edition of the New Testament in Greek in 1516, the Euthalian hypotheses for the Pauline letters together with Latin argumenta were printed before the beginning of each epistle.[113] In the *Apologia ad Fabrum*, Erasmus appeals directly to the argumenta as support for the idea of a Lucan translation of Hebrews.[114] While Erasmus would go on to develop his own argumenta for the Pauline epistles, the migration of the Euthalian hypotheses from manuscript to print edition speaks to their enduring importance and the lingering legacy of Origen.

The Pauline History of Hebrews. Warren Campbell, Oxford University Press. © Oxford University Press 2025.
DOI: 10.1093/9780197769287.003.0005

---

[113] Desiderius Erasmus, *Novum instrumentum omne* (Basel: Johann Froben, 1516), 132. In the 1519 edition, Erasmus included his own hypotheses; cf. Riemer A. Faber, "The Argumentum as Paratext: Editorial Strategies in the Novum Testamentum," *Erasmus of Rotterdam Society Yearbook* 37.2 (2017): 161–75.

[114] See R. P. Guy Bedouelle, *Controversies: Apologia ad Fabrum, Appendix de scriptis Clithovei, Dilutio, Responsio ad disputaationem de divortio*, vol. 83 (Toronto: Toronto University Press, 1998), 67: "But does not the preface to this Epistle contained in our manuscripts clearly support it?"

Epilogue

> Behold how much harm a book causes without the title of the author.
> —Thomas Cajetan, 1529[1]

Thomas Cajetan was one of many sixteenth-century commentators with a renewed sense of criticism of the Pauline authorship of Hebrews. The idea of a Hebrew original was increasingly difficult to defend, and the typical explanation of Paul's anonymity slowly lost its appeal. In a moment of aggravation, Cajetan laments the "harm" that anonymity causes, inflicting such a lengthy history of dispute. Cajetan's exclamation, and its underlying assumptions, relates to one of the core questions of this book. What if the anonymity of Hebrews was not a harm (*malus*) but an enduring feature of the text that uniquely illuminates how Pauline authorship is created and sustained, together with the shifting perceptions of Paul and Jews that arise along the way, as Hebrews is accounted for and engaged as Pauline? With this perspective on the Pauline history of Hebrews, and at the end of this project, a series of conclusions emerge.

First, the earliest Pauline features of our anonymous text arise from the editorial strategies used to unify Pauline letters together as a corpus. Discussions of Pauline authorship in second-century Egypt and Palestine are explanations of the material conditions of Paulinity exemplified by the title, "To the Hebrews," together with other literary resources at a writer's disposal and in conversation with the ever-growing discussion of Pauline authorship. While the earliest stages of this authorial ascription lie beyond the horizon of our lingering pieces of evidence, the first readers available to us are already attempting to account for "To the Hebrews" as a previously titled and currently circulating Pauline letter. Tertullian exemplifies this same practice but with a different textual scenario requiring interpretation. Rather than Paul, it is Barnabas' letter *Ad Hebraeos* that must be explained.

---

[1] *Opera omnia quotquot in Sacrae Scripturae expositionem reperiuntur, Tomas Quintus: In omnes Pauli et aliorum Apostolorum epistolas Commentarrii* (Lyons: Prost, 1639) 329: *Ecce quantum parit malum liber sine authoris titulo*. Translation, Kenneth Hagen, *Hebrews Commenting from Erasmus to Bèze 1516–1598*, BGBE 23 (Tübingen: Mohr Siebeck, 1981), 19, slightly modified.

The addition of the title *Pros Hebraious* is, then, our earliest interpretive reading of this text and the central piece of information that governed subsequent discourse about the letter. In fact, it is the Jewish context that is made to explain the other lingering difficulties. Anonymity is necessary because of the hostilities between Hebrew Christians and Paul, and the stylistic difference of Hebrews is a byproduct of the text's originally Jewish language. Both ideas emerge from a reading of Acts 21.

One of the early "Pauls" to emerge as the author of Hebrews is the Paul of Acts 21, who addresses Jews in Jerusalem in the Ἑβραΐδι διαλέκτῳ amid intense clashes surrounding Paul's teaching about the Law. In fact, this narrated Paul of Acts never disappears from the tradition and continues to explain the strange features of Hebrews throughout its afterlife. The importance of this narrated apostle in the reception of Hebrews invites further work on the driving force of the Paul in Acts upon subsequent interpretative tradition, perhaps especially on questions of how Paul relates to and thinks about fellows Jews.

Second, active participation within the discourse surrounding the Pauline authorship of Hebrews does not begin to describe how readers may configure and appropriate Hebrews as a Pauline letter to Jews. Clement's (dis)interest in Hebrews as a Pauline letter is conditioned by his image of Paul as a former Jew turned expert of scriptural mysteries, his image of Jews as earthly and bodily readers of texts, and his aim to establish links between Christianity and Greek philosophy. While the use of Acts to think about the origins of Hebrews would prove lasting and formative, Clement has little need for a Paul who writes to Hebrews. For Origen, however, Hebrews is made to be a pivotal text in articulating the core difference between Christianity and Judaism precisely because it is Paul's letter to the Hebrews. Origen has *every need* for a Paul who wrote to Hebrews, for here he finds a Jewish apostle who was able to take up Jesus' hermeneutic, namely, how the Jewish shadows really point to the Christian forms. What Clement and Origen reveal to us is that the ways in which readers incorporate the Pauline and Jewish resonances of Hebrews are open. In this sense, the "Paulinity" of Hebrews continually fluctuates, and the degrees of synthesis and unification are conditioned upon the prevailing interests and influences of a given reader. Yes, for Clement and Origen, Hebrews was authored by Paul, yet their readings are marked by resistance and embrace of the Pauline and Jewish coordinates. The hermeneutical posture that Clement and Origen adopt for reading Hebrews is conditioned by their need for a Jewish apostle in conceptualizing the difference between Christianity and Judaism.

Together with the narrated Paul of Acts, then, is this other "Paul" who follows along throughout the history of Hebrews. This is the Paul within the corpus of later readers who may align, resist, inform, or otherwise engage with the image of Paul as an author of Hebrews. Observing how the Letter to the Hebrews is appropriated within these later contexts magnifies these images of Paul, together with the concomitant images of Jews. Other Pauline texts might similarly be "weighed" within the context of later corpora. Ephesians, for example, is read by Greg Sterling as a *vita contemplativa* of Paul, designed to address a less specific audience with a universalizing Pauline message by picturing Paul as the recipient of revelation and as accessible only through his remaining epistolary corpus.[2] What role does the Paul of Ephesians together his vision of Jew and Gentile co-participation have upon later (re)appropriations of the Pauline corpus?[3] From this angle, the reception of a corpus need not only be a barrier to an elusive authenticity, but can also be the window through which to observe how configurations of Paul emerge from prioritizing certain epistolary texts along with narrative depictions and what issues these configurations of Paul are made to address.

Third, the prefatory practices that facilitate discourse about the Pauline authorship of Hebrews in the fourth century and beyond are the literary placeholders for earlier traditions of reading typified in Clement and Origen. These prefatory *hypothéseis* institutionalize the "Pauline authorship of Hebrews" despite never fully realizing Paul as the author. Hebrews is only ever a *disputed* Pauline text, hanging onto its affiliation with the apostle despite constant reminders of all the ways in which it is un-Pauline. As the reading traditions of the second, third, and fourth centuries fold back upon the transmission history of Hebrews in the form of hypotheses or argumenta, we observe the return of the reader in material history and the

---

[2] Gregory E. Sterling, "From Apostle to the Gentiles to Apostle of the Church: Images of Paul at the End of the First Century," *ZNW* 99 (2008): 97, also argues that "Acts is a narrative parallel to the theological construct of Ephesians." See also Christine Gerber, "Paulus als Ökumeniker: Die Interpretation der paulinischen Theologie durch den Epheserbrief," in *Receptions of Paul in Early Christianity: The Person of Paul and His Writings Through the Eyes of His Early Interpreters*, ed. J. Schröter, S. Butticaz, and A. Dettwiler (Berlin: de Gruyter, 2018), 317–54.

[3] See, for example, Benjamin H. Dunning, "Strangers and Aliens No Longer: Negotiating Identity and Difference in Ephesians 2," *HTR* 99 (2006): 1–16; James A. Kelhoffer, "The Ecclesiology of 2 Clement 14: Ephesians, Pauline Reception, and the Church's Preexistence," in Schröter et al., *Receptions of Paul*, 377–408.

closure of an *inclusio* for the project as a whole. Hebrews first emerges as a text fitted with Pauline marks that prepare the text for inclusion with a corpus, while the very readers who respond to that configuration become the means by which Hebrews is configured as Pauline in the transmission of that corpus. In this institutionalizing practice, we find Origen's interpretive legacy that Hebrews is a Pauline statement to Jews about the shadow of the Law given particular prominence. The Euthalian prologue championing this reading is extensively attested and also transmitted within the subsequent and no less popular Oecumenian catena commentary on Paul. Erasmus' appeal to the argumenta of Hebrews in his dispute with Lefèvre noted in the previous chapter is but one confession of the influence of these prefatory texts in the interpretation of Hebrews. Certainly, one might press further into the influences of Origen's hermeneutic in various exegetical projects, following this language of the shadow as a way of configuring the relationship between Christians and Jews.

Rather than a legacy that terminates in the sixteenth century as the "depaulinization" of Hebrews gets thoroughly underway, Origen's reading of anonymity is appreciated all the more and allows the Pauline connection to linger on in new ways. Hebrews may lose its Pauline author, but its Pauline "thoughts" remain. Erasmus is credited as one of the earliest voices to question the Pauline authorship of Hebrews, although these criticisms are put forward strategically and selectively.[4] In following Jerome (and Origen before him), Erasmus, and others like Cajetan, continue to evoke the name "Paul" when using Hebrews despite registering significant criticisms of the traditional explanations of Pauline authorship. And yet, with a newfound freedom from Paul, Hebrews is able to become transcendently Pauline. "It could be," Erasmus ponders, "that the letter is not by Paul and yet is even better than the Pauline letters."[5] Without the limitations of an author, Hebrews is free to *epitomize* the apostle's thought. Take, for example, B. F. Wescott's consideration of Hebrews long after Erasmus and on the other side of the century that criticized Pauline authorship most vigorously:

---

[4] Erasmus' criticisms of Hebrews are focalized in the *Apologia ad Fabrum*. See R. P. Guy Bedouelle, *Controversies: Apologia ad Fabrum, Appendix de scriptis Clithovei, Dilutio, Responsio ad disputaationem de divortio*, CWE 83 (Toronto: University of Toronto Press, 1998); as well as Hagen, *Hebrews Commenting*, 4–8.

[5] Erasmus, *Apologia ad Fabrum*. Translation, Bedouelle, *Controversies*, 81.

There is unquestionably a sense in which Origen is right in saying that "the thoughts" of the Epistle are the thoughts of St. Paul. The writer shews the same broad conception of the universality of the Gospel as the Apostle of the Gentiles, the same grasp of the age-long purpose of God wrought out through Israel, the same trust in the atoning work of Christ, and in His present sovereignty. He speaks with the same conscious mastery of the Divine Counsel. But he approaches each topic from a different side. He looks at all as from within Israel, and not as from without. He speaks as one who step by step had read the fulfillment of the Old Covenant in the New without any rude crisis of awakening or any sharp struggle with traditional errors. His Judaism has been all along the Judaism of the prophets and not of the Pharisees, of the O. T. and not of the schools.[6]

Wescott's evocation of Origen is fitting. Even if Hebrews no longer has "Paul," it may yet have a deeply Pauline author. As Paul recedes, the anonymous "he" who wrote the epistle captures the apostle's thought. This new, nondescript, and anonymous author of Hebrews is also the empty container that later readers may fill with an image of Paul as they describe its Paulinity. Hebrews never fully obtains Paul as its author, nor is it ever fully released from the apostle's legacy.

The Pauline History of Hebrews. Warren Campbell, Oxford University Press. © Oxford University Press 2025.
DOI: 10.1093/9780197769287.003.0006

---

[6] B. F. Westcott, *The Epistle to the Hebrews* (London: Macmillin 1892), lxxviii.

Appendix

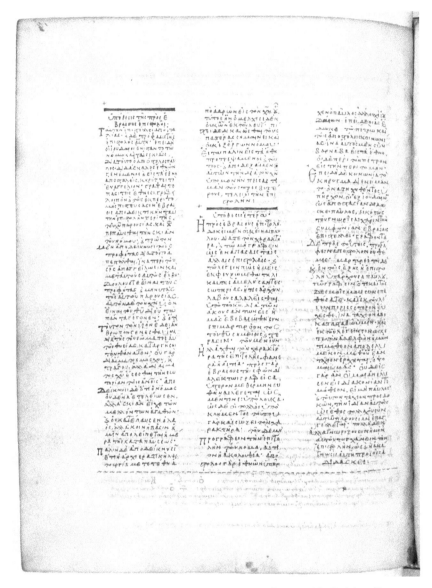

Figure 5 Euthalian and ἕτερα in Paris grec. 224 A f.188v with division line at the bottom. Courtesy of the Bibliothèque nationale de France (Archives et Manuscrits)

Figure 6 Paris. grec. 224, f. 7r (GA 1934). From left to right, Oecumenius, Chrysostom, and Theodoret. Courtesy of the Bibliothèque nationale de France (Archives et Manuscrits)

Bibliography

Aland, Kurt. "Die Entstehung des Corpus Paulinum." In *Neutestamentliche Entwürfe*, ed. Kurt Aland, 302–50. Munich: Chr. Kaiser Verlag, 1979.
Aland, Kurt. "Methodische Bemerkungen zum Corpus Paulinum bei den Kirchenvätern des zweiten Jahrhunderts." In *Kerygma und Logos: Beiträge zu den geistesgeschichtlichen Beziehungen zwischen Antike und Christentum*, ed. Adolf Martin Ritter, 29–48. Göttingen: Vandenhoeck & Ruprecht, 1979.
Aland, Kurt, Annette Benduhn-Merz, Gerd Mink, and Horst Bachmann, eds. *Text und Textwert der griechischen Handschriften des Neuen Testaments II: Die Paulinischen Briefe*. Vol. 4, *Kolosserbrief bis Hebräerbrief*. ANTF 19. Berlin: de Gruyter, 1991.
Albl, M. C. *"And Scripture Cannot Be Broken": The Form and Function of Early Christian Testamonia Collections*. NovTSup 96. Leiden: Brill, 1999.
Alexander, Philip. "'In the Beginning': Rabbinic and Patristic Exegesis of Genesis 1:1." In *The Exegetical Encounter Between Jews and Christians in Late Antiquity*, ed. Emmanouela Grypeou and Helen Spurling, 1–29. Leiden: Brill, 2009.
Allen, Bronwen Neil, and Wendy Mayer, eds. *Preaching Poverty in Late Antiquity: Perceptions and Realities*. Arbeiten zur Kirchen- und Theologiegeschichte 28. Leipzig: Evangelische Verlagsanstalt, 2009.
Allen, Garrick V. "Titles in the New Testament Papyri." *NTS* 68 (2022): 156–71.
Allen, Pauline, and Wendy Mayer. "The Homilist and the Congregation: A Case-Study of Chrysostom's Homilies on Hebrews." *Augustinianum* 36 (1996): 397–421.
Allen, Pauline, and Wendy Mayer. "The Thirty-Four Homilies on Hebrews: The Last Series Delivered by Chrysostom in Constantinople?" *Byzantion* 65 (1995): 309–48.
Amato, Eugenio, and Jacques Schamp. *Ethopoiia: La représentation de caractères entre fiction scolaire et réalité vivante à l'époque impériale et tardive*. Université de Fribourg. Groupe de recherches sur les rhétoriques de l'antiquité tardive, Cardo 3. Salerno: Helios editrice, 2005.
Anderson, C. P. "The Epistle to the Hebrews and the Pauline Letter Collection." *HTR* (1966): 429–38.
Anderson, C. P. "Hebrews among the Letters of Paul." *SR* 5 (1975–76): 258–66.
Anderson, Graham. *The Second Sophistic: A Cultural Phenomenon in the Roman Empire*. London: Routledge, 1993.
Antonova, Stamenka E. *Barbarian or Greek? The Charge of Barbarism and Early Christian Apologetics*. Leiden: Brill, 2019.
Arnott, W. G., trans. and ed. *Meander, Aspis. Georgos. Dis Exapaton. Dyskolos. Encheiridion. Epitrepontes*. LCL 132. Cambridge, MA: Harvard University Press, 1979.
Ashwin-Siejkowski, Piotr. *Clement of Alexandria: A Projection in Christian Perfection*. London: T&T Clark, 2008.
Assmann, Jan. "Text und Kommentar: Einführung." In *Text und Kommentar*, ed. Jan Asmman and Burkhard Gladigow, 9–33. Beiträge zur Archäologie der literarischen Kommunikation 4. Munich: Fink, 1995.
Ast, Rodney. "A New Fragment from Herodas' 'Mimes' and a Snippet of Homer (P.CtYBR inv.457)." *Museum Heveticum* 70.2 (2013): 145–56.
Attridge, Harold W. *Hebrews: A Commentary on the Epistle to the Hebrews*. Hermeneia. Philadelphia: Fortress, 1989.

Auerbach, Erich. "Figura." In *Scenes from the Drama of European Literature*, ed. W. Godzich and J. Schulte-Sasse, trans. R. Manheim, 11–71. Minneapolis: University of Minnesota Press, 1984.

Aune, David E. "Reconceptualizing the Phenomenon of Ancient Pseudepigraphy: An Epilogue." In *Pseudepigraphie und Verfasserfiktion in frühchristlichen Briefen*, ed. J. Frey, J. Herzer, M. Janßen, and C. Rothschild, 789–824. WUNT 246. Tübingen: Mohr Siebeck, 2009.

Baarda, T. "Marcion's Text of Gal 1:1 Concerning the Reconstruction of the First Verse of the Marcionite Corpus Paulinum." *VC* 42 (1988): 236–56.

Bacher, Wilhem. "The Church Father Origen and Rabbi Hoshaya." *JQR* 3 (1891): 357–60.

Backhaus, Knut. "Der Hebräerbrief und die Paulus-Schule." *BZ* 37 (1993): 183–208.

Baehrens, W. A., ed. *Origenes Werke VI, Homilien zum Hexateuch in Rufins Übersetzung. Teil 1: Die Homilien zu Genesis, Exodus und Leviticus.* GCS 29. Leipzig: J. C. Hinrichs, 1929.

Baehrens, W. A., ed. *Origenes Werke VII, Homilien zum Hexateuch in Rufins Übersetzung. Teil 2: Die Homilien zu Numeri, Josua und Judices.* GCS 30. Berlin: de Gruyter, 1921.

Baehrens, W. A., ed. *Origenes Werke VIII, Hömilien zu Samuel I, zum Hohelied und zu den Propheten Kommentar zum Hohelied in Rufins und Hieronymus' Übersetzungen.* GCS 33. Leipzig: J. C. Hinrichs, 1925.

Bagnall, Roger S. *Early Christian Books in Egypt.* Princeton: Princeton University Press, 2009.

Bammel, Ernst. "Die Zitate in Origenes' Schrift wider Celsus." In *Judaica et Paulina 2*, 57–61. WUNT 91. Tübingen: Mohr Siebeck, 1997.

Bandt, Cordula, and Franz Xaver Risch. "Das Hypomnema des Origenes zu den Psalmen—eine unerkannte Schrift des Eusebius." *Adamantius* 19 (2013): 395–410.

Banev, Krastu. *Theophilus of Alexandria and the First Origenist Controversy: Rhetoric and Power.* Oxford: Oxford University Press, 2015.

Bardy, Gustave. "Aux origines de l'école d'Alexandrie." *RSR* 27 (1937): 65–90.

Bardy, Gustave. "Les traditions juives dans l'oeuvre d'Origène." *RB* 34 (1925): 217–52.

Barkley, Gary Wayne. *Origen: Homilies on Leviticus: 1–16.* FC 83. Washington, DC: Catholic University of America Press, 1992.

Barrett, C. K. "Pauline Controversies in the Post-Pauline Period." *NTS* 20 (1974): 229–45.

Bartoletti, Vittorio. *Papiri greci e latini della Società Italiana.* Vol. 14, 5–7. Florence: Ariani, 1957.

Bastianini, Guido, ed. "1497. NT HEBR. 13:12–13; 19–20." In *Papiri Greci e Latini*, Vol. 15, *PSI*, 171–72. Florence: Istituto papirologico G. Vitelli, 2008.

Batovici, Dan. "Hermas in Clement of Alexandria." *StPatr* 66 (2013): 41–51.

Bauernfeind, Otto. *Der Römerbrieftext des Origenes nach dem Codex von der Goltz (cod. 184, B64 des Athosklosters Lawra.* TUGAL 3. Leipzig: Hinrichs, 1923.

Baum, Armin D. "Authorship and Pseudepigraphy in Early Christian Literature: A Translation of the Most Important Source Texts and an Annotated Bibliography." In *Paul and Pseudepigraphy*, ed. Stanley E. Porter and Gregory P. Fewster, 11–63. Pauline Studies 8. Leiden: Brill, 2013.

Beare, Frank W. "The Text of the Epistle to the Hebrews in P[46]." *JBL* 63.4 (1944): 379–96.

Beatrice, P. F. "Porphyry at Origen's School at Caesarea." In *Origeniana Duodecima: Origen's Legacy in the Holy Land—a Tale of Three Cities: Jerusalem, Caesarea and Bethlehem, Proceedings of the 12th International Origen Congress, Jerusalem, June 25–29, 2017*, ed. Brouria Bitton-Ashkelony, Oded Irshai, Aryeh Kofsky, Hillel Newman, and Lorenzo Perrone, 267–83. BETL 302. Leuven: Peeters, 2019.

Beattie, D. R. G., and P. R. Davies. "What Does Hebrew Mean?" *JSS* 56 (2011): 71–83.

Becker, Eve-Marie. "Von Paulus zu 'Paulus': Paulinische Pseudepigraphie-Forschung als literaturgeschichtliche Aufgabe." In *Pseudepigraphie und Verfasserfiktion in frühchristlichen Briefen*, ed. J. Frey, J. Herzer, M. Janßen, and C. Rothschild, 363–86. WUNT 246. Tübingen: Mohr Siebeck, 2009.

Bedu-Addo, J. T. "Recollection and the Argument 'from a Hypothesis' in Plato's Meno." *JHS* 54 (1984): 1-14.
Behr, John. *Origen: On First Principles*. Vols. 1-2. Oxford: Oxford University Press, 2017.
Berchman, Robert M. "The Categories of Being in Middle Platonism: Philo, Clement, and Origen of Alexandria." In *The School of Moses: From Philo to Origen. Middle Platonism in Transition*, ed. John Peter Kenney, 89-140. Chico: Scholar's Press, 1984.
Berger, Johann Gottfried Immanuel. "Der Brief an die Hebräer: Eine Homilie." In *Göttingische Bibliothek der neuesten theologischen Literatur, Dritter Band*, ed. J. F. Schleusner and Carl F. Stäudlin, 449-69. Göttingen: Vandenhoeck & Ruprecht, 1797.
Berger, Klaus. "Zur diskussion über die Herkunft von 1 Kor. 2:9." *NTS* 24 (1978): 270-83.
Bergjan, Silke-Petra. "Celsus the Epicurean? The Interpretation of an Argument in Origen, Contra Celsum." *HTR* 94.2 (2001): 179-204.
Beyschlag, Karlmann. *Clemens Romanus und der Frühkatholizismus*. BHT 35. Tübingen: Mohr Siebeck, 1966.
Bickerman, Elias J. "En marge de l'écriture." *RB* 88 (1981): 39-40.
Bietenhard, Hans. *Caesarea, Origenes und die Juden*. Stuttgart: Kohlhammer, 1974.
Bigg, Charles. *Christian Platonists of Alexandria*. Oxford: Clarendon, 1913.
Bingham, D. Jeffery. "Irenaeus and Hebrews." In *Christology, Hermeneutics, and Hebrews: Profiles from the History of Interpretation*, ed. Jon C. Laansma and Daniel J. Treier, 65-80. London: T&T Clark, 2012.
Bird, Michael F., and Joseph R. Dodson, eds. *Paul and the Second Century*. London: T&T Clark, 2011.
Birdsall, J. Neville. "The Text and Scholia of the Codex von der Goltz and Its Allies, and Their Bearing upon the Texts of the Works of Origen, Especially the Commentary on Romans." In *Origeniana: Premier colloque international des etudes origéniennes, Montserrat, 18-21 septembre 1973*, ed. Henri Crouzel, Gennaro Lomiento, and Josep Rius-Camps, 215-22. Bari: Instituto di Letteratura Christiana Antica, 1975.
Blaski, Andrew. "Jews, Christians, and the Conditions of Christological Interpretation in Origen's Work." In *Origeniana Duodecima: Origen's Legacy in the Holy Land—a Tale of Three Cities: Jerusalem, Caesarea and Bethlehem, Proceedings of the 12th International Origen Congress, Jerusalem, June 25-29, 2017*, ed. Brouria Bitton-Ashkelony, Oded Irshai, Aryeh Kofsky, Hillel Newman, and Lorenzo Perrone, 505-17. BETL 302. Leuven: Peeters, 2019.
Blaski, Andrew. "The *Philocalia of Origen:* A Crude or Creative Composition?" *VC* 73 (2019): 174-89.
Bleek, F. *Brief an die Hebräer*. Berlin: Dümmler, 1828.
Blomkvist, Vemund. *Euthalian Traditions: Text, Translation and Commentary*. TU 17. Berlin: de Gruyter, 2012.
Blönnigen, Christoph. *Der griechische Ursprung der jüdisch-hellenistischen Allegorese und ihre Rezeption in der alexandrinischen Patristik*. Europäische Hochschulschriften XV, KSL 59. Frankfurt am Main: Peter Lang, 1992.
Blowers, P. M. "Origen, the Rabbis, and the Bible: Toward a Picture of Judaism and Christianity in Third-century Caesarea." In *Origen of Alexandria: His World and His Legacy*, ed. C. Kannengiesser and W. L. Petersen. Notre Dame: University of Notre Dame Press, 1988.
Boccaccini, Gabriele, and Carlos A. Segovia. *Paul the Jew: Rereading the Apostle as a Figure of Second Temple Judaism*. Minneapolis: Fortress, 2016.
Bockmuehl, Marcus. "The Dead Sea Scrolls and the Origins of Biblical Commentary." In *Text, Thought, and Practice in Qumran and Early Christianity: Proceedings of the Ninth International Symposium of the Orion Center for the Study of the Dead Sea Scrolls and Associated Literature, Jointly Sponsored by the Hebrew University Center for the Study of Christianity, 11-13 January, 2004*, ed. Ruth A. Clements and Daniel R. Schwartz, 3-29. Leiden: Brill, 2009.

Bockmuehl, Marcus. "The Making of Gospel Commentaries." In *The Written Gospel*, ed. Marcus Bockmuehl and Donald A. Hagner, 274-95. Cambridge: Cambridge University Press, 2005.
Bokedal, Tomas. "The Rule of Faith: Tracing Its Origins." *JTS* 7.2 (2013): 223-55.
Boucaud, Pierre. "The *Corpus Paulinum*: Greek and Latin Exegesis of the Epistles in the First Millennium." *RHR* 230 (2013): 299-332.
Bousset, Wilhelm. *Die Religion des Judentums im neutestamentlichen Zeitalter*. Berlin: Reuther & Reichard, 1903.
Bovon, François. "Paul comme Document et Paul comme Monument." In *Chrétiens en conflit: L'Épître de Paul aux Galates*, ed. J. Alaaz, 54-65. Essais bibliques 13. Geneva: Labor et Fides, 1987.
Boyarin, Daniel. *Intertextuality and the Reading of Midrash*. Bloomington: Indiana University Press, 1994.
Boyarin, Daniel. "Philo, Origen, and the Rabbis on Divine Speech and Interpretation." In *The World of Early Egyptian Christianity: Language, Literature, and Social Context*, ed. James E. Goehring and Janet A. Timbie, 113-29. Washington, DC: Catholic University of America Press, 2007.
Boyarin, Daniel. "Plato's Soul and the Body of the Text in Philo and Origen." In *Interpretation and Allegory: Antiquity to the Modern Period*. ed. Jon Whitman, 89-107. Leiden: Brill, 2000.
Brakke David. "Jewish Flesh and Christian Spirit in Athanasius of Alexandria." *JECS* 9 (2001): 453-81.
Braun, Herbert. *An die Hebräer*. HNT 14. Tübingen: Mohr Siebeck, 1984.
Bremmer, Jan N. "The First Pogrom? Religious Violence in Alexandria in 38 CE?" In *Alexandria: Hub of the Hellenistic World*, ed. Benjamin Schliesser, Jan Rüggemeier, Thomas J. Kraus, and Jörg Frey, 245-59. WUNT 460. Tübingen: Mohr Siebeck, 2021.
Brennecke, Hanns Christof. "Die Anfänge einer Paulusverehrung." In *Biographie und Persönlichkeit des Paulus*, ed. E.-M. Becker and P. Pilhofer, 295-305. WUNT 187. Tübingen: Mohr Siebeck, 2005.
Brennecke, Hanns Christof, Uta Heil, Annette von Stockhausen, and Angelika Wintjes, eds. *Athanasius Werke, III/1: Dokumente zur Geschichte des arianischen Streites*. Vols. 1-5. Berlin: de Gruyter, 1934, 2007, 2014, 2021.
Brésard, L., and H. Crouzel, eds. *Origène: Commentaire sur le Cantique des Cantiques*. Vol. 1. SC 375. Paris: Cerf, 1991.
Brésard, L., and H. Crouzel, eds. *Origène: Commentaire sur le Cantique des Cantiques*. Vol. 2. SC 376. Paris: Cerf, 1992.
Bright, Pamela. "The Epistle to the Hebrews in Origen's Christology." In *Origeniana Sexta: Origène et la Bible / Origen and the Bible. Actes du Colloquium Origenianum Sextum Chantilly, 30 août-3 septembre 1993*, ed. Gilles Dorival and Alain Le Boulluec, 559-65. Leuven: Peeters, 1995.
Brooks, James A. "The Text of the Pauline Epistles in the Stromata of Clement of Alexandria." ThD diss., Princeton University, 1966.
Brooks, Roger. "Straw Dogs and Scholarly Ecumenism: The Appropriate Jewish Background for the Study of Origen." In *Origen of Alexandria: His World and His Legacy*, ed. Charles Kannengiesser and William L. Petersen, 63-95. Notre Dame: Notre Dame University Press, 1988.
Broudehoux, J. P. *Mariage et famille chez Clément d'Alexandrie*. Théologie historique 11. Paris: Beauschesne et ses fils, 1970.
Brox, Norbert. *Falsche Verfasserangaben: Zur Erklärung der frühchristlichen Pseudepigraphie*. Stuttgarter Bibelstudien 79. Stuttgart: Katholisches Bibelwerk, 1975.
Bruce, F. F. "'To the Hebrews': A Document of Roman Christianity?" *ANRW* 2.25.4 (1987): 3496-521.
Bruce, F. F. "'To the Hebrews' or 'To the Essenes.'" *NTS* 9 (1963): 217-32.

Bucchi, F. ed. *Commentarii in epistulas Pauli apostoli ad Titum et ad Philemonem*. CCSL 77C. Turnhout: Brepols, 2003.

Buchanan, G. W. *To the Hebrews*. AB 36. New York: Doubleday, 1972.

Buchheit, Vinzenz. "Rufinus von Aquileja als Fälscher des Adamantiosdialogs." *ByzZ* 51 (1958): 314–28.

Buchinger, Harald. "Origenes und die Quadragesima in Jerusalem ein Diskussionsbeitrag." *Adamantius* 13 (2007): 174–217.

Buck, Charles H. "The Early Order of the Pauline Corpus." *JBL* 68.4 (1949): 351–57.

Bucur, Bogdan Gabriel. "The Place of the Hypotyposeis in the Clementine Corpus: An Apology for 'The Other Clement of Alexandria.'" *JECS* 17 (2009): 313–35.

Buell, Denise Kimber. "Race and Universalism in Early Christianity." *JECS* 10.4 (2002): 429–68.

Buell, Denise Kimber. *Why This New Race? Ethnic Reasoning in Early Christianity*. New York: Columbia University Press, 2005.

Burch, Vacher. "Two Notes on Euthalius of Sulci." *JTS* 17 (1916): 176–79.

Buri, Fritz. *Clemens Alexandrinus und der Paulinische Freiheitsbegriff*. Zurich: Niehans, 1939.

Burnet, Régis. "La finale de l'épître aux Hébreux: Une addition alexandrine de la fin du IIe siècle." *RB* 120 (2013): 423–40.

Buth, Randall, and Chad Pierce. "*Hebraisti* in Ancient Texts: Does Ἑβραϊστί Ever Mean 'Aramaic'?" In *The Language Environment of First Century Judaea*, ed. Randall Buth and R. Steven Notley, 66–190. Leiden: Brill, 2014.

Butler, H. E. ed. *Quintilian. Institutio Oratoria*. Vol 1. LCL 124. Cambridge, MA: Harvard University Press, 1920.

Butterworth, G. W. *Clement of Alexandria*. LCL 92. New York: G. P. Putnam, 1919.

Butticaz, Simon. "Paul et le judaïsme: Des identités en construction." *RHPR* 94 (2014): 253–73.

Cadiou, René. "La bibliothèque de Césarée et la formation des chaînes." *RevScRel* 16 (1936): 474–83.

Cadiou, René. *La jeunesse d'Origène: Histoire de l'École d'Alexandrie au début du IIIe siècle*. Paris: Bauschesne, 1936.

Cain, Andrew. *Jerome's Commentaries on the Pauline Epistles and the Architecture of Exegetical Authority*. Oxford: Oxford University Press, 2022.

Carr, David M. *The Formation of Genesis 1–11*. Oxford: Oxford University Press, 2020.

Casey, Robert. *The excerpta ex Theodoto of Clement of Alexandria*. London: Christophers, 1934.

Chadwick, Henry. *Origen: Contra Celsum*. Cambridge: Cambridge University Press, 1953.

Chadwick, Henry. "Rufinus and the Tura Papyrus of Origen's Commentary on Romans." *JThS* n.s. 10 (1959): 10–42.

Chin, C. Michael. "Rufinus of Aquileia and Alexandrian Afterlives: Translation as Origenism." *JECS* 18 (2010): 617–47.

Choat, Malcolm, and Rachel Yuen-Collingridge. "Texts Without Authors: Unidentified Texts in the Christian Tradition from Roman Oxyrhynchus." *EC* 10 (2019): 56–71.

Clark, Elizabeth. "Comment: Chrysostom and Pauline Social Ethics." In *Paul and the Legacies of Paul*, ed. W. S. Babcock, 193-99. Dallas: Southern Methodist University Press, 1990.

Clark, Elizabeth. "Origen, the Jews, and the Song of Songs: Allegory and Polemic in Christian Antiquity." In *Perspectives on the Song of Songs / Perspektiven der Hoheliedauslegung*, ed. John Barton, Reinhard G. Kratz, Choon-Leong Seow, and Markus Witte, 274–93. BZAW 346. Berlin: de Gruyter, 2005.

Clark, Elizabeth. *The Origenist Controversy: The Cultural Construction of an Early Christian Debate*. Princeton: Princeton University Press, 1992.

Clements, Ruth. "Origen's *Hexapla* and Christian-Jewish Encounter in the Second and Third Centuries." In *Religious Rivalries and the Struggle for Success in Caesarea Maritima*, ed. Terence L. Donaldson, 303–29. ESCJ 8. Waterloo: Wilfrid Laurier University Press, 2000.

Clements, Ruth. "Origen's Readings of Romans in *Peri Archon*: (Re)Constructing Paul." In *Early Patristic Readings of Romans*, ed. Kathy L. Gaca and L. L. Welborn, 159-79. New York: T&T Clark, 2005.

Clements, Ruth. "Peri Pascha: Passover and the Displacement of Jewish Interpretation Within Origen's Exegesis." ThD diss, Harvard Divinity School, 1997.

Clements, Ruth. "τέλειος ἄμωμος: The Influence of Palestinian Jewish Exegesis on the Interpretation of Exodus 12.5 in Origen's Peri Pascha." In *The Function of Scripture in Early Jewish and Christian Tradition*, ed. Craig A. Evans and James A. Sanders, 285-311. Sheffield: Sheffield Academic Press, 1998.

Clivaz, Claire. "(According) to the Hebrews: An Apocryphal Gospel and a Canonical Letter Read in Egypt." In *Between Canonical and Apocryphal Texts*, ed. Frey Jörg, Clivaz Claire, Nicklas Tobias, and Röder Jörg, 271-88. WUNT 1.419. Tübingen: Mohr Siebeck, 2019.

Clivaz, Claire. "A New NT Papyrus: P126 (PSI 1497)." *EC* 1 (2010): 158-62.

Clivaz, Claire. "The New Testament at the Time of the Egyptian Papyri: Reflections Based on P12, P75 and P126 (P. Amh. 3b, P. Bod. XIV-XV and PSI 1497)." In *Reading New Testament Papyri in Context—Lire les papyrus du Nouveau Testament dans leur contexte. Actes du colloque des 22-24 octobre 2009 à l'université de Lausanne*, ed. C. Clivaz and J. Zumstein, 41-51. Leuven: Peeters, 2011.

Cockerill, G. L. "Heb 1:1-14, *1 Clem*. 36:1-6, and the High Priest Title." *JBL* 97 (1978): 437-40.

Cockle, W. E. H. "4498. Epistle to the Hebrews I 7-12." In *The Oxyrhynchus Papyri*, vol. 66, ed. N. Gonis, J. Chapa, W. E. H. Cockle, D. Obbink, P. J. Parsons, and J. David Thomas, 9-11. London: Egypt Exploration Fund, 1999.

Cody, Aelrod. *Heavenly Sanctuary and Liturgy in the Epistle to the Hebrews*. St. Meinrad: Grail Publications, 1960.

Cohen, Shaye J. D. "Sabbath Law and Mishnah Shabbat in Origen De Principiis." *JSQ* 17 (2010): 160-89.

Comfort, Philip W., and David P. Barrett. *The Text of the Earliest New Testament Greek Manuscripts*. Wheaton: Tyndale House, 2001.

Conybeare, Fred C. "The Date of Euthalius." *ZNW* 5 (1904): 39-52.

Conybeare, Fred C. "On the Codex Pamphili and the Date of Euthalius." *Journal of Philology* 23 (1895): 241-59.

Coogan, Jeremiah. *Eusebius the Evangelist*. Oxford: Oxford University Press, forthcoming.

Cook, James D. *Preaching and Popular Christianity: Reading the Sermons of John Chrysostom*. Oxford Theology and Religion Monographs. Oxford: Oxford University Press, 2018.

Cosaert, Carl P. "Clement's of Alexandria's Gospel Citations." In *The Early Text of the New Testament*, ed. Charles E. Hill and Michael J. Kruger, 393-413. Oxford: Oxford University Press, 2012.

Cosaert, Carl P. *The Text of the Gospels in Clement of Alexandria*. SBLNTGF 9. Atlanta: Society of Biblical Literature, 2008.

Cox, Patricia. "Origen and the Bestial Soul: A Poetics of Nature." *VC* 36.2 (1982): 115-40.

Cramer, John A. *Catenae Graecorum patrum in Novum Testamentum*. Vols. 1-7. Oxford: Oxford University Press, 1842-44.

Crawford, Matthew R. "Tatian, Celsus, and Christianity as 'Barbarian Philosophy' in the Late Second Century." In *The Rise of the Early Christian Intellectual*, ed. Lewis Ayres and H. Clifton Ward, 45-80. AK 139. Berlin: de Gruyter, 2020.

Criboire, Raffaella. *Writing, Teachers, and Students in Graeco-Romans Egypt*. American Studies in Papyrology. Atlanta: Scholars Press, 1996.

Crouzel, Henri, ed. *Grégorie le Thaumaturge: Remerciement a Origène suivi de la Lettre d'Origène a Grégoire*. SC 148. Paris: Cerf, 1969.

Crouzel, Henri. "L'École d'Origène à Césarée: Postscriptum à une édition de Grégoire le Thaumaturge." *BLE* 71 (1970): 15-27.

Crouzel, Henri. "Les condemnations subies par Origène et sa doctrine." In *Origeniana Septima*, ed. W. A. Bienert and U. Kühnweg, 311–15. Belgium: Leuven University Press, 1999.
Crouzel, Henri. *Origène et la "Connaissance Mystique"*. Paris: Desclée de Brouwer, 1961.
Crouzel, Henri. *Origène et la philosophie*. Théologie 52. Paris: Aubier, 1962.
Crouzel, Henri, and Manilo Simonetti, eds. *Origène Traité des Principes*. SC 268. Paris: Cerf, 1980.
Cyril of Alexandria. *Commentary on the Letter to the Hebrews: Armenian Critical Text*. Ed. Xač'ik Grigoryan. Yerevan: Ankyunacar, 2020.
Czajkowski, Kimberley. "Jewish Associations in Alexandria?" In *Private Associations and Jewish Communities in the Hellenistic and Roman Cities*, ed. Benedikt Eckhardt, 76–96. JSJSup 191. Leiden: Brill, 2019.
Dahl, Nils. "The 'Euthalian Apparatus' and 'Affiliated Argumenta.'." In *Studies in Ephesians: Introductory Questions, Text- & Edition-Critical Issues, Interpretation of Texts and Themes*, ed. D. Hellholm, V. Blomkvist, and T. Fornberg, 234–40. Tübingen: Mohr Siebeck, 2000.
Dahl, Nils. "The Origin of the Earliest Prologues to the Pauline Letters." *Semeia* 12 (1978): 233–77.
Dahl, Nils. "The Particularity of the Pauline Epistles as a Problem in the Ancient Church." In *Neotestamentica et Patristica: Eine Freundesgabe, Herrn Professor Dr. Oscar Cullmann zu seinem 60 Geburtstag überreicht*, 261–71. NovTSup 6. Leiden: Brill, 1962.
Daly, Brian. "What Did Origenism Mean in the Sixth Century?" In *Origene et la Bible / Origen and the Bible*, ed. Gilles Dorival and Alain Le Boulluec, 627–38. BETL, 118. Leuven: Leuven University Press, 1995.
Danéliou, Jean. *Origène*. Paris: Table Ronde, 1948.
Dassmann, Ernst. *Der Stachel im Fleisch: Paulus in der frühchristlichen Literatur bis Irenäus*. Münster: Aschendorff, 1979.
Dawson, David. *Allegorical Readers and Cultural Revision in Ancient Alexandria*. Berkeley: University of California Press, 1991.
Dawson, David. *Christian Figural Reading and the Fashioning of Identity*. Berkeley: University of California Press, 2001.
Dawson, John. "Allegorical Reading and the Embodiment of the Soul in Origen." In *Christian Origins: Theology, Rhetoric, and Community*, ed. G. Jones and L. Ayres, 26–43. London: Routledge, 1988.
de Boer, E. A. "Tertullian on 'Barnabas' Letter to the Hebrews' in *De pudicitia* 20.1-5." *VC* 68 (2014): 243–63.
de Boer, Martinus C. "Comment: Which Paul?" In *Paul and the Legacies of Paul*, ed. William S. Babcock, 45–54. Dallas: Southern Methodist Press, 1990.
de Boer, Martinus C. "Images of Paul in the Post-Apostolic Period." *CBQ* 42 (1980): 359–80.
de Boor, C. Carl Gotthard, ed. *Nicephori archiepiscopi Constantinopolitam opuscula historica*. Leipzig: Teubner, 1880.
de Bruyn, Theodore. *Making Amulets Christian: Artefacts, Scribes, and Contexts*. Oxford: Oxford University Press, 2017.
de Bruyn, Theodore, and Jitse H. F. Dijkstra. "Greek Amulets and Formularies from Egypt Containing Christian Elements: A Checklist of Papyri, Parchments, Ostraka, and Tablets." *BASP* 48 (2011): 96–197.
de Bruyne, Donatien. "Prologues bibliques d'origin Marcionite." *RBén* 24 (1907): 1–16.
de Bruyne, Donatien. "Un prologue inconnu des épitres catholiques." *RBén* 23 (1906): 82–87.
de Groote, Marc. "Des prologues bibliques d'origine chrysostomienne: Les arguments attribués à Théodoret et à Théophylacte sur les épîtres pauliniennes." *ZAC* 19 (2015): 481–501.
de Groote, Marc. "Die Kirchenväter in Oecumenius' *Scholia in Iohannem Chrysostomum*." *VC* 55 (2001): 191–200.

de Lange, Nicholas. "Origen and the Jewish Bible Exegesis." *JJS* 22 (1971): 31–52.
de Lange, Nicholas. *Origen and the Jews: Studies in Jewish-Christian Relations in Third-Century Palestine*. Cambridge: Cambridge University Press, 1976.
de Lange, Nicholas. "Origen and the Rabbis on the Hebrew Bible." *StPatr* 14 (1976): 117–21.
de Lange, Nicholas. "The Revival of the Hebrew Language in the Third Century CE." *JSQ* 3 (1996): 342–58.
de Wette, W. M. L. *Kurze Erklärung der Briefe an Titus, Timotheus und die Hebräer*. Leipzig: Weidmannische Buchhandlung, 1844.
DeCock, Miriam. *Interpreting the Gospel of John in Antioch and Alexandria*. Atlanta: Society of Biblical Literature Press, 2020.
DeCock, Miriam. "Theodoret of Cyrus and His Exegetical Predecessors: A Study of His Biblical Commentary Prefaces." *Open Theology* 7 (2021): 445–60.
Demura, Miyako. "Origen's Allegorical Interpretation and the Philological Tradition of Alexandria." In *Origeniana Nona: Origen and the Religious Practice of His Time. Papers of the 9th International Origen Congress, Pécs, Hungary, 29 August–2 September 2005*, ed. György Heidl and Róbert Somos, 149–58. Leuven: Peeters, 2009.
den Boer, W. "De allegorese in het werk van Clemens Alexandrinus." PhD diss., University of Leiden, 1940.
Déroche, Vincent. "La politique anti-judaïque au VIe et au VIIe siècle un memento inédit, les képhalaia." *Travaux et Mémoires* 11 (1991): 275–311.
Devreesse, Robert. "Chaines exégétiques grecques." In *Dictionnaire de la Bible: Supplément*, ed. Louis Pirot, coll. 1084–233. Paris, 1928.
Dhôtel, Jean-Claude. "La 'sanctification' du Christ d'après Hébreux, II,11: Interprétations des Pères et des scolastiques médiévaux." *RSR* 47 (1959): 515–43.
Dhôtel, Jean-Claude. "La 'sanctification' du Christ d'après Hébreux II,11. Seconde partie: L'exégèse de Heb. II,11 dans les commentaires de l'épître aux Hébreux de saint Jean Chrysostome à saint Thomas." *RSR* 48 (1960): 420–52.
Dickey, Eleanor. *Ancient Greek Scholarship. A Guide to Finding, Reading, and Understanding Scholia, Commentaries, Lexica, and Grammatical Treatises, from Their Beginnings to the Byzantine Period*. New York: Oxford University Press, 2007.
Diekamp, Franz. *Die origenistischen Streitigkeiten im sechsten Jahrhundert und das fünfte allgemeine Concil*. Münster: Aschendorff, 1899.
Diekamp, Franz."Mittheilungen über den neuaufgefundenen Commentar des Oekumenius zu Apokalypse." *Sitzungsberichte der Königlichen Preussischen Akademie der Wissenschaften zu Berlin* (1901): 1046–58.
Dinan, Andrew. "Αἴνιγμα and Αἰνίττομαι in the Works of Clement of Alexandria." *StPatr* 46 (2010): 175–80.
Dively Lauro, Elizabeth Ann. *The Soul and the Spirit of Scripture Within Origen's Exegesis*. Leiden: Brill, 2005.
Dochhorn, Jan. "Jüdisch-alexandrinische Literatur? Eine Problemanzeige und ein Überblick über diejenige Literatur, die potentiell dem antiken Judentum entstammt." In *Alexandria*, ed. Tobias Geogres, Felix Albrecht, and Reinhard Feldmeier, 285–312. COMS 1. Tübingen: Mohr Siebeck, 2013.
Dontatus, Bernardus. *Expositiones antiquae ex diversis sanctorum patrum commentariis ab Oecumenio et Aretha collectae in hosce Novi Testamenti tractatus. Oecumenii quidem in Acta Apostolorum. In septem Epistolas quae Catholicae dicuntur. In Pauli omnes. Arethae vero in Ioannis Apocalypsim*. Verona: Apud Staphanum & fratres Sabios, 1532.
Dooley, Timothy W. "Marcionite Influences in the Primum Quaeritur Preface to Vulgate Paul." *StPatr* 99 (2018): 139–56.
Dorival, Gilles. "Biblical Catenae: Between Philology and History." In *Commentaries, Catenae and Biblical Tradition*, ed. H. A. G. Houghton, 65–81. Piscataway: Gorgias, 2016.

Dorival, Gilles. "The Bible, Commentaries, Scholia, and Other Literary Forms." In *On the Fringe of Commentary: Metatextuality in Ancient Near Eastern and Ancient Mediterranean Cultures*, ed. S. H. Aufrère, P. S. Alexander, and Z. Pleše, 163-74. Leuven: Peeters, 2014.

Dorival, Gilles. "Des commentaires de l'Écriture aux chaînes." In *Le monde grec ancien et la Bible: Bible de tous les temps I*, ed. Claude L. Mondésert, 361-86. Paris: Beauchesne, 1984.

Dorival, Gilles. "L'apport des Synopses transmises sous le nom d'Athanase et de Jean Chrysostome à la question du Corpus Littéraire de la Bible?" In *Qu'est-ce qu'un corpus littéraire? Recherches sur le corpus biblique et les corpus patristiques*, ed. Gilles Dorival, Christian Boudignon, Florence Bouet, and Claudine Cavalier, 53-93. Leuven: Peeters, 2005.

Dorival, Gilles. "Les formes et modèles littéraires." In *Histoire de le littérature grecque chrétienne: Introduction*, ed. Bernard Pouderon and Enrico Norelli, 139-88. Paris: Cerf, 2008.

Dorival, Gilles, and Ron Naiweld. "Les interlocuteurs hébreux et juifs d'Origène à Alexandrie et à Césarée." In *Caesarea Maritima: A Retrospective After Two Millennia*, ed. Kenneth G. Holum and Avner Raban, 121-38. Leiden: Köln, 1998.

Dörrie, Heinrich. "Ammonios der Lehrer Plotins." *Hermes* 83 (1955): 439-77.

Dörrie, Heinrich, and Matthias Batles. *Der Platonismus im 2. Und 3. Jahrhundert nach Christus: Bausteine 73-100, Übersetzung, Kommentar*. Stuttgart: Bad Cannstatt, 1993.

Dothan, Moshe. *Hammath Tiberias: Early Synagogues and the Hellenistic and Roman Remains*. Jerusalem: University of Haifa, 1983.

Droge, Arthur J. *Homer Or Moses? Early Christian Interpretations of the History of Culture*. Tübingen: Mohr Siebeck, 1989.

Duff, Jeremy. "P46 and the Pastorals: A Misleading Consensus." *NTS* 44 (1998): 578-90.

Dunn, James D. G. *The New Perspective on Paul: Collected Essays*. WUNT 185. Tübingen: Mohr Siebeck, 2005.

Dyer, Brian R. "The Epistolary Closing of Hebrews and Pauline Imitation." In *Paul and Pseudepigraphy*, ed. Stanley E. Porter and Gregory P. Fewster, 269-85. Leiden: Brill, 2013.

Eastman, David. *The Death of the Apostles: Ancient Accounts of the Martyrdoms of Peter and Paul (Latin, Greek, Syriac)*. Atlanta: Society of Biblical Literature, 2015.

Eastman, David. *Paul the Martyr: The Cult of the Apostle in the Latin West*. Atlanta: Society of Biblical Literature, 2011.

Edsall, Benjamin. "Clement and the Catechumenate in the Late Second Century." In *The Rise of the Early Christian Intellectual*, ed. Lewis Ayers and H. Clifton Ward, 100-127. AK 139. Berlin: de Gruyter, 2020.

Edsall, Benjamin. *The Reception of Paul and Early Christian Initiation: History and Hermeneutics*. Cambridge: Cambridge University Press, 2019.

Edwards, Mark. "Ammonius, Teacher of Origen." *JEH* 44 (1993): 169-81.

Edwards, Mark. "Christ or Plato? Origen on Revelation and Anthropology." In *Christian Origins: Theology Rhetoric and Community*, ed. Lewis Ayers and Gareth Jones, 11-25. London: Routledge, 1998.

Edwards, Mark. "Clement of Alexandria and his Doctrine of the Logos." *VC* 54 (2000): 159-77.

Edwards, Mark. "Gnostics and Valentinians in the Church Fathers." *JTS* 40 (1989): 25-47.

Edwards, Mark. *Origen Against Plato*. Aldershot: Ashgate, 2002.

Edwards, Robert G. T. "Clement of Alexandria's Anti-Valentinian Interpretation of Gen 1:26-27." *ZAC* 18 (2014): 365-89.

Ehrhard, Albert. "Der Codex H ad epistulas Pauli und 'Euthalius diaconos.'" *Centralblatt für Bibliothekwesen* 8 (1891): 385-411.

Ehrman, Bart, ed. *The Apostolic Fathers*. Vol. 1. LCL 24. Cambridge, MA: Harvard University Press, 2001.

Eisenbaum, Pamela. "Locating Hebrews Within the Literary Landscape of Christian Origins." In *Hebrews: Contemporary Methods, New Insights*, ed. Gabriella Gelardini, 213-38. BibInt 75. Leiden: Brill, 2005.

Eisenbaum, Pamela. *Paul Was Not a Christian: The Original Message of a Misunderstood Apostle*. New York: HarperCollins, 2009.
Ellingworth, Paul. "Hebrews and *1 Clement*: Literary Dependence or Common Tradition?" *BZ* 23 (1979): 262–69.
Ephrem Armenius. Սրբոյն Եփրեմի մատենագրութիւնք. Venice: Tparani Srboyn Ghazaru, 1836.
Erasmus, Desiderius. *Novum instrumentum omne*. Basel: Johann Froben, 1516.
Erlemann, Kurt. "Alt und neu bei Paulus und im Hebräerbrief: Frühchristliche Standortbestimmung im Vergleich." *TZ* 54 (1998): 345–67.
Faber, Riemer A. "The Argumentum as Paratext: Editorial Strategies in the Novum Testamentum." *Erasmus of Rotterdam Society Yearbook* 37 (2017): 161–75.
Faye, Eugène de. *Origène, sa vei, son oeuvre, sa pensée*. Vol. 1. Paris: Ernest Leroux, 1923.
Ferguson, Evert. "Canon Muratori: Date and Provenance." *StPatr* 17 (1982): 677–83.
Fewster, Gregory. "Archiving Paul: Manuscripts, Religion, and the Editorial Shaping of Ancient Letter Collections." *Archivaria* 81 (2016): 101–28.
Fewster, Gregory. "Authoring Manuscripts." In *The Oxford Handbook of the New Testament in Roman Empire*, ed. Harry O. Maier, Heid Wendt, and Emiliano Rubens Urcuioli. Oxford: Oxford University Press, forthcoming.
Fewster, Gregory. "Dying and Rising with the Author: Specters of Paul and the Material Text." In *Biblical Exegesis Without Authorial Intention? Interdisciplinary Approaches to Authorship and Meaning*, ed. Clarissa Breu, 169–73. BibInt 172. Leiden: Brill, 2019.
Fewster, Gregory. "Finding Your Place: Developing Cross-Reference Systems in Late Antique Biblical Codices." In *The Future of New Testament Textual Scholarship: From H. C. Hoskier to the Editio Critica Maior and Beyond*, ed. Garrick V. Allen, 155–79. Tübingen: Mohr Siebeck, 2019.
Fewster, Gregory. "Forgers and Critics of the Corpus Paulinum." PhD diss., University of Toronto, 2020.
Finegan, Jack. "The Original Form of the Pauline Collection." *HTR* 49.2 (1956): 85–103.
Fletcher, Angus John Stewart. *Allegory: The Theory of a Symbolic Mode*. Ithaca: Cornell University Press, 1964.
Fox, Michael. "Alcuin's Expositio in epistolam ad Hebraeos." *JML* 18 (2008): 326–45.
Frede, Hermann Josef. *Altlateinische Paulus-Handschriften*. Freiburg: Verlag Herder, 1964.
Frede, Hermann Josef. "Die Ordnung der Paulusbriefe und der Platz des Kolosserbriefs im Corpus Paulinum." In *Vetus Latina: Die Reste der altlateinischen Bibel*, 24/2, Lief. 4, 290–303. Freiburg: Herder, 1969.
Frede, Michael. "Celsus's Attack on the Christians." In *Philosophia Togata II: Plato and Aristotle at Rome*, ed. Jonathan Barnes and Miriam T. Griffin, 232–40. Oxford: Clarendon, 1997.
Fredriksen, Paula. "The Birth of Christianity and the Origins of Christian Anti-Judaism." In *Jesus, Judaism, and Christian Anti-Judaism: Reading the New Testament After the Holocaust*, ed. Paula Fredriksen and Adela Reinhartz, 8–30. Louisville: Westminster John Knox Press, 2002.
Fredriksen, Paula. "How Jewish Is God? Divine Ethnicity in Paul's Theology." *JBL* 137 (2018): 193–212.
Fredriksen, Paula. "Paul's Letter to the Romans, the Ten Commandments, and Pagan 'Justification by Faith.'" *JBL* 133 (2014): 801–8.
Fredriksen, Paula. "Why Should a 'Law-Free' Mission Mean a 'Law-Free' Apostle?" *JBL* 134 (2015): 637–50.
Fredriksen, Paula. *Paul, the Pagans' Apostle*. New Haven: Yale University Press, 2017.
Frey, Jörg. "Das Judentum des Paulus." In *Paulus.Leben—Umwelt—Werk—Briefe*, ed. Oda Wischmeyer, 25–65. UTB 2767. Tübingen: FranckeVerlag,[2]2012.
Fritzsche, Otto Fridolin. *Theodori episcopi Mopuesteni In novum testamentum commentariorum quae reperiri potuerunt*. Turici: Meyer et Zeller, 1847.

Froehlich, Karlfried. "Which Paul? Observations on the Image of the Apostle in the History of Biblical Exegesis." In *New Perspectives on Historical Theology: Essays in Memory of John Meyendorff*, ed. Bradley Nassif, 279-99. Grand Rapids: Eerdmans, 1996.

Ferguson, John. *Clement of Alexandria: Stromateis Books One to Three*. FC 85. Washington, D.C: Catholic University of America Press, 1991.

Fürst, A., and H. Strutwolf. *Der Kommentar zum Hohelied, Eingeleitet und übersetzt*. Origenes Werke mit deutscher Übersetzung, vol. 9.1. Berlin: de Gruyter, 2016.

Fürst, Alfons. *Christentum als Intellektuellen-Religion: Die Anfänge des Christentums in Alexandria, 36-42*. SBA 213. Stuttgart: Katholisches Bibelwerk, 2007.

Fürst, Alfons. "Origen: Exegesis and Philosophy in Early Christian Alexandria." In *Interpreting the Bible and Aristotle in Late Antiquity: The Alexandrian Commentary Tradition Between Rome and Baghdad*, ed Josef Lössl and John W. Watt, 13-32. Burlington: Ashgate, 2011.

Gäbel, Georg. "The Text of Hebrews in GA 1739, in Selected Other Greek Manuscripts, and in Works of Origen: Preliminary Quantitative Assessments." In *The New Testament in Antiquity and Byzantium: Traditional and Digital Approaches to Its Texts and Editing. A Festschrift for Klaus Wachtel*. ed. H. A. G. Houghton, D. C. Parker, and H. Strutwolf, 147-63. ANTF 52. Berlin: de Gruyter, 2019.

Gager, John. *The Origins of Anti-Semitism*. Oxford: Oxford University Press, 1983.

Gager, John. *Reinventing Paul*. Oxford: Oxford University Press, 2000.

Gager, John. *Who Made Early Christianity? The Jewish Lives of the Apostle Paul*. New York: Columbia University Press, 2017.

Gallagher, Edmon L. *Hebrew Scripture in Patristic Biblical Theory: Canon, Language, Text*. VCSup 114. Leiden: Brill, 2012.

Gallagher, Edmon L., and John D. Meade. *The Biblical Canon Lists from Early Christianity: Texts and Analysis*. Oxford: Oxford University Press, 2017.

Gamble, Harry Y. *Books and Readers in the Early Church: A History of Early Christian Texts*. New Haven: Yale University Press, 1995.

Gamble, Harry Y. *The New Testament Canon: Its Making and Meaning*. Philadelphia: Fortress, 1985.

Gamble, Harry Y. "The Redaction of the Pauline Letters." *JBL* 94 (1975): 409-14.

Gaston, Lloyd. "Paul and the Torah." In *Antisemitism and the Foundations of Christianity*, ed. Alan T. Davies, 48-71. New York: Paulist Press, 1979.

Gaston, Lloyd. *Paul and the Torah*. Vancouver: University of British Columbia Press, 1987.

Gathercole, Simon. "The Alleged Anonymity of the Canonical Gospels." *JTS* 69.2 (2018): 447-76.

Gathergood, Emily. "Papyrus 32 (Titus) as a Multi-Text Codex: A New Reconstruction." *NTS* 59 (2013): 588-606.

Gelardini, Gabriella. "'As If by Paul?' Some Remarks on the Textual Strategy of Anonymity in Hebrews." In *The Early Reception of Paul the Second Temple Jew: Text, Narrative and Reception History*, ed. Isaac W. Oliver and Gabriele Boccaccini, 267-86. London: T&T Clark, 2018.

Gelardini, Gabriella. "Hebrews, an Ancient Synagogue Homily for *Tisha be-Av*: Its Function, Its Basis, Its Theological Interpretation." In *Hebrews: Contemporary Methods—New Insights*, ed. Gabriella Gelardini, 107-27. Leiden: Boston, 2005.

Gelardini, Gabriella. *Verhärtet eure Herzen nicht: Der Hebräer, eine Synagogenhomilie zu Tischa be-Aw*. BibInt 83. Leiden: Brill, 2007.

Georgi, Dieter. "Hebrews and the Heritage of Paul." In *Hebrews: Contemporary Methods—New Insights*, ed. Gabriella Gelardini, 239-44. BIS 75. Leiden: Brill, 2005.

Geue, Tom. *Author Unknown: The Power of Anonymity in Ancient Rome*. Cambridge, MA: Harvard University Press, 2019.

Gibson, Roy. "On the Nature of Ancient Letter Collections." *JRS* 102 (2012): 56-78.

Gnilka, Joachim. "Das Paulusbild im Kolosser- und Epheserbrief." In *Kontinuität und Einheit: Festschrift für Franz Mussner*, ed. Paul-Gerhard Müller, Werner Stenger, and J. C. van Kesteren, 179-93. Freiburg: Herder, 1981.

Gögler, Rolf. *Zur Theologie des biblischen Wortes bei Origenes.* Düsseldorf: Patmos, 1963.
Gonnet, D. "L'utilisation christologique de l'Épître aux Hébreux dans les orations contra Arianos d'Athanase d'Alexandrie." *StPatr* 32 (1997): 19–24.
Goodspeed, Edgar J. *The Formation of the New Testament.* Chicago: University of Chicago Press, 1926.
Gotshtein, Alon Goshen. "Polemomania—Methodological Reflection on the Study of the Judeo-Christian Controversy Between the Talmudic Sages and Origin [sic] over the Interpretations of the Song of Songs / פולמוסומניה—הרהורים מיתודיים על חקר הוויכוח היהודי-נוצרי בעקבות פירושי חז"ל ואוריגנס לשיר-השירים." *JS* 42 (2003–4): 119–90.
Graetz, Heinrich. "Hillel, der Patriarchensohn." *MGWJ* 25 (1881): 433–34.
Grafton, Anthony, and Megan Williams. *Christianity and the Transformation of the Book: Origen, Eusebius, and the Library of Caesarea.* Cambridge, MA: Harvard University Press, 2006.
Grappe, Christian. "De quelques images de Paul et da la manière dont elles se déploient au cours de deuz premiers siècles." *FoiVie* 94 (1995): 49–59.
Grappe, Christian. "Hébreux et la tradition paulinienne." In *Receptions of Paul in Early Christianity: The Person of Paul and His Writings Through the Eyes of His Early Interpreters,* ed. J. Schröter, S. Butticaz, and A. Dettwiler, 461–83. Berlin: de Gruyter, 2018.
Gräßer, Eric. *An die Hebräer, 1 Teilband (Hebr 1–6).* EKKNT 17/1. Zurich: Benziger, 1990.
Graumann, Thomas. "Origenes—ein Kirchenvater? Vom Umgang mit dem origeneischen Erbe im frühen 4. Jahrhundert." In *Origeniana Octava: Origen and the Alexandria Tradition; Papers of the 8th International Origen Congress, Pisa 27–31 August 2001,* ed. Lorenzo Peroone, 877–88. Leuven: Leuven University Press, 2003.
Gray, Patrick. "The Early Reception of Hebrews 6:4–6." In *Scripture and Traditions: Essays on Early Judaism and Christianity in Honor of Carl R. Holladay,* ed. Patrick Gray and Gail R. O'Day, 321–39. Leiden: Brill, 2008.
Greer, Rowan A. *The Captain of Our Salvation: A Study in the Patristic Exegesis of Hebrews.* BGBE 15. Tübingen: Mohr Siebeck, 1973.
Gregory, Andrew. "First Clement and the Writings That Later Formed the New Testament." In *The Reception of the New Testament in the Apostolic Fathers,* ed. Andrew Gregory and Christopher Tuckett, 129–57. Oxford: Oxford University Press, 2005.
Gregory, Andrew. *The Gospel According to the Hebrews and the Gospel of the Ebionites.* Oxford: Oxford University Press, 2017.
Grenfell, B. P., and A. S. Hunt, *The Amherst Papyri I.* London: Oxford University Press, 1900.
Grenfell, B. P., and A. S. Hunt. "657. Epistle to the Hebrews." In *The Oxyrhynchus Papyri. Part IV,* 36–48. London: Egypt Exploration Fund, 1904.
Gruen, Erich. "Christians as a 'Third Race': Is Ethnicity at Issue?" In *Christianity in the Second Century: Themes and Developments,* ed. James Carleton Paget and Judith Lieu, 235–49. Cambridge: Cambridge University Press, 2017.
Gruen, Erich. *Ethnicity in the Ancient World—Did It Matter?* Berlin: de Gruyter, 2020.
Grünstäudl, Wolfgang. "The Quest for Pantaenus: Paul Collomp, Wilhelm Bousset, and Johannes Munck on an Alexandrian Enigma." In *Alexandria: Hub of the Hellenistic World,* ed. Benjamin Schliesser, Jan Rüggemeier, Thomas J. Karus, and Jörg Frey, 413–39. WUNT 460. Tübingen: Mohr Siebeck, 2021.
Guignard, Christophe. "The Muratorian Fragment as a Late Antique Fake? An Answer to C. K. Rothschild." *RevSR* 93 (2019): 73–90.
Guignard, Christophe. "The Original Language of the Muratorian Fragment." *JTS* 66.2 (2015): 596–624.
Guinot, Jean-Noël. "La christologie de Théodoret de Cyr dans son commentaire sur le Cantique." *VC* 39 (1985): 256–72.
Gwynn, David M. *The Eusebians: The Polemic of Athanasius and the Construction of the "Arian Controversy".* Oxford: Oxford University Press, 2006.

Habermehl, Peter, ed. *Origenes Werke, Band 6 Homilien zum Hexateuch in Rufins Übersetzung, Teil 1: Die Homilien zu Genesis.* GCS Neue Folge 17. Berlin: de Gruyer, 2012.

Hadot, I. "Les introductions aux commentaires exégétiques chez les auteurs néoplatoniciens et les auteurs chrétiens." In *Les règles de l'interpretation*, ed. M. Tardieu, 99–122. Paris: Cerf, 1987.

Hagner, Donald A. *The Use of the Old and New Testaments in Clement of Rome.* NovTSup 34. Leiden: Brill, 1973.

Hahneman, Geoffrey Mark. "More on Redating the Muratorian Fragment." *StPatr* 19 (1988): 359–65.

Hahneman, Geoffrey Mark. *The Muratorian Fragment and the Development of the Canon.* Oxford: Clarendon Press, 1992.

Haidacher, S. "Rede des Nestorius über Hebr. 2,1 überliefert unter dem Namen des hl. Chrysostomus." *ZKT* 29 (1905): 192–95.

Hallman, Joseph M. "The Communication of Idioms in Theodoret's Commentary on Hebrews." In *In Dominico Eloquio = In Lordly Eloquence: Essays on Patristic Exegesis in Honour of Robert Louis Wilken*, ed. Paul M. Blowers, Angela Russell Christman, David G. Hunter, and Robin Darling Young, 369–79. Grand Rapids: Eerdmans, 2002.

Halperin, David J. "Origen, Ezekiel's Merkabah, and the Ascension of Moses." *CH* 50 (1981): 261–75.

Hammond, Caroline P. "The Last Ten Years of Rufinus's Life and the Date of His Move South from Aquileia." *JTS n.s.* 28 (1977): 327–429.

Hammond Bammel, Caroline P. *Der Römerbrief des Rufin und seine Origenes-Übersetzung.* AGLB 10. Freiburg: Hinrichs, 1985.

Hammond Bammel, Caroline P. *Der Römerbriefkommentar des Origenes: Kritische Ausgabe der Übersetzung Rufins, Buch 4–6.* Vetus Latina 33. Frieburg: Herder, 1998.

Hammond Bammel, Caroline P. *Der Römerbriefkommentar des Origenes: Kritische Ausgabe der Übersetzung Rufins, Buch 7–10.* Vetus Latina 34. Frieburg: Herder, 1998.

Hammond Bammel, Caroline P. "A New Witness to the Scholia from Origen in the Codex von der Goltz." In *Origeniana Quinta: Papers of the 5th International Origen Congress, Boston College, 14–18 August 1989*, ed. Robert Daly, 137–41. BETL 105. Leuven: Peeters, 1992.

Hammond Bammel, Caroline P. "Origen's Pauline Prefaces and the Chronology of His Pauline Commentaries." In *Origeniana Sexta: Origène et la Bible / Origen and the Bible. Actes du Colloquium Origenianum Sextum Chantilly, 30 août–3 septembre 1993*, ed. Gilles Dorival and Alain Le Boulluec, 509–10. Leuven: Peeters, 1995.

Hanson, R. P. C. *Origen's Doctrine of Tradition.* London: SPCK, 1954.

Harl, Marguerite. "Structure et cohérence du *Peri Archôn*." In *Origeniana, Premier colloque international des études origéniennes (Montserrat, 18–21 septembre 1971)*, ed. Henri Crouzel, Gennaro Lomiento, and Josep Rius-Camps, 11–32. Bari: Università di Bari, 1975.

Harl, Marguerite. *Origène et la fonction révélatrice du Verbe Incarné.* Patristica Sorbonensia 2. Paris: Éditions du Seuil, 1958.

Harl, Marguerite, and Nicholas de Lange, eds. *Origène, Philocalie 1–20 sur les Écritures et La Lettre à Africanus sur l'histoire de Suzanne.* SC 302. Paris: Cerf, 1983.

Harnack, Adolf von. *Die Briefsammlung des Apostels Paulus und die anderen vorkonstantinischenchristlichen Brief Sammlungen.* Leipzig: Hinrichs, 1926.

Harnack, Adolf von. "Ein neues Fragment aus den Hypotyposen des Clemens." *Sitzungsberichte der Berliner Akademie der Wissenschaften* (1904): 901–8.

Harnack, Adolf von. "Probabilia über die Adresse und den Verfasser des Hebräerbriefs." *ZNW* 1 (1900): 16–41.

Harris, James Rendel. "Euthalius and Eusebius." In *Hermas in Arcadia and Other Essays*, ed. James Rendel Harris, 60–83. Cambridge: Cambridge University Press, 1896.

Harris, James Rendel. *Stichometry.* London: C. J. Clay & Sons, 1893.

Hart, Patrick. *Prolegomena to the Study of Paul.* SuppMTSR 15. Leiden: Brill, 2020.

Harvey, Graham. *The True Israel: Uses of the Names Jew, Hebrew, and Israel in Ancient Jewish and Early Christian Literature.* Leiden: Brill, 2001.

Hatch, William Henry Paine. "The Position of Hebrews in the Canon of the NT." *HTR* 29 (1936): 133–51.

Hatch, William Henry Paine. "A Redating of Two Important Uncial Manuscripts of the Gospels—Codex Zacynthius and Codex Cyprius." In *Quantulacumque: Studies Presented to Kirsopp Lake,* ed. R. P. Casey, S. Lake, and A. K. Lake, 333–38. London: Christophers, 1937.

Hatch, William Henry Paine, and C. Bradford Wells. "A Hitherto Unpublished Fragment of the Epistle to the Ephesians." *HTR* 51.1 (1958): 33–37.

Havrda, Matyáš. *The So-Called Eighth "Stromateus" by Clement of Alexandria: Early Christian Reception of Greek Scientific Methodology.* Philosophia antiqua, 144. Leiden: Brill, 2016.

Head, P. M., and M. Warren. "Re-Inking the Pen: Evidence from P. Oxy. 657 (P13) Concerning Unintentional Scribal Errors." *NTS* 43 (1997): 469–73.

Heath, Jane. *Clement of Alexandria and the Shaping of Christian Literary Practice: Miscellany and the Transformation of Greco-Roman Writing.* Cambridge: Cambridge University Press, 2020.

Hegermann, Harald. *Der Brief an die Hebräer.* ThHKNT 16. Berlin: Evangelische, 1988.

Heine, Ronald. *Origen: Homilies on Genesis and Exodus.* FC 71. Washington, DC: Catholic University of American Press, 1982.

Heine, Ronald. "Origen and the Eternal Boundaries." In *Die Septuaginta und das frühe Christentum / The Septuagint and Christian Origins,* ed. Thomas Scott Caulley and Hermann Lichtenberger, 393–409. WUNT 277. Tübingen: Mohr Siebeck, 2011.

Heine, Ronald. *Origen Commentary on the Gospel According to John Books 13–32.* FC 89. Washington, DC: Catholic University of America Press, 1993.

Heine, Ronald. *Origen: Scholarship in the Service of the Church.* Oxford: Oxford University Press, 2010.

Heither, Theresia. "Origenes als Exeget: Ein Forschungsüberblick." In *Stimuli: Exegese und ihre Hermeneutik in Antike und Christentum, Festschrift für Ernst Dassmann,* ed. Georg Schöllgen and Clements Scholten, 141–53. Münster: Aschendorff, 1996.

Heither, Theresia. *Translatio Religionis: Die Paulusdeutung des Origenes in seinem Kommentar zum Römerbrief.* Bonner Beiträge zur Kirchengeschichte 16. Cologne: Boehlau, 1990.

Hemmerdinger, Bertrand. "Euthaliana." *JTS* 11 (1960): 349–55.

Hemmerdinger, Bertrand. "L'auteur de l'édition 'Euthalienne.'" In *Acten des XI. Internationalen Byzantinistenkongresses, München 1958,* ed. by Franz Dölger and Hans-Georg Beck, 227–31. Munich: C. H. Beck, 1960.

Hengel, Martin. *Between Jesus and Paul.* Philadelphia: Fortress, 1983.

Henne, Philippe. "La datation du canon de Muratori." *RB* 100 (1993): 54–75.

Héring, Jean. *L'Épître aux Hébreux.* CNT 12. Neuchatel-Paris, 1954.

Hilgenfeld, Adolf. *Historisch-kritische Einleitung in das Neue Testament.* Leipzig: R. Reisland, 1875.

Hill, C. C. *Hellenists and Hebrews.* Minneapolis: Fortress, 1992.

Hirshman, Marc. "Origen and the Rabbis on Leviticus." *Adamantius* 11 (2005): 93–100.

Hirshman, Marc. "Reflections on the Aggada of Caesarea." In *Caesarea Maritima: A Retrospective after Two Millennia,* ed. Kenneth G. Holum and Avner Raban, 469–75. Leiden: Köln, 1998.

Hofius, Otfried. *Der Vorhang vor dem Thron Gottes: Eine exegetish-religionsgeschichtliche Untersuchung zu Hebräer 6,19f. und 10,19ff.* WUNT 14. Tübingen: Mohr Siebeck, 1971.

Holl, Karl. ed. *Epiphanius Dritter Band: Panarion haer. 65–80.* GCS 37. Leipzig: Hinrichs, 1933.

Hombergen, Daniel. *The Second Origenist Controversy: A New Perspective on Cyril of Scythopolis' Monastic Biographies as Historical Sources for Sixth-Century Origenism*. Rome: Pontificio Ateneo S. Anselmo, 2001.
Honoratus, Maurus Servius. *In Vergilii carmina comentarii. Servii Grammatici qui feruntur in Vergilii carmina commentarii*. Ed. Georgius Thilo. Leipzig: Teubner, 1881.
Horbury, William. "Origen and the Jews: Jewish-Greek and Jewish-Christian relations." In *The Jewish-Greek Tradition in Antiquity and the Byzantine Empire*, ed. James K. Aitken and James Carleton Paget, 79–90. Cambridge: Cambridge University Press, 2014.
Hornschuh, Manfred. "Das Leben des Origenes und die Entstehung der alexandrinischen Schule." *ZKG* 71 (1960): 1–25, 193–214.
Horsley, Richard. "Pneumatikos vs. Psychikos Distinctions of Spiritual Status among the Corinthians." *HTR* 69 (1976): 269–88.
Hoskier, H. C. "A Commentary on the Various Readings in the Text of the Epistle to the Hebrews in Chester-Beatty." *RB* 46 (1937): 58–82.
Hoskier, H. C. *A Commentary on the Various Readings in the Text of the Epistle to the Hebrews in the Chester-Beatty Papyrus* $\mathfrak{P}^{46}$ *(circa 200 A.D.)*. London: Bernard Quaritch, 1938.
Hoskier, H. C. "The Lost Commentary of Oecumenius on the Apocalypse." *AJP* 34 (1913): 300–314.
Hoskier, H. C. ed. *The Complete Commentary of Oecumenius on the Apocalypse*. Ann Arbor: University of Michigan, 1928.
Houghton, H. A. G. "The Layout of Early Latin Commentaries on the Pauline Epistles and Their Oldest Manuscripts." *StPatr* 91 (2017): 71–112.
Hovhanessian, Vahan. *Third Corinthians: Reclaiming Paul for Christian Orthodoxy*. StBibLit 18. New York: Peter Lang, 2000.
Huffman, Carl. *Philolaus of Croton: Pythagorean and Presocratic. A Commentary on the Fragments and Testimonia with Interpretive Essays*. Cambridge: Cambridge University Press, 1993.
Hunt, Arthur S. "1078. Epistle to the Hebrews IX." In *The Oxyrhynchus Papyri. Part VIII*, ed. Arthur Hunt, 11–13. London: Egypt Exploration Fund, 1911.
Hurtado, Larry. *The Earliest Christian Artifacts Manuscripts and Christian Origins*. Grand Rapids: Eerdmans, 2006.
Hyldahl, Niels. "The Reception of Paul in the Acts of the Apostles." In *The New Testament as Reception*, ed. Mogens Müller and Henrik Tronier, 101–19. JSNTSup 230. Sheffield: Sheffield Academic Press, 2002.
Inowlocki, Sabrina. "Eusebius of Caesarea's *Interpretatio Christiana* of Philo's De vita contemplative." *HTR* 97.3 (2004): 305–28.
Irvine, Martin. *The Making of Textual Culture: "Grammatica" and Literary Theory, 350–1100*. Cambridge: Cambridge University Press, 1994.
Īshoʻdād of Merv, *The Commentaries of Ishoʻdad of Merv: Bishop of Hadatha (c. 850 A.D.) in Syriac and English*. Vol 5, Part 2. Ed. Margaret Dunlop Gibson and J. Rendel Harris. Cambridge University Press, 1916.
Itter, Andrew. *Esoteric Teaching in the "Stromateis" of Clement of Alexandria*. Leiden: Brill, 2009.
Jacobs, Andrew. "A Jew's Jew: Paul and the Early Christian Problem of Jewish Origins." *JR* 86 (2006): 258–86.
Jacobs, Andrew. "The Lion and the Lamb: Reconsidering 'Jewish-Christian Relations' in Antiquity." In *The Ways That Never Parted: Jews and Christians in Late Antiquity and the Early Middle Ages*, ed. A. H. Becker and A. Y. Reed, 95–118. Tübingen: Mohr Siebeck, 2003.
Jacobs, Andrew. *Remains of the Jews: The Holy Land and Christian Empire in Late Antiquity*. Stanford: Stanford University Press, 2004.
Jacobsen, Anders-Christian. *Christ—the Teacher of Salvation: A Study on Origen's Christology and Soteriology*. Münster: Aschendorff Verlag, 2015.

Jakab, Attila. *Ecclesia alexandrina: Evolution sociale et institutionelle du christianisme alexandrine (IIe et IIIe siècles)*. Christianismes anciens 1. Bern: Peter Land, 2001.

Jervell, J. "Paulus in der Apostelgeschichte und die Geschichte des Urchristentums." *NTS* 32 (1986): 378–92.

Johnston, Steve. "La Correspondance apocryphe entre Paul et les Corinthiens: Un pseudépigraphe paulinien au service de la polémique anti-gnostique de la fin du IIe siècle." In *Colloque international "L'Évangile selon Thomas et les textes de Nag Hammad"*, ed. Louis Painchaud and Paul-Hubert Poirier, 226–29. BCNH 8. Quebec: Presses Université Laval, 2007.

Jones, E. D. "The Authorship of Hebrews xiii." *ExpTim* (1934–35): 562–67.

Kaestli, Jean-Daniel. "La place du Fragment de Muratori dans l'histoire du canon: À propos de la thèse de Sundberg et Hahnemann." *CrSt* 15.3 (1994): 609–34.

Kaler, Michael, Louis Painchaud, and Marie-Pierre Bussières. "The Coptic Apocalypse of Paul, Irenaeus' Adversus Haereses 2.30.7, and the Second-Century Battle for Paul's Legacy." *JECS* 12 (2004): 173–93.

Karo, Georg, and Hans Lietzmann. *Catenarum Graecarum Catalogus*. Nachrichten der Akademie der Wissenschaften zu Göttingen, Philologisch-historische Klasse. Göttingen: Lüder Horstmann, 1902.

Kasher, Aryeh. *The Jews in Hellenistic and Roman Egypt: The Struggle for Equal Rights*. TSAJ 7. Tübingen: Mohr Siebeck, 1978.

Kenyon, Frederic G. *Books and Readers in Ancient Greece and Rome*. Oxford: Clarendon, 1932.

Kenyon, Frederic G., ed. *The Chester Beatty Biblical Papyri: Descriptions and Texts of Twelve Manuscripts on Papyrus of the Greek Bible. Fasciculus III Supplement Pauline Epistles, Plates*. London: Emery Walker, 1937.

Kenyon, Frederic G., ed. *The Chester Beatty Biblical Papyri: Descriptions and Texts of Twelve Manuscripts on Papyrus of the Greek Bible. Fasciculus III Supplement Pauline Epistles, Text*. London: Emery Walker, 1934.

Kettler, F. H. "War Origenes Schüler des Ammonios Sakkas?" In *Epektasis: Mélanges patristiques offerts au Cardinal Jean Daniélou*, ed. J. Fontaine and C. Kannengiesser, 327–35. Paris: Beauchesne, 1972.

Kibbe, Michael. "Is It Finished? When Did It Start? Hebrews, Priesthood, and Atonement in Biblical, Systematic, and Historical Perspective." *JTS* 65 (2014): 25–61.

Kim, K. W. "Codices 1582, 1739, and Origen." *JBL* 69 (1950): 167–75.

Kim, Young Kyu. "Palaeographical Dating of P[46] to the Later First Century." *Bib* 69 (1988): 248–57.

Kimelman, Reuven. "Rabbi Yohanan and Origen on the Song of Songs: A Third-Century Jewish-Christian Disputation." *HTR* 73 (1980): 567–95.

Kindiy, Oleh. "Approximating Church and School in Clement of Alexandria's Stromateis VII." In *The Seventh Book of the Stromateis: Proceedings of the Colloquium on Clement of Alexandria, Olomouc, October 21–23, 2010*, ed. Matyáš Havrda, Vít Hušek, and Jana Plátová, 291–98. VCSup. 117. Leiden: Brill, 2012.

Kindiy, Oleh. *Christos Didaskalos: The Christology of Clement of Alexandria*. Saarbrücken: Verlag Dr. Müller, 2008.

King, J. Christopher. *Origen on the Song of Songs as the Spirit of Scripture: The Bridegroom's Perfect Marriage-Song*. Oxford: Oxford University Press, 2005.

Kinzig, Wolfgang. "Καινὴ διαθήκη: The Title of the New Testament in the Second and Third Centuries." *JTS* 45 (1994): 519–44.

Kister, Menahem. "Allegorical Interpretations of Biblical Narratives in Rabbinic Literature, Philo, and Origen: Some Case Studies." In *New Approaches to the Study of Biblical Interpretation in Judaism of the Second Temple Period and in Early Christianity*, ed. Gary Anderson, Ruth Clements, and David Satran, 133–83. Leiden: Brill, 2013.

Klauck, Hans-Josef. *Allegorie und Allegorese in synoptischen Gleichnistexten*. NA 13. Münster: Aschendorff 1978.

Klauck, Hans-Josef. *Die antike Briefliteratur und das Neue Testament: Ein Lehr und Arbeitsbuch*. Paderborn: Ferdinand Schöningh, 1998.
Klijn, A. F. J. "Jewish Christianity in Egypt." In *The Roots of Egyptian Christianity*, ed. Birger A. Pearson and James E. Goehring, 161–75. Studies in Antiquity and Christianity. Philadelphia: Fortress, 1986.
Klostermann, Erich, ed. *Origenes Werke X, Matthäuserklärung I*. GCS 40. Berlin: de Gruyter, 1935.
Klostermann, Erich, and Pierre Nautin, ed. *Origenes Werke III. Jeremiahomilien. Klageliederkommentar. Erklärung der Samuel- und Königsbücher*. GCS 6. Berlin: de Gruyter, 1983.
Knauber, Adolf. "Das Anliegen der Schule des Origenes zu Cäsaraea." *Münchener Theologische Zeitschrift* 19 (1968): 182–203.
Knauber, Adolf. "Katechetenschule oder Schulkatechumenat? Um die rechte Deutung des 'Unternehmens' der ersten grossen Alexandriner." *TThZ* 60 (1951): 243–66.
Knox, John. *Philemon Among the Letters of Paul: A New View of Its Place and Importance*. Chicago: University of Chicago Press, 1939.
Koch, Hal. *Pronoia und Paideusis: Studien über Origenes und sein Verhältnis zum Platonismus*. Berlin: de Gruyter, 1932.
Koetschau, Paul, ed. *Origenes Werke I, Die Schrift vom Martyrium, Buch I–IV gegen Celsus*. GCS 2. Berlin: de Gruyer, 1899.
Koetschau, Paul, ed. *Origenes Werke V, De Principiis*. GCS 22. Berlin: de Gruyter, 1913.
Kovacs, Judith. "Clement of Alexandria and Valentinian Exegesis in the Excerpts from Theodotus." *StPatr* 41 (2006): 187–200.
Kovacs, Judith. "Concealment and Gnostic Exegesis: Clement of Alexandria's Interpretation of the Tabernacle." *StPatr* 31 (1997): 414–37.
Kovacs, Judith. "Divine Pedagogy and the Gnostic Teacher According to Clement of Alexandria. *JECS* 9.1 (2001): 3–25.
Kovacs, Judith. "Echoes of Valentinian Exegesis in Clement of Alexandria and Origen: The Interpretation of 1 Cor 3.1–3." In *Origeniana Octava: Origen and the Alexandria Tradition; Papers of the 8th International Origen Congress, Pisa 27–31 August 2001*, ed. Lorenzo Peroone, 317–29. Leuven: Peeters, 2003.
Kovacs, Judith. "Grace and Works: Clement of Alexandria's Response to Valentinian Exegesis of Paul." In *Ancient Perspectives on Paul*, ed. Tobias Nicklas, Andreas Merkt, and Joseph Verheyden, 191–210. NTOA/SUNT 102. Göttingen: Vandenhoeck & Ruprecht, 2013.
Kovacs, Judith. "Reading the 'Divinely Inspired' Paul: Clement of Alexandria in Conversation with 'Heterodox' Christians, Simple Believers, and Greek Philosophers." In *Clement's Biblical Exegesis: Proceedings of the Second Colloquium on Clement of Alexandria (Olomouc, May 29–31, 2014)*, ed. Veronika Cernuskova, Judith L. Kovacs, and Jana Plátová, 325–43. Leiden: Brill, 2017.
Kovacs, Judith. "Saint Paul as Apostle of Apatheia: Stromateis VII, Chapter 14." In *The Seventh Book of the Stromateis: Proceedings of the Colloquium on Clement of Alexandria, Olomouc, October 21–23, 2010*, ed. Matyáš Havrda, Vít Hušek, and Jana Plátová, 199–216. VCSup 117. Leiden: Brill, 2012.
Kovacs, Judith. "Was Paul an Antinomian, a Radical Ascetic, or a Sober Married Man? Exegetical Debates in Clement of Alexandria's *Stromateis* 3." In *Asceticism and Exegesis in Early Christianity: The Reception of New Testament Texts in Ancient Ascetic Discourses*, ed. Hans-Ulrich Weidemann, 186–202. NTOA/SUNT 101. Göttingen: Vandenhoeck & Ruprecht, 2013.
Kraft, Robert. "Barnabas' Isaiah Text and the 'Testimony Book' Hypothesis." *JBL* 79.4 (1960): 336–50.
Kraus, Wolfgang. "Zu Absicht und Zielsetzung des Hebräerbriefes." *KD* 60 (2014): 250–71.
Krauss, Samuel. "The Jews in the Works of the Church Fathers." *JQR* o.s. 5 (1893): 122–57.

Kutter, Hermann. *Clemens Alexandrinus und das Neue Testament: Eine Untersuchung.* Giessen: J. Richer Buchhandlung, 1897.
Lake, Kirsopp. *The Earlier Epistles of St. Paul: Their Motive and Origin.* London: Rivingtons, 1911.
Lake, Kirsopp, and Silva Lake. "The Scribe Ephraim." *JBL* 62 (1943): 263–68.
Lake, Kirsopp, Johannes de Zwaan, and Morton S. Enslin. "Athos, Laura 184 [B'64] (Greg. 1739; von Soden α78), Acts, Catholic Epistles, Paul." In *Six Collations of New Testament Manuscripts*, ed. Kirsopp Lake and Silva New, 216–17. HTS 17. Cambridge, MA: Harvard University Press, 1932.
Lamberton, Robert D. *Homer the Theologian: Neoplatonist Allegorical Reading and the Growth of the Epic Tradition.* Berkeley: University of California Press, 1986.
Lamoreaux, J. C. "The Provenance of Ecumenius' Commentary on the Apocalypse." *VC* 52 (1998): 88–108.
Landmesser, Christof. "Ferdinand Christian Baur as Interpreter of Paul: History, the Absolute, and Freedom." In *Ferdinand Christian Baur and the History of Early Christianity*, ed. Martin Bauspiess, Christof Landmesser, and David Lincicum, 147–76. Oxford: Oxford University Press, 2017.
Lang, Manfred, ed. *Paulus und Paulusbilder: Konstruktion—Reflexion—Transformation.* ABG 31. Leipzig: Evangelische Verlagsanstalt, 2013.
Lang, T. J. "Arts of Memory, Ancient Manuscript Technologies, and the Aims of Theology." *Religions* 13 (2022): 1–13.
Lang, T. J., and Matthew Crawford. "The Origins of Pauline Theology: Paratexts and Priscillian of Avila's Canons on the Letters of the Apostle Paul." *NTS* 63 (2017): 125–45.
Langton, Daniel R. *The Apostle Paul in the Jewish Imagination: A Study in Modern Jewish-Christian Relations.* Cambridge: Cambridge University Press, 2014.
Larcher, Richard, trans., *Aquinas, Commentary on the Letter of Saint Paul to the Hebrews*, ed. J. Mortensen. Lander: Aquinas Institute for the Study of Sacred Doctrine, 2012.
Larsen, Matthew D. C., and Mark Letteney. "Christians and the Codex: Generic Materiality and Early Gospel Traditions." *JECS* 27.3 (2019): 383–415.
Laub, Franz. "'Ein für allemal hineingegangen in das Allerheiligste' (Hebr 9,12)—Zum Verständnis des Kreuzestodes im Hebräerbrief." *BZ* 35 (1991): 65–85.
Laub, Franz. "Verkündigung und Gemeindeamt: Die Autorität der ἡγούμενοι Hebr 13, 7.17.24." *SNTSU* 6–7 (1981–82): 169–90.
Lawson, R. P. *Origen: The Song of Songs Commentary and Homilies.* ACW 26. Westminster: Newman Press, 1957.
Layton, Richard A. "Catenae." In *The Oxford Handbook of Early Christian Biblical Interpretation.* ed. Paul M. Blowers and Peter M. Martens, 220–28. Oxford: Oxford University Press, 2019.
Le Boulluec, Alain. "Aux origins, encore, de l'école' d'Alexandrie." *Adamantius* 5 (1999): 7–36.
Le Boulluec, Alain. "Clement d'Alexandrie." In *Dictionnaire des philosophes antiques*, vol. 2, *Babélyca d'Argos à Dyscolius*, ed. Richard Goulet, 426–31. Paris: Brepols, 1994.
Le Boulluec, Alain. "De l'usage de titres 'néotestamentaires' chez Clément." In *La formation des canons scripturaires*, ed. M. Tardieu, 191–202. Paris: Cerf, 1993.
Le Boulluec, Alain. "De Paul à Origène: Continuité ou divergence?" In *Allégorie des poètes, allégorie des philosophes: Études sur la poétique et l'herméneutique de l'allégorie de l'antiquité à la réforme*, ed. Gilbert Dahan and Richard Goulet, 113–32. Fédération de recherche 33 du C.N.R.S., Textes et traditions 10. Paris: Vrin, 2005.
Le Boulluec, Alain. "L'école d'Alexandrie: De quelques aventures d'un concept." In *ΑΛΕΞΑΝΔΡΙΝΑ: Hellénisme, judaïsme et christianisme à Alexandrie. Mélanges offerts au P. Claude Mondésert*, 403–17. Paris: Les Editions du Cerf, 1987.
Le Boulluec, Alain. *La notion d'hérésie dans la littérature grecque IIe-IIIe siècles.* Vol. 2. Paris: Études Augustiniennes, 1985.

Le Boulluec, Alain. "La rencontre de l'hellénisme et de la 'philosophie barbare' selon Clément d'Alexandrie." In *Alexandrie: Une mégapole cosmopolite*, ed. Jean Leclant, 186–88. Paris: de Boccard, 1999.
Levey, Irving M. "Caesarea and the Jews." In *The Joint Expedition to Caesarea Maritima*, vol. 1, ed. C. T. Fritsch, 43–78. Missoula: Scholars Press, 1975.
Levine, Lee I. *The Ancient Synagogue: The First Thousand Years*. New Haven: Yale University Press, 2000.
Levine, Lee. *Caesarea under Roman Rule*. SJLA 7. Leiden: Brill, 1975.
Levine, Lee. "Synagogue Leadership: The Case of the Archisynagogue." In *Jews in a Graeco-Roman World*, ed. Martin Goodman, 181–94. Oxford: Oxford University Press, 1998.
Leyerle, Blake. "John Chrysostom on Almsgiving and the Use of Money." *HTR* 87 (1994): 29–47.
Lietzmann, Hans. *Catenen: Mitteilungen über ihre Geschichte in handschriftlicher Überlieferung*. Freiburg: Mohr Siebeck, 1897.
Lieu, Judith M. "'As Much My Apostle as Christ Is Mine': The Dispute over Paul Between Tertullian and Marcion." *EC* 1 (2010): 41–59.
Lieu, Judith M. "The Battle for Paul in the Second Century." *ITQ* 75 (2010): 3–14.
Lieu, Judith M. *Image and Reality: The Jews in the World of the Christians in the Second Century*. Edinburgh: T&T Clark, 1996.
Liljeström, Kenneth, ed. *The Early Reception of Paul*. Helsinki: Finnish Exegetical Society, 2011.
Lilla, S. R. C. *Clement of Alexandria: A Study in Christian Platonism and Gnosticism*. Oxford: Oxford University Press, 1971.
Lindemann, Andreas. *Apostel und Lehrer der Kirche: Studien zu Paulus und zum frühen Paulusverständnis*. Tübingen: Mohr Siebeck, 1999.
Lindemann, Andreas. "Der Apostel Paulus im 2 Jahrhundert." In *The New Testament in Early Christianity, La reception des écrit néotestamentaires dans le christianisme primitif*, ed. Jean-Marie Sevrin, 39–67. BETHhL 86. Leuven: Leuven University Press, 1989.
Lindemann, Andreas. *Paulus im ältesten Christentum: Das Bild des Apostels und die Rezeption der paulinischen Theologie in der frühchristlichen Literatur bis Marcion*. BHT 58. Tübingen: Mohr Siebeck, 1979.
Lindl, Ernest. *Die Oktateuchcatene des Prokop von Gaza und die Septuagintaforschung*. Munich: Hermann Lukaschik, 1902.
Lods, Marc. "Étude sur les sources juives de la polémique de Celse contre les chrétiens." *RHPR* 21 (1941): 1–33.
Löhr, Winrich. *Basilides und seine Schule*. WUNT 83. Tübingen: Mohr Siebeck, 1996.
Löhr, Winrich. "Christian Gnostics and Greek Philosophy in the Second Century." *EC* 3 (2012): 349–77.
Lohse, Bernhard. "Beobachtungen zum Paulus-Kommentar des Marius Victorinus und zur Wiederentdeckung des Paulus in der lateinischen Theologie des vierten Jahrhunderts." In *Kerygma and Logos: Beiträge zu den geistesgeschichtlichen Beziehungen zwischen Antike und Christentum. Festschrift für Carl Andresen zum 80. Geburtstag*, ed. Adolf Martin Ritter, 351–66. Göttingen: Vanderhoeck & Ruprecht, 1979.
Lona, E. *Der erste Clemensbrief*. Göttingen: Vandenhoeck & Ruprecht, 1998.
Lorrain, Agnès. "Autour du Vaticanus gr. 762: Notes pour l'étude des chaînes à présentation alternante." *Byzantion* 90 (2020): 67–95.
Lorrain, Agnès. "Des prologues bibliques d'origine chrysostomienne: Les arguments attribués à Théodoret et à Théophylacte sur les épîtres pauliniennes." *ZAC* 19 (2015): 481–501.
Lubac, Henri. *Histoire et esprit: L'intelligence de l'écriture d'après Origène*. Paris: Aubier, 1950.
Lüdemann, Gerd. *Paulus, der Heidenapostel*. Vol. 2, *Antipaulinismus im frühen Christentum*. FRLANT 130. Göttingen: Vandenhoeck & Ruprecht, 1983.
Luijendijk, Annemarie. "Sacred Scriptures as Trash: Biblical Papyri from Oxyrhynchus." *VC* 64 (2010): 217–54.

Lünemann, Gottlieb. *Kritisch Exegetisches Handbuch über den Hebräerbrief.* KEK 13. Göttingen: Vandenhoeck & Ruprecht, 1855.
Machiela, Daniel A., and Robert Jones. "Was There a Revival of Hebrew During the Hasmonean Period? A Reassessment of the Evidence." *JAJ* 12 (2021): 217–80.
MacLachlan, R. F. "The Context of Commentary: Non-Biblical Commentary in the Early Christian Period." In *Commentaries, Catenae and Biblical Tradition,* ed. H. A. G. Houghton, 37–64. Texts and Studies 13. Piscataway: Gorgias, 2016.
Manns, Frédéric. "Une tradition juive dans les Commentaires du Cantique des Cantiques d'Origène." *Antonianum* 65 (1990): 3–22.
Mansfeld, Jaap. *Prolegomena: Questions to Be Settled Before the Study of an Author, or a Text.* PhA 61. Leiden: Brill, 1994.
Manson, William. *The Epistle to the Hebrews: An Historical and Theological Reconsideration.* 2nd ed. London: Hodder & Stoughton, 1953.
Mantovani, Dario. *Les juristes écrivains de la Rome antique: Les oeuvres des juristes comme litterature.* Docet omnia 3. Paris: Les Belles Lettres, 2018.
Marguerat, Daniel. "Paul après Paul: Une histoire de réception." *NTS* 54 (2008): 317–37.
Marguerat, Daniel. *Paul in Acts and Paul in His Letters.* WUNT 310. Tübingen: Mohr Siebeck, 2013.
Markschies, Christoph. "Valentinian Gnosticism: Towards the Anatomy of a School." In *The Nag Hammadi Library After Fifty Years,* ed. John D. Turner and Anne McGuire, 401–38. NHMS 44. Leiden: Brill, 1997.
Marmorstein, A. "Deux renseignements d'Origène concernant les juifs." *REJ* 71 (1920): 190–99.
Marrou, Henri-Irénée. *Histoire de l'education dans l'antiquité.* Paris: Seuil, 1956.
Marrou, Henri-Irénée, and Marguerite Harl, eds. *Le Pédagogue.* Vol. 1. SC 70. Paris: Éditions du Cerf, 1949.
Marshall, John. "From Small Words: Reading Deixis and Scope in Romans." *JJMJS* 4 (2017): 1–20.
Marshall, John. "Misunderstanding the New Paul: Marcion's Transformation of the Sonderzeit Paul." *JECS* 20 (2012): 1–29.
Martens, Peter. "The Modern Receptions of Origen's Biblical Scholarship: A Bibliographic Essay." In *Origeniana Undecima: Origen and Origenism in the History of Western Thought; Papers of the 11th International Origen Congress, Aarhus University, 26–31 August 2013,* ed. Ander-Christian Jacobsen, 67–86. BETL 279. Leuven: Peeters, 2016.
Martens, Peter. *Origen and Scripture: The Contours of the Exegetical Life.* Oxford: Oxford University Press, 2012.
Martens, Peter. "Revisiting the Allegory/Typology Distinction: The Case of Origen." *JECS* 16 (2008): 283–317.
Martens, Peter. "Why Does Origen Accuse the Jews of 'Literalism'? A Case Study of Christian Identity and Biblical Exegesis in Antiquity." *Adamantius* 13 (2007): 218–30.
Mason, Eric. *"You Are a Priest Forever": Second Temple Jewish Messianism and the Priestly Christology of the Epistle to the Hebrews.* STDJ 74. Leiden: Brill, 2008.
Maxwell, Jaclyn L. *Christianization and Communication in Late Antiquity: John Chrysostom and His Congregation in Antioch.* Cambridge: Cambridge University Press, 2009.
Mayer, Wendy. *The Homilies of St John Chrysostom—Provenance: Reshaping the Foundations.* Orientalia Christiana Analecta 273. Rome: Pontificium Institutum Orientalium Studiorum, 2005.
Mayer, Wendy. "Les Homélies de Jean Chrysostome: Problèmes concernant la provenance, l'ordre et la datation." *REAug* 52 (2006): 329–53.
McGuckin, John. "Caesarea Maritima as Origen Knew It." In *Origeniana Quinta, Origenism and Later Developments, Papers of the 5th International Origen Congress, Boston, 14–18 August 1989,* ed. R. J. Daly, 3–25. Leuven: Leuven University Press, 1992.

McGuckin, John. "Origen as a Literary Critic in the Alexandrian Tradition." In *Origeniana Octava: Origen and the Alexandria Tradition; Papers of the 8th International Origen Congress, Pisa 27–31 August 2001*, ed. Lorenzo Perrone, 121–36. Leuven: Peeters, 2003.
McGuckin, John. "Origen on the Glory of God." *StPatr* 21 (1989): 316–24.
McGuckin, John. "Origen on the Jews." In *Christianity and Judaism: Papers Read at the 1991 Summer Meeting and the 1992 Winter Meeting of the Ecclesiastical History Society*, ed. D. Wood, 1–13. Studies in Church History 29. Oxford: Blackwell, 1992.
McKechnie, Paul. *Christianizing Asia Minor: Conversion, Communities, and Social Change in the Pre-Constantinian Era*. Cambridge: Cambridge University Press, 2019.
Mees, Michael. "Die Hohepriester-Theologie des Hebräerbriefes im Vergleich mit dem Ersten Clemensbrief." *BZ* 22 (1978): 115–24.
Mees, Michael. *Die Zitate aus dem Neuen Testament bei Clements von Alexandrien*. Quoaderni di "Vetera Christianorum" 2. Rome: Istituto die Letteratura Cristiana Antica, 1970.
Méhat, André. *Étude sur les "Stromates" de Clément d'Alexandrie*. Patristica Sorbonensia 7. Paris: Éditions du Seuil, 1966.
Méhat, André. "L'Hypothèse des 'Testimonia' à l'épreuve des Stromates: Remarques sur les citations de l'Ancien Testament chez Clément d'Alexandrie." In *La Bible et les Pères: Colloque de Strasbourg 1-3 octobre 1969*, 229–42. Paris: Presses universitaires de France, 1971.
Mekitharistes, Patres. *S. Ephræm Syri commentarii in epistolas D. Pauli nunc primum ex armenio in Latinum sermonem a patribus Mekitharistis translate*. Venice: Ex Typographia Sancti Lazari, 1893.
Méndez, Hugo. "Revising the Date of the Armenian Lectionary of Jerusalem." *JECS* 291 (2021): 61–92.
Merz, Annette. *Fiktive Selbstauslegung des Paulus: Intertextuelle Studien zur Intention und Rezeption der Pastoralbriefe*. NTOA 52. Göttingen: Vandenhoeck & Ruprecht, 2004.
Metzger, Bruce M. *Canon of the New Testament: Its Origin, Development and Significance*. Oxford: Clarendon Press, 1987.
Metzger, Bruce M. *A Textual Commentary on the Greek New Testament*. 2nd ed. Stuttgart: 1994.
Meyer, Barbara U. *Jesus the Jew in Christian Memory*. Cambridge: Cambridge University Press, 2020.
Michel, Otto. *Der Brief an die Hebräer*. KEK 13. Göttingen: Vandenhoeck & Ruprecht, 1947.
Migne, J.-P. *Patrologiae cursus completus*. Series Graeca 82. Paris: Migne, 1864.
Migne, J.-P. *Patrologiae cursus completus*. Series Graeca 63. Paris: Migne, 1862.
Mimouni, Simon. "Le 'grand prêtre' Jésus 'à la manière de Melchisédech' dans l'Épître aux Hébreux." *Annali di Storia dell'Esegesi* 33 (2016): 79–105.
Mitchell, Margaret M. "Paul and Judaism Now, Quo vadimus?" *JJMJS* 5 (2018): 55–78.
Mitton, C. L. *The Formation of the Pauline Corpus*. London: Epworth, 1955.
Moffatt, James. *The Epistle to the Hebrews*. ICC. Edinburgh: T&T Clark, 1924.
Moffit, David M. *Atonement and the Logic of Resurrection in the Epistle to the Hebrews*, NovTSup. 141. Leiden: Brill, 2011.
Moffit, David M. "Jesus' Heavenly Sacrifice in Early Christian Reception of Hebrews: A Survey." *JTS* 68.1 (2017): 46–71.
Moore, Nicholas. "Heaven and Temple in the Second Temple Period: A Taxonomy." *JSP* 33.1 (2023): 75–93.
Moreschini, Claudio, and D. A. Sykes, eds. *St Gregory of Nazianzus: Poemata arcana*. Oxford Theological Monographs. Oxford: Clarendon Press, 1997.
Mortley, Raoul. *The Idea of Universal History from Hellenistic Philosophy to Early Christian Historiography*. Lewiston: E. Mellen Press, 1996.
Mortley, Raoul. "The Mirror and I Cor 13, 12 in the Epistemology of Clement of Alexandria." *VC* 30 (1976) 109–20.

Mortley, Raoul. "The Past in Clement of Alexandria: A Study of an Attempt to Define Christianity in Socio-Cultural Terms." In *Jewish and Christian Self-Definition*, vol. 1, *The Shaping of Christianity in the Second and Third Centuries*, ed. E. P. Sanders, 186–200. Minneapolis: Fortress, 1980.
Mühlenberg, E. "Katenen." In *Theologische Realenzyclopädie 18*, ed. Gerhard Krause and Gerhard Müller, 14–20. Berlin: de Gruyter, 1989.
Murphy, Francis X. *Rufinus of Aquileia (345–410): His Life and Works*. Washington, DC: Catholic University of America Press, 1945.
Murphy, H. S. "On the Text of Codices H and 93." *JBL* 78 (1959): 228–37.
Murray, Michele. "Jews and Judaism in Caesarea Maritima." In *Religious Rivalries and the Struggle for Success in Caesarea Maritima*, ed. Terence L. Donaldson, 127–52. ESCJ 8. Waterloo: Wilfrid Laurier University Press, 2000.
Najman, Hindy, and Irene Peirano Garrison. "Pseudepigraphy as an Interpretive Construct." In *The Old Testament Pseudepigrapha: Fifty Years of the Pseudepigrapha Section at the SBL*, ed. Matthias Henze and Liv Ingeborg Lied, SBLEJL 50, 331–55. Atlanta: Society of Biblical Literature, 2019.
Nanos, Mark D., Magnus Zetterholm, eds. *Paul Within Judaism: Restoring the First-Century Context to the Apostles*. Minneapolis: Fortress, 2015.
Nasrallah, Laura. "'Out of Love for Paul': History and Fiction and the Afterlife of the Apostle Paul." In *Early Christian and Jewish Narrative: The Role of Religion in Shaping Narrative Forms*, ed. Judith Perkins and Ilaria Ramelli, 73–96. Tübingen: Mohr Siebeck, 2015.
Nauck, A. *Tragicorum Graecorum fragmenta*. Leipzig: Teubner, 1889.
Nautin, Pierre. "La fin des *Stromates* et les *Hypotyposes* de Clément d'Alexandrie." *VC* 30 (1976): 268–302.
Nautin, Pierre. "Les citations de la Prédication de Pierre dans Clément D'Alexandrie, Strom, VI. V. 39–41." *JTS* 25.1 (1974): 98–105.
Nautin, Pierre. *Origène: Sa vie et son œuvre*. Christianisme Antique I. Paris: Bauchesne, 1977.
Neeb, John H. C. "Origen's Interpretation of Genesis 28:12 and the Rabbis." In *Origeniana Sexta: Origène et la Bible / Origen and the Bible. Actes du Colloquium Origenianum Sextum Chantilly, 30 août–3 septembre 1993*, ed. Gilles Dorival and Alain le Boulluec, 71–80. Leuven: Peeters, 1995.
Neuschäfer, Bernhard. *Origenes als Philologe*. Basel: Friedrich Reinhardt Verlag, 1987.
Neyrey, H. "Syncrisis and Encomium: Reading Hebrews Through Greek Rhetorics." *CBQ* 82 (2020): 276–99.
Nicklas, Tobias. "Jews and Christians? Sketches from Second Century Alexandria." In *Jews and Christians: Parting Ways in the First Two Centuries CE? Reflections on the Gains and Losses of a Model*, ed. Matthias Konradt, Judith Lieu, Laura Nasrallah, Jens Schröter, and Gregory E. Sterling, 347–79. BZNW 253. Berlin: de Gruyter, 2021.
Nicklas, Tobias, Andreas Merkt, and Joseph Verheyden, eds. *Ancient Perspectives on Paul*. Göttingen: Vandenhoeck & Ruprecht, 2013.
Niehoff, Maren R. "Auf den Spuren des hellenistischen Judentums in Caesarea: Ein Jüischer Psalmenforscher in Origenes' Glosse im Kontext Rabbinischer Literatur." *ZAC* 27.1 (2023): 31–76.
Niehoff, Maren. "A Jewish Critique of Christianity from the Second Century: Revisiting the Jew Mentioned in Contra Celsum." *JECS* 21 (2013): 151–75.
Niehoff, Maren. *Philo of Alexandria: An Intellectual Biography*. New Haven: Yale University Press, 2018.
Nongbri, Brent. *Before Religion: A History of a Modern Concept*. New Haven: Yale University Press, 2015.
Nongbri, Brent. *God's Library: The Archaeology of the Earliest Christian Manuscripts*. New Haven: Yale University Press, 2018.
Nongbri, Brent. "Grenfell and Hunt on the Dates of Early Christian Codices: Setting the Record Straight." *BASP* 48 (2011): 149–62.

Nongbri, Brent. "Losing a Curious Christian Scroll but Gaining a Curious Christian Codex." *NovT* 55.1 (2013): 77–88.
Norelli, Enrico. "La tradition paulinienne dans les lettres d'Ignace." In *Receptions of Paul in Early Christianity: The Person of Paul and His Writings Through the Eyes of His Early Interpreters*, ed. J. Schröter, S. Butticaz, and A. Dettwiler, 519–51. Berlin: de Gruyter, 2018.
Novenson, Matthew. *Paul, Then and Now*. Grand Rapids: Eerdmans, 2022.
Novenson, Matthew. "Whither the Paul Within Judaism Schule?" *JJMJS* 5 (2018): 79–88.
O'Leary, J. S. "The Recuperation of Judaism." In *Origeniana Sexta: Origène et la Bible / Origen and the Bible. Actes du Colloquium Origenianum Sextum Chantilly, 30 août–3 septembre 1993*, ed. Gilles Dorival and Alain le Boulluec, 373–79. Leuven: Peeters, 1995.
Oberg, Eberhard, ed. *Amphilochii Iconiensis iambi ad Seleucum*. PTS 9. Berlin: de Gruyter, 1969.
Ohme, Heinz. *Kanon ekklesiastikos: Die Bedeutung des Altkirchlichen Kanonbegriffs*. Arbeiten zur Kirchengeschichte 67. Berlin: de Gruyter, 1998.
Oliver, Isaac W., and Gabriele Boccaccini, eds. *The Early Reception of Paul the Second Temple Jew*. LSTS 92. London: Bloomsbury, 2018.
Omont, Henri. "Notice sur un très ancien manuscrit grec en onciales des Épîtres de Saint Paul conservé à la Bibliothèque Nationale (H ad epistulas Pauli) par H.O." *NEMBM* 33 (1890): 141–90.
Opelt, I. "Das Ende von Olympia: Zur Entstehungszeit der Predigten zum Hebräerbrief des Johannes Chrysostomos." *ZKG* 81 (1970): 64–69.
Osborn, Eric. "Arguments for Faith in Clement of Alexandria." *VC* 48.1 (1994): 3–7.
Osborn, Eric. *Clement of Alexandria*. Cambridge: Cambridge University Press, 2005.
Osborn, Eric. "Paul and Plato in Second-Century Ethics." *StPatr* 15 (1984): 474–85.
Osborn, Eric. "Teaching and Writing in the First Chapter of the 'Stromateis' of Clement of Alexandria." *JTS* 10.2 (1959): 335–39.
Otto, Jennifer. *Philo of Alexandria and the Construction of Jewishness in Early Christian Writings*. Oxford: Oxford University Press, 2018.
Oulton, J. E. L. "Rufinus's Translation of the Church History of Eusebius." *JThS* 30 (1929): 150–74.
Outler, A. C. "The Platonism of Clement of Alexandria." *JR* 20 (1940): 217–40.
Overbeck, Franz. *Zur Geschichte des Kanons: Zwei Abhandlungen*. Chemnitz: Ernst Schmeitzner, 1880.
Paget, James Carleton. "Anti-Judaism and Early Christian Identity." *ZAC* 1 (1997): 195–225.
Paget, James Carleton. "The Christian Exegesis of the Old Testament in the Alexandrian Tradition." In *Hebrew Bible / Old Testament: The History of Its Interpretation*, vol. 1, *From the Beginnings to the Middle Ages (Until 1300)*, ed. Magne Sæbø with C. Brekelmans and M. Haran, 508–15. Göttingen: Vandenhoeck & Ruprecht, 1996.
Paget, James Carleton. "Clement of Alexandria and the Jews." *SJT* 51 (1998): 86–94.
Paget, James Carleton. "The Jew of Celsus and *adversus Judaeos* literature." *ZAC* 21.2 (2017): 201–42.
Paget, James Carleton. "Jews and Christians in Ancient Alexandria from the Ptolemies to Caracalla." In *Alexandria, Real and Imagined*, ed. Anthony Hirst and Michael Silk, 143–66. Aldershot: Ashgate, 2004.
Panella, Theodora. "The Pseudo-Oecumenian Catena on Galatians." PhD diss., University of Birmingham, 2017.
Parker, D. C. *An Introduction to the New Testament Manuscripts and Their Texts*. Cambridge: Cambridge University Press, 2008.
Parker, D. C., and J. N. Birdsall. "The Date of Codex Zacynthius (Ξ): A New Proposal." *JTS* 55 (2004): 117–31.
Parpulov, G. "An Unknown Catena on the Pauline Epistles." *Byzantine Review* 2 (2020): 9–16.
Parvis, P. M. "The Commentary on Hebrews and the Contra Theodorum of Cyril of Alexandria." *JTS* 26 (1975): 415–19.

Patrich, Joseph. "Caesarea Maritima in the Time of Origen." In *Origeniana Duodecima: Origen's Legacy in the Holy Land—a Tale of Three Cities: Jerusalem, Caesarea and Bethlehem, Proceedings of the 12th International Origen Congress, Jerusalem, June 25–29, 2017*, ed. Brouria Bitton-Ashkelony, Oded Irshai, Aryeh Kofsky, Hillel Newman, and Lorenzo Perrone, 375–409. BETL 302. Leuven: Peeters, 2019.

Penniman, John David. *Raised on Christian Milk: Food and the Formation of the Soul in Early Christianity*. New Haven: Yale University Press, 2017.

Penny, Donald N. "The Pseudo-Pauline Letters of the First Two Centuries." PhD diss., Emory University, 1979.

Pépin, Jean. *Mythe et allegorie: Les origines grecques et les contestations judéochrétiennes*. Paris: Etudes Augustiniennes, 1976.

Perdelwitz, Richard. "Das literarische Problem des Hebräerbriefs." *ZNW* 11 (1910): 59–78.

Perrone, Lorenzo, ed., with Marina Molin Pradel, Emanuela Prinzivalli, and Antonio Cacciari. *Origenes Werke*. Vol. 13, *Die neuen Psalmenhomilien: Eine kritische Edition des Codex Monacensis Graecus 314*. GCS Neue Folge 19. Berlin: de Gruyter, 2015.

Perrone, Lorenzo. "Die 'Verfassung der Juden': Das biblische Judentum als politisches Modell in Origenes' *Contra Celsum*." *ZAC* 7 (2003): 310–28.

Peterson, Jacob W. "Patterns of Correction as Paratext: A New Approach with Papyrus 46 as a Test Case." In *The Future of New Testament Textual Scholarship: From H. C. Hoskier to the Editio Critica Maior and Beyond*, ed. Garrick Allen, 201–29. Tübingen: Mohr Siebeck, 2019.

Philippou, A. J. "Origen and the Early Jewish-Christian Debate." *GOTR* 15 (1970): 140–52.

Photiades, Penelope J. "Pan's Prologue to the 'Dyskolos' of Menander." *Greece & Rome* 5 (1958): 108–22.

Pintaudi, Rosario. "N.T. Ad Hebraeos VI, 7–9; 15–17." *ZPE* 42 (1981): 42–44.

Pitts, Andrew W., and Joshua F. Walker. "The Authorship of Hebrews: A Further Development in the Luke-Paul Relationship." In *Paul and His Social Relations*, ed. Stanley E. Porter and Christopher D. Land, 143–84. Leiden: Brill, 2013.

Plátovaá, Jana. "Bemerkungen zu den Hypotyposen-Fragmenten des Clemens Alexandrianus." *SP* 46 (2010): 181–87.

Porter, Stanley E. "When and How Was the Pauline Canon Compiled? An Assessment of Theories." In *The Pauline Canon*, ed. Stanley E. Porter, 95–127. Leiden: Brill, 2004.

Prigent, Pierre. *Les Testimonia dans le christianisme primitive: L'Épître de Barnabé i–xvi et ses sources*. Études Bibliques. Paris: Lecoffre, 1961.

Prokop von Gaza. *Eclogarum in libros historicos Veteris Testamenti epitome, Teil I: Des Genesiskommentar*. Ed. Karim Metzler. GCS N.F. 22. Berlin: de Gruyter, 2015.

Pusey, P. E. *Sancti patris nostri Cyrilli archiepiscopi Alexandrini in D. Joannis evangelium*. Vol. 3. Oxford: Clarendon, 1872.

Ramelli, Ilaria. "Origen, Patristic Philosophy, and Christian Platonism: Re-Thinking the Christianisation of Hellenism." *VC* 63 (2009): 217–63.

Ramelli, Ilaria. "Origen the Christian Middle/Neoplatonist: New Arguments for a Possible Identification." *JECH* 1.1 (2011): 98–130.

Ramelli, Ilaria. "Origen's Allegoresis of Plato's and Scriptures' 'Myths.'" In *Religious Competition in the Greco-Roman World*, ed. Nathaniel DesRosiers and Lily C. Vuong, WGRWSup 10, 85–107. Atlanta: SBL Press, 2016.

Ramelli, Ilaria. "Philo as Origen's Declared Model: Allegorical and Historical Exegesis of Scripture." *SCJR* 7 (2012): 1–17.

Ramelli, Ilaria, and Giulio A. Lucchetta. *Allegoria*. Vol. 1. *L'età classica: Introduzione e cura di R. Radice*. Milan: Vita e Pensiero Università, 2004.

Raspanti, G., ed. *Commentarii in epistulam Pauli apostoli ad Galatas*. CCSL 77A. Turnhout: Brepols, 2006.

Redepenning, Ernst. *Origenes: Eine Darstellung seines Lebens und seiner Lehre*. Bonn: Verlag, 1846.

Reece, Steve. *Paul's Large Letters: Paul's Autographic Subscriptions in the Light of Ancient Epistolary Conventions*. LNTS 561. London: T&T Clark, 2017.
Rehm, Bernhard, ed. *Die Pseudoklementinen II: Rekognitionen*. GCS 51. Berlin: Akademie Verlag, 1965.
Renner, Frumentius. *"An die Hebräer"—ein pseudepigraphischer Brief*. Münsterschwarzacher Studien 14. Münsterschwarzach: Vier-Türme, 1970.
Renoux, Charles. "Origène dans la liturgie de l'Église de Jérusalem." *Adamantius* 5 (1999): 37–52.
Rensberger, David. "As the Apostle Teaches: The Development of the Use of Paul's Letters in Second-Century Christianity." PhD diss., Yale University, 1981.
Reynolds, Leighton Durham, and Nigel Guy Wilson. *Scribes and Scholars: A Guide to the Transmission of Greek and Latin Literature*. Oxford: Oxford University Press, 1968.
Ribbens, Benjamin J. *Levitical Sacrifice and Heavenly Cult in Hebrews*. BZNW 222. Berlin: de Gruyter, 2016.
Richard, Marcel. "Les citations de Théodoret conservées dans la chaîne de Nicétas sur l'Évangile selon Saint Luc." *RB* 43 (1934): 88–96.
Richards, E. R. "The Codex and the Early Collection of Paul's Letters." *BBR* 8 (1998): 151–66.
Ridings, Daniel. *The Attic Moses: The Dependency Theme in Some Early Christian Writers*. SGLG LIX. Göteborg: Acta Universitatis Gothoburgensis, 1995.
Ridolfini, Francesco Pericoli. "Le origini della scuoladi Alessandria." *RSO* 37 (1962): 211–30.
Riggenbach, Eduard. *Der Brief an die Hebräer*. KNT 14. Leipzig: Deichert, 1913.
Riggenbach, Eduard. *Historische Studien zum Hebräer brief*. Vol. 1, *Die ältesten lateinischen Kommentare zum Hebräerbrief*. Vol. 8.1 of *Forschungen zur Geschichte des neutestamentlichen Kanons und der altkirchlichen Literatur*, ed. Theodor Zahn. Leipzig: Deichert, 1907.
Rives, J. B. "The Decree of Decius and the Religion of Empire." *JRS* 89 (1999): 135–54.
Rizzi, Marco. "The End of *Stromateis* VII and Clement's Literary Project." In *The Seventh Book of the Stromateis: Proceedings of the Colloquium on Clement of Alexandria, Olomouc October 21–23, 2010*, ed. M. Havrda, V. Hušek, and J. Plátová, 299–311. VCSup 117. Leiden: Brill, 2012.
Rizzi, Marco. "The Literary Problem in Clement of Alexandria: A Reconsideration." *Adamantius* 17 (2011): 154–63.
Roberts, Charles. "The Christian Book and Greek Papyri." *JTS* 50.199–200 (1949): 155–68.
Roberts, Charles, and T. C. Skeat. *The Birth of the Codex*. London: Oxford University Press, 1983.
Roberts, Louis. "The Literary Form of the Stromateis." *Second Century* 1.4 (1981): 211–22.
Robinson, Joseph Armitage. *Euthaliana*. Texts and Studies 3.3. Cambridge: Cambridge University Press, 1895.
Rodenbiker, Kelsie. "The Claromontanus Stichometry and Its Canonical Implications." *JSNT* 44.2 (2021): 240–53.
Romeny, Bas ter Haar. "Procopius of Gaza and His Library." In *From Rome to Constantinople: Studies in Honour of Averil Cameron*, ed. Hagit Amirav and Bas ter Haar Romeny, 173–90. Late Antique History and Religion 1. Leuven: Peeters, 2007.
Roncaglia, Martiniano Pellegrino. "Pantène et le Didascalée d'Alexandrie: Du Judéochristianisme au christianisme hellénistique." In *A Tribute to Arthur Vööbus: Studies in Early Christian Literature and Its Environment, Primarily in the Syrian East*, ed. Robert H. Fischer, 211–33. Chicago: Lutheran School of Theology, 1977.
Roose, Hanna. "Der 2. Thessalonicherbrief im Verhältnis zum 1. Thessalonicherbrief: Ein Gedankenexperiment." In *Receptions of Paul in Early Christianity: The Person of Paul and His Writings Through the Eyes of His Early Interpreters*, ed. J. Schröter, S. Butticaz, and A. Dettwiler, 443–59. Berlin: de Gruyter, 2018.
Roose, Hanna. "2 Thessalonians as Pseudepigraphic 'Reading Instruction' for 1 Thessalonians: Methodological Implications and Exemplary Illustration of an Intertextual

Concept." In *The Intertextuality of the Epistles: Explorations of Theory and Practice*, ed. D. R. McDonald, S. E. Porter, and T. L. Brodie, 133–51. Sheffield: Sheffield Phoenix, 2006.

Rosenmeyer, Patricia A. *Ancient Epistolary Fictions: The Letter in Greek Literature*. Cambridge: Cambridge University Press, 2001.

Rothschild, Clare K. "Hebrews as a Guide to Reading Romans." In *Pseudepigraphie und Verfasserfiktion in Frühchristlichen Briefen: Pseudepigraphy and Author Fiction in Early Christian Letters*, ed. Jörg Frey, Jens Herzer, Martina Janßen, and Clare K. Rothschild, 537–73. WUNT 246. Tübingen: Mohr Siebeck, 2009.

Rothschild, Clare K. "Hebrews as an Instructional Appendix to Romans." In *Paul and Pseudepigraphy*, ed. Stanley E. Porter and Gregory P. Fewster, 245–68. PAST 8. Leiden: Brill, 2013.

Rothschild, Clare K. *Hebrews as Pseudepigraphon: The History and Significance of the Pauline Attribution of Hebrews*. WUNT 235. Tübingen: Mohr Siebeck, 2009.

Rothschild, Clare K. "The Muratorian Fragment as Roman Fake." *NovT* 60 (2018): 55–82.

Roukema, Riemer. "Origen, the Jews, and the New Testament." In *The "New Testament" as a Polemical Tool: Studies in Ancient Christian Anti-Jewish Rhetoric and Beliefs*, ed. Rimer Roukema and Hagit Amirav, 241–53. NTOA 118. Göttingen: Vandenhoeck & Ruprecht, 2018.

Royse, James R. "The Early Text of Paul (and Hebrews)." In *The Early Text of the New Testament*, ed. Charles E. Hill and Michael J. Kruger, 175–203. Oxford: Oxford University Press, 2013.

Royse, James R. *Scribal Habits in Early Greek New Testament Papyri*. Leiden: Brill, 2008.

Runia, David T. "Ancient Philosophy and the New Testament: 'Exemplar' as Example." In *Method and Meaning: Essays on New Testament Interpretation in Honor of Harold W. Attridge*, ed. Andrew B. MacGowan and Kent Richards, 347–61. SBL Resources for Biblical Study 67. Atlanta: Society of Biblical Literature, 2011.

Runia, David T. "Philo and Origen: A Preliminary Survey." In *Origeniana Quinta, Origenism and Later Developments, Papers of the 5th International Origen Congress, Boston, 14–18 August 1989*, ed. R. J. Daly, 333–39. Leuven: Leuven University Press, 1992.

Runia, David. *Philo in Early Christian Literature*. Assen: Van Gorcum, 1993.

Russell, D. A. *Quintilian, Institutio Oratoria*. LCL 124. Cambridge, MA: Harvard University Press, 2002.

S. Ephræm Syri Commentarii in Epistolas D. Pauli nunc primum ex armeno in latinum sermonem a Patribus Mekitharistis translate. Venice: Typographia Sancti Lazari, 1893.

Sagnard, F. *Clément d'Alexandrie: Extraits de Théodote*. SC 23. Paris: Cerf, 1970.

Sanders, Henry A. *A Third Century Codex of the Epistles of Paul*. University of Michigan Studies, Humanistic Series 38. Ann Arbor: University of Michigan Press, 1935.

Schäfer, Karl Theodor. "Marius Victorinus und die Marcionitischen Prologe zu den Paulusbriefen." *RBén* 80 (1970): 7–16.

Schäfer, Karl Theodor. *Untersuchungen zur Geschichte der lateinischen Übersetzung des Hebräerbriefs*. Römische Quartalschrift 23, Supplementheft. Freiburg: Herder, 1929.

Schäfer, Peter. *Two Gods in Heaven: Jewish Concepts of God in Antiquity*. Trans. Allison Brown. Princeton: Princeton University Press, 2020.

Scheck, Thomas P, trans. *Origen: Commentary on the Epistle to the Romans, Books 1–5*. FC 103. Washington, DC: Catholic University of America Press, 2001.

Scheck, Thomas P. *Origen: Homilies on Numbers*. Downers Grove: IVP Academic, 2009.

Schenck, Kenneth. *A New Perspective on Hebrews: Rethinking the Parting of the Ways*. Minneapolis: Fortress, 2019.

Schenke, Hans-Martin. "Mittelägyptischen 'Nachlese' I. Bermerkungen zum Adverb ϩⲓⲧⲣⲟⲩⲡ 'schnell' anlässlich der Edition von Restfragmenten in der Mailänder Handschrift der Paulusbriefe mit einem neuen Beleg." *ZÄS* 116 (1989): 160–74.

Scherbenske, Eric. *Canonizing Paul: Ancient Editorial Practice and the Corpus Paulinum*. Oxford: Oxford University Press, 2013.

Schiele, F. M. "Harnack's 'Probabilia' Concerning the Address and the Author of the Epistle to the Hebrews." *AJT* 9 (1905): 290–308.
Schille, G. *Das älteste Paulus-Bild: Beobachtungen zur lukanischen und zur deuteropaulinischen Paulus-Darstellung*. Berlin: Evangelische Verlagsanstalt, 1979.
Schironi, Francesca. *The Best of the Grammarians: Aristarchus of Samothrace on the Iliad*. Ann Arbor: University of Michigan Press, 2018.
Schironi, Francesca. "Greek Commentaries." *DSD* 19 (2012): 399–441.
Schironi, Francesa. *ΤΟ ΜΕΓΑ ΒΙΒΛΙΟΝ: Book-Ends, End-Titles, and Coronides in Papyri with Hexametric Poetry*. Durham, NC: American Society of Papyrologists, 2010.
Schlossnikel, R. F. *Der Brief an die Hebräer und das Corpus Paulinum: Eine linguistische "Bruchstelle" im Codex Claromontanus (Paris, Bibliothèque Nationale Grec 107 + 107A + 107B) und ihre Bedeutung im Rahmen von Text- und Kanongeschichte*. Freiburg: Herder, 1991.
Schluze, J. L., ed. *Interpretatio Epistolae Ad Hebraeos*. Patrologia Graecae 82. Paris: J.-P. Migne, 1859.
Schmeller, Thomas. "Ungetrennt und unvermischt? Die Frage nach Kompilationen und Interpolationen in den echten Paulusbriefen." In *Receptions of Paul in Early Christianity: The Person of Paul and His Writings Through the Eyes of His Early Interpreters*, ed. J. Schröter, S. Butticaz, and A. Dettwiler, 751–77. Berlin: de Gruyter, 2018.
Schmithals, Walter. "Der Hebräerbrief als Paulusbrief: Beobachtungen zur Kanonbildung." In *Die Weltlichkeit des Glaubens in der Alten Kirche: Festschrift für Ulrich Wickert zum siebzigsten Geburtstag*, ed. Dietmar Wyrwa, 319–37. Berlin: de Gruyter, 1997.
Schmithals, Walter. *Paul and the Gnostics*. Nashville: Abingdon, 1972.
Schmithals, Walter. "Über Empfänger und Anlass des Hebräerbriefs." In *Eschatologie und Schöpfung: FS für Erich Grässer zum siebzigsten Geburtstag*, ed. M. Evang, H. Merklein, and M. Wolter, 321–42. BZNW 89. Berlin: de Gruyter, 1997.
Schmithals, Walter. "Zur Abfassung und ältesten Sammlung der paulinischen Hauptbriefe." *ZNW* 51 (1960): 225–45.
Schnabel, Eckhard J. "The Muratorian Fragment: The State of Research." *JETS* 57 (2014): 231–64.
Schniedewind, William. "Aramaic, the Death of Written Hebrew, and Language Shift in the Persian Period." In *Margins of Writing, Origins of Cultures*, ed. Seth L. Sanders, 141–51. OIS 2. Chicago: Oriental Institute of the University of Chicago, 2006.
Scholten, Clemens. "Die alexandrinische Katechetenschule." *JAC* 38 (1995): 16–37.
Schröger, Friedrich. "Der Hebräerbrief-paulinisch?" In *Kontinuität und Einheit: Festschrift für Franz Mussner*, ed. P. G. Müller and W. Stenger, 211–22. Freiburg: Herder, 1981.
Schröter, Jens. "Kirche im Anschluss an Paulus: Aspekte der Paulusrezeption in der Apostelgeschichte und in den Pastoralbriefen." *ZNW* 98 (2007): 77–104.
Schröter, Jens, Simon Butticaz, and Andreas Dettwiler, eds. *Receptions of Paul in Early Christianity: The Person of Paul and His Writings Through the Eyes of His Early Interpreters*. Berlin: de Gruyter, 2018.
Schürer, Emil. *Geschichte des jüdischen Volkes im Zeitalter Jesu Christi*. Leipzig: Hinrichs, 1866–90.
Schwartz, Eduard, and Theodore Mommsen, eds. *Eusebius Werke II/1: Die Kirchengeschichte*. 2nd ed. GCS N.F. 6.1. Berlin: Akademie Verlag, 1999.
Schwartz, Seth. "Language, Power and Identity in Ancient Palestine." *Past & Present* 148 (1995): 3–47.
Seesemann, Heirich. "Das Paulusverständnis des Clemens Alexandrinus." *TSK* 107 (1936): 312–46.
Sickenberger, Joseph. *Die Lukaskatene des Niketas von Herakleia*. TUGAL, 22.4. Leipzig: J.C. Hinrichs, 1902.
Sieben, Hermann Josef. *Kirchenväterhomilien zum Neuen Testament: Ein Repertorium der Textausgaben und Übersetzungen. Mit einem Anhang der Kirchenväterkommentare*. Instrumenta Patristica 11. The Hague: Martinus Nijhoff International, 1991.

Slater, William J., ed. *Aristophanis Byzantii Fragmenta post A. Nauck collegit, testimoniis ornavit, brevi commentario instruxit.* Berlin: de Gruyter, 1986.
Souter, Alexander. *The Earliest Latin Commentaries on the Epistles of St. Paul.* Oxford: Clarendon, 1999.
Sparks, H. F. D. "The Order of the Epistles in P46." *JTS* 42 (1941): 180–81.
Spicq, Ceslas. "L'authenticité du chapitre XIII de l'Épître aux Hébreux." *ConNT* (1947): 226–36.
Spicq, Ceslas. *L'Épître aux Hebreux, I. Introduction, II. Commentaire.* Études Bibliques. Paris: Libraire Lecoffre, 1952.
Staab, Karl. "Die griechischen Katenenkommentare zur den katholischen Briefe." *Bib* 5 (1924): 296–353.
Staab, Karl. *Die Pauluskatenen nach den handschriftlichen quellen untersucht.* Rome: Verlag des Päpstlichen Bibelinstituts, 1926.
Staab, Karl. *Pauluskommentare aus der Griechischen Kirche aus Katenenhandschriften gesammelt und herausgegeben.* NTA 15. Münster: Aschendorff, 1933.
Stählin, Otto. *Clemens Alexandrinus und die Septuaginta.* Nürnberg, 1901.
Stählin, Otto. *Clemens Alexandrinus erster Band: Protreptikos und Paedagogus.* GCS 12. Berlin: Akademie-Verlag, 1972.
Stählin, Otto. *Clemens Alexandrinus vierter Band: Register.* GCS 39.1. Akademie-Verlag, 1980.
Stählin, Otto, Ludwig Früchtel, and Ursula Treu. *Clemens Alexandrinus dritter Band: Stromata Buch VII und VIII; Excerpta ex Theodoto; Eclogae Propheticae; Quis dives salvetur; Fragmente.* GCS 17. Berlin: Akademie-Verlag, 1970.
Stählin, Otto, Ludwig Früchtel, and Ursula Treu. *Clemens Alexandrinus zweiter Band: Stromata Buch I–VI.* GCS 15. Berlin: Akademie-Verlag, 1985.
Staples, Jason. *The Idea of Israel in Second Temple Judaism: A New Theory of People, Exile, and Israelite Identity.* Cambridge: Cambridge University Press, 2021.
Steidle, B. "Neue Untersuchungen zu Origenes's Περὶ ἀρχῶν." *ZNW* 40 (1941): 236–43.
Stemberger, Günter. "Ebraismo a Caesarea Maritima: Personalità rabbinico a Caesarea Maritima." In *Caesarea Maritima e la Scuola Origeniana: Multiculturalità, forme di competizione culturale e identità Cristiana*, ed. Osvalda Andrei, 96–102. Supplementi Adamantius 3. Brescia: Morcelliana, 2013.
Stendahl, Krister. "The Apocalypse of John and the Epistles of Paul in the Muratorian Fragment." In *Current Issues in New Testament Interpretation*, ed. W. Klassen and G. F. Snyder, 239–45. New York: Harper and Row, 1962.
Sterling, Gregory E. "Ontology versus Eschatology: Tensions Between Author and Community in Hebrews." *SPhilo* 13 (2001): 190–211.
Stern, David. "Ancient Jewish Interpretation of the Song of Songs in Comparative Context." In *Jewish Biblical Interpretation and Cultural Exchange*, ed. Natalie B. Dohrmann and David Stern, 87–107. Philadelphia: University of Pennsylvania Press, 2013.
Stern, David. "The First Jewish Books and the Early History of Jewish Reading." *JQR* 98.2 (2008): 163–202.
Stevens, Luke J. "The Evangelists in Clement's *Hypotyposes*." *JECS* 26.3 (2018): 353–79.
Stevens, Luke J. "The Two-Volume Archetype of the Pauline Corpus." *JSPL* 8.1 (2018): 102–26.
Steyn, Gert J. "The Ending of Hebrews Reconsidered." *ZNW* 103 (2012): 235–53.
Steyn, Gert J. "Hebrews in an Egyptian Setting?" In *The Epistle to the Hebrews: Writing at the Borders*, ed. Régis Burnet, Didier Luciani, and Geert Van, 103–22. BET 85. Leuven: Peeters, 2016.
Stowers, Stanley. *A Rereading of Romans: Justice, Jews, Gentiles.* New Haven: Yale University Press, 1994.
Strecker, Georg, and Bernhard Rehm. *Die Pseudoklementinen I. Homilien.* 2nd ed. GCS 42. Berlin: Akademie Verlag, 1992.
Streeter, B. H. *The Four Gospels: A Study of Origins.* London: Macmillan, 1930.

Stroumsa, Guy. *Barbarian Philosophy: The Religious Revolution of Early Christianity.* Tübingen: Mohr Siebeck, 1999.
Stroumsa, Guy. *Hidden Wisdom: Esoteric Traditions and the Roots of Christian Mysticism.* SHR 70. Leiden: Brill, 2005.
Struck, Peter T. *The Birth of the Symbol: Ancient Readers at the Limits of Their Texts.* Princeton: Princeton University Press, 2004.
Suggit, J. trans., *Oecumenius, Commentary on the Apocalypse.* Washington, DC: Catholic University of America Press, 2006.
Sundberg, Albert C. "Canon Muratori: A Fourth Century List." *HTR* 66 (1973): 1–41.
Swete, H. B. *Theodori Episcopi Mopsuesteni in epistolas B. Pauli Commentarii: The Latin Version with the Greek Fragment.* 2 vols. Cambridge: Cambridge University Press, 1880, 1882.
Sykes, Alistair Stewart. *From Prophesy to Preaching: A Search for the Origins of Christian Homily.* VCSup. 59. Leiden: Brill, 2001.
Taylor, Miriam. *Anti-Judaism and Early Christian Identity: A Critique of the Scholarly Consensus.* Leiden: Brill, 1995.
Theißen, Gerd. *Untersuchungen zum Hebräerbrief.* StNT 2. Gütersloh: Mohn, 1969.
Thiessen, Matthew. "Conjuring Paul and Judaism Forty Years After Paul and Palestinian Judaism." *JJMJS* 5 (2018): 6–20.
Thiessen, Matthew. *Contesting Conversion: Genealogy, Circumcision, and Identity in Ancient Judaism and Christianity.* Oxford: Oxford University Press, 2011.
Thiessen, Matthew. *Paul and the Gentile Problem.* Oxford: Oxford University Press, 2016.
Thomas, Matthew J. "Origen on Paul's Authorship of Hebrews." *NTS* 65 (2019): 598–609.
Thompson, James W. "The Epistle to the Hebrews in the Works of Clement of Alexandria." In *Transmission and Reception: New Testament Text-Critical and Exegetical Studies,* ed. J. W. Childers and D. C. Parker, 239–54. TS 3.4. Piscataway: Gorgias Press, 2006.
Thompson, Trevor. "As If Genuine: Interpreting the Pseudepigraphic 2 Thessalonians." In *Pseudepigraphie und Verfasserfiktion in frühchristlichen Briefen,* ed. Jörg Frey, Jens Herzer, Martina Janssen, and Clare Rothschild, 471–88. Tübingen: Mohr Siebeck, 2009.
Thümmel, Hans Georg. "Philon und Origenes." In *Karpoi: Ausgewählte Aufsätze; Patristik—Philosophie—christliche Kunst (1966–2004),* ed. Christfried Böttrich, 78–91. Greifswalder theologische Forschungen 14. Frankfurt am Main: Peter Lang, 2007.
Thurén, Jukka. *Das Lobopfer der Hebräer: Studien zum Aufbau und Anliegen von Hebräerbrief 13.* Acta Academiae Aboensis 47. Åbo: Akademi, 1974.
Thyen, Hartwig. *Der Stil der jüdisch-hellenistischen Homilie.* FRLANT 47. Göttingen: Vandenhoeck & Ruprecht, 1955.
Tischendorf, C. *Apocalypses Apocryphae, Mosis, Esdrae, Pauli, Iohannis, item Mariae Dormitio, additis evangeliorum et actuum apocryphorum suplementis.* Leipzig: Mendelssohn, 1866.
Torjesen, Karen Jo. "'Body,' 'Soul,' and 'Spirit' in Origen's Theory of Exegesis." *ATR* 67 (1985): 17–30.
Torjesen, Karen Jo. *Hermeneutical Procedure and Theological Method in Origen's Exegesis.* Patristische Texte und Studien 38. Berlin: de Gruyter, 1986.
Torrey, C. C. "The Authorship and Character of the So-Called 'Epistle to the Hebrews.'" *JBL* 30 (1911): 137–56.
Trapp, M. B. "Images of Alexandria in the Writings of the Second Sophistic." In *Alexandria, Real and Imagined,* ed. Anthony Hirst and Michael Silk, 113–32. Aldershot: Ashgate, 2004.
Tregelles, S. P. *Codex Zacynthius E or Greek Palimpsest Fragments of the Gospel of St. Luke, Deciphered, Transcribed, and Edited.* London: Samuel Bagster and Sons, 1861.
Trobisch, David. *Die Entstehung der Paulusbriefsammlung: Studien zu den Anfängen christlicher Publizistik.* NTOA10. Göttingen: Vandenhoeck & Ruprecht, 1989.
Trudinger, L. Paul. "'ΚΑΙ ΓΑΡ ΔΙΑ ΒΡΑΧΕΩΝ ΕΠΕΣΤΕΙΛΑ ΥΜΙΝ': A Note on Hebrews XIII.22." *JTS* 23 (1972): 128–30.

Turner, C. H. "Greek Patristic Commentaries on the Pauline Epistles." In *A Dictionary of the Bible*, vol. 5, *Supplement*, ed. James Hastings. Edinburgh: Clark, 1898.

Tzvetkova-Glaser, Anna. *Pentateuchsauslegung bei Origenes und den frühen Rabbinen*. Frankfurt am Main: Peter Lang, 2010.

Tzvetkova-Glaser, Anna. "Polemics against Judeo Christian Practices in Origen's Homilies." StPatr 46 (2010): 217–22.

Übelacker, Walter. *Der Hebräerbrief als Appel: Untersuchungen zur Exordium, Narratio und Postscriptum (Hebr 1–2 und 13,22–25)*. ConB 21. Stockholm: Almqvist & Wiksell, 1989.

Übelacker, Walter. "Paraenesis or Paraclesis—Hebrews as a Test Case." In *Early Christian Paraenesis in Context*, ed. James Starr and Troels Engberg-Pedersen, 319–52. BZNW 125. Berlin: de Gruyter, 2012.

Urbach, Ephraim. "Homiletical Interpretations of the Sages and the Expositions of Origen on the Canticles, and the Jewish-Christian Disputation." ScrHier 22 (1971): 247–75.

Urbach, Ephraim. "Rabbinic Exegesis and Origen's Commentary on the Song of Songs and Jewish-Christian Polemics / דרשות חז״ל ופירושי אוריגינס לשיר השירים והוויכוח נוצרי-היהודי". *Tarbiz*/תרביץ 30 (1960): 148–70.

Uthemann, Karl-Heinz. "Was verraten die Katenen über die Exegeseihre Zeit?" In *Stimuli: Exegese und ihre Hermeneutik in Antike und Christentum: Festschrift für Ernst Dassmann*, ed. Georg Schöllgen and Clemens Scholten, 284–96. Münster: Aschendorff, 1996.

van de Bunt (Hoek), Annewies. "Milk and Honey in the Theology of Clement of Alexandria." In *Fides Sacramenti—Sacramentum Fidei: Studies in Honour of Pieter Smulders*, ed. Hans Jorg Auf der Maur, L. Bakker, A. van de Bunt, and J. Waldram, 27–39. Assen: Van Gorcum, 1981.

van den Broek, Roelof. "The Christian 'School' of Alexandria in the Second and Third Centuries." In *Centers of Learning: Learning and Location in Pre-Modern Europe and the Near East*, ed. J. W. Drijvers and A. A. McDonald, 39–47. Leiden: Brill, 1995.

van den Broek, Roelof. "Juden und Christen in Alexandrien im 2. und 3. Jahrhundert." In *Studies in Gnosticism and Alexandrian Christianity*, 179–96. Leiden: Brill, 1996.

van den Hoek, Annewies. "The 'Catechetical' School of Early Christian Alexandria and Its Philonic Heritage." HTR 90.1 (1997): 59–87.

van den Hoek, Annewies. *Clement of Alexandria and His Use of Philo in the Stromateis: An Early Christian Reshaping of a Jewish Mode*. Leiden: Brill, 1988.

van den Hoek, Annewies. "The Concept of *soma tōn graphōn* in Alexandrian Theology." StPatr 19 (1989): 250–54.

van den Hoek, Annewies. "Mistress and Servant: An Allegorical Theme in Philo, Clement, and Origen." In *Origeniana Quarta: Die Referate des 4. Internationalen Origeneskongresses (Innsbruck, 2.–6. September 1985)*, ed. Lothar Lies, 344–48. Innsbrucker theologische Studien Bd. 19. Innsbruck: Tyrolia, 1987.

van den Hoek, Annewies. "Techniques of Quotation in Clement of Alexandria: A View of Ancient Literary Working Methods." VC 50 (1996): 223–43.

Vanhoye, Albert. *Exegesis Epistulæ ad Hebræos [ad usum privatum auditorum]*. Rome: Pontificium Institutum Biblicum, 1968.

Verhasselt, Gertjan. "The Hypotheses of Euripides and Sophocles by 'Dicaearchus.'" GRBS 55 (2015): 608–36.

Verheyden, Joseph. "The Canon Muratori: A Matter of Dispute." In *The Biblical Canons*, ed. J.-M. Auwers and H. J. De Jonge, 500–550. Leuven: Leuven University Press, 2003.

Verheyden, Joseph. "Origen on the Origin of 1 Cor 2,9." In *The Corinthians Correspondence*, ed. R. Bieringer 491–511. BETL 125. Leuven: Peeters, 1996.

Vessella, Carlo. *Sophisticated Speakers: Atticistic Pronunciation in the Atticist Lexica*. Trends in Classics—Supplementary Volume 55. Berlin: de Gruyter, 2018.

Vogels, Heinricus Iosephus, ed. *Ambrosiaster, Commentarius in xii epistulas Paulinas*. CSEL 81/1–3. Vindobonae: Hoelder, 1966–69).

Vogt, Hermann Josef. "Die Juden beim späten Origenes." In *Origenes als Exeget*, ed. Wilhelm Geerlings, 225–39. Paderborn: Ferdinand Schöningh, 1999.
Völker, W. *Der wahre Gnostiker nach Clemens Alexandrinus*. TU 57.2. Berlin: Akademie, 1952.
Vollenweider, Samuel. "Paul entreexégèse et histoire de la réception." In *Paul, une théologie en construction*, ed. Andreas Dettwiler, Jean-Daniel Kaestli, and Daniel Marguerat, 441–59. MoBi 51. Geneva: Labor et Fides, 2004.
Vollenweider, Samuel. "Paulus zwischen Exegese und Wirkungsgeschichte." In *Die prägende Kraft der Texte: Hermeneutik und Wirkungsgeschichte des Neuen Testaments. Ein Symposium zu Ehren von Ulrich Luz*, ed. Moises Mayordomo, 115–37. SBS 199. Stuttgart: Katholisches Bibelwerk, 2005.
von der Goltz, Eduard. *Eine textkritische Arbeit des zehnten bezw. sechsten Jahrhunderts*. TU 17.4. Leipzig: Hinrichs, 1899.
von Dobschütz, Ernst. *Das Kerygma Petri kritisch untersucht*. TU 11.1. Leipzig: Hinrichs, 1893.
von Dobschütz, Ernst. "Ein Beitrag zur Euthaliusfrage." *Zentralblatt für Bibliothekswesen* 10 (1893): 49–70.
von Johannes, Arnold. "Mit Platon zur Erkenntnis Gottes? Der 'philosophische Exkurs' des Siebten Briefs bei Kelsos und Origenes." *ThPh* 95.3 (2020): 321–61.
von Soden, Hermann Freiherr. *Die Schriften des Neuen Testaments in ihrer ältesten erreichbaren Textgestalt hergestellt auf Grund ihrer Textgeschichte. I. Teil: Untersuchungen, I. Abteilung: Die Textseugen*. Göttingen: Vandenhoeck and Ruprecht, 1911.
von Soden, Hermann Freiherr. *Hebräerbrief, Briefe des Petrus, Jakobus, Judas*. HCNT 3/2. Leipzig: Mohr Siebeck, 1899.
Wagner, Monica. *Rufinus the Translator: A Study of His Theory and Practice as Illustrated in His Version of the Apologetica of St. Gregory Nazianzen*. Washington, DC: Catholic University of America Press, 1945.
Wagner, Walter. "Another Look at the Literary Problem in Clement of Alexandria's Major Writings." *CH* 37 (1968): 251–60.
Ward, H. Clifton. "'Symbolic Interpretation Is Most Useful': Clement of Alexandria's Scriptural Imagination." *JECS* 25.4 (2017): 531–60.
Wasserstein, Abraham. "A Rabbinic Midrash as a Source of Origen's Homily on Ezekiel / מדרש יהודי אצל אוריגנים." *Tarbiz*/תרביץ 46 (1977): 317–18.
Waszink, J. H. "Some Observations on the Appreciation of 'the Philosophy of the Barbarians' in Early Christian Literature." In *Mélanges offerts à Mademoiselle Christine Mohrmann*, 41–56. Utrecht: Spectrum, 1963.
Watts, E. J. *City and School in Late Antique Athens and Alexandria*. Berkeley: University of California Press, 2006.
Weber, Ferdinand. *System der altsynagogalen palätinischen Theologie aus Targum, Midrash und Talmud*. Leipzig: Dörffling & Franke, 1880.
Wedderburn, A. J. M. "'Letter' to the Hebrews and Its Thirteenth Chapter." *NTS* 50 (2004): 390–405.
Wegenast, Klaus. *Das Verständnis der Tradition bei Paulus und in den Deuteropaulinen*. Neukirchen-Vluyn: Neukirchener Verlag, 1962.
Weise, B. *Kritisch exegetisches Handbuch über den Brief an die Hebräer*. Göttingen: Vandenhoeck and Ruprecht, 1888.
Weiss, Hans-Friedrich. *Der Brief an die Hebräer*. KEK 13. Göttingen: Vandenhoeck & Ruprecht, 1991.
Wendt, Heidi. *At the Temple Gates: The Religion of Freelance Experts in the Roman Empire*. Oxford: Oxford University Press, 2016.
Werline, Rodney. "The Transformation of Pauline Arguments in Justin Martyr's Dialogue with Trypho." *HTR* 92 (1999): 79–93.
Westcott, B. F. *The Epistle to the Hebrews*. London: Macmillian 1892.

Wettstein, J. *Novum Testamentum Graecum*. Amsterdam: Dommeriana, 1752.
White, Benjamin L. "Reclaiming Paul? Reconfiguration as Reclamation in 3 Corinthians." *JECS* 17 (2009): 497-523.
White, Benjamin L. *Remembering Paul: Ancient and Modern Contests over the Image of the Apostle*. New York: Oxford University Press, 2014.
Whitmarsh, Timothy. *The Second Sophistic*. New Surveys in the Classic 35. Cambridge: Cambridge University Press, 2005.
Wieseler, Karl. *Eine Untersuchung über den Hebräerbrief namentlich seinen Verfasser und seine Leser. Erste Hälfte*. Kiel: C. F. Mohr, 1860.
Wilcox, Max. "'According to the Pattern (TBNYT)...': Exodus 25, 40 in the New Testament and Early Jewish Thought." *RevQ* 13 (1988): 647-56.
Wilde, Robert. *The Treatment of the Jews in the Greek Christian Writers of the First Three Centuries*. SP 81. Washington, DC: Catholic University of America Press, 1949.
Wiles, Maurice. *Archetypal Heresy: Arianism Through the Centuries*. Oxford: Oxford University Press, 2001.
Wilken, Robert L. *The Christians as the Romans Saw Them*. 2nd ed. New Haven: Yale University Press, 2003.
Wilken, Robert L. "Origen's Homilies on Leviticus and Vayikra Rabbah." In *Origeniana Sexta: Origène et la Bible/Origen and the Bible. Actes du Colloquium Origenianum Sextum Chantilly, 30 août-3 septembre 1993*, ed. Gilles Dorival and Alain le Boulluec, 81-91. Leuven: Peeters, 1995.
Willard, Louis Charles. *A Critical Study of the Euthalian Apparatus*. ANTF 41. Berlin: de Gruyter, 2009.
Williams, Frank, trans. *The Panarion of Epiphanius of Salamis: Book 1 (Sects 1-46)*. NHMS 63. Leiden: Brill, 2009.
Wills, Lawrence. "The Form of the Sermon in Hellenistic Judaism and Early Christianity." *HTR* 77 (1984): 277-99.
Wilson, N. G. "A Chapter in the History of Scholia." *CQ* 17 (1967): 244-56.
Windisch, Hans. *Der Hebräerbrief*. HNT 14. Tübingen: Mohr Siebeck, 1913.
Winkelmann, F. "Einige Bemerkungen zu den Aussagen des Rufinus von Aquileia und des Hieronymus über ihre Übersetzungstheorie und Methode." In *Kyriakon: Festschrift Johannes Quasten*, ed. P. Granfield and J. Jungmann, 532-47. Münster: Verlag Aschendorff, 1970.
Wischmeyer, Wolfgang Karl. "Bemerkungen zu den Paulusbriefkommentaren des G. Marius Victorinus." *ZNW* 63 (1972): 108-20.
Witherington III, Ben. "The Influence of Galatians on Hebrews." *NTS* 37 (1991): 146-52.
Wolfsdorf, David. "The Method ἐξ ὑποθέσεως at *Meno* 86e1-87d8." *Phronesis* 53 (2008): 35-64.
Wolfson, Harry Austryn. *Philo: Foundations of Religious Philosophy in Judaism, Christianity, and Islam*. Vol. 1. Cambridge, MA: Harvard University Press, 1962.
Wolter, Michael. "Die anonymen Schriften des Neuen Testaments Annäherungsversuch an ein literarisches Phänomen." *ZNW* 79 (1988): 1-16.
Wordsworth, Johannes, and Henricus Julianus White, eds., with Alexandro Ramsbotham, Hedley Friderico Davis Sparks, and Claudio Jenkins. *Novum Testamentum Domini Nostri Iesu Christi Latine, Pars Secunda—Epistulae Paulinae*. Oxford: Clarendon, 1913-41.
Wordsworth, John, and Henry Julius White. *Nouum Testamentum Latine. Secundum Editionem Sancti Hieronymi*. London: Simon Wallenerg, 1911.
Wrede, William. *Das literarische Rätsel des Hebräerbriefs*. FRLANT 8. Göttingen: Vandenhoeck & Ruprecht, 1906.
Wyrwa, Dietmar. *Die christliche Platonaneignung in den Stromateis des Clemens von Alexandrien*. Berlin: de Gruyter, 2011.

Wyrwa, Dietmar. "Religiöses Lernen im Zweiten Jahrhundert und die Anfänge der alexandrinischen Katechetenschule." In *Religiöses Lernen in der biblischen, frühjüdischen und frühchristlichen Überlieferung*, ed. Beate Ego and Helmut Merkel, 291–301. WUNT 1/180. Tübingen: Mohr Siebeck, 2005.

Yee, Tet-Lim N. *Jews, Gentiles and Ethnic Reconciliation: Paul's Jewish Identity and Ephesians*. Cambridge: Cambridge University Press, 2005.

Young, David. *The Concept of Canon in the Reception of the Epistle to the Hebrews*. London: T&T Clark, 2021.

Young, Frances M. *Biblical Exegesis and the Formation of Christian Culture*. Cambridge: Cambridge University Press, 1997.

Young, Frances M. "Christological Ideas in the Greek Commentaries on the Epistle to the Hebrews." *JTS* 20 (1969): 150–63.

Yuen-Collingridge, R. "Between Autograph and Copy: Writing as Thinking on Papyrus." *Book History* 21 (2018): 1–28.

Zacagni, Lorenzo Alessandro. *Collectanea monumentorum veterum Ecclesiae graecae ac latinae quae hactenus in Vaticana bibliotheca delituerunt. Tomus primus*. Rome: Sacred Congregation for the Propagation of the Faith, 1698.

Zahn, Theodor. *Geschichte des neutestamentlichen Kanons, Erster Band: Das Neue Testament vor Origenes. Erste Hälfte*. Erlangen: Deichert, 1888.

Zahn, Theodor. *Geschichte des neutestamentlichen Kanons, Zwieter Band: Urkunden und Belege zum ersten und dritten Band. Erste Hälfte*. Leipzig: Deichert, 1890.

Zahn, Theodore. *Introduction to the New Testament*. 2nd ed. Ed. Melancthon Williams Jacobus, trans. John Trout, William Mather, Louis Hodous, Edwards Worcester, William Hoyt Worrell, and Rowland Dodge from the third German edition. New York: Scribner, 1917².

Zawadzki, Konrad. "Der verlorene Schluss des Codex Vaticanus Graecus 762. Eine Rekonstruktion anhand der Codices Pantokratoros 28 und Vaticanus Graecus 692." *Museum Helveticum* 77 (2020): 277–96.

Zuntz, Günther. *The Ancestry of the Harklean New Testament*. British Academy, Supplemental Papers 7. London: Oxford University Press, 1945.

Zuntz, Günther. "Euthalius = Euzoius?" *VC* 7 (1953): 16–22.

Zuntz, Günther. *The Text of the Epistles: A Disquisition upon the Corpus Paulinum*. Schweich Lectures 1946. London: Oxford University Press, 1953.

Index

Since the index has been created to work across multiple formats, indexed terms for which a page range is given (e.g., 52–53, 66–70, etc.) may occasionally appear only on some, but not all of the pages within the range.

1 Clement 41–2, 44–8

Acts of the Apostles, Ch 21 39–41, 167–8, 181–2
   Paul's law obedience in chapter 21 174
   Confrontation between Paul and Jews from Asia 151–2, 154–5, 181–2
Adolf von Harnack 5–6, 34–5, 40–1
Alain Le Boulluec 69–70, 77–8
Alexandria 1, 20, 28–9, 60–1, 90–1, 100–1
Allegory 110–11, 119–20, 130–1, 134–6, 139–40
Andreas Lindemann 6–7
Andrew Jacobs 36, 127
Annewies van den Hoek 65, 79, 82–3, 103–4, 133–6
Anonymity of Hebrews 1, 3–4, 25–6, 151–4, 167–8, 181

Benjamin White 7–9
Brent Nongbri 31–2, 122–3

Canon List 50–1, 55–8
Codex 28–31
   Codex Vaticanus 55–7
   Codex Coislinianus 14–15, 27, 155
Catena Manuscripts 18, 162–5, 169–71, 176
   Pauline Catena 165
   Oecumenius/Oecumenian Catena 171–2
Christian Grappe 6–7, 26
Christopher Guignard 37–8, 53–4
Claire Clivaz 29–30
Clare Rothschild 23, 32–3, 46–50
Contra Celsum 115–16, 118–19, 126–7, 133–4, 137–9
corpus Paulinum 4, 13–16, 27–9, 47, 53–4, 57, 66–8, 151

Daniel Boyarin 107, 110–11, 136–7
David Dawson 70–2, 134–6

David Runia 133–4
Denise Kimber Buell 94–8
Donatien de Bruyn 50–1, 54

Elizabeth Clark 125–6, 149–50
Ephrem the Syrian 27, 148, 151–4, 174
Epistle of Barnabas 16–17, 34–5, 78–9, 81–2
   Hebrews as the Letter of Barnabas 16–17, 23–4, 49–52, 147–8, 181–2
   Figure of Barnabas 1–2, 50–1, 72–3, 77–8
Erasmus of Rotterdam 20, 111–12, 146–7, 178–9, 183–4
Eric Osborn 68, 74, 86–7
Eusebius of Caesarea 1–3, 18–20, 35–40, 44–5, 47, 51–2, 100, 151–4
Euthaliana 156–9, 161, 170–2

Frances Young 103–4, 128, 134–6
Frederic Kenyon 28–9, 31–2

Gabriella Gelardini 23–6, 32–3
Gaius of Rome 19–20, 48, 51–2
Giles Dorival 147–8, 158–9, 163–5
Greek Philosophy 83–7, 91, 94–5, 98–9, 182–3
Gregory Fewster 14–15, 29–30, 158–9
Günther Zuntz 156, 160
Gustave Bardy 60–1, 127

Hauptbriefe 5–6, 11
Heavenly temple 17–18, 105–9
Hebrews (persons/ethnicity) 37–9, 94–7
   Ἑβραΐδι (language) 16–17, 36, 40–2, 182
Hebrews as translation 40, 45, 152, 162–3, 168
Henri Crouzel 101
Herman Hoskier 21–2, 171
hypóthesis / hypothéseis 144–6, 159–60, 162–3, 166–8
   Argumenta 54, 158–9, 178–9, 183–4

INDEX

Ilaria Ramelli 134–6
Image of Paul 3, 10, 12, 15–17, 77–8, 95–6, 98, 141–2, 182–3, 185
Irenaeus of Lyons 7–9, 19–20, 48–9

James Carleton Paget 69–70, 90–1, 109–10, 115–16
Jennifer Otto 97–8, 114–15, 131, 133–4
Jerome 20, 44, 50–1, 55–7, 147–8
Jew (ethnicity) 17, 36, 98
John Chrysostom 18, 27, 148–51, 153–4, 161–3, 166
John Gager 10–13
John McGuckin 100–1, 123–4, 128, 132–3
Joseph Verheyden 53–4, 74–5
Josephus 35–6, 89–90, 121–2, 160
Judith Kovacs 67–8, 73–4
Judith Lieu 4–7, 13–14

Karl Staab 154, 164–5, 167–72
Kirsopp Lake 28–9, 161–2

Latin reception of Hebrews 48–58
Law as a shadow 107–10, 114–15, 117, 121–2, 150, 159
Lee Levine 25–6, 124–7
Logos 25–6, 61–2, 66, 69–72, 77–8, 96, 103–4, 107–8, 136–7
Lorenzo Perrone 100, 118–19, 132

Manuscript placement, Hebrews 55–8
Marcion 8–9, 12–13, 15, 20, 52–4, 56–7, 70–1, 118–19
Maren Niehoff 115–16, 129–30, 134
Marguerite Harl 109–10, 139–40
Mark Edwards 61, 67–8, 128, 134–6
Matthew Thiessen 10–11, 75
Melchizedek 52–3, 63–5, 114
Mimicking Pauline Citations 69–70, 72–81
Miriam DeCock 103–4, 162–3
Muratorian Fragment 20, 53–4

Nicholas de Lange 127–8, 130–3
Nils Dahl 53–4, 157–9

Pantaenus the Elder 39–40, 100
Papyrus 46 21–2, 27, 29–33
Paratextual framing 14–15, 146, 158–9
Paul within Judaism 10–11
Paul, Jewishness 12, 92–4, 119–23
Paula Fredriksen 10–13
Paulinity 3–4, 9, 15–17, 20, 23–7, 31–3, 38–9, 43, 46–7
Peter Martens 128, 131–2, 139–40
Philo of Alexandria 19–20, 35–6, 79, 132–9, 160
Pierre Nautin 62, 72–3, 100–2, 128
Porphyry 134–6, 139–40, 145
postscript (Hebrews 13) 16–17, 21–7
Pseudepigraphy 23–6

Quintilian 28–9, 128–9

Raoul Mortley 69–70, 83–4
Robert Wilken 124–5, 136–7
Roelof van den Broek 60–1, 90–1
Rome 19–20, 34–5, 45–8
Ronald Heine 105, 124–5, 127
Rowan Greer 102–4, 111, 143–4
Rufinus 111–12, 122–3, 148, 151–4, 161–2
Ruth Clements 111, 126–7, 129, 136–7

Seneca 12
Seven-letter theory 53–5
Spiritual reading 109–11, 134–6
Superscription 4, 14–16, 27, 29–30, 158–9

T. J. Lang 14–15, 143
Tabernacle (Exodus) 17–18, 105–6
Testimonia 82–3
Theodor Zahn 27, 34–5, 37, 147–8, 158–9
Theodore of Mopsuestia 166–8, 170–1
Theodoret of Cyrrhus 143–6, 153–4, 162–3, 169–70, 172
Theophylact of Ohrid 165, 174–6
Third Corinthians 7–10
Titles of Pauline letters 33, 35
Title of Hebrews 34–5

Walter Schmithals 1–2, 21–3
Wendy Mayer 148–9